CONFLICT RESOLUTION
AND
UNITED STATES HISTORY

VOLUME ONE:

The Colonial Period through Reconstruction

by

John Whiteclay Chambers II and Arlene L. Gardner

Rutgers, The State University of New Jersey
New Brunswick/Piscataway, New Jersey

Conflict Resolution and United States History: The Colonial Period through the Twentieth Century is published in 2 volumes, each with accompanying CD and DVD, by the New Jersey Center for Civic and Law-Related Education, Rutgers, The State University of New Jersey, New Brunswick/Piscataway, New Jersey:

    Volume One, *The Colonial Period through Reconstruction,* ISBN 978-0-9794811-0-9
    Volume Two, *The Gilded Age through the Twentieth Century,* ISBN 978-0-9794811-1-6

For more information: Contact the New Jersey Center for Civic and Law-Related Education at Rutgers University, Lucy Stone Hall B303, Piscataway, NJ 08854. Phone: 732-445-3413. Email address: civiced@njclre.rutgers.edu. Website: http://civiced.rutgers.edu/CONFLICT/index.htm.

Sources and credits for illustrations are listed at the end of each chapter.

Cover and layout design by Marian Olivas of the National Center for the Study of History in the Schools at University of California, Los Angeles.

ISBN   978-0-979811-0-9

Printed in the United States of America
10 9 8 7 6 5 4 3 2 1

For

Alison R. Bernstein

Vice President, the Ford Foundation
Historian, Visionary, Humanitarian,

without whose faith in the program, this never would have been achieved.

TABLE OF CONTENTS

Preface and Acknowledgments..vii

The Authors...xi

Foreword by Gary Nash..xii

Chapter One: Conceptual Context for Conflict Resolution and History.......................................1

Chapter Two: Developing Skills for Resolving Conflicts..21

Chapter Three: How to Use the Curriculum Package...59

Chapter Four: **Native Americans and European Colonists**...73

                    Part One: *The Puritans and King Philip's War, 1675-76*

                    Prepared with the help of Jill Lepore, Harvard University; and Gary Nash, University of California, Los Angeles

                    Part Two: *The Quakers and the Lenni Lenape Indians, 1682–84*

                    Prepared with the help of Max Carter, Guilford College; James Merrell, Vassar College; and Gary Nash, University of California, Los Angeles

Chapter Five: **Could the American Revolution Have Been Avoided?**...105

                    Part One: *First Continental Congress debates how to respond to Britain in 1774*

                    Part Two: *Mock Negotiations between Britain and the American Colonies in 1775*

                    Prepared with the help of Pauline Maier, Massachusetts Institute of Technology

Chapter Six: **Issues of Slavery at the Federal Convention, 1787**..135

                    Prepared with the help of Paul Finkelman, University of Tulsa Law School; and Jack Rakove, Stanford University

Chapter Seven: **The Cherokee Indian Removal**..159

Prepared with the help of J.B. Finger, University of Tennessee, Knoxville; and
James Merrell, Vassar College

Chapter Eight: **War Between Mexico and the United States**....................................179
Prepared with the help of George Sanchez, University of Southern California;
and Pedro Santoni, California State University at San Bernardino

Chapter Nine: **The Compromise of 1850**...199

Prepared with the help of Michael Holt, University of Virginia

Chapter Ten: **The Struggle for Women's Rights in the Nineteenth Century**...........................223

Prepared with the help of Margaret Crocco, Teachers College, Columbia University;
Nancy Hewitt, Rutgers, The State University of New Jersey, New Brunswick; and
Linda Kerber, University of Iowa

Chapter Eleven: **Post-Civil War Reconstruction**...249

Prepared with the help of Eric Foner, Columbia University; and Clement
Alexander Price, Rutgers, The State University of New Jersey, Newark

Index...279

Supplementary Materials (located inside back cover):

CD: **"Conflict Resolution and United States History Resource Materials for Volume One"**
Includes primary source documents as well as teacher overheads/student handouts
in both Microsoft Word and Microsoft PowerPoint.

DVD: **"Historical Roleplaying Using Conflict Resolution Skills"**
Visually demonstrates students engaged in classroom activities using conflict
resolution skills and playing roles of historical figures in case studies from this
curriculum package.

PREFACE AND ACKNOWLEDGMENTS

The *Conflict Resolution and United States History* curriculum package—the two-volume book and the accompanying CD and DVD—is designed to make American history more relevant, interesting and motivating for students. It is also designed to integrate skills for resolving conflicts into learning about the history of the United States. Since much of American history concerns conflict, our case studies deal with a variety of different conflicts in the American past. Some case studies involve conflicts between different cultures (for example, between seventeenth-century Native Americans and European colonists). Others focus on clashes between different ethnic or racial groups (e.g., the conflicts resulting in the National Origins Act of 1924, the Montgomery Bus Boycott in 1955, and the Los Angeles Riots of 1992). Some involve feuds between nations (for example, the American colonies and Britain, the United States and Mexico, the United States and Spain). Still other case studies examine conflicting economic interests (e.g., labor and management in the Pullman Strike and the Paterson Silk Strike), or clashing philosophies or ideologies (e.g., the debate over slavery at the Constitutional Convention of 1787, over the Compromise of 1850, over multiracial democracy during Reconstruction, or differences over the role of women in society and the workforce in the nineteenth and twentieth centuries).

This innovative curriculum provides teachers with an understanding and ability to teach conflict resolution skills to their students and to have them apply these skills to better understand American history as well as everyday conflicts. The goal is both academic and pragmatic: to give students an appreciation of the complexity of historical conflicts and an ability to resolve conflicts in their own lives. The materials provide a comprehensive teacher supplement for U.S. history courses from grades 5 through 12, including gifted students, special education students, and advanced placement students. It can also be used in introductory American History courses in college.

Supported by the Ford Foundation, this curriculum is the result of a collaboration by the Rutgers Center for Historical Analysis and the New Jersey Center for Civic and Law-Related Education, both located at the New Brunswick/Piscataway campus of Rutgers, The State University of New Jersey. These materials are the culmination of ten years of curriculum development, teacher institutes, and classroom piloting. The two-volume curriculum package includes the following:

- The latest historical scholarship from more than 25 prominent historians from leading universities around the country.
- Historical background, directions for role-playing activities, comparisons with what really happened in history, questions for discussion and bibliographies for 20 major conflicts in the American past. Each case study is correlated with the National Standards for United States History.
- Practical lessons and materials on conflict resolution skills.
- A CD containing reproducible teacher overheads, student handouts, maps and primary source documents for each case study.
- A DVD that shows actual classes demonstrating case studies, using conflict resolution skills in the roles of historical figures, and including instructions and debriefing by the teachers.

Volume One includes ten case studies of historical conflicts, ranging from the Colonial Period to post-Civil War Reconstruction. Volume Two includes ten case studies, starting with the Pullman Strike of 1894 and concluding with the Los Angeles Riots of 1992. Credits for illustrations are included at the end of each chapter. Chapter One of each volume offers an overview of violence in American society, the development of alternatives, including conflict resolution skills, an examination of the value of teaching history, and a discussion of why history is not inevitable. It also contains suggestions of how the *Conflict Resolution and United States History* curriculum package may help to motivate your students to learn a richer, deeper understanding of history as well as skills for resolving conflicts in their daily lives. Chapter Two offers background materials and lessons to help your students learn conflict resolution skills. Chapter Three provides suggestions on how to do historical role-playing using conflict resolution skills.

Teachers from middle and high schools who participated in more than a dozen institutes that we held around the country between 1995 and 2005 subsequently piloted early versions of the curricular materials and provided invaluable suggestions for improvement. They used the materials with their students and integrated lessons to develop conflict resolution skills with role-playing activities, historical research and analysis. Teachers and students using the *Conflict Resolution and United States History* materials and teaching strategies reported the following advantages over traditional lecture-style history classes:

- **Increased student motivation**. Teachers uniformly reported that their students were more motivated to learn history and to do historical research when the interactive role-playing activities were used.

- **Greater mastery of history.** Teachers noted that their students obtained a greater understanding of the complexity of the historical subject matter.

- **Richer understanding of history**. Many of the teachers reported that their students gained a deeper appreciation of historical developments and the interplay of individual actions and events than the seemingly inevitable flow of history that characterizes many textbooks.

- **Improved critical thinking and problem solving skills**. Many of the teachers concluded that this curriculum's theoretically open-ended approach to history and exploration of conflict resolution encouraged their students to use critical thinking and problem-solving skills.

- **Improved conflict resolution skills**. Most students indicated that the skills they learned were useful in their daily lives as well as in assessing larger conflicts.

- **Improved classroom management skills for teachers.** Several teachers, especially those in urban school districts, reported that they used the negotiation and mediation skills they learned from the summer institutes to resolve conflicts in their classrooms.

Many people have believed in this project and given it their time, ideas and support to bring it to fruition. We would like to thank the following historians for their invaluable insights and suggestions. In Volume One, those historians include Max Carter, Guilford College; Margaret Crocco, Teachers College, Columbia University; J.B. Finger, University of Tennessee, Knoxville; Paul Finkelman, University of Tulsa Law School; Eric Foner, Columbia University; Nancy Hewitt, Rutgers University, New Brunswick; Michael Holt, University of Virginia; Jill Lepore, Harvard University; Linda Kerber, University of Iowa; Pauline Maier, Massachusetts Institute of Technology; James Merrell, Vassar College, Gary Nash, University of California, Los Angeles; Clement Alexander Price, Rutgers University, Newark; Jack Rakove, Stanford University; George Sanchez, University of Southern California; and Pedro Santoni, California State University at San Bernardino.

In Volume Two, the historians include Harriet Hyman Alonso, City College, City University of New York; Steve Golin, Bloomfield College, Bloomfield, New Jersey; Linda Kerber, University of Iowa; Alice Kessler-Harris, Columbia University; Thomas Paterson, University of Connecticut, Storrs; Louis Peréz, University of North Carolina, Chapel Hill; Jan Reiff, University of California, Los Angeles; George Sanchez, University of Southern California; Melvin Small, Wayne State University, Detroit; Shelton Stromquist, University of Iowa; J. Mills Thornton, University of Michigan; Deborah Gray White, Rutgers University, New Brunswick; and Virginia Yans, Rutgers University, New Brunswick.

In addition, we would like to thank the following conflict resolution practitioners for their assistance and expertise: Linda Lantieri, at the Resolving Conflict Creatively Program; Mickey Pepera, Lesley University, Cambridge, Massachusetts; Judy Zimmer at Street Law, Inc., and Linda Stamato and Sanford M. Jaffe, at the Rutgers Center for Negotiation and Conflict Resolution.

While recognizing the valuable contributions made by many historians, political scientists, conflict resolution practitioners and others, the authors are solely responsible for any errors or inaccuracies that remain.

We would like to recognize the assistance provided by the program committees that included our project among the sessions at various annual meetings of the American Historical Association, the Organization of American Historians, and the National Council for the Social Studies. For hosting our workshops or teacher workshops at their institution, we also thank Sibyl Brownlee at Fitchburg College in Fitchburg, Massachusetts; the Constitutional Rights Foundation in Chicago; Margaret Crocco at Columbia University; the Harvard Program on Negotiation, Cambridge, Massachusetts; Gary Nash at the University of California, Los Angeles; G. Kurt Piehler at University of Tennessee at Knoxville; Melvin Small at Wayne State University in Detroit; David Trevaskis at Temple University, Philadelphia, Pennsylvania; and the staff at the Rutgers University Inn and Conference Center for many valuable and comfortable Summer Institutes in New Brunswick, New Jersey.

We are deeply grateful to the many teachers--too many to name-- who participated in our institutes. We would like to express special appreciation to Barry Bachenheimer, supervisor for curriculum, Caldwell-West Caldwell Public Schools, New Jersey; Patricia Franklin, Percy Julian Middle School, Oak Park, Illinois; Stephanie King, North Miami High School, North Miami, Florida; and Nancy Wallace, Freehold Township High School, Freehold, New Jersey, who provided valuable feedback as we prepared these chapters, and some of whom, along with their students, demonstrated the teaching strategies on our DVD. Special thanks also to Jim Daly, professor of education at the College of Education and Human Service, Seton Hall University, South Orange, New Jersey; John Calimano, retired teacher East Brunswick High School, New Jersey; John Cartaina, retired social studies supervisor, Paterson Public Schools, New Jersey; and Lynnette Poag, retired middle school teacher, Vineland, New Jersey.

At Rutgers University, we received essential support from Executive Dean Holly Smith, Dean Barry Qualls, the chairs of the History Department over the past ten years--Ziva Galili, John Chambers, David Oshinsky, Deborah Gray White, and Paul Clemens--plus Rutgers Center for Historical Analysis Administrator Lynn Shanko and her assistant, Tim Alves. Over the years, we have had a number of graduate and undergraduate assistants, who helped to check facts, find quotations, maps, documents and illustrations, and do other assorted tasks. They rightly deserve a special thanks, and we gratefully acknowledge the help of Brian Adkins, Lisa-Marie Batelli, Matthew Cheser, Nancy Gonzalez Lopez, Richard Mizelle, Martin Summers, and Brandon Wright. We also thank those wonderful people who were crucial in the final process of turning this project into a book: Marian Olivas at the National Center for History in the Schools at the University of California, Los Angeles and, especially, Matthew Gazda, Rutgers undergraduate student, and Marika Dunn, Rutgers graduate student, and Lisa Kruger at the Rutgers Graduate School of Education. Marian, Matt, Marika and Lisa were vital in helping us turn a raw manuscript into an elegant book.

We would offer a special word of appreciation to our families who suffered through the lengthy process and the trials and tribulations, excitement and frustrations that this project has involved. Thus a big thanks to our spouses: Amy Piro Chambers and Edward Israelow, and our children: Tacy Chambers, and Hannah and David Israelow.

Our greatest debt is to the Ford Foundation, which, under the presidency of Susan Berresford, supported our project for a decade as we tested and turned our concept into this curriculum. We would like to thank Dr. Berresford; Dr. Joseph Aguerrebere, Jr., director, Education and Culture Programs; and most of all, Dr. Alison Bernstein, vice president at the Ford Foundation and historian, humanist, and visionary, who originally saw the potential in our idea. We are proud to dedicate this volume to Dr. Bernstein as a small acknowledgment of our debt for her many years of faith and support for this project.

We hope that these materials and innovative teaching methodologies will help create a better insight into the past and its relevance to the present as well as a deeper understanding of conflict resolution skills that can help to achieve safer schools and society. We hope that in the long run, this project and these materials may contribute, if only in a small way, to building a better future for Americans and all humankind.

John Whiteclay Chambers II
Arlene L. Gardner
New Brunswick, New Jersey
May 2007

THE AUTHORS

John Whiteclay Chambers II is a prize-winning scholar/teacher. He is Distinguished Professor of History and former Chair of the History Department at Rutgers University, New Brunswick, New Jersey, where he has taught since 1982. He received an Outstanding Teaching Award there in 2005. He has a B.A. from Temple University in Philadelphia, an M.A. from San Francisco State University, and Ph.D. in History from Columbia University. He spent six years as a reporter for newspapers in Los Angeles and Marin counties in California, and as a news writer/producer at KRON-TV, the NBC affiliate in San Francisco. After receiving his Ph.D., Dr. Chambers taught from1972-82 at Columbia University's Barnard College, where he won an Outstanding Teaching Award in 1975. Dr. Chambers has written or edited a dozen books on war and peace, several of them prize-winning studies. Among these are *The Eagle and the Dove: The American Peace Movement and U.S. Foreign Policy, 1900-1922* (1976, 2nd edition, 1991); *The Tyranny of Change: America in the Progressive Era, 1900-1920* (1st edition, 1980, 2nd edition, 1992, 3rd edition, 2000); *To Raise an Army: The Draft Comes to Modern America* (1987), which won the Best Book Award from the American Military History Institute; *The New Conscientious Objection* (1993); *World War II, Film, and History* (1996); *The Oxford Companion to American Military History* (1999), which won the first Best Reference Book Award from the Society for Military History; and *George Washington in Cranbury: The Road to the Battle of Monmouth* (2003),which won First Prize from the N.J. League of Historical Societies. He is a past president of the Peace History Society. Dr. Chambers has received fellowships or grants from the Rockefeller Foundation, the National Endowment for the Humanities, the Organization of American Historians, the National Park Service, and the Ford Foundation. He was a fellow at the Institute for Advanced Study in Princeton, a Fulbright Fellow at the University of Rome, and a Visiting Lecturer at the University of Tokyo.

Arlene L. Gardner is a lawyer and a prominent educational consultant. She is the Executive Director of the New Jersey Center for Civic and Law-Related Education, which is located at Rutgers, The State University of New Jersey, New Brunswick/Piscataway campus. She is a graduate of Douglass College at Rutgers University, and Georgetown University School of Law. She worked as a legal intern at the Agency for International Development and with corporate law firms in San Francisco and New Jersey. Ms. Gardner served as an assistant counsel to the governor of New Jersey for four years, specializing in education, health and human services issues. In 1990, she founded the New Jersey Center for Civic and Law-Related Education in order to provide materials and training in civic and law-related education for New Jersey teachers and students. In addition to an article in the *Georgetown International Business and Law Review* (1976), she has written several articles about school partnerships and law-related education, and a book, *School Partnerships: A Handbook for School and Community Leaders* (1990). She also wrote an article, "Conflict Resolution and History: The War with Mexico as a Case Study" for *Social Education,* the Journal of the National Council for the Social Studies (2001). She has organized hundreds of professional development institutes, workshops, and conferences for teachers over the past fifteen years. In addition, she has taught graduate courses and conducted workshops across the country and at numerous international sites on conflict resolution, prejudice reduction, the Constitution and the Bill of Rights, New Jersey government, controversial issues, rights and responsibilities, and interdisciplinary teaching. Ms. Gardner served as a member and president of the Board of Education of Westfield, New Jersey, helping to achieve high standards, good morale and excellent working relations among teachers, administrators and the school board.

FOREWORD

It is widely agreed that knowledge of history is a precondition of an informed citizenry. Particularly, we assume, every would-be citizen should understand what decisions made in the past account for today's circumstances. Without understanding our history, and the histories of other countries, it is difficult to be clear-minded about our responsibilities as citizens of the world's most venerable democracy. To be historically literate, a citizen must graduate from the passive absorption of dates, names, facts, places, and events to a more active engagement with the historical record. Such engagement involves raising questions about how individuals, groups, and societies have made decisions in the past and analyzing their solutions to knotty problems.

In creating the *National Standards for History*, first published in 1994, a small battalion of teachers, curriculum specialists, and academic historians crafted five standards in historical thinking. The fifth standard, of great relevance to this innovative approach to American history, is "Historical Issues-Analysis and Decision-Making." Endorsed by thirty professional organizations involved in history education, the standard states:

> Issue-centered analysis and decision-making activities place students squarely at the center of historical dilemmas and problems faced at critical moments in the past and the near-present. Entering into such moments, confronting the issues or problems of the time, analyzing the alternatives available to those on the scene, evaluating the consequences that might have followed those options for action that were not chosen, and comparing with the consequences of those that were adopted, are activities that foster students' deep personal involvement in these events.

> If well chosen, these activities also promote capacities vital to a democratic citizenry; the capacity to identify and define public policy issues and ethical dilemmas; analyze the range of interests and values held by the many persons caught up in the situation and affected by its outcome; locate and organize the data required to assess the consequences of alternative approaches to resolving the dilemma; assess the ethical implications as well as the comparative costs and benefits of each approach; and evaluate a particular course of action in light of all of the above and, in the case of historical issues-analysis, in light also of its long-term consequences revealed in the historical record.

The twenty case studies in these two volumes of *Conflict Resolution and United State History* provide classroom teachers with highly teachable moments in American history that amply fulfill the historical thinking standards that were set to help young learners become historically literate. There is one additional advantage in engaging students in these critical moments of United States history–the opportunity to clear students' minds from the noxious idea of historical inevitability. Implicit in each case study is the belief that history is not predetermined, that each violent encounter in the American past could have had a different outcome.

The idea of historical inevitability is as old as the tales told by conquerors. In the earliest Puritan writings of the late seventeenth century, the religious immigrants to New England were God's earthly agents, so their conflicts with Algonkian people were God's will. If heathens could not be Christianized, they should be banished from the land. This "providential history," which also explained epidemics, earthquakes, flood and famine as the intervening hand of an angry God, gave way to a secularized version of historical inevitability. By the mid-nineteenth century, an angry Jehovah did not dictate the course of history but larger forces did, whether environmental and geographic, moral and political, or economic and social. The view arose, as Isaiah Berlin has written of modern history in general, that "the behaviour of men is . . . made what it is by factors largely beyond the control of individuals." Thus, historians writing in the late nineteenth and early twentieth centuries deployed terms such as "the march of events," "the spirit of the age," the "laws of history," "the tide of human affairs," and–the most familiar of all–"manifest destiny." Such phrases connote the inevitability of events, the irresistible rhythms of human life, and the unswervable forces that dictate the way humans act, individually and collectively.

In a democratic society, the notion of historical inevitability is profoundly antidemocratic because it contradicts what almost all teachers tell the students sitting in their classrooms: that the individual matters, that any young American can make a difference, that the student's life and the life of American society is not predetermined. The individual in history, often cast as a hero or leader, is the person who makes history rather than succumbing to larger forces. That is the potency of the innovative approach to teaching history offered by *Conflict Resolution and United States History*.

Gary B. Nash
Director
National Center for History in the Schools
University of California, Los Angeles
July 10, 2006

CHAPTER ONE

CONCEPTUAL CONTEXT FOR CONFLICT RESOLUTION AND HISTORY

The goals of this book are to help students understand conflicts in history and also to assist them in managing conflicts, large and small, in their daily lives. In *Conflict Resolution and United States History*, we use history to look at conflict and conflict to look at history. Conflict has been a large part of our past history, and conflict continues to be a part of current-day politics and society. Focusing on past episodes of discord is one way to try to understand history. This curriculum seeks to integrate into the teaching of history an understanding and appreciation of conflict resolution and to provide students with opportunities to practice using practical conflict resolution skills. At the same time, it aims to encourage students to become more engaged and more skillful in the critical analysis of historical developments. Thus, it enhances the intellectual process of historical analysis while also offering practical skills to help students in resolving conflicts they encounter in their everyday lives.

This curriculum package is the culmination of ten years of work, supported by the Ford Foundation, to determine whether conflict resolution skills might be successfully integrated into the teaching of American history and whether such integration would be valuable for students. The response has been a resounding "yes"! The materials wed the conflict resolution techniques of "interest-based" negotiation and mediation with the instructional techniques of historical analysis and historical roleplaying. We ask students to learn about the past by playing the roles of actual individuals involved in significant conflicts in the American past. We have selected twenty major conflicts in American history as case studies for students to explore and understand the causes of the conflicts, the possible alternative resolutions, and the consequences of the choices made by the individuals and groups in each of these historical conflicts. The case studies draw upon the experience and advice of leading university historians as well as teachers who have utilized the materials in their classrooms.

Our case studies include major historical conflicts over three centuries of American history. Some involve international crises, among them the American Revolution, the Mexican War, the War with Spain in 1898, U.S. entry into World War I, the Cuban Missile Crisis of 1962, and the Vietnam War. Others focus on major national political clashes, such as the issue of slavery at the U.S. Constitutional Convention of 1787, the expansion of slavery and the Compromise of 1850, and the issue of multiracial democracy during Reconstruction. Industrial labor strife in the late nineteenth and early twentieth centuries is dealt with via the Pullman strike and boycott and the Paterson silk strike. The issue of immigration is confronted by focusing on immigration restrictions proposed in the 1920s. Desegregation and non-violent civil disobedience are explored in the Montgomery Bus Boycott of 1955-56. Some case studies deal with conflicts with Native Americans: King Philip's War, 1675-76 in New England; William Penn and the Lenni Lenape in Pennsylvania, 1682-84; and the issue of removal of the Cherokees from their homelands in the 1830s. Two case studies directly address conflicts involving the status of women in America: the struggle for women's rights in the nineteenth century and the fight for equal wages and opportunities for women in the paid workforce after World War II. Finally, economic, ethnic, and racial conflict in the nation's cities is illustrated in a case study of the Los Angeles Riots of 1992. In many of the case studies, the domestic concerns and international issues are interrelated. Some of the larger issues of equality and justice remain with us to the present day.

This chapter will provide a scholarly context for our creative approach to teaching U.S. history: intertwining conflict resolution techniques and historical roleplaying as a way to learn a richer, deeper understanding of history and to enhance critical thinking, conflict resolution, communication and citizenship skills.

Violence in America

It has been said that "violence is as American as cherry pie."[1] Violence is and has been pervasive in American history and is seem by many as part of America's national character.[2] Yet, despite a high level of individual acts of violence (such as assaults, shootings and murders),[3] most Americans recognize and respect the rule of law, unless and until the law is seen by many as unjust and oppressive.[4] Among diverse communities of individuals, modern democracies emphasize consensual, non-violent methods of allocating, monitoring and adjusting political power. In spite of their differences in culture and moral values, the multiethnic and multicultural members of America's heterogeneous society are legally equal as citizens of the nation. At the very least, this system of government by consent of the citizenry requires respect for others with differing values and views. The vitality of modern democracy is not derived solely from its elected representatives. It is, perhaps more importantly, rooted in the dispersal of political influence and the commitment and ability of citizens to resolve conflicting interests nonviolently for the common good of the community. Without a commitment to nonviolent conflict resolution, we would have a coercive polity rather than a consensual democracy.[5]

While there are certainly many different causes of violence, whether by individuals or by groups, what has struck us is how much American mass culture has glamorized violence, and how very little it has emphasized non-violent means of dealing with conflict. There is a long history of celebrating the violent hero, from the rugged, early frontiersman, cowboy, gunfighter or western sheriff or marshal to the modern warrior or detective, or futuristic "Jedi", to the animated figures of current video games (whether "macho" man or, more recently, "macho" woman, such as the movie and video heroine Lara Croft). American popular culture has mythologized the uncompromising

---

[1] Although it is sometimes remembered as "Violence is as American as *apple* pie," the actual quotation attributed to H. Rap Brown, black civil rights activist in the late 1960s, was "Violence is as American as cherry pie." See "The Quotations Home Page," http://theotherpages.org/topic-v2.html (accessed September 22, 2006); and also Jerome C. Weeks, "Cherry Pie," letter to the editor, *New York Review of Books,* September 23, 1982.

[2] A recent poll by the Pew Research Center revealed that a majority of respondents in foreign countries as well as nearly a majority of Americans themselves continue to view American national character as violent. Andrew Kohut and Michele Norris, "World Takes Dim View of the U.S. " *All Things Considered*, June 23, 2005, (National Public Radio) www.npr.org; Brian Knowlton, "Polls Shows Modest Changes in Levels in Anti-US Mood," *New York Times*, June 24, 2005, A10.

[3] Although the basis for crime statistics varies, the United States usually ranks high, if not highest, among western, industrialized countries in its crime and murder rates. For example, the United States ranks first among sixty countries in "Total Crimes by Country," and twenty-fourth in murders per capita by country, in the Seventh United Nations Survey of Crime Trends and Operations of Criminal Justice Systems, 1998-2000 (United Nations Office on Drugs and Crimes, Centre for International Crime Prevention) at www.nationmaster.com. In a 2004 "List of Countries by Murder Rate," the United States ranks eleventh out of sixty. Widipedia.com (Both accessed 13 January 2007).

[4] The "rule of law" has alternatively been viewed by individuals, political leaders and scholars as: the protection of individual rights; another word for democracy; laws clearly set out in advance and equally applied to all; more broadly, the social, economic, educational and cultural conditions under which legitimate individual aspirations and dignity may be realized; a political ideal only; or simply the fact that everyone should obey the law. See Brian Z. Tamanaha, *On The Rule of Law: History, Politics and Theory* (New York: Cambridge University Press, 2004). Also see "Constitutionalism," *The Oxford Companion to the Supreme Court of the United States*, Kermit L. Hall, ed. (New York: Oxford University Press, 1992) 190-192 and Ian Shapiro, ed., *The Rule of Law* (New York: New York University Press, 1994).

[5] For a recent exploration of this idea, see John Keane, *Violence and Democracy* (New York: Cambridge University Press, 2004).

hero who uses force or the threat of force to overcome "evil" adversaries.[6] Violence is bound up with the very definition of the American nation. The nation came into being as a result of the violent overthrow of British rule. It was redefined again in the mid-nineteenth century as a result of the Civil War. America's sense of moral superiority and world leadership was confirmed by our victory in World War II. These conflicts have been seen by most Americans as "just wars," and our involvement in them is celebrated.

Traditional American values stress individualism, freedom, and national power and greatness. These values have often been achieved and defended through force or the threat of force—whether taming the frontier or conquering peoples seen as standing in the way of American interests or ideology. In a culture emphasizing power and coercion, victory has been and remains a primary value. "Winning isn't everything, it is the only thing!"[7] Although this aphorism comes from the playing field, it has become the mantra for American competitiveness everywhere—in entertainment, politics, the courtroom, financial markets, and international relations. This emphasis on total victory generally requires a defeated and vanquished adversary. American youth absorb this ideology with its emphasis on the use of power and force and its definition of success as total victory.

We began this project in 1994 as a response to a rise of violence in America's schools in the early 1990s. This was several years before the mass shootings at Columbine High School in 1999, a tragedy that focused national attention on the subject.[8] School shootings are relatively rare, and youth violence has actually declined from the historic high rates of the last decade of the twentieth century.[9] Yet the persistence of tragic episodes of

---

[6] Richard Slotkin, *Regeneration through Violence: The Mythology of the American Frontier, 1600-1860* (Middletown, CT: Wesleyan University Press, 1973); and *Gunfighter Nation: The Myth of the Frontier in Twentieth Century America* (New York: Atheneum, 1992). A number of studies have condemned the media's glorification of violence. Some have sought, with varying degrees of success, to make causal links between media depictions and actual perpetrators of violence. See for example, Laurie Mifflin, "Many Researchers Say Link is Already Clear on Media and Violence," *New York Times*, May 9, 1999, A28; John Cloud, "Taking Aim at Show Biz: Most of the Post-Littleton Lawmaking Has Focused on Guns. Now It's Hollywood's Turn to Squirm," *Time*, June 21, 1999, 42-43; Anahad O'Connor, "Really? The Claim: Violent Video Games Make Young People Aggressive," *New York Times*, August 30, 2005, F5.

[7] Since the late 1960s, the aphorism, linked in the public mind to Vince Lombardi, coach of the Green Bay Packers professional football team, has become part of the debate over American culture. Steven J. Overman, "'Winning isn't Everything. It's the Only Thing': The Origin, Attributions and Influence of a Famous Football Quote," *Football Studies* 2, no 2 (October 1999): 77-99; David Maraniss, *When Pride Still Mattered: A Life of Vince Lombardi* (New York: Simon and Schuster, 2000), chs. 21-22.

[8] Our project began with a grant in 1994 from the Ford Foundation, which was already concerned with the increase in youth violence. Five years later in 1999, the killing of 13 students and teachers at Columbine High School in Littleton, an affluent suburb of Denver, Colorado, by two youths who then killed themselves was the worst school shooting in U.S. history to that date and brought the issue of school violence to the national agenda. See Robert McFadden, "Violence, Real and Imagined, Sweeps Through the Schools," *New York Times*, April 30, 1999, A1; "Special Report: Massacre in Colorado: Why? Portraits of the Killers; the Science of Teen Violence," *Newsweek*, May 3, 1999, 22-40; "Pain Still Fresh 5 Years after Columbine Massacre," *New York Times*, April 21, 2004, B11.

[9] Nancy D. Brener, Thomas R. Simon, Etienne G. Krug, and Richard Lowry, "Recent Trends in Violence-Related Behaviors among High school Students in the United States," *Journal of the American Medical Association*, 282 (August 1999): 440-46, an analysis of four biennial Youth Risk Behavior surveys between 1991 and 1997, which indicated significant decreases in percentages of students who reported carrying a weapon or engaging in a physical fight or being injured in one, but which showed little change in the percentages of students reporting feeling unsafe to go to school, being threatened or injured with a weapon on school property, or having property stolen or deliberately damaged at school. For evidence that violence continued to rise, see Charisse Jones, "Report Shows Violence Rising in Schools," *New York Times*, August 13, 1994, A25.

violence at schools continues to remind us of the violent impulses and behavior among youths.[10] Such violent urges and actions threaten our schools and our communities. Young people in the United States, especially those in urban areas, are at great risk of being victims or perpetrators of violence. This potential for violence creates a pervasive sense or perception of insecurity, if not outright fear, even in locations where the risk of violence is low.[11] Thus, we need to provide alternative ways for youths and adults to manage conflict and prevent it from emerging into violence, even where actual violence is not yet intense or persistent.

Some schools have responded to violence or the perception of violence by imposing greater discipline, which appears on the surface to be an effective manner of controlling violence, at least in the short run. Following the Columbine shootings, schools imposed so-called "zero-tolerance" policies against threats, whether verbal or otherwise, of violence.[12] However, external discipline alone fails to deal with the root causes of violent behavior or to teach students how to resolve conflicts without violence. Without addressing the roots of potentially violent behavior, administrators are, in effect, simply shifting the problem of violence to outside of the school building.[13] Violence is deflected into the community as a whole where it can, in fact, grow worse. The best long-term approach to violence, it seems to us, is, first, to create a climate in which students themselves understand the importance of identifying and reporting potentially dangerous conflicts before they erupt into violence. Second, and even more important in the long run, we believe that it is vital to have students learn ways—including conflict resolution techniques—to deal with aggressive and violent impulses and behavior in themselves and with others in their schools and their communities.

But, is American society more violent than other societies? Some question this conclusion, including neoconservative scholar and political commentator Robert Kagan, who contends that while Europeans may generally see Americans as having a "warlike temperament" and "Americans generally favor policies of coercion rather than persuasion, emphasizing punitive sanctions over inducements to better behavior, the stick over the carrot," this is not because Americans are inherently more violent but because the United States is militarily strong while Europe is not.[14] If violence is not a particular characteristic of Americans, perhaps human beings are

---

[10] Todd S. Purdum, "Shooting at School Leaves 2 Dead and 13 Hurt," *New York Times*, March 6, 2001, A1. "Louisiana: One Killed in Trade School Shooting," *New York Times*, April 8, 2003; "Minnesota: School Shooting is a Murder Case," *New York Times*, September 28, 2003; "Nebraska Student Found with Bombs Outside High School," *New York Times*, March 19, 2004; Jodi Wilgoren, "Shooting Rampage by Student Leaves 10 Dead on Reservation [Red Lake High School, Minnesota]," *New York Times*, March 22, 2005; William Yardley, "Boy, 17, Dies in School Shooting in Takoma, and Student Is Held," *New York Times*, January 4, 2007, A20; Kate Zerike, "Violent Crime in Cities Show Sharp Rise, Reversing Trend," *New York Times*, March 9, 2007, A14; and John M. Broder, "32 Shot Dead in Virginia; Worst U.S. Gun Rampage," *New York Times*, April 17, 2007, A1. For an analysis, see, Greg Winter, "Why Educators Falter before the Enigma of Violence," *New York Times*, March 30, 2005, B7.

[11] Katherine S. Newman, *Rampage: The Social Roots of School Shootings* (New York: Basic Books, 2004); Mohammad Shafii and Sharon Lee Shafii, eds., *School Violence: Assessment, Management, Prevention* (Washington, DC: American Psychiatric Press, 2001); Peter Applebome, "For Youths, Fear of Crime Is Pervasive and Powerful: Worries Force New Behavior, Study Finds," *New York Times*, January 12, 1996, A12; Evelyn Nieves, "An Inner-City Perspective on High School Violence," *New York Times*, March 18, 2001, A12. Some authorities combine the problem of violence with problems of incivility, intolerance, and undisciplined behavior in the schools.

[12] John Leland, "Zero Tolerance Changes Life at One School," *New York Times*, April 8, 2001, XI-1. However, the "zero tolerance" policy has led to a dispute over what constitutes a threat worthy of suspension or expulsion. In support of free speech, the American Civil Liberties Union has challenged disciplinary action taken, for example, against a student for wearing a t-shirt endorsing anarchy.

[13] See, e.g., John Holl, "Students Shot After School in Jersey City," *New York Times*, January 4, 2006, B-3.

[14] Robert Kagan, "Power and Weakness," *Policy Review* 113 (June/July 2002): 3-28.

simply, inherently violent. This question has been debated by philosophers, psychologists, sociologists, anthropologists, biologists and paleontologists for years. Seventeenth-century British political philosopher Thomas Hobbes argued famously that all men in society are inherently brutish, self-interested and prone to violence, and it requires great control to prevent their passions and desires from plunging society into anarchy.[15] French philosopher Jean-Jacques Rousseau alternatively proposed that human nature is essentially peaceful and that it is civilization that corrupts otherwise peaceful human existence.[16] Both Sigmund Freud and ethnologist Konrad Lorenz concluded that humans were inherently aggressive.[17] The debate about the sources of human violence--whether it is biologically driven or externally conditioned or motivated--continues to the present day.[18]

Gender analysis also has been involved in the debate over human nature. It has been argued that the female half of humankind seems to be less directed towards violence. Confronting the industrial arms race and war at the beginning of the twentieth century, Jane Addams, reformer, peace activist, suffragist, and one of the founders of modern social work, was one of many who argued that women's maternal instincts could lead to a nurturing rather than warring society and to a peaceful world.[19] More recently, Judith Hand, a biologist at UCLA, reasserted this view, contending that women are less inclined to be combative and less likely to engage in wars than men because their biological role as mothers necessitates that they protect their young.[20] Alternatively, others have emphasized culture over biology. For example, Linda Stamato, Co-Director of the Center for Negotiation and Conflict Resolution at Rutgers, The State University of New Jersey, has suggested that the socialization of

---

[15] Thomas Hobbes (1588-1679), wrote that men in a state of nature, without civil government, are in a war of all against all. See *The Leviathan* (1651) and *Of Liberty and Necessity* (1654).

[16] Jean-Jacques Rousseau (1712-1778) held that humans were good by nature but corrupted by the harmful influences of civilization. See *Emile, or l'education* (1762) and *Social Contract* (1762).

[17] In his *Civilization and its Discontents* (1929), Sigmund Freud identified the source of much human unhappiness as the result of efforts of individuals to stifle their aggressive tendencies in order to live in an organized society. In *On Aggression* (1966), Konrad Lorenz studied the instinctive behavior of animals and concluded that animals, especially males, were biologically programmed to use aggression in response to challenges from other animals for critical resources.

[18] While archeologists Debra Martin and David Frayer in *Troubled Times: Violence and Warfare in the Past* (Australia: Gordon and Breach Publishers, 1997) and Lawrence Keeley in *War Before Civilization* (New York: Oxford University Press, 1996) believe that the available archeological evidence confirms the existence of prehistoric violence, renowned South African paleontologist Philip Tobias notes that Homo erectus and Homo habilis both lived in the same areas of Africa for more than a million years without any fossil records of violence between them (see Philip V. Tobias, *Man's Past and Future*. Johannesburg: Witwatersrand University Press, 1969). Finnish developmental psychologist Kaj Bjorkqvist argues that human conflict does not necessarily lead to violence. See Douglas Fry and Kaj Bjorkqvist, eds., *Cultural Variation in Conflict Resolution: Alternatives to Violence* (Mahwah, NJ: Lawrence Erlbaum, 1997). Anthropologist and conflict resolution practitioner William Ury hypothesizes that once humans moved from nomadic hunting and gathering to farming, centuries of human cooperation changed to conflict and violence because of increased population and reduced opportunities to "walk away" with families increasingly tied to the land. See *William Ury, Getting to Peace: Transforming Conflict at Home, at Work, and in the World* (New York: Viking, 1999). Columbia University psychologist and educator Morton Deutsch makes similar conjectures. See "Oppression and Conflict," plenary address at the annual meetings of the International Society of Justice Research in Skovde, Sweden, June 17, 2002.

[19] Jane Addams dealt extensively with the connection between women and peace in *The Long Road of Women's Memory* (New York: Macmillan, 1916), as did English pacifist and suffragist leader, Emmeline Pethick Lawrence in "Motherhood and War," *Harper's Weekly* 59 (December 5, 1914): 542-45.

[20] Judith L. Hand, *Women, Power and the Biology of Peace* (San Diego: Questpath, 2003). See also Stephen P. Rosen, *War and Human Nature.* (Princeton, NJ: Princeton University Press, 2007).

women tends to lead them to focus on long-term relationships over short-term power issues that are traditionally of more concern to men.[21]

Violence also can simply be a result of poor judgment. In a book she entitled, *The March of Folly*, noted historian Barbara Tuchman reviewed several famous episodes in history, each of which led to violence and bloodshed that she contends were unnecessary because viable non-violent alternatives were available. She argues that the policies that led to such avoidable bloodshed occurred because of "the pursuit by government of policies contrary to their own interest." Why, Tuchman asks, "did the Trojan rulers drag the suspicious-looking horse into their walls despite every reason to suspect a trick by the Greeks in the Trojan War?" Why did King George III continue to undertake policies that were contrary to British self interest in maintaining goodwill with her American colonies that benefited Britain economically, politically and morally? Why did the United States not continue to support anti-colonial efforts by the Vietnamese to obtain self-rule immediately after World War II? In each case, Tuchman concludes that the answer lies in "woodenheadedness" by leaders who were guilty of either "assessing a situation in terms of preconceived fixed notions while ignoring or rejecting any contrary signs" or "the refusal to benefit from experience."[22] This problem continues to the present.[23] Alternatives to violence are often ignored because the threat or actual use of violence appears to promise swift and decisive results.

Alternatives to Violence

We are not recommending that Americans should be submissive. The idea is not to appease or capitulate in order to avoid violence. Nor are we arguing that violence is never warranted. Violence *is* sometimes justified. We believe that violence may be warranted, indeed might be necessary, under limited circumstances where no reasonable alternative exists. As prescribed in "just war" theory, organized violence should be employed only as a last resort and in carefully defined circumstances, with the means employed proportional to the threat.[24] One of the main problems with violence as a means of resolving conflict is that it often does *not* resolve the underlying conflict. In fact, it may simply postpone resolution or even make the conflict worse by aggravating the situation and inducing further violence in retaliation. In addition, violence often produces unanticipated results and sometimes irreparable consequences.

In contrast to America's predominately power-oriented culture, there has been a less recognized peace-oriented subculture in America since the colonial times. This peace subculture has focused less on the dominant concerns of power, coercion, and victory; instead it has put more emphasis on persuasion, cooperation, mutual consent, and sustained harmony. Not surprisingly, the peace subculture has emphasized inducements rather than threats, persuasion rather than coercion, conciliation or reconciliation rather than victory and defeat. Most of those who have been part of the peace subculture and the most vocal critics of the raw use of power have often

---

[21] Linda Stamato, "The New Age of Negotiation," *Ivey Business Journal Online*, July 1, 2004. The direction of women's studies in recent years has emphasized women's connection to peace as deriving from their social and political acculturation rather than from any innate biological characteristics. See, e.g., the survey in Berenice A. Carroll, "Feminism and Pacifism: Historical and Theoretical Connections," in *Women and Peace: Theoretical, Historical and Practical Perspectives*, Ruth Roach Pierson, ed. (London: Croom Helm, 1987), 2-28.

[22] Barbara Tuchman, *March of Folly: From Troy to Vietnam* (New York: Ballantine Books, 1984); see especially pages 4, 7, 128 and 234-235.

[23] See, Nicholas D. Kristof, "Et Tu, George?" *New York Times,* January 23, 2007, A19, for the example of the U.S. and the quagmire in Iraq.

[24] See, for example, Michael Walzer, *Just and Unjust Wars: A Moral Argument with Historical Illustrations*, 2nd ed. (New York: Basic Books, 1992); and Walzer, *Arguing about War* (New Haven, CT: Yale University Press, 2005).

been activists seeking to make society more equitable and compassionate. Some people were led to this peace subculture through religious beliefs; others came to it through personal experience and secular attitudes. Some were pacifists or humanists with views about common membership in society; some were simply seeking to maintain harmony within the immediate or extended family. The influence of this subculture can be seen through the pacifistic religious faiths, such as the Quakers and Mennonites. The subculture of peace has a long history in the American past that included the nonsectarian peace movement, the Women's Rights Movement and other social reform movements of the nineteenth century; and through some of the non-violent groups within the broader civil rights, women's, peace, anti-nuclear, and environmental movements in the twentieth century.[25]

The American Civil Rights Movement is a successful example of a peaceful resolution to a conflict. Nonviolent protests in the streets helped to frame and press the moral issues underlying segregation that were raised and ultimately decided by Congress and the courts. Writing in 1958 about the Montgomery Bus Boycott three years earlier, the Reverend Martin Luther King, Jr., warned against the dangers of resorting to violence, even when used against oppression:

> Violence as a way of achieving racial justice is both impractical and immoral. It is impractical because it is a descending spiral ending in destruction for all. The old law of an eye for an eye leaves everybody blind. It is immoral because it seeks to humiliate the opponent rather than win his understanding; it seeks to annihilate rather than to convert. Violence is immoral because it thrives on hatred rather than love. It destroys community and makes brotherhood impossible. It leaves society in monologue rather than dialogue. Violence ends by defeating itself. It creates bitterness in the survivors and brutality in the destroyers. A voice echoes through time saying to every potential Peter, "Put up your sword." History is cluttered with the wreckage of nations that fail to follow this command.[26]

South Africa after apartheid provides one of the best and most surprising success stories of nonviolent reconciliation. Although it was widely expected that apartheid would be overthrown by violence and that a bloody race war would result, instead black and white South Africans found a way to peacefully share the same land together. Despite his long years of imprisonment by the white Afrikaner regime, Nelson Mandela, once liberated, chose to focus on reconciliation rather than retribution. He reframed the issue from one of *fault* to one of cooperation and reconciliation through the establishment of a Truth and Reconciliation Commission. Although not totally without violence, this unexpectedly peaceful result demonstrates both the positive impact that an individual leader can have and the value of creatively reframing an issue to preserve rather than demolish a relationship. In his autobiography, *Long Walk to Freedom,* Mandela emphasized the need to appreciate the humanity of those who might seek to hurt or destroy you and concluded that: "to be free is not merely to cast off one's chains, but to live in a way that respects and enhances the freedom of others."[27]

---

[25] On the peace subculture, see, for example, Charles DeBenedetti, *The Peace Reform in American History* (Bloomington: Indiana University Press, 1980); Charles Chatfield, *The American Peace Movement: Ideals and Activism* (New York: Twayne, 1992); Harriet Hyman Alonso, *Peace as a Women's Issue: A History of the U.S. Movement for World Peace and Women's Rights* (Syracuse, NY: Syracuse University Press, 1993); James C. Junke and Carol M. Hunter, *The Missing Peace: The Search for Nonviolent Alternatives in United States History* (Scottdale, PA.: Herald Press, 2001); Viktoria Hertling, "Countering a 'Culture of Violence.' Can it be Done?" *Peace & Change,* 32/1 (January 2007): 78-88.

[26] Martin Luther King, Jr., *Stride Toward Freedom: The Montgomery Story* (New York: Harper and Row, 1958), 213.

[27] See Nelson Mandela's own description of this process and his conclusions in *Long Walk to Freedom: The Autobiography of Nelson Mandela* (Boston: Little Brown, 1994), 624-25. Gail M. Presbey, "Evaluating the Legacy of Nonviolence in South Africa," *Peace & Change,* 31/2 (April 2007): 141-174.

The Dalai Lama provides yet another example of a peaceful approach to conflict resolution by a strong and enlightened leader. Much like Mandela, the current Dalai Lama has been trying to reclaim his historic country of Tibet by gaining moral support from other countries and peoples. He has emphasized inner peace and empathy with others. Explaining his philosophy in a speech at Rutgers University in September 2005, Tenzin Gyatso, the fourteenth Dalai Lama, spoke out against anger and violence. "Anger blinds you to the real issues," he said. It prevents the mind from seeing clearly and distorts reality by emphasizing the negative. Instead, he asserted, one needs calmness and compassion with mutual regard, mutual trust in order to open one's "inner door" and develop "internal disarmament." Individuals with "internal disarmament" focus on emotions that are beneficial and constructive rather than hostile and aggressive and find peaceful solutions to conflicts.[28]

Although media emphasis has been on violence in the world, the *Human Security Report* published by Oxford University Press in 2005 indicates that global violence has, in fact, decreased. The report concluded that since the end of the Cold War in 1991, armed conflict and nearly all other forms of political violence have diminished. Worldwide, there were 40 percent fewer conflicts in 2003 than there had been in 1992. With the demise of the Soviet Union and the end of the Cold War, big power "proxy wars" ended and the United Nations was freed to focus on peacekeeping. This resulted in quiet peacekeeping successes in Namibia, El Salvador, Mozambique, eastern Slovenia, and East Timor, achievements that went largely unheralded because of press focus on the horrific failures in Rwanda, Serbia, and Darfur. Despite such failures, a 2005 Rand Corporation study found that United Nations peace-building operations had a two-thirds success rate.[29] International terrorism is the only type of political violence that has increased, yet terrorists kill only a fraction of the number killed in wars. Despite this, the dominant public perception is of an immediate threat, far beyond its actual lethality.[30]

German philosopher Immanuel Kant had predicted an era of perpetual peace and relative prosperity once monarchies had been replaced by liberal, self-governing republics.[31] With the end of the Cold War, political scientists have resurrected Kant's idea of perpetual peace, asserting that liberal democracies do not fight each other. Conservative American political scientist Robert Kagan contends, however, that while Europe is headed in the direction of peaceful international cooperation, the United States "remains mired in history, exercising power in the anarchic Hobbesian world...."[32] Having popularized the idea of "the end of history" with the triumph of liberal democracy, Francis Fukuyama fears that our liberal emphasis on rights and shared interests will fall before societies focused on self-discipline and duty to the community.[33] Even more fearful is conservative political

---

[28] Speech by Tenzin Gyatso, the Dalai Lama, "Peace, War and Reconciliation," at Rutgers, The State University of New Jersey, New Brunswick, NJ, September 25, 2005. See also, Dalai Lama, *Ethics for the New Millennium* (New York: Riverhead, 1999).

[29] Both reports cited in Andrew Mack, "Our Peaceful Planet," Op-Ed, *Newark Star-Ledger*, Jan. 1, 2006, X-1; the article originally appeared in the *Washington Post*. The deadliest conflicts—those with 1,000 or more battle deaths—fell by some 80 percent. The number of genocides and other mass slaughters of civilians also dropped by 80 percent, while core human rights abuses declined in five out of six regions of the developing world since the mid-1990s.

[30] James Traub, "Wonderful World? Since the cold war, the earth has become more peaceful. Why doesn't it feel that way?" *New York Times Magazine,* March 19, 2006, 13-14.

[31] Immanuel Kant, "Perpetual Peace: A Philosophical Sketch" (1795). This urgent plea for international cooperation, written when Kant was 71, sets forth ways for achieving such a peace through nations with civil constitutions, republican governments, and a federation of free states. It has been viewed as an argument for the creation of liberal republics in order to limit war.

[32] Kagan, "Power and Weakness," 3. For a more liberal view, see Spencer R. Weart, *Never at War: Why Democracies Will Not Fight One Another* (New Haven, CT: Yale University Press, 1998)

[33] Francis Fukuyama, *The End of History and the Last Man* (New York: The Free Press, 1992).

scientist Samuel P. Huntington of Harvard University, who views what he calls a "clash of civilizations" (or cultures) as even more likely today than during the Cold War. However, even he notes that whether we live in war or peace will depend on how our leaders respond to what they perceive as threats.[34]

Conflict Resolution Theory and Skills

In recent years, there has been much research on conflict resolution theory and techniques, especially "principled" or "interest-based" negotiation and mediation that produces a so-called "win-win" solution.[35] Principled or interest-based negotiation seeks "to decide issues on their merits rather than through a haggling process."[36] This process can be applied to third-party mediation as well as to direct negotiation between or among disputing parties. It identifies and focuses on key needs or vital interests—material and emotional—that underlie the rhetoric, posturing, positions or hostility of the disputing parties. It seeks to identify the degree to which the dispute is not a "zero-sum" situation, so that it is not necessary for one side to lose for the other side to win.[37] Perhaps the resources are not finite. Perhaps not all parties really want the same thing. Our book, *Conflict Resolution and United States History,* draws upon this body of conflict resolution theory and practice to show how to work creatively to resolve conflict nonviolently and reach solutions that are produced by agreement rather than by coercion and that may be mutually beneficial and long-lasting.

Conflict resolution techniques emphasize communication, active listening, identifying key issues and needs, separating positions and interests, and creative reframing of issues. Using such techniques, successful interest-based negotiation or mediation can move beyond initial anger and hostility to achieve a resolution in which each party achieves his or her most important needs and interests and which is fair, practical, stable and lasting, or at least has provisions for periodic reexamination and renewal of consensus as circumstances change. Chapter Two of this book deals specifically and practically with these techniques.

Although people have been using non-violent conflict resolution techniques for centuries, alternative dispute resolution or conflict resolution as a formal theory is a relatively recent concept. Some of the pioneering research in the development of dispute resolution theory was done in response to the threat of nuclear warfare

---

[34] Samuel P. Huntington, *The Clash of Civilizations and the Remaking of World Order* (New York: Simon and Schuster, 1996).

[35] "Win-win" is the name given to the process of conflict resolution that seeks to maximize the results for all disputants. See Fred E. Jandt, *Win-Win Negotiating: Turning Conflicts into Agreements* (New York: John Wiley and Sons, 1985).

[36] The phrase "principled negotiation" was popularized by Roger Fisher and William Ury, founders of the Program on Negotiation (www.pon.org) at the Harvard Law School. See Fisher and Ury, with Bruce Patton, *Getting to Yes: Negotiating Agreement Without Giving In*, 2nd ed. (New York: Penguin Books, 1991). More recent works include Roger Fisher and Scott Brown, *Getting Together: Building Relationships As We Negotiate* (New York: Penguin, 1988); William Ury, *Getting Past No: Negotiating Your Way from Confrontation to Cooperation* (New York: Bantam, 1991); William Ury, et al., *Getting Disputes Resolved: Designing Systems to Cut the Costs of Conflict* (Cambridge: Harvard Project on Negotiation, 1993); and William Ury, *Getting to Peace: Transforming Conflict at Home, at Work and in the World* (New York: Penguin Putnam, Inc., 1999). Other sources include: Phyllis Beck Kritek, *Negotiating at an Uneven Table: A Practical Approach to Working with Difference and Diversity* (San Francisco: Jossey-Bass, 1994); Morton Deutsch and Peter T. Coleman, *The Handbook of Conflict Resolution: Theory and Practice* (San Francisco: Jossey-Bass, 2000); Deborah M. Kolb, Judith Williams, and Carol Frohlinger, *Her Place at the Table: A Woman's Guide to Negotiating Five Key Challenges to Leadership Success* (San Francisco: Jossey-Bass, 2004); and Michael L. Moffitt and Robert C. Bardone, eds., *The Handbook of Dispute Resolution* (San Francisco: Jossey-Bass, 2005).

[37] "Zero sum" describes the situation in which a participant's gain or loss is exactly balanced by the losses or gains of the other participants. When the total gains are added up and the total losses are subtracted, the sum will be zero. Chess is an example of a zero-sum game: it is impossible for both players to win.

during the Cold War. The plunge to the brink of nuclear catastrophe in the Cuban Missile Crisis of 1962 led some to explore ways to curtail escalating threats of violence.[38] More recently, the continuing crisis in the Middle East, as well as the rash of ethnic civil wars that followed the breakup of the Soviet Empire and the end of the Cold War in 1991, gave further impetus to work on negotiation and mediation.[39]

The shocking waves of urban violence that rocked American society in the late 1960s and early 1970s led to domestic efforts to develop negotiation and mediation programs and to enhance conflict resolution theory. Mediation and arbitration had been part of labor management relations for decades. But beginning in the late 1960s, interest rapidly expanded in negotiation and especially in mediation as alternatives to violence or to settlements imposed by the courts, an arbitrator or a legislature. Most dramatically, as a result of major urban riots, community mediation emerged as a possible mechanism to deal with interpersonal and inter-group conflicts underlying the violence. In the top-down models, business, civic, and governmental organizations sought to resolve major and minor community disputes through mediation rather than legal action. In contrast, in the grass-roots models, activist organizations tried a style of community-based mediation patterned after various non-Western dispute resolution traditions and institutions such as the informal, harmony-oriented African "moots."[40]

As litigation proliferated in the United States in the late twentieth century, the mediation movement spread to areas that had previously been under the jurisdiction of the courts. Burdened by drastically increased case loads, the judiciary encouraged litigants to try to resolve their disputes through mediation rather than going to trial. The trend toward mediation expanded rapidly to include such areas as divorce, child custody, and landlord-tenant relations. In the final decades of the twentieth century, the mediation movement grew to include costly litigation, such as products liability and environmental issues. The idea was to involve the people who would be affected by and would have to live with decisions. Mediation held out the promise of practical, acceptable, and stable solutions to policy needs and enforcement problems.[41]

---

[38]See, e.g., Robert Jervis, *Perception and Misperception in International Politics* (Princeton, NJ: Princeton University Press, 1976); Richard Smoke, *War: Controlling Escalation* (Cambridge, MA: Harvard University Press, 1977). For more recent work since the end of the Cold War, particularly on civil and ethnic wars, see Roy E. Licklider, *Stopping the Killing: How Civil Wars End* (New York: New York University Press, 1993); John Darby and William J. Long and Peter Brecke, *War and Reconciliation: Reason and Emotion in Conflict Resolution* (Cambridge, MA: M.I.T. Press, 2003); and Joseph S. Nye, Jr., *Understanding International Conflicts: An Introduction to Theory and History*, 6th ed., (New York: Pearson Longman, 2007).

[39] See e.g., J. Bercovitch, "International Mediation: A Study of the Incidence, Strategies, and Conditions of Successful Outcomes," *Cooperation and Conflict* 21 (1986): 155-168 (Bercovitch studied 210 mediation efforts in 72 international disputes occurring between 1945 and 1984 and drew a number of conclusions about what conditions—nature of the parties as well as the mediator—were most conducive to international mediation) and John A. Vasquez, James Turner Johnson, Sanford Jaffe, and Linda Stamato, eds., *Beyond Confrontation: Learning Conflict Resolution in the Post-Cold War Era* (Ann Arbor: University of Michigan Press, 1995).

[40] The African "moots," despite regional differences, share similarities as informal, ad hoc, mediated assemblies of neighbors in a village setting that allows a full airing of domestic and other grievances and seeks to achieve a consensual solution, reconciling the temporarily aggrieved parties with positive rewards rather than negative sanctions, rehabilitating the offending party and restoring the solidarity of the group. For a detailed analysis of one such moot, see James L. Gibbs, "The Kpelle Moot," *Africa*, 33, no. 1 (1963), reprinted in Aaron Podolefsky and Peter J. Brown, eds., *Applying Anthropology: An Introductory Reader*, 3rd ed. (New York: McGraw-Hill, 1994). One of the present co-authors, Arlene Gardner, learned during a visit to Senegal in March 2005 as part of a civic education exchange program of the current use of consensual airing of grievances in which the parties continue a respectful dialogue until the dispute is resolved.

[41] Particularly informative on this history is Robert A. Baruch Bush, "Dispute Resolution—the Domestic Arena: Methods, Applications, and Critical Issues," in Vasquez, Johnson, Jaffe and Stamato, eds., *Beyond Confrontation* (Ann Arbor, MI:

During the 1980s and 1990s, some public and private schools added "peer mediation" programs to their curricula in a laudable attempt to provide alternatives to student violence. Peer mediation enables trained student mediators to help their peers to identify the problem underlying the conflict and ways to solve it.[42] However, there are limitations to most peer mediation programs in schools. According to teachers and school administrators involved with peer mediation programs, one of the main problems with such programs is the difficulty in finding time in an already full curriculum and teaching schedule to include another course, even one that teachers and principals believe is as worthwhile as conflict resolution. Another problem is that in many peer mediation programs, only a few students are selected and trained to be peer mediators. Often, the teacher or school administrator who makes the selection will choose those students who excel academically and have very good social skills. These may not, however, be students who other students view as peers. More importantly, students identified as "troublemakers," who are often those most in need of conflict resolution insights and skills, are usually not the students identified for peer mediation training.[43] However, when teachers select students who represent a cross-section of the student body, training is broadly provided to teachers, administrators, students and parents, and the program is integrated into the academic day, a peer mediation program can be effective in building student confidence and conflict resolution skills.[44]

Our *Conflict Resolution and United States History* program offers a different approach. It integrates conflict resolution into a core curriculum—U.S. history. In our method, *all* of the students in the U.S. history classes participate in learning conflict resolution skills and applying them to disputes in the distant and recent American past. This approach has a serious academic component: students learn conflict resolution skills and history, and their proficiency in both is tested and graded. There is also a practical aspect: our curriculum prescribes first teaching conflict resolution skills by using hypothetical examples from everyday life—such as a

---

University of Michigan Press, 1995), 9-38; John Lande, "Getting the Faith: Why Business Lawyers and Executives Believe in Mediation," *Harvard Negotiation Law Review* 5 (2000): 201; Robert A. Baruch Bush and Joseph P. Folger, *The Promise of Mediation: The Transformative Approach to Conflict*, 2nd ed. (San Francisco: Jossey-Bass, 2004); and Stamato, "The New Age of Negotiation."

[42] See, for example, the Resolving Conflict Creatively Program, an initiative of Educators for Social Responsibility, Cambridge, Massachusetts, the largest peer mediation program in the country, begun in 1985 and now working with over 400 schools across the nation, at www.esrnational.org/about-rccp.html; National Association of Peer Programs in Gladstone, Missouri, which offers training for peer program trainers and program evaluators at www.peerprograms.org; Managing Student Behavior in Today's Schools, College of Education, University of Florida, Gainesville at http://education.ufl.edu/web/?pid=305; CRU Institute in Bellevue, Washington, which runs programs for faculty and students at www.cruinstitute.org; Life Trax in Aurora, Colorado, which offers peer mediation training to schools in the greater Denver area at www.schoolmediationcenter.org.

[43] Marie Koch (student assistance counselor and peer mediation director, Westfield Public Schools, Westfield, NJ), in discussion with co-author, Arlene Gardner, March, 2006.

[44] The Resolving Conflict Creatively Program provides training to teachers, administrators, students and parents to foster emotional and social development by focusing on the skills and practices of conflict resolution and diversity education. The peer mediators are selected by application or nomination and the teachers ensure that the mediators selected represent a cross-section of the student body. The peer mediations often take place during lunch. The positive results appear to flow from the fact that the program is aimed at changing the school culture by comprehensively working with administrators, teachers, students and parents. See the evaluation by William DeJong, *Building the Peace: The Resolving Conflict Creatively Program* (Washington, DC: National Institute of Justice, 1993). For an account of the program by its founders, see Linda Lantieri and Janet Patti, *Waging Peace in Our Schools* (Boston: Beacon Press, 1996).

dispute in a video store or with noisy neighbors. After that introduction, the conflict resolution skills are then applied to historical case studies. The case studies provide practice in using conflict resolution skills and an analytical framework for better understanding the sources of the conflict, its historical context, and plausible options that might have been available.

Understanding and using conflict resolution skills as applied both to daily life and historical events can help to build students' confidence in their problem-solving abilities and improve their social and academic skills. Furthermore, active engagement in the process of historical roleplaying can help students appreciate the degree to which individuals or groups can make a difference in the course of events. If students recognize that the direction of human history is not inevitable, they may feel empowered and motivated rather than apathetic and powerless, as unfortunately so many students feel today. By enabling teachers to provide instruction in conflict resolution and in American history at the same time, many of the problems associated with some peer mediation programs are alleviated. The curriculum approach in *Conflict Resolution and United States History* can demonstrate the importance of negotiation and mediation, significantly increase the number of students who are taught conflict resolution skills, and stimulate and enhance the learning of American history.

Why We Study the Past

There is great value in studying the past, and there are many reasons for teaching American history. The most commonly asserted rationale for studying history is to provide lessons for the present. In the often repeated words of the American philosopher George Santayana: "Those who cannot remember the past are condemned to repeat it."[45] Although many argue that studying the past will not help us to avoid making errors in the future,[46] this utilitarian justification is a powerful one, and our curriculum does emphasize the usefulness of the past in understanding the present. Sophisticated analysis of the past teaches that in many cases plausible alternatives existed. Various choices could have been made and might have made a difference. Such analysis of the past reinforces the importance of organization, action and leadership. It warns us of the dangers of unintended consequences. The past provides us with vicarious experiences that we can learn from. It also is humbling for those in the present to learn about obstacles that others overcame in the past—whether it be the achievements of immigrants, the triumph of the Civil Rights movement or, more theoretically, the rise—and fall—of whole societies and civilizations.[47] It is important to remember the past, in part, to avoid the hubris of the present. The past may be a guide to navigation, as suggested by historian David McCullough, it helps to tell us who we are, as individuals, as members of groups, and as a nation. We have to know who we *were*, if we want to know who we are and where we are going.[48]

We may look at history not only as events that happened and seek to understand why, but also to praise, condemn or simply remember what happened. Memory is, of course, an essential part of history. Collective memory—or public memory as it is often called—has for centuries been used to give meaning to peoples and

---

[45] George Santayana, *The Life of Reason* (New York: Charles Scribner's Sons, 1905); or as Malcolm X phrased it: "History is a people's memory, and without memory man is demoted to the lower animals."

[46] See, for example, Henry Steele Commager, *The Nature and the Study of History* (Columbus, OH: Charles E. Merrill, 1965); and Peter J. Lee, "Why Learn History?" in *Learning History*, A.K. Dickinson, P.J. Lee and P.J. Rogers, eds. (London: Heinemann Education, 1984).

[47] See, e.g., Jared Diamond, *Collapse: How Societies Choose to Fail or Succeed* (New York: Viking, 2005).

[48] David McCullough, Commencement Address, Wesleyan University, Middletown, Connecticut, June 3, 1984.

their place in the world. "History is to a nation as memory is to the individual," declared American historian Arthur M. Schlesinger Jr., "so a nation denied a conception of the past will be disabled in dealing with its present and its future."[49]

From the beginning of the republic through the mid-twentieth century, national history and national icons were emphasized as part of building a unified identity and public memory for Americans.[50] However, since the 1960s, this kind of unified national history has been seriously challenged as simplistic in neglecting the pluralism of the American people and their experiences. Instead, we began to also look at the memories and histories offered by the various ethnic and racial groups that compose American society and to celebrate them as part of the American experiment in a pluralistic, multicultural democracy.[51] By the 1980s, a struggle began over the definition of the nature of America society and the national memory, including the kind of history that should be taught. These so-called "culture wars" pitted "traditional" American history, which was focused on national political, economic and military history and foreign relations and the roles of influential national leaders, against the new social and cultural history and multicultural history, which emphasized the common people, including women and minorities and the perspectives of the many different groups that comprise our society.[52] History as now widely studied includes an appreciation of the multiplicity of perspectives on events in the past.

We also can look at history as fascinating literature in the humanistic tradition as old as Homer and Thucydides. In the hands of compelling narrative historians such as Stephen Ambrose, Doris Kearns Goodwin, David McCullough, Arthur Schlesinger, and Barbara Tuchman, the past becomes an inherently fascinating account filled with dramatic characters and storylines as well as useful examples. Not simply a compilation of facts, history can come alive and be an engaging rendition of high emotion, especially when students are put into the places of people, who were just as human as they are. History can provide us with insight into the human condition and the complexity of human motivation.

Studying history also can help to develop critical thinking skills. Historian Antulio J. Echevarria II has recommended that students study history to "rigorously scrutinize facts and sources," detect "biases and specious arguments" and penetrate "the myths that surround the past."[53] Equipping students to examine historical interpretations rigorously moves students from simple recall of information to synthesis and evaluation--the

---

[49] Arthur M. Schlesinger Jr., "Folly's Antidote," *New York Times*, January 1, 2007, p. A19.

[50] See George Lipsitz, *Time Passages: Collective Memory and American Popular Culture* (Minneapolis: University of Minnesota Press, 1990); Michael G. Kammen, *In the Past Lane: Historical Perspectives on American Culture* (New York: Oxford University Press, 1997); G. Kurt Piehler, *Remembering War the American Way* (Washington, DC: Smithsonian Institution Press, 1995); Eric Foner, *The Story of American Freedom* (New York: W.W. Norton, 1998); David W. *Blight, Race and Reunion: The Civil War in American Memory* (Cambridge, MA: Harvard University Press, 2001).

[51] John Bodnar, *Remaking America: Public Memory, Commemoration, and Patriotism in the Twentieth Century* (Princeton, NJ: Princeton University Press, 1992).

[52] For examples of the contending schools of thought, see Lynne V. Cheney, "The End of History," *Wall Street Journal*, October 20, 1994, A22; Gary B. Nash, Charlotte Crabtree and Ross E. Dunn, *History on Trial: Culture Wars and the Teaching of the Past* (New York: Knopf, 1999); and James Leming, Lucien Ellington and Kathleen Porter, *Where Did Social Studies Go Wrong?* (Washington, DC: Thomas B. Fordham Foundation, 2003).

[53] Antulio J. Echevarria II, "The Trouble with History, " *Parameters*, 35/ 2 (Summer 2005): 78-90.

highest levels of Bloom's Taxonomy of Cognitive Outcomes.[54] Echevarria is reflecting longtime concerns, such as those articulated by John Dewey a century ago, that our beliefs should be grounded in evidence.[55] We study history to learn how to think, to inquire into the causation of events and the motivation of individuals, as well as to understand the past.

We might study history in order to enlarge, or possibly transform, American culture from one that practices, encourages and even celebrates violence to one that can practice, encourage and celebrate non-violence. Thomas Merton, noted American religious writer and poet, wrote before his death in 1968, "Nonviolent action must establish itself in the minds and memories of modern man not only as *conceivable* and *possible*, but as a *desirable alternative* to what he now considers the only realistic possibility: namely, political technique backed by force."[56]

Perhaps, most importantly, we study history in order to have the knowledge and skills to be informed, engaged citizens in a democratic society. In their recent book, *Teaching History for the Common Good*, Keith C. Barton and Linda S. Levstik systematically review the various purposes for studying history. They conclude, correctly in our view, that knowledge of history and a critical understanding of the past are crucial for an educated individual and essential to a well functioning democracy. Focusing on the intersection of goals, content and pedagogy, they stress that teachers need to understand both the structures and principles of their disciplines—in this case history—and how to transform the methods, concepts and knowledge of that discipline in ways that will make sense to students.[57]

But, there are numerous problems that confront history teachers in their classrooms: the lack of knowledge and interest, as well as widespread apathy and cynicism among many students. Too many Americans are essentially historically illiterate. They know virtually nothing about their nation's past. According to the National Assessment of Educational Progress, more than half of America's high school seniors do not know basic facts about American history.[58] They do not know the intent of the Monroe Doctrine or the primary goal of U.S. foreign

---

[54] Lorin W. Anderson, et. al., *A Taxonomy for Learning, Teaching and Assessing: A Revision of Bloom's Taxonomy of Educational Objectives* (Boston: Allyn and Bacon, 2001). See also Marcy P. Driscoll, *Psychology of Learning for Instruction*, 3d ed.(Boston: Allyn and Bacon, 2005).

[55] John Dewey, *How We Think* (New York: D.C. Heath, 1910).

[56] Thomas Merton, "Blessed Are the Meek: The Roots of Christian Nonviolence," *Fellowship* (May 1967): 20.

[57] Keith C. Barton and Linda S. Levstik, *Teaching History for the Common Good* (Mahwah, NJ: Lawrence Erlbaum Associates, 2004).

[58] The most recent nationwide evaluations by the U.S. Department of Education, the *National Assessment of Educational Progress, 2006* (released on May 16, 2007) indicated that the percentage of 12th graders scoring at or above the basic level in U.S. History increased from 43 percent in 2001 to 47 percent in 2006. (Institute of Education Sciences, U.S. Department of Education) http://nationsreportcard.gov/ushistory_2006. There was no change in the scores of 12th graders in civics from 2001. Only 27% of twelfth-graders reached a "proficient" mastery of civics. (Institute of Education Sciences, US Department of Education) http://nationsreportcard.gov/civics_2006. In a 2006 study by the McCormick Tribune Freedom Museum, only one in 1000 Americans could name the five fundamental freedoms included in the First Amendment to the U.S. Constitution (speech, religion, press, assembly, petition), but 22 percent knew the names of the five Simpson cartoon characters. See "Characters from 'The Simpsons' More Well known to Americans than their First Amendment Freedoms, Survey Finds," news release, March 1, 2006, (McCormick Tribune Foundation) www.mccormicktribune.org. Not only do our young people lack basic knowledge about U.S. history, civics and government, but they tend to vote at a much lower rate than their parents and they are distrustful of government. See, e.g., *The Civic Mission of Schools* (New York: CIRCLE and the Carnegie Corporation of New York, 2003).

policy after World War II. They cannot explain or interpret a complex historical event, such as Western expansion, the decimation of Native Americans, or the nature of the Civil Rights movement.[59] Many adult Americans are also woefully uninformed about the past. Polls show that a majority of adults do not know what "D-Day" means or even which countries the United States fought against in World War II.[60]

Not only do our young people know little about American history, but also many of them complain that studying history is "boring." Some dismiss history as irrelevant or as manipulated by the government, media or other powerful forces. Many feel helpless because of the overwhelming power of immense institutions and the seemingly inevitable flow of history. Cynics, such as the French philosopher Voltaire, see history as "the lie commonly agreed upon" and "a bag of tricks we play upon the dead,"[61] but understanding how individuals influence history can help students "to overcome the powerful pull of cynicism."[62] Manipulative, nonobjective reconstruction and interpretation of the past can, of course, be a trick played on the living. The past has certainly been unscrupulously used by some to manipulate the present in the interest of a particular policy. However, historical awareness can avoid or at least minimize the impact of such manipulation.

Students may be bored, apathetic or cynical about history because the study of the past is often presented as a long and seemingly inevitable sweep of past occurrences. To bring history alive, students need to understand and appreciate that individuals *can* have an impact on the course of events. The approach in *Conflict Resolution and United States History* confronts both students' lack of interest and their apathy or cynicism. It does so through historical roleplaying techniques that insert students into the past and help them to understand historical figures as people living in their own times.

Historical roleplaying can interest and involve students in studying and understanding the past. It can also broaden their views about their roles and the nature of society today and in the future. Too many young people see history and even future developments as following some kind of inevitable course of events. This sense of inevitability reinforces existing feelings of powerlessness and apathy. However, if we can show young people how choices and actions did or could have made a difference in the past, we can help them to better comprehend the richness of the past and also to better understand themselves as well as their responsibilities. Most importantly, we may be able to encourage a belief in the utility and value of being an informed and engaged citizen contributing in constructive ways to a better American society.

Historical Inevitability vs. Considering Alternatives in History

History textbooks too often seem to imply inevitability, and many students see history as an continuous chain of events. But, history is *not* inevitable. Complex events are not predetermined. Instead, individuals (such as presidents, kings, congresses, leaders of social movements or other influential individuals or groups) make decisions at points in time in the unfolding development of a conflict which may narrow the range of options for resolving the conflict. By not giving the alternative possibilities, the implicit view offered by the textbook is that the

---

[59] "Most 12th Graders Know Little American History, Survey Says," *New York Times*, November 2, 1995, A22.

[60] Ann Cronin, "America's Grade on 20th Century European Wars: F," *New York Times*, December 3, 1995, IV-5.

[61] Both quotes are commonly attributed to Voltaire, however, the original source is unknown, (website of the University of Notre Dame, Department of Philosophy) http://philosophy.nd.edu (accessed September 27, 2006).

[62] The phrase is from David Cortright, *Gandhi and Beyond: Nonviolence for an Age of Terrorism* (Boulder, CO: Paradigm Publishers, 2006), 2.

resulting resolution (often wars) was inevitable. In reality, up to the moment blood is shed, it often may be possible to follow a different option than the one that led to violence. For example, in the presidential election of 1844, Whig candidate Henry Clay lost to the Democrat James Polk because 5000 Whig voters in New York bolted and voted for a third-party candidate, costing Clay the state and the election. If Clay had won, perhaps war with Mexico over Texas and the southwest in 1846-48 might well have been avoided, since the Whig Party philosophy was to gradually expand westward through settlement rather than war.[63] Earlier, in 1776, war between Britain and her North American colonies was not inevitable: the British and the colonists could have made different decisions. Reconstruction of the South after the American Civil War did not have to unfold as it did: it was the result of choices made by individuals and groups at that time. We are not slaves to immutable historical forces. People can make a difference in the course of human events.

Since the course of human history is not inevitable, we believe that it is both legitimate and valuable to explore the options that existed at a given point in time, options that might have led to a different outcome. Reopening the past gives students a sense of the possibilities that existed and the excitement and drama of history. Involving students as actual participants in efforts to resolve significant conflicts in history piques their interest, challenges their curiosity, encourages them to raise questions about the causation and consequences of particular actions and events. Most importantly, this approach enables students to better understand what actually happened in history.

We are not advocating "imaginary" history, the kind of wild conjecture, such as "what would have happened to the development of the Roman Empire if Antony had not been smitten by Cleopatra's beauty?" or "what would have happened if the Confederacy had won the Civil War?" Such questions lead to mere speculation, ungrounded in any empirical data and, therefore, are beyond the realm of historical analysis. British historian E.H. Carr, famously dismissed such speculation as "a parlour game with the might-have-beens of history."[64] However, several prominent historians, such as Harvard's Niall Ferguson and Princeton's John Murrin, have suggested that studying carefully controlled hypothetical or alternative history can help to better understand what actually happened and why.[65] Historian Robert Crowley called alternative history an "historical can opener" and a useful tool for understanding historical developments.[66] We are using the term, "alternative history," to mean the process of examining or exploring options that might have realistically been available at the time. The value of considering alternative history can be seen in the work of noted anthropologist Jared Diamond, who argues in *Guns, Germs and Steel: The Fates of Human Societies* that the evolution of a particular society is not an inevitable response to

---

[63] Jeffrey B. Morris and Richard B. Morris, eds. *Encyclopedia of American History*, 7th ed., (New York: Harper Collins, 1996), 212-213. See generally Michael F. Holt, *The Rise and Fall of the American Whig Party* (New York: Oxford University Press, 1999).

[64] Edward Hallett Carr, *What Is History?* 2nd ed. (New York: Knopf, 1965), 127. While condemning the idea, Carr did suggest it in his history of the Soviet Union, asking, for example, what would have happened if Lenin had not had a paralyzing stroke and had survived? Would Stalin still have come to power with his ruthless regime?

[65] For recent explorations in counterfactual history, see Niall Ferguson, ed., *Virtual History: Alternatives and Counterfactuals* (New York: Basic Books, 1999); John M. Murrin, "The French and Indian War, the American Revolution, and the Counterfactual Hypothesis: Reflections on Lawrence Henry Gipson and John Shy," *Reviews in American History* 1 (September 1973): 307-318; and the papers presented at "What If: Counterfactualism and Early American History," conference honoring Professor John M. Murrin, held at Princeton University, March 30-31, 2001; Gary J. Kornblith, "Rethinking the Coming of the Civil War: A Counterfactual Exercise," *Journal of American History*, 90/1 (June 2003): 76-105.

[66] Robert Crowley presentation at "Not Just a 'Parlour Game' Anymore: Counterfactual History in the Historical Mainstream--A Roundtable, "Annual Meeting of the American Historical Association, Philadelphia, PA, January 6, 2006.

migration or other external factors but rather the result of the decisions made by leaders regarding the use of their environmental as well as human resources.[67]

In his valedictory lecture as Regius Professor of Modern History at Oxford University in 1980, Hugh R. Trevor-Roper summarized the value of reopening the past:

At any given moment in history there are real alternatives, and to dismiss them as unreal because they were not realized...is to take the reality out of the situation. How can we 'explain what happened and *why*' if we only look at what happened and never consider the alternatives, the total pattern of forces whose pressure created the event? Take the case of revolutions. We all know the revolutions which happened. But how can we 'explain' them unless we can compare them with the revolutions which have not happened—that is, with those moments in history when similar circumstances and similar forces existed and yet revolution did not break out? To assume that 'what happened was bound to happen' is to beg the question of why it happened: it is what happened in the context of what might have happened... It is only if we place ourselves before the alternatives of the past, as of the present, only if we live for a moment, as the men of the time lived, in its still fluid context and among its still unresolved problems, if we see those problems coming upon us, as well as look back on them after they have gone away, that we can draw useful lessons from history."[68]

Plausibility is the key to the legitimacy of alternative or hypothetical history. It is essential that students understand the difference between alternatives that were plausible (that is, they had the distinct possibility of happening) and alternatives that were implausible (they had little or no chance of occurring). Students need to appreciate the difference and the reasons why some things actually happened, others might plausibly have happened, and still others could not possibly have happened.[69] In so doing, they learn much more about an historical situation and the complexity of causation. They also learn about the subjectivity of historians' re-creation of the past, an important lesson in itself--how the writing of history is a continual dialogue of the present with the past.[70] The greatest plausibility would be given to options that were advocated by participants at the time. Such analysis also will help students to appreciate that there are frequently unanticipated consequences to our actions. Things do not always turn out as planned. It is instructive to comprehend the options put forward and not taken and the reasons for that. This analysis will help us to better understand what actually happened and why.[71]

---

[67]Jared Diamond, *Guns, Germs and Steel: The Fates of Human Societies* (New York: W.W. Norton, 1997). After carefully analyzing the impact of animal and plant domestication on the development of a variety of societies, Diamond concludes that the way individuals and leaders respond to the availability or limitations of resources, not the existence of natural resources or other external factors, is what makes a difference in the direction or development of a society.

[68] Hugh Trevor-Roper, *History and Imagination* (Oxford: Clarendon Press, 1980) 12-13, 16.

[69] A conceptualization nicely stated by Isaiah Berlin in *Historical Inevitability* (London: Oxford University Press, 1959), 31.

[70] Peter Novick, *That Noble Dream: The "Objectivity Question" and the American Historical Profession* (Cambridge: Cambridge University Press, 1988); and John Lewis Gaddis, *The Landscape of History: How Historians Map the Past* (New York: Oxford University Press, 2002).

[71] Indeed, equal importance should be given to all of the major possibilities that contemporaries contemplated before the fact; otherwise, we become victims of the most elementary teleological error of examining only the evidence that proves the result.

Historical Roleplaying and Conflict Resolution

What we are proposing in *Conflict Resolution and United States History* is to "reopen" the past through historical roleplaying and the application of conflict resolution skills. Roleplaying is inherently interesting, so that students forget that history is supposed to be "boring." Unlike historical simulations where the students reenact what actually happened in history, historical roleplaying offers a more engaging challenge to the students. Our historical roleplaying scenarios provide parameters for the students to replay and theoretically even redirect the course of history. Students are encouraged to analyze the historical situation and to seek plausible alternatives or options to what actually happened. The value of this exercise is that it gives the students considerable insight into the historical actors, their interests, their positions and their circumstances. Thus, it enables students to achieve a deeper, richer understanding of history. The use of conflict resolution skills adds to the interest, as well as to an understanding of alternatives. Together, the historical roleplaying and the conflict resolution skills directly address the issues of motivation and apathy by enabling students to see how individuals and groups can, and do, have a major impact on the direction of social progress.

In consultation with teachers and scholars, we have selected twenty important conflicts in American history as case studies. More than half of these ultimately led to violence. While the violence may produce a temporary solution, it rarely resolves the underlying conflict. For example, although the military defeat of Germany in World War I put a temporary halt to German expansionist goals, it ultimately contributed to a second World War because it did not address the underlying feelings of "victimhood". While the American Civil War resolved the issues of secession and slavery, it left the underlying problem of the place of African Americans in a multiracial democracy for future generations to determine. On rare occasions, violence resolved the specific issues. For example, the American Revolution settled the conflict between Britain and her American colonies by removing the colonies from the control of the British government (although it did not determine the nature of the freedom and liberty that the colonists claimed for themselves). More often, the results of violence are not just. For example, it is difficult to view the Mexican War or Cherokee Removal as just or fair, although they were viewed a such by many people at the time.

The case studies in *Conflict Resolution and United States History* also include several conflicts that were resolved without significant violence; for example, the struggles involving women's rights, immigration, and racial integration in the twentieth century. Some of the case studies include compromises that ultimately turned out to be unsuccessful, such as the compromises over slavery at the Federal Convention of 1787 and the Compromise of 1850, both of which ultimately failed because they did not address the underlying issues and interests concerning slavery. Although the Cuban Missile Crisis in 1962 brought the world frightening close to nuclear war, leaders committed to averting such a disaster were able to defuse the immediate situation and even to address some of the underlying issues. While violent behavior often has been an important part of the nation's part, it is critical to note that the majority of political, economic or ideological conflicts in American history have been resolved without violence.

The next two chapters more fully explain how to teach conflict resolution skills (Chapter Two) and how to use these skills while doing historical roleplaying (Chapter Three). Chapter Two: "Developing Skills for Resolving Conflicts," provides background about the origins, responses and nature of conflict and the value of conflict resolution skills. Chapter Three: "How to Use the Curriculum Package," describes in detail the steps and materials for utilizing the case studies and our methodology of intertwining conflict resolution skills and historical roleplaying. The remaining chapters are the case studies in American history. They provide a full historical background prepared with the help of leading scholars of American history for each of the case studies. The accompanying CD, "*Conflict Resolution and United States History* Resource Materials," includes primary source documents, maps, charts, photographs and other illustrations as well as student handouts and teacher overheads that can be printed, copied and used in the classroom. The accompanying DVD, "Historical Roleplaying Using Conflict Resolution Skills," provides a visual demonstration by middle and high school students of our historical roleplaying and conflict resolution methodology in practice.

The Value of this Approach

Conflict Resolution and United States History helps to address the widespread lack of interest and the woeful lack of knowledge about history, as well as the lack of skills for resolving conflicts without violence. Americans have always been an especially forward-looking people, but since the cataclysmic 1960s, in particular, there has been an extensive belief that the past is irrelevant. This is stated most tellingly in the words of one highly popular song, "Don't stop thinking about tomorrow. Yesterday is gone."[72]

Intertwining historical roleplaying with the use of conflict resolution skills encourages students to look at and appreciate various perspectives. It enables teachers to motivate students by involving them in "reliving" history. Reopening the possibilities of the past by doing historical roleplaying makes learning history more interesting, challenging, and more likely to be retained by students. It follows the basic theory of John Dewey that students learn best "by doing," which has been confirmed by a century of research. A "Learning Pyramid" developed by the National Teaching Laboratory indicates that people, on average, retain 5 percent of what they hear in a lecture but 75 percent of what they learn by doing something. Historical roleplaying enables students to learn history by doing it.[73]

This methodology allows students to explore the past as a way of understanding the range of opportunities available within the limitations of the cultural context and historical circumstances of the time. At the same time, these instructional strategies offer the possibility of teaching conflict resolution skills through real conflicts whose consequences are now, given distant historical perspective, clearer to us. Through the process of learning and using conflict resolution skills, separating interests and positions, and comparing the results of their roleplaying with what actually happened in history, students learn not only history and conflict resolution skills but also important critical thinking skills that can serve them well in life.

Several hundred teachers have participated in the institutes, workshops, and conferences sponsored by the *Conflict Resolution and United States History* project. Teachers anonymously responding to surveys or participating in focus group discussions were nearly unanimous in applauding the strengths of the *Conflict Resolution and United States History* curriculum. They uniformly reported that when the interactive roleplaying activities were used, their students were more motivated to learn history and to do historical research. Student surveys confirmed that these teaching strategies resulted in greater interest in learning and greater retention of knowledge than through traditional classroom lectures. Many teachers reported that their students obtained a greater comprehension of the complexity and nuances of the historical subject matter and a deeper appreciation of the interplay of individual actions and events than the seemingly inevitable flow of events that characterizes the narrative in many history textbooks.

----

[72]This refrain, from the popular 1977 Fleetwood Mac song, "Don't Stop," has been used extensively by politicians and in commercials. Four decades before the 1960s, Henry Ford, automobile manufacturer and a largely self-educated and self-made millionaire, had famously declared "History is more or less bunk. It's tradition. We don't want tradition. We want to live in the present and the only history that is worth a tinker's dam is the history we made today."

[73] The Learning Pyramid has been in use (with various modifications) since 1954. It was developed and used by the National Teaching Laboratory Institute (NTL) at their Bethel, Maine campus in the early 1960s. Currently, the NTL Institute for Applied Behavior Science is at 300 North Law Street, Suite 300, Alexandria, Virginia 22314, www.ntl.org.

Many of the teachers concluded that the theoretically open-ended approach to history and the goal of resolving conflicts encouraged their students to use critical thinking skills and an interest-based, problem-solving approach to resolving conflicts. Most students indicated that the skills they learned were useful in their daily lives as well as in the classroom. Students who were taught negotiation skills were more likely to use such skills to resolve their everyday conflicts than were the students who were not exposed to negotiation skills. Some teachers even reported that the conflict resolution skills helped them with classroom management as well as in their own daily lives. Several of the teachers commented that they used the negotiation and mediation skills that they learned in the program's summer institutes directly in their schools to resolve conflicts with and among their students. The teachers noted that they were better able to resolve student conflicts through negotiation and mediation than by the imposition of authoritarian disciplinary actions.

These results were confirmed by an "Evaluation of the Conflict Resolution and United States History Project," prepared by the Graduate School of Education at Rutgers, the State University of New Jersey. Due to their use of the Conflict Resolution and U.S. History materials and methodology, 90 percent of responding teachers indicated that their history courses were richer; 80 percent of the teachers indicated that their students gained a richer understanding of history; and more than 80 percent of teachers reported that their students could use the conflict resolution skills they had been taught. In addition, two-thirds of the teachers concluded that their teaching had become more effective as a result of the knowledge and skills they gained from using the *Conflict Resolution and United States History* materials and methodology.[74]

Traditionally, a primary goal of teaching history has been to impart a body of knowledge about the past. If, however, the goal of teaching history in the schools is not simply to learn history for its own sake but rather to develop citizens who have the knowledge and skills to effectively contribute to a participatory, pluralistic democracy, then teaching methodologies that fully engage students in inquiry and critical thinking are required.[75] By vigorously engaging students directly in the process of understanding and interpreting the past, the materials and teaching methodologies in *Conflict Resolution and United States History* can help to counteract students' lack of historical awareness as well as their apathy and cynicism about history and politics. Students engaged in historical roleplaying are motivated to learn history, develop a deeper understanding of historical change, and appreciate that individuals and groups can have an effect on the direction of history. Learning conflict resolution skills gives young people tools that they can use in their daily lives as well as in analyzing and understanding the dynamics of public policy in the past and in the present. By combining conflict resolution skills with historical roleplaying activities, *Conflict Resolution and United States History* demonstrates that while conflicting interests, needs, attitudes, or ideas are an inherent part of human life, many conflicts can be resolved creatively and non-violently to the benefit of the individuals, the community or the larger society or nation. Most importantly, the skills of analytical thinking, problem-solving and public speaking, as well as the understanding of our past, which form the core of *Conflict Resolution and United States History,* are critical for students to become the informed, engaged citizens required for a vital and enduring democracy.

---

[74] Deanna Lewis and John. W. Young, Graduate School of Education, Rutgers University, "Evaluation of the Conflict Resolution and United States History Project," February 2006, 1-15.

[75] As is suggested by Howard Gardner in *The Disciplined Mind: What All Students Should Understand* (New York: Simon and Schuster, 1999) p. 157. See also Barton and Levstik, *Teaching for the Common Good*; Joseph J. Onosko, "Barriers to the Promotion of Higher-Order Thinking in Social Studies," *Theory and Research in Social Education* 19 (Fall 1991): 341-366; Stephen J. Thornton, "Curriculum Consonance in United States History Classrooms," *Journal of Curriculum and Supervision* 3 (Summer 1998): 308-20; Bruce Fehn and Kim E. Koeppen, "Intensive Document-Based Instruction in a Social Studies Methods Course," *Theory and Research in Social Education* 4 (Fall 1998) 461-484; S.G. Grant, *History Lessons: Teaching, Learning and Testing in U.S. High School Classrooms* (Mahwah, NJ: Lawrence Erlbaum Associates, 2003), 3-28.

CHAPTER TWO

DEVELOPING SKILLS FOR RESOLVING CONFLICTS

It is unavoidable that people and nations will face conflicts in their lives. Disputes naturally arise over interests, needs, and desires. If we look at the history of national or international interactions over the years, we see a recurrence of conflicts, which are sometimes resolved by diplomacy or negotiations, but more frequently lead to violence, wars, riots, strikes or other less peaceful processes that are costly in terms of lives, property and social progress. While conflict may be an inevitable part of national as well as personal life, its escalation to violence is not. If we can understand the sources of conflict and develop skills to deal with conflict constructively and nonviolently, we may be able to resolve the underlying causes of conflicts rather than escalating them—whether the disputants are siblings, neighbors or nations.

It is our belief that teachers, students, indeed everyone, should learn how to be proactive and skillful in negotiating or mediating the conflicts that they confront in their daily lives and to encourage groups and nations to do the same. This approach calls not simply for empathy and understanding but also for realism and hard-thinking about real needs and vital interests. It requires a long-term view about continuing relationships and goals rather than a short-term focus on anger and immediate results. The purpose of this chapter is to provide background materials for understanding conflict and ways to resolve it and a series of activities to engage your students in using practical skills for resolving hypothetical conflicts that happen in our everyday lives. By first applying conflict resolution skills to hypothetical everyday conflicts, students learn to use such skills as active listening, which they can then apply to historical conflicts and perhaps to their own lives.

The *Conflict Resolution and United States History* curriculum package draws upon recent work in conflict or alternative dispute resolution to show how to approach conflicts so that they can be resolved by agreements that are mutually acceptable, mutually beneficial and long-lasting. This process of managing conflict—a problem-solving or interest-based approach—provides an alternative to a coercive solution in which one side compels, at least temporarily, the other to accept its will. A problem-solving or interest based approach to conflict involves identifying your real interests rather than taking a position from which you can't move without feeling that you are giving in. This approach is based on the "principled negotiation" model from the Harvard Negotiation Project.[1] However, we prefer the terminology, "interest-based" negotiations because it better captures the core of the process, which is to identify and seek common interests rather than to bargain from positions.[2]

Much like the personal pride that interferes with our individual ability to step back and apologize to a friend or spouse, national pride often prevents countries from stepping back from the brink of war. Interest-based negotiation requires disputants, first and foremost, to identify their interests and needs—emotional as well as material. The disputants should seek to understand the underlying interests of the other party or parties as well as

---

[1] See, Roger Fisher, William Ury and Bruce Patton, *Getting to Yes: Negotiating Agreement Without Giving In,* 2nd ed. New York: Penguin Books, 1991); Roger Fisher and Scott Brown, *Getting Together: Building Relationships as We Negotiate* (New York: Penguin Books, 1989); William Ury, *Getting Past No: Negotiating Your Way from Confrontation to Cooperation* (New York: Bantam Books, 1993); and the website for the Harvard Negotiation Project at www.pon.org.

[2] Interest-Based Negotiation is the terminology that has been used in labor-management contract negotiations since the late 1980s. See John R. Stepp, Kevin M. Sweeney and Robert L. Johnson, "Interest-Based Negotiation: An Engine-Driving Change, *The Journal for Quality and Participation*, (Sept/Oct 1998).

their own. Then, the parties should brainstorm a variety of solutions that might meet their interests. As long as there is a basis of trust and an appreciation that both or all sides want to continue an ongoing relationship, the process should result in solutions that are satisfactory to all the disputants. Sharing information, working to meet each other's interests, exploring new or creative ideas are the ingredients of successful negotiations and mediations. The agreed upon solution may not be perfect or ideal for each party; however, it cannot be viewed as a compromise where one or all of the parties surrender some key interests. Rather, the goal of 'interest-based" negotiation is a "win-win" solution in which each participant satisfies his or her most important basic interests and, therefore, has a stake in the outcome and the continuing maintenance and monitoring of the agreement.

It is valuable to understand conflict and learn conflict resolution skills both on a personal level for everyday life and on an academic level for better understanding of conflicts in history. This chapter will provide a context for understanding the typical sources and responses to conflict and a series of lessons for practicing the skills for resolving conflicts peacefully and effectively. The lessons are focused on everyday conflicts and include hypothetical roleplaying activities. The lessons follow a rational development of key concepts or skills from the value of using negotiating skills through activities to practice the steps involved in resolving conflicts. You may want to use the activities as prepared or develop your own scenarios for your students to use. Although we offer a step by step process for your students to understand the process and to practice the skills involves, we are not suggesting that the steps must be adhered to rigidly.

To fully implement and discuss all of the conflict resolution skills identified in Chapter Two would take approximately six hours or six class periods. It might be more effective to do the lessons in pieces, such as one per week. Conflict resolution lessons are probably most useful when periodically reintroduced and expanded during the school year. For example, you may want to spend a class period introducing negotiation skills immediately before you have your students use them in roleplaying an historical case study, such as the one involving the American Revolution. You may want to wait to introduce mediation skills until you need to use them in a different historical case study. Understanding and practicing skills for peacefully resolving conflicts will not only provide your students with useful life skills but also will enrich your students' understanding of history and may even help you with classroom management.

This chapter includes fifteen lessons or activities for you to use with your students. They are organized to allow your students to reach conclusions about the sources of and responses to conflict; to understand and appreciate a series of conflict resolution skills or techniques that will improve their chances of arriving at satisfactory, nonviolent solutions; and to practice a series of roleplaying activities using the conflict resolution skills.

Lesson One: Conflict is everywhere

Before you start any lessons about conflict resolution, you may want to have your students complete the "Student Attitudes about Conflict" Pre-Test (student handout #1 on the CD). It takes approximately 10 minutes to complete. It will help you ascertain your students' attitudes regarding conflict. Collect the completed forms and hold them until the end of the school year. After you have completed the conflict resolution unit and done several of the historical conflict resolution roleplaying activities, you should have your students complete the same test as a Post-test. You may find the results interesting. Teachers using the *Conflict Resolution and United States History* materials have reported that many of their students do, in fact, change their approach to resolving conflict.

You may want to introduce the subject of conflict and conflict resolution by having your students think about everyday conflicts and negotiations. One way to do this is to use the "Conflict Resolution Bingo Game," which is on the CD as student handout #2 and also reproduced below. The purpose of the Conflict Resolution Bingo Game is to enable your students to quickly appreciate that conflict is everywhere and that, in fact, they engage in informal negotiations probably on a daily basis, whether with their parents, siblings, teachers, or peers.

Simply living with another person, going to class, driving a car or crossing a busy street can be a source of conflict. Serving on a committee, working in a group or deciding what to do together with another person all involve negotiations. We resolve small and large disputes several times each day without even thinking about it (of course, that's part of the problem!). This activity should take approximately 20 minutes. It also is a great activity to help your students to get to know each other at the beginning of the school year and for you to learn something about their background and experiences in dealing with conflict, as well as a way to set some rules for classroom management.

Student handout/Teacher Overhead #2

Conflict Resolution Bingo

Try to fill every square.
You can sign your card once.
You can sign other people's cards twice.

Has gone shopping	Has taken part in a debate	Has a sibling	Has a pet	Has waited on a long line
Has played a video game with a partner	Has gone on a family trip	Has shared a bedroom with a sibling	Has a curfew	Has planned a party or event
Has received a report card	Has chores to do around the house	Has never had a conflict	Earns an allowance	Has watched TV with another person
Has been a member of a committee	Has not been aggravated with anyone this month	Has worked on a group project for school	Lives with another person	Has a home computer
Has a part-time job	Plays a sport	Has eaten lunch in the school cafeteria	Rides on a school bus	Has run for an elected position in school

Here are the directions for playing **Conflict Resolution Bingo**:

1. Hand out the "Bingo cards" to your students.

2. Explain that the goal is to completely fill each square with names.

3. Explain that students in the class should sign their name to those squares where they have done the activity mentioned.

4. Each person may sign two squares.

5. Have your students take ten minutes to mill around the room, talk with each other and get signatures on their "Bingo cards".

6. At the end of ten minutes at least one student should have all of the squares on his or her bingo card filled, with the exception of the center square, which reads: "Has never had a conflict."

7. At this point, ask the students to be seated and discuss the bingo cards.

8. Ask who was able to fill the entire bingo card. No one should have signed the center square, which reads "Never had a conflict." If no one signed this square, discuss why not: humans have conflicts all of the time. If someone signed the center square, prod gently to allow the student to appreciate that even if all of his or her conflicts have been peacefully resolved, he or she has still had conflicts.

9. Conclude that conflicts are a natural and unavoidable part of human existence.

Lesson Two: Conflict can serve positive purposes

As an anticipatory lesson, ask your students what comes to mind when they hear the word, "conflict"? Most responses will undoubtedly be negative, such as wars, violence, yelling, anger, etc. Perhaps there might be few more positive responses, such as change, problem solving. After listing all of your students' responses on a chalkboard or whiteboard, circle all of the "negative" responses and discuss why there are so many negative views of conflict. Then discuss the positive words and why students associate them with conflict. Conclude that, although conflicts may be unpleasant, difficult, painful and even violent, they also serve useful purposes, such as spurring creative thinking and helping to solve problems.

The English word, "conflict," is from the Latin, "conflictus," which means the act of striking together. This derivation is fairly straight forward, since conflicts involve people clashing. However, compare this meaning with the Chinese characters for "conflict," which are "danger" and "opportunity".[3] You may want to use the following overhead:

---

[3] See http://chineseculture.about.com/library/symbol/blcc_conflict.htm; http://www.hrea.org/erc/Library/primary/Opening_the_Door/part4.html; and http://www.mediate.ca/conflict-overview.htm. However, there is some dispute as to the accuracy of taking Chinese ideograms out of their cultural context. See J. Marshall Unger, *Ideogram: Chinese Characters and the Myth of Disembodied Meaning*, (Honolulu: University of Hawaii Press, 2003) and the summary on http://www.pinyin.info/readings.ideogram.html.

Student handout/Teacher Overhead #3: *What is conflict?*

In Chinese, the word "conflict" is the union of the symbols for "Opportunity" and "Danger".

We usually see the danger, but not the opportunity.[4]   Since conflicts are a part of daily life and not likely to disappear, what is important is *how* we respond to conflicts. Can we use the opportunities that they provide to solve the problem that created the conflict? Will the potential for danger spur us to think creatively for constructive and effective solutions?

Lesson Three: What are the sources of conflict?

Since conflicts can arise at any moment in any place, why do some people seem to be more prone to fights than others and some countries more frequently involved in wars, coups or revolutions? Why do some people seem to be able to resolve their conflicts easily and peacefully? Can we identify any themes about the sources of conflict that might help us to better understand why conflicts occur?

Activity # 1: We don't listen to each other

We suggest that you involve your students in a hypothetical roleplaying activity, "The Bloody Conflict," which involves two highly competitive and long-term rivals who are both seeking the same materials in order to achieve personal and public goals. You should provide only enough direction for your students to be able to try to find a solution to their problem. The objective of the activity is for your students to appreciate how people normally negotiate: by taking positions, perhaps seeking compromises, but not carefully listening to each other or sharing information. Too often, we talk past each other and misunderstand each other. We also tend *not* to reveal much information about our underlying interests when we are in a situation where we are arguing or disagreeing with someone. This human tendency to withhold information when we believe that we are "bargaining" or negotiating and to fail to seek a full understanding of what is being said often leads to misunderstandings that may mask the real issues, make negotiations difficult or skew the results.

"The Bloody Conflict" involves a complex set of hypothetical personal, professional and ideological factors that pit a hypothetical Dr. Runcible and a hypothetical Dr. Quarg against each other for blood for research on cancer or AIDS.[5] The directions are below as student handout/teacher overhead #4. Student handout #5: Fact sheet for Dr. Runcible and student handout #6: Fact sheet for Dr. Quarg are included in the student handouts on the CD. The hypothetical facts are summarized below:

---

[4] This idea was suggested to us by Sanford Jaffe and Linda Stamato, co-directors of the Rutgers Center for Negotiation and Conflict Resolution, at our July 1995 Summer Institute on Conflict Resolution and United States History.

[5] This activity was developed by Alice Haller, an attorney in Summit, New Jersey, for our July 1997 Summer Institute on Conflict Resolution and United States History.

After years of effort, Dr. Runcible is close to finding a cure for cancer but needs vast amounts of blood supplies to complete her research. At the same time, Dr. Quarg, who is the world's leading AIDS researcher, is closing in on a cure for AIDS. They have been professional rivals for years and each hopes to obtain a Nobel Prize for his or her research efforts. Dr. Quarg believes that he needs all of the blood supply that is held by one company, Plasmotek, in order to produce enough of his AIDS drug to end AIDS. Dr. Runcible believes that she needs all of the blood supply to develop enough of the cancer drug to cure cancer worldwide. They are both aware that the other is seeking the entire blood supply. What they are not aware of (and this is revealed only on the separate fact sheets) is that Dr. Quarg only needs the part of the white blood cells called the "killer cell" and Dr. Runcible only needs the part of the white blood cell called the "helper cell." (Do not share this information with your students-- one of the purposes of the activity is to see if they will share it).

Student Handout/Teacher Overhead #4: *"The Bloody Conflict"*

The Facts:

Dr. Margaret Runcible has devoted her entire career to finding a cure for cancer and is one of the world's leading cancer researchers. After years of dedication and hard work, she has finally developed a drug that is effective in curing cancer. Dr. Ozwald Quarg has devoted his entire career to AIDS research and is one of the leading scientists in the field. He has developed a serum that effectively eliminates all forms of the HIV virus. Since there is a global shortage of reliable blood, each needs the entire supply of blood that is held by one laboratory, Plasmotek. Dr. Quarg and Dr. Runcible have been intense rivals since medical school. They are aware of each other's urgent need for Plasmotek's blood supply. They agree to meet with each other to see if they can work out a solution.

Directions

1. Divide into pairs
2. Hand out fact sheets (#5 for Dr. Runcible and #6 for Dr. Quarg)
3. This information is fictional.
4. Do NOT share your fact sheet with the other person
5. After you each read your fact sheet, speak with each other and see if you can come to an agreement that meets the needs of both parties.
6. Allow 10-15 minutes for reading and negotiating.

Debriefing:

1. Who was NOT able to come to resolution? Why?
2. Who was able to come to a resolution? What was it?
3. What was making it difficult to come to a resolution?
   a. Lack of trust—rivals, competitors
   b. Failure to disclose—taught not to reveal
   c. Not really listening to what the other person was saying
   d. Focus on the person rather than the interests
   e. What does this tell us about conflicts?

You may want to circulate around the room to listen to what solutions the pairs of students are reaching. In "The Bloody Conflict," if Dr. Runcible and Quarg shared information and carefully listened to each other they would discover that one only needs the "helper" cells and the other only needs the "killer" cells. A few pairs of students may actually listen carefully and discover that. Most probably will not.

In the debriefing, you should ask those students who were *unable* to come to a resolution to respond first. This allows the issues of lack of time (interest-based negotiation takes patience and time), and perhaps lack of listening to be raised and discussed. Then ask those students who reached an agreement based on compromises, such as sharing the blood supply, to explain how their agreement would work. This is what most students will immediately see as solutions. These are not "wrong" answers. They are simply not the optimal answers because each party gets *less* of what he or she is seeking. Finally, ask those students who were able to discern that their needs were, indeed, *not* incompatible, how they discovered this. They will tell you that either one party asked the other whether they needed a killer or helper cells, or that one party volunteered the information that he or she only needed the killer or helper cells. If no one comes to this resolution, then offer it as an option and see what the class response is. Full disclosure enables the two doctors to both achieve their goals—obtaining all of the available blood. Doing the activity reveals one truth about why conflicts are not always resolved to the optimal resolution of both parties: because we do not listen to each other.

Admittedly, the activity contains a "magic bullet": when Dr. Runcible and Dr. Quarg learn that one needs the "helper cells" and the other the "killer cells," an optimal solution where they are both able to have exactly what they want becomes available. Clearly, the real world does not usually work so neatly. The activity was constructed so that your students can appreciate that we often fail to carefully listen to each other and to share information. Active listening by paraphrasing or questioning and voluntarily providing information may lead to more optimal resolutions to conflicts because both or all parties better understand everyone's interests and needs.

Activity #2: Why do most conflicts occur?

Following "The Bloody Conflict" activity, your class should be ready to discuss the sources of conflict. As an anticipatory lesson, ask your students *why* they think most conflicts occur and list their responses on a board. If this question does not elicit responses, you may want to specifically ask about conflicts in their lives, e.g., with their parents, with their siblings, with their friends, in school, etc. There is a value in allowing your students to consider their own lives and to think about why they as individuals have been involved in conflicts. You will discover that they may be using other words, but that conflicts basically occur for some combination of the following reasons: struggle for power or control; economic, social, political or personal interests; expectations; misunderstandings; feelings of anger, hostility or fear; competition; prejudice; irritating behavior; and pride.

After the group discussion, you may want to share handout/overhead #7 with your class and circle those items that your students have suggested that you want to emphasize.

Students should understand that conflicts happen all the time because there are real and legitimate reasons for differences: competing efforts for control or power, competing economic, social, political or personal interests, values and needs.[6] Beyond these objective differences in interests, conflicts also often arise, and

---

[6] Historians, sociologists, psychologists and political scientists over the millennia have provided similar summaries of the causes of conflicts in interpersonal, national and international situations. Thucydides argued that the increasing power of Athens led to the Peloponnesian War. Noted historian Barbara Tuchman concluded that wars from the Greek states in the fifth century to the United States in the twentieth century have resulted from lack of trust, miscommunication, misunderstanding, and misperception. See footnote 21 in Chapter One. Stephen Van Evera, political scientist at MIT, stresses that a misperception can fuel deep conflict escalating into war. See Stephen Van Evera. *Causes of War: Power and the Roots of Conflict* (Ithaca: Cornell University Press,

---

Student Handout/Teacher Overhead #7: *Sources of Conflict*

1. Goals, ideologies—struggles for control, power

2. Interests—economic, social, political, personal

3. Opinions, feelings—arguments, hostility

4. Expectations—competition, jealousy, disappointment, anger

5. Perception—misunderstanding, failure to communicate

6. Behavior—irritation, fear, triggers

7. Culture—prejudice, fear, competitive culture

8. PRIDE—personal and national

---

sometimes expand, simply because of our emotions or our behavior. There may be no real differences of opinion or interests, yet we may feel hostile towards another person because of past history, or we may be acting in response to fears, anger or disdain, or behaving in such a way that irritates the other person. So, a conflict is actually created by interpersonal behavior—by our emotional responses—where none really exists. Similarly, we may have differing expectations that are in conflict or we may misperceive the other person's real interests or concerns. It is the misperception or lack of communication that has created the conflict. Once the misperception or lack of communication has been resolved by disclosure and discussion, the conflict itself may be resolved or at least be on its way to resolution.

Finally, there is the problem of "pride." How many times in your life have you been in a situation where you have taken a position and found that your self-pride would not let you retreat from it? How many wars have been fought because "national pride" would not allow defeat without battle (such as the Mexican War in 1845 and the Spanish-American War in 1898)?[7] How many wars have continued beyond the point of "victory" because "national pride", or perhaps the personal pride of the leaders, blinded them to creative exit strategies that might have served their underlying interests (such as the British in America in 1775, the United States in Vietnam in the 1960s)?

1999). Harvard political scientist Samuel P. Huntington summarizes the causes of international conflict as: perception, fear, lack of trust, difficulty with communication, lack of familiarity with …other people" as well as influence, military power, discrimination, values and culture and "occasionally, territory." See Huntington, *The Clash of Civilizations and the Remaking of World Order* (New York: Simon & Schuster, 1996), 129 and 208. Morton Deutsch, professor of psychology and education at Columbia University notes that "perceptions, values, ideology, motivations and other psychological states" as well as "social, economic and political factors" are all ingredients for conflicts. See Morton Deutsch, "Social Psychology's Contributions to the Study of Conflict Resolution," *Negotiation Journal* (October 2002): 307-320.

[7] When several groups of teachers at one of our Institutes resolved the War with Mexico in 1845 by agreeing to exchange Mexican land for U.S. dollars, Professor George Sanchez, an historian at the University of Southern California who had helped to prepare the background materials and was at the Institute, stressed that although this seemed like a rational solution, it would never have happened unless there was some way for Mexico to maintain its national pride. Mexican leaders knew in 1845 that they could not defeat the United States but they could not simply give the United States the land that it wanted "without a fight" because of national pride. The same was true in 1898. Spain knew that it could not defeat the United States but it could not simply give up Cuba without going to war with the United States because of national pride. To a large extent, the continued involvement of the United States in Vietnam and perhaps Iraq beyond the time when it was clear that the United States was not going to "win the war" and achieve its proclaimed goal there was due to pride.

It is important to lay the background for an appreciation of the sources of conflict and the impediments to easy resolutions to conflict. Use the examples that your students raise to make the discussion concrete and useful on a personal level.

Lesson Four: Responding to Conflict

Ask your students how they usually respond to conflict. Write their responses on a board or chart. Then ask more broadly how they think most people respond to conflicts and write these responses on a board or chart. Finally, ask what institutions or processes exist in society to help people resolve conflicts and write these responses on a board or chart. If the following are not on your list, suggest or lead your students to appreciate the following responses to conflict and show them teacher overhead/student handout #8 below.

"Prehistoric Firing Squad"
www.CartoonStock.com

Explain that litigation requires a third party (a judge) to resolve the conflict for the disputants. In arbitration, a third party selects the best solution offered by the disputants. In mediation, a third party helps the disputants to come to an agreement. Negotiation leaves the disputants to work out their own solution.

Student Handout/Teacher Overhead #8: *Responses to Conflict*

- FIGHT

- FLIGHT/AVOIDANCE

- COMPROMISE

- LITIGATION

- ARBITRATION

- MEDIATION

- NEGOTIATION

Let's go back and analyze the advantages and disadvantages of each of these methods of resolving conflicts in terms of:

- Control by the disputants

- Cooperation by the disputants

- Resolution of the conflict

- Win/win or lose/lose

- Understanding of self and others

- Use of critical thinking and problem solving skills

- Framework for continued relationship

"Fastest Gun in the West"
Nevada Historical Society

FIGHT. Perhaps the disputants maintain control when they fight, but they certainly are not cooperating (or perhaps they are, if we assume that it takes two to fight?), and the resolution is at best win/lose, if not lose/lose. There is no understanding gained about oneself or the other person, no use of critical thinking and problem solving skills, and most certainly, no framework for a continued relationship (other than to come back for a rematch). So, does fighting solve the problem? It is hard to conclude anything but no.

FLIGHT. How about flight or avoidance? Perhaps control of the dispute is maintained by the disputants if avoidance can be seen as control, but there is certainly no cooperation and, more importantly, no resolution. Avoiding the issue appears to result in a lose/lose situation for everybody: there is no understanding gained of oneself or the other, no use of critical thinking or problem solving skills and no framework for a continued relationship. So, does flight or avoidance solve the problem? No, what it does is force the disputants to continue to carry their "hostile baggage."

COMPROMISE. Many believe that the best solution to conflicts is to simply compromise. A compromise is controlled by the disputants, requires cooperation by the disputants and resolves the conflict. If there was no coercion and all parties are satisfied with the compromise, then it is a win/win. However, if any of the disputants feels that he or she was taken advantage of or made a bad deal, then the compromise is a lose/lose and will probably lead to further conflict.

LITIGATION. Societies have set up mechanisms, such as litigation, arbitration and mediation, to help disputants resolve their conflicts without violence. In litigation, the parties present their cases to an independent examiner—a judge—who makes a decision which is legally binding on the parties. The disputants lose control of the resolution and put it in the hands of a third party. There is not usually a great deal of cooperation and although there is a resolution, it is usually favorable to one side (win/lose). Litigation does not usually result in a greater understanding of oneself or others and does not usually offer a framework for a continued relationship. But it does resolve the issue.

ARBITRATION. Arbitration is very similar to litigation. Both parties to a dispute agree to have an independent examiner—an arbitrator—listen to their arguments and make a decisions for them. The solution is placed in the hands of the arbitrator—who usually selects an option from among those offered by the disputants. Arbitration is common in labor and contract disputes. As with litigation, the resolution is in the hands of a third party rather than the disputants, there is no cooperation, little opportunity for gaining an understanding of oneself or others, and no framework for a continued relationship. As with litigation, the parties do have a resolution, which is legally binding, but the decision is usually hailed by one side and blasted by the other (win/lose).

MEDIATION. Mediation also involves a disinterested third-party—a mediator. However, the mediator does not make the decision about the outcome of the conflict but rather helps the disputants to come to a resolution. Mediation is frequently employed to settle disputes between husbands and wives, landlords and tenants, and consumers and businesses. Control is maintained by the disputants, the process requires a certain amount of cooperation by the disputants, and the mediator's questions and suggestions might help in self-understanding and understanding of other points of view. Since there is no resolution unless the parties agree, the solution should be win/win and should provide a framework for a continued relationship.

NEGOTIATION. Finally, negotiation enables disputants to work out their own solution. Control is maintained by the disputants, their cooperation is required, critical thinking and problem-solving skills are employed, and there is an opportunity to gain understanding of oneself and others. Since the resolution is the result of the parties directly talking with each other, it should be a win/win and it should provide a framework for a continued relationship.

Student Handout/teacher Overhead #9: ***Advantages and Disadvantages of Responses to Conflict***

- **FIGHT**—win/lose—does it resolve the problem?

- **FLIGHT/AVOIDANCE**—("hostile baggage") lose/lose—does it resolve the problem?

- **COMPROMISE**—lose/lose or win/win or give in win/lose

- **LITIGATION**—judge decides—win/lose—rights-based

- **ARBITRATION**—third party selects best solution offered by the disputants—win/lose

- **MEDIATION**—third party HELPS disputants come to an agreement—win/win

- **NEGOTIATION**—disputants work out their own solution—win/win

---

Please keep in mind that these are generalizations. We do not mean to suggest that every negotiation will result in a win-win solution or that litigation always will result in one party leaving unhappy. You may want to use handout #9 to as a summary to conclude this lesson.

Note that when *fundamental rights* are involved, a rights-based system, such as litigation, *should* be used to resolve the issues. You do not want to negotiate away fundamental rights (such as the constitutional right to equal protection raised in the Montgomery Bus Boycott). When teachers mediated this conflict at the Teacher Institute where we first introduced it, they followed the steps in mediation and developed a variety of compromises, such as designating the number of rows that would be designed for whites only or for flexible seating depending on the number of whites and blacks on a particular bus. Such compromise solutions made sense from the perspective of negotiations, but they failed to account for the underlying issue, which was whether it was constitutional for African Americans to be discriminated against in terms of their usage of public transportation.

In reality, the legal issue was resolved in the courts, although it was the bus boycott on the streets that brought the issue to national attention and framed the social and political context for the legal decision.[8] Therefore, we have added a moot court activity[9] to the Pullman Strike (Volume Two, Chapter Four) as well as the Montgomery Bus Boycott (Volume Two, Chapter Nine) activities. The court hearings are included as counterpoints to the mediations to show that conflicts over fundamental rights should be adjudicated by the courts, based on constitutional principles, rather than potentially "negotiated away." Although we are trying to promote the use of conflict resolution skills, it is important for you and your students to appreciate that not every conflict is subject to negotiation and that the legal system is particularly important for affirming fundamental rights.

Most conflicts, however, do not involve issues of fundamental human rights but rather issues of self-esteem, identity, pride (on a personal or national level), or competing economic or political interests. Where differing interests are involved (such as competing economic needs), interest-based negotiation or mediation can help the disputing parties to see each other's point of view, to delineate possible solutions and to move the parties towards a resolution that is mutually acceptable and lasting.[10]

Lesson Five: Overview of Conflict Resolution Skills

Hand out student handout/teacher overhead #10: "Steps in Conflict Resolution." This summary is based on *Getting to Yes*, by Roger Fisher and William L. Ury, as well as information from professional mediators, and the experience of one of the co-authors, Arlene Gardner, in working on school board negotiations and years of workshops with teachers and students. Discuss the importance of each step with your class.

Student Handout/Teacher Overhead #10: *Steps in Conflict Resolution*

1. Recognize emotions and avoid having them interfere

2. Use active listening skills

3. Identify the underlying interests

4. Seek (Brainstorm) possible solutions

5. Use objective criteria to evaluate possible solutions

6. Identify solutions that all parties can accept (meet common interests)

7. Agree on the best solution and to come back to the problem if the solution does not work

8. Look long-term to preserve the relationship.

---

[8] While the news media, particularly television news, emphasized the dramatic images of African Americans nonviolently protesting segregated buses by walking and using group cabs, the core issue of whether public transportation should be segregated by race was resolved in court in real life. This should not diminish the importance of the moral protest by masses of desegregationists in providing a context for the court's opinion mandating desegregation on public transportation in *Browder v. Gayle*, 142 F. Supp 707 (1956), following the decision in *Brown v. Board of Education*, 347 U.S. 483 (1954).

[9] A moot court is a mock appellate hearing. Directions for conducting a moot court are included in the Montgomery Bus Boycott and the Pullman Strike activities.

[10] Fisher, Ury and Patton, 17-39; Street Law and National Crime Prevention Council, *Community Works: Smart Teens Make Safer Communities*, 2nd ed. (Washington, DC: National Crime Prevention Council, 2004), 124-126.

1.   *Recognize emotions and avoid having them interfere with the negotiations.*

The need to identify the emotions that underlie the conflict has been alternatively characterized by Fisher and Ury as "separating the people from the problem" and by several student mediation manuals as "recognizing and avoiding triggers.[11] Angry feelings are often the biggest impediment to resolving a conflict. Recall from our list of Sources of Conflict (overhead #7) that one of the main sources of conflict is feelings—angry, hostile or fearful feelings. Fisher and Ury note that: "Emotions on one side will generate emotions on the other. Fear may breed anger, and anger, fear. Emotions may quickly bring a negotiation to an impasse or an end." To avoid this, they suggest explicitly acknowledging emotions, "theirs and yours," and recognizing them as legitimate; allowing the other side to let off steam and not responding to emotional outbursts.[12]

Focusing on the issues causing the conflict rather than the people involved or any hostility, fear or dislike is clearly more difficult than it sounds. If you are upset with another person, it is difficult to put your emotions aside. However, that is exactly what needs to be done. Step back and recognize and understand your emotions and those of the disputing parties. Is it fear? Is it anger? What has caused these emotions to exist? Acknowledge the emotions (again, yours and theirs) as legitimate. Don't pretend that they don't exist.

For example, instead of yelling, "I hate you," which escalates a dispute to a totally emotional level without any understanding of the issues, explain that "I hate when you dismiss what I have said without even considering it because it makes me feel bad," which identifies both your emotions and the problems and enables a discussion to follow on the issue rather than just raw emotions. It may be difficult to acknowledge your fears or anger, but they will interfere less with the negotiations once they are acknowledged. Similarly, it may be difficult to listen to the person with whom you are having a dispute tell you how angry he or she is or how unfair he or she feels you have treated him or her. However, by allowing the emotion to surface and to be expressed, the air can be cleared and the disputants can focus on seeking ways to resolve the substance of their conflict.

Overhead #7 lists "irritation, fear and triggers" as contributing to conflicts. Triggers are those things that make you angry. We need to recognize when others are saying or doing things that make us angry and to control our anger, by explicitly stating that a certain action or phrase is making you angry (shouting, ignoring you, speaking in a sarcastic tone of voice, poking a finger in your face, getting too close) and that you would appreciate it if the person would stop it. You also need to recognize when your words or actions are angering others.

Included is an activity to help your students to identify their "triggers" and how they can respond to avoid escalating a conflict or bringing negotiations to an end. See Lesson 6: Triggers and Student Handout/Teacher Overhead #12).

2.   *Use active listening skills.*

Active listening means not just hearing what the speaker is saying to you but also communicating to that person your understanding of what he or she has said. The goal is to avoid misunderstandings and perhaps to even find a point of commonality by ensuring that everyone understands what has been said. By "active listening" we mean that the person listening not only hears what is said but also provides clear feedback to the speaker so that the speaker and the listener both understand the same thing.

---

[11] Fisher, Ury and Patton, 17-39; Street Law and National Crime Prevention Council, 124-126.

[12] Fisher, Ury and Patton, 107-129.

How can you tell when someone has heard and *understood* what you have said? While shaking your head might seem to indicate that you have understood and agree with what has been said, in actuality, we shake our heads merely to acknowledge that we have been listening. The same is true with eye contact. Although it is important to maintain eye contact, eye contact alone does not communicate what you understand, only that you have been looking at the speaker. To make sure that your understanding of what has been said is communicated back to the speaker, paraphrase what has been said, or ask a question, or restate what your understanding is. For example, in a landlord-tenant lease agreement, the potential lessee might say, "So let me understand you, you mean that you are afraid that I might ruin something at the apartment, so you are requiring a $500 deposit that will be returned if there is no damage?"

An active listening activity to help your students practice active listening skills is included as Lesson 7: "Do I Understand You?" and Student Handout/Teacher Overhead #13.

3. *Identify the underlying interests.*

It is crucial in this methodology (and in real life!) to separate interests from positions, both your own and those of the other disputants. Positions are what a person is demanding or seeking. Interests are what motivates him or her, the reasons WHY he or she is taking a particular position. For example, perhaps you state that you would like to walk to dinner. I state that I would prefer to drive to dinner. These are our positions and they are mutually incompatible. However, if we each try to find out the reason for our positions rather than simply repeating them, perhaps there is an easy resolution. Perhaps you want to drive because you think that the walk is too far and I want to walk because I am looking for a little exercise and fresh air. Although the two positions seem irreconcilable, there are numerous possible solutions once we understand the underlying interests: we can drive part of the way to dinner and walk the rest; we can walk a little after dinner; we can drive to dinner and walk earlier in the day, etc.

Many people believe that they should negotiate by demanding more than they really need or want or that they can "win" by "sticking to their guns" and refusing to budge from their positions. This is "positional negotiation." To some extent, it has become ritualized as part of many labor negotiations. In some cases, the positional negotiating or bargaining merely makes the process longer since first both sides need to go through the "rituals" of putting forward their positions before they seriously negotiate. In other cases, digging into positions rather than trying to identify and meet the underlying interests results in an end to the negotiations. Such a stalemate may force the negotiators to give up control of the process for a decision by an arbitrator.

For example, in the fall of 2005, the New York Metropolitan Transit Authority (MTA) and the Transit Workers Union were involved in contract negotiations. The points of contention included wages, pensions, workers' healthcare contributions, and disciplinary actions against workers. Believing that their demands were not being addressed, the transit workers decided to strike. For the first time in 25 years they closed the entire MTA bus and subway system December 20-22, 2005. The transit workers returned to their jobs after three days and the union and MTA met and work out a contract. In January 2006, the proposed contract was voted down by the transit workers union by a seven vote margin. The MTA petitioned for an order for binding arbitration while the union scrambled to develop a revised contract. Although the transit workers union later approved the contract it had narrowly rejected earlier, the MTA rejected it in favor of arbitration. In December 2006, the arbitration panel ruled that both sides must abide by the contract proposed by the MTA and later approved by the transit union just prior to arbitration. The contract provided raises for transit workers as the union requested and also required that the workers pay a certain percentage of their wages toward health insurance as the MTA had insisted. [13]

---

[13] Adam Lisberg and Pete Donohue, "Digging their Wheels," *New York Daily News*, December 16, 2005, News section, City Final Edition.; Janny Scott and Sewell Chan, "Stakes Climb on Day 2 of Strike," *New York Times*, December 22, 2005, Section A, Late Edition-Final; Sewell Chan, "Deal Voted Down At Last Moment," *New York Times*, January 22, 2006, Section 1, Late Edition-

Student Handout/Teacher Overhead #11: *Positions and Interests*

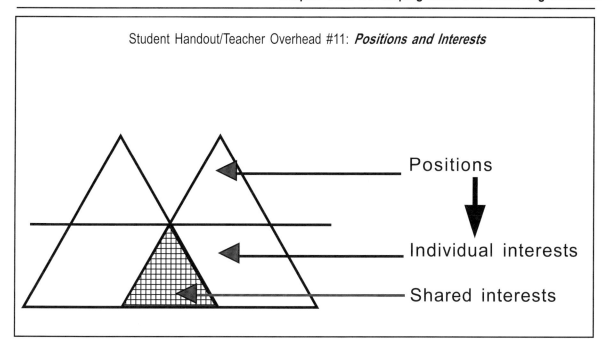

As the schematic above (Student Handout/Teacher Overhead #11) visually demonstrates,[14] there is usually little meeting ground for opposing positions. However, the underlying interests are usually broader needs or desires that may be met in several different ways, and there is often an area of overlapping of shared interests that can satisfy the most important needs of all of the disputants. The focus on interests rather than positions enables the parties to explore possible solutions and to seek to find a solution that satisfies the most important interests of all or a large number of the parties involved.

An example frequently used to illustrate the difference between positions and interests is the negotiation between Egypt and Israel at Camp David in 1978. Egyptian President Anwar Sadat insisted that all of the Sinai must be returned to Egypt while Israeli Prime Minister Menachem Begin insisted that Israel needed to keep some of the Sinai. Redrawing the map to return only part of the Sinai was not an option for Egypt. Redrawing the map to return all of Sinai was not an option for Israel. The parties managed to get beyond these totally incompatible positions by focusing on the underlying interests. Israel's main interest was security, while Egypt's main interest was sovereignty. The Israeli Prime Minister finally agreed to a plan that would return all of the Sinai to Egypt but would assure Israeli security by providing Egypt's official recognition of and relations with Israel and by having troops from the United States and elsewhere as monitors in a demilitarized buffer zone between the two countries.[15]

Final; "MTA asks for binding arbitration in contract dispute," Associated Press, January 25, 2006, State and Local Wire; Steven Greenhouse, "Long After Strike Shut Subways, Dispute Heads Into Arbitration," *New York Times*, March 24, 2006, Section B, Late Edition-Final; Ray Sanchez, "Union OKs deal, but MTA doesn't," *Newsday*, April 19, 2006, News section, City Edition; Sewell Chan, "Transit Deal Is No Closer After 6 Days of Arbitration," *New York Times*, August 14, 2006, Section B, Late Edition-Final; Steven Greenhouse and William Neuman, "Arbitrators Rule on Deal for Transit," *New York Times*, December 16, 2006.

[14] This schematic was suggested as a way of conceptualizing the area of shared interests once the underlying interests have been identified by Stakeholder Negotiation Services International Limited (SNSI) and can be found at http://www.snsi.org/negotiation.php.

[15] The Israeli-Egyptian Peace Treaty was signed in March 1979 and the staged withdrawal completed by early 1982. For details and consequences of the Camp David negotiations, see especially William B. Quandt, *Camp David: Peacemaking and Politics* (Washington, D.C.: Brookings Institution, 1986).

On a more local level, negotiations between local boards of education and unions are often contentious, fail to appreciate that the bottom-line goals are the same (providing the best education for students at a reasonable cost) and that good ongoing relations are important. As president of a local board of education, one of the authors negotiated with the unions representing teachers, administrators, secretaries and custodians. In one of the negotiations with the school secretaries, the secretaries sought a larger increase than had been granted to the teachers (3.9%) arguing that they had a much lower base of pay. The negotiators for the school board agreed with the underlying premise but did not want to start spiraling increases above four percent. The main goal of the school board was to encourage the secretaries to improve their computer skills. After much discussion, the two sides found an agreement that met the interests of both sides: a "merit" increase plan whereby the secretaries could earn an extra $100 for each specific computer program for which they demonstrated mastery. This provided a small amount of extra funding that met the interests of the secretaries and also met the interests of the school board by provided an incentive for the secretaries to improve their computer skills at minimal additional cost to the district. Equally important, good working relations were maintained.[16]

The most powerful interests are basic human needs, such as security, economic well-being, a sense of belonging, recognition, and control over one's life. Yet, we often do not see these and instead focus on concerns about money or power. Lesson 8 provides an activity for your students to practice separating interests and positions (also brainstorming and evaluating possible solutions). See Student Handout/Teacher Overhead #14.

4. *Seek (Brainstorm) possible solutions.*

Once the parties have identified their interests, they can seek to answer the question: "What do you think would be a good solution to the problem?" Brainstorming involves open-mindedly identifying a variety of options without judging them. Our tendency in negotiations is to search for a single answer, assume that there is a fixed pie and prematurely judge and discard options. Instead we need to identify a variety of possible options and not judge them until after we have identified the issues and the interests involved as well as the range of options available. Remember how Dr. Quarg and Dr. Runcible were stuck arguing about whether AIDS or cancer research was more important? And the result was that the limited pie was split rather than having a more far-ranging discussion that revealed that the underlying interests could be fully satisfied.

Sometimes an idea that initially sounds crazy, upon discussion and reflection, can lead to a positive solution. That is, an idea that has some merit but also has some problems might be improved upon so that it works! Sometimes, the disputants can brainstorm ideas on their own and bring them to the negotiation session. Alternatively, or in addition, the disputants might brainstorm together. Lesson 8 and Lesson 9 provide activities for your students to practice identifying the underlying interests, brainstorming possible solutions and using objective criteria to evaluate the solutions.

5. *Use objective criteria to evaluate possible solutions.*

Using objective criteria to evaluate possible solutions to a conflict is the reason why the Harvard Negotiation Program calls this "principled negotiation." Rather than following positional negotiation where the most persistent person will probably gain his goal, they argue that by referring to objective criteria, the solution is "based on principle, not pressure". There is a basis of reason for the solution, it is less open to attack, consistent with precedent and more objective.[17]

---

[16] See "Agreement Between the Westfield Association of Educational Secretaries and the Westfield Board of Education, July 1, 2006-June 30, 2009," Article VIII, Section D.

[17] Fisher, Ury and Patton, 83-85.

How do you determine what objective criteria to use? Usually, by asking the question, "what have others done in similar situations?" Similar situations may be what other similarly situated school districts have done on a particular issue or policy, the market value of real or personal property, scientific judgment, professional standards, precedent, tradition, equal treatment, or efficiency. While the seller of a house wants the highest price and the buyer wants the lowest one that they can negotiate, the issue instead is what a fair price would be. Since market value is something fairly easy to ascertain by reference to selling prices of similar homes recently sold in the same or similar locations, this is usually the way that a fair price is determined for a house or commercial building. The same is true for selling a used car. A "Blue Book", which lists the value of autos by year and model is (or probably should be) the basis for the sale of a used car. However, even in these fairly clear-cut cases, there is always room for discussion about the condition of the house or the car, which may vary dramatically and change the value accordingly.

6. *Identify solutions that meet common interests and all parties can accept.*

How can you identify solutions that meet common interests? How do you avoid accepting a solution that may not meet your needs? Fisher and Ury suggest that especially in situations where the other person is more powerful or has a stronger bargaining position, you should know your BATNA, that is, the Best Alternative To a Negotiated Agreement.[18] In some cases, the best alternative may also be the worst alternative (WANTA). In all cases it is important to know what you have to offer and when it is better *not* to come to a resolution. If their needs were really mutually exclusive rather than compatible, perhaps Dr. Quarg or Dr. Runcible could find an alternative way to conduct their research or find some alternative way to get the materials that they need, much as the medical research community in the United States has sought to find alternative sources for stem cell research once the use of stem cells culled by destroying embryos was banned by the federal government. Lesson 8: "John and Matt" and Lesson 9: "Going to the Cleaners" provide activities for your students to practice identifying the underlying interests, brainstorming and evaluating possible solutions and seeking solutions that all parties can accept.

7. *Agree on the best solution and to come back to the problem if the solution does not work.*

Even when both sides come to an agreement that they believe is fair, there may be unforeseen circumstances that upset it or one or more parties may simply decide they can no longer abide by the agreement. Therefore, it is prudent to spell out what will happen if the agreement is not followed. Perhaps the Second World War could have been avoided if the Treaty of Versailles, the peace settlement following the First World War, had included a provision that required the parties to meet again if there were changed circumstances or if the treaty was no longer being followed.[19]

8. *Look long-term to preserve the relationship.*

Although listed last, an understanding that looking long-term towards continuing a relationship with your "opponent" is very important and something that should be remembered throughout the process of negotiation or

---

[18] Fisher, Ury and Patton, 97-106.

[19]The Treaty of Versailles did contain provisions for a Commission of Enquiry (Article 412) to receive complaints regarding possible treaty violations and for the Commission to investigate, issue a report and suggest economic sanctions (Article 414). However, these were all punitive provisions. There were no positive provisions for revisiting the treaty. President Woodrow Wilson had hoped the worst provisions of the treaty would be revised through the League of Nations, whose founding covenant was made part of the Treaty of Versailles. The full treaty and a listing of readings about the Versailles Treaty may be found at http://history.acusd.edu/gen/text/versaillestreaty/vercontents.html.

mediation. If you are part of a family that includes competitive, obstinate people, this is sometimes difficult to remember. You may tend to fall into arguments where no one will budge and you may remain on nonspeaking terms for month or years. What is lost—the continuing relationship—is probably far more important than the issue in dispute. But we all too often forget this in our daily lives. Similarly, parties to hard-fought litigation rarely remain on friendly terms. Labor negotiations are sometimes very contentious and lose track of the fact that management and employees must continue to work together afterwards. Preserving the relationship does not mean that we should avoid disagreement since differences of opinion can lead to opportunities for creative thinking and new ways to approach and resolve problems. It does mean that we should treat those with differing views with respect, rationality, good communication and non-coercive persuasion.[20]

Lesson Six: Triggers

This lesson is designed to help your students identify those verbal or nonverbal behaviors that result in anger or other negative emotional reactions. The purpose is not only to gain an appreciation of what behaviors act as triggers to anger them, but also to gain an understanding of how their behavior might negatively impact negotiations with others. Hand out or use overhead #12. Explain that "triggers" are verbal or nonverbal behaviors that result in anger or other negative emotional reactions that interfere with the communication between two (or more) people. Note that everyone has triggers and that it is important to recognize them. Engage your students in the "Triggers" activity and discussion.[21] Ask your students to answer each question individually, then have them discuss their responses in pairs or groups of three, then as whole class.

Student Handout/Teacher Overhead #12: *Triggers*

Triggers are verbal or nonverbal behaviors that result in anger or other negative emotional reactions and interfere with the communication between two (or more) people.

Directions:

1. What are trigger words for me?
2. What kind of body language is a trigger for me?
3. How do I know when I'm angry?
4. How do I react to my triggers?

Debriefing:

1. Do we see any common themes?
2. It's important to recognize when someone's behavior is angering you and to AVOID body language or Words that will trigger conflict.
3. It's also important to recognize when you are saying or doing something that is triggering someone else (pointing, etc.) and AVOID such statements or actions.

---

[20] See Roger Fisher and Scott Brown. *Getting Together: Building Relationships as We Negotiate* (Boston: Houghton Mifflin, 1988).

[21] This activity is based on an activity from *Community Works: Smart Teens Make Safer Communities*, 2nd ed., 2004.

Write your students' responses to the question, "What are trigger words for me" on a chart or board. Then write their responses to the question, "What kind of body language is a trigger for me?" After you have listed all the responses, ask your students if they see any common themes. Circle the words or body language that they see as common theme. You will probably notice that the common themes involve tone of voice, words or body language that is disrespectful, dismissive, sarcastic or otherwise negative. Conclude with the idea that it is important to recognize when someone's behavior is angering you and to *avoid* body language or words that will trigger conflict. It is also important to recognize when you are saying or doing something that is triggering someone else (pointing, etc.) and avoid such language or actions.

Lesson Seven: Active Listening Skills

The most important skill involved in resolving conflicts is to actively listen to what the other person is saying. *Active listening* means listening *and* communicating to the other person your understanding of what was said and your view of it, that is, providing *feedback*.

As an anticipatory activity, ask your students, "How can you tell when someone is listening to what you are saying?" List the responses on a board or chart and then consider their effect. The responses will probably include the following:

- ✓   Body language: Eye contact, Nodding, Shaking head
- ✓   Verbal : Saying yes or no
- ✓   Seeking information—asking a question
- ✓   Seeking confirmation—rephrasing or paraphrasing

Ask the students which of these responses clearly indicates to the speaker that you understand or don't understand what he or she has said? The response should be: questioning, paraphrasing, restating. Simply shaking your head or making eye contact indicates that you are listening, but does not indicate to the speaker that you understand what the speaker has said.

The active listening activity below, "Do I Understand You," forces students to paraphrase, question or restate what they have heard before they can respond. We usually are busy constructing our response rather than listening to what the speaker has to say. A large amount of misunderstanding occurs simply because we are not providing adequate feedback. "Do I Understand You" is not a game of telephone where the message is repeated until it is garbled beyond recognition. In fact, it is just the opposite: your students must repeat, paraphrase and ask a question about what the prior speaker said before they can make their own statement or comment.

Select a controversial topic and four students (or volunteers) to begin the discussion. Place four chairs in front of the classroom and have pairs of students sit in teams next to each other and across from the two students on the team with opposing views. Assign a position to each team and identify the person to begin the discussion. For example, if you select the topic of gun control, the two students on the pro-gun control team will argue in support of it and the two students seated across from them on the anti-gun control team will argue in opposition to it. Let's assume that you start with those supporting it. One team member will explain why he or she supports gun control. A member of the team opposing gun control must paraphrase, repeat or question what the pro-gun control team member has said before he or she can respond to it. After hearing the anti-gun control view, the other pro-gun control team member must similarly paraphrase, restate or question the anti-gun control view before making his or her own statement. The second anti-gun control team member will do the same.

Student Handout/Teacher Overhead # 13: *"Do I Understand You?"*

Directions:

1. Select a controversial issue—gun control, abortion, gay marriage, immigration, or brainstorm with your students to pick an issue that interests them
2. Place four chairs in front of the classroom.
3. Form teams of two students to argue the same side (Ask for four volunteers or pick them)
4. Have students who will be arguing the same side sit next to each other across from the team of students arguing the opposing side of the issue
5. Select one side and a particular individual to start the discussion
6. No one should interrupt
7. First person from the state viewpoint.
8. Before the person across from him or her on the opposing team can respond, <u>he or she must in some way restate his or her understanding of what has been said</u>, by asking a question, restating what has been said, or paraphrasing what he or she has heard using phrases such as, "in other words..., you are saying....", "so your point is...").
9. Then, the person from the opposing team may state his or her viewpoint
10. After both members of both teams have gone back and forth four times, other stduents from the class may be assigned to continue the discussion until the entire class has been involved.
11. Alternatviely, the original four students may demonstrate this process for the entire class.

Debriefing:

1. With each set of questions and paraphrasing, the issue is clarified.
2. The activity hones in on possible definitial problems that may stand in the way of understanding each other.
3. The active listening also helps to elad toward possible resolutions.
4. We usually are busy thinking of responses to others rather than carefully listening to what has been said and providing feedback about what we heard.

This process may be a bit repetitive; however, you will find that there is very little misunderstanding even if all four people are not in total agreement. And the activity is great practice for active listening. You may want to have the same four students, in pairs on teams of two, model the process for the rest of the class and actually begin and conclude the discussion. This may take anywhere from ten minutes to an entire class period. Or you may want to bring in new team members to replace the initial students to continue the discussion until all members of the class have been involved. This will ensure that the rest of your class has been listening carefully since they will have to pick up the discussion where the prior team members left it. This may take an entire class period.

Lesson Eight: Identify the underlying interests, brainstorm and evaluate possible solutions.

To practice identifying the underlying interests, brainstorming and evaluating possible solutions, use the simple fact pattern below, in handout #14. John and Matt share a locker and John often borrows things that belong to Matt and forgets to return them. Matt is upset. They are about to have a fight and are brought to the school principal's office.[22] The principal has asked John and Matt to identify their interests, brainstorm and evaluate possible solutions. Divide half of your class into groups of two and have them roleplay the scenario as John and Matt. John and Matt should identify their underlying interests, brainstorm and evaluate possible solutions. Divide the other half into groups of three and have them roleplay a trip to the principal's office where the principal decides what should be done in the situation. In the groups of three, the student playing the role of a "typical" principal should either impose his or her own solution for the situation (authoritarian) or help the students come to their own resolution (mediative).

Student Handout/Teacher Overhead #14: *John and Matt at the Locker*

John and Matt go to a crowded high school. They have been assigned to share a locker because there are only a limited number of lockers available. They are both on the wrestling team and also have some classes together. They have known each other since grade school and hang out with the same crowd. John often borrows items that Matt has put in the locker—a book for class, a comb for his hair, gum, a CD, a pen or pencil. He frequently forgets to return what he borrows until Matt reminds him. One day after John borrows a CD, Matt shouts at him: "Start bringing your own stuff to school." John promises to do so but a couple of days later he asks to borrow a book for class. Matt slams the locker door and shoves John, shouting, "I've had it with you, man. Quit bugging me! Don't ever ask me for anything again!" John lunges back at Matt and punches him. A teacher steps in to break up the fight and both boys are sent to the principal's office.

Directions:

1. Divide half the class into groups of two to roleplay Matt and John.
2. Divide the other half into groups of three to roleplay Matt, John and the principal.
3. Identify the underlying interests
4. Brainstorm solutions
5. Evaluate the solutions

Debriefing:

1. What are the underlying interests of Matt and John?
2. What are some possible solutions?
3. How realistic and workable are the solutions?

---

[22] This activity is based on "John and Abel," from *Marshall Croddy, ed., The Streets, the Courts and the Community* (Los Angeles: Constitutional Rights Foundation, 1992), 62.

After allowing the groups of students to roleplay for approximately ten minutes, ask members from each group to list the interests and possible solutions and write them on a board or chart. Since John and Matt are friends, they should both have an interest in continuing their relationship. They also have a mutual interest in solving the locker problem. The possible solutions might include: asking to be assigned other locker partners, agreeing that they will not borrow any of each others' belongings in the locker, setting aside specific space in the locker for each of them. Your students will probably have more creative ideas. It is important for your students to brainstorm without evaluating the possible solutions and then to consider all of the possible solutions side-by-side. List all of the possible solutions raised in the groups and have the entire class evaluate them.

As part of the debriefing, compare the process and results in the direct discussion between Matt and John and the one with the principal. From an early age, we teach young people that conflicts are mostly resolved by authorities: parents, teachers, leaders; or by a judge, police officer, boss, director or president. It will be interesting to compare the results of a resolution by an authority (the principal), or with the aid of a third-party (the principal as a mediator), or by the students themselves. The authoritarian solution might be the same as what the boys might agree upon (no borrowing or different locker partners), or it may involve punitive measures. Ask the students playing the roles of Matt and John how the felt about the solutions and see if there is any difference between those solutions that were generated by the two boys and the ones imposed by the principal.

Lesson Nine: Negotiating

Your students are ready to negotiate now (in fact, they just have!). Review with your class the steps involved in negotiations and tips from professional negotiators. Steps in a typical negotiating include the following:

1. The disputants agree to ground rules: they will avoid triggers, put-down, interruptions and other language or behavior that will interfere with the negotiations.

2. Each side tells the story from his or her perspective

3. The disputants use active listening skills

4. The disputants identify the issues and interests.

5. They brainstorm possible solutions without judging them

6. They evaluate the options, using objective criteria.

Student Handout/Teacher Overhead #15: ***Steps in Negotiations***

1. The disputants agree to ground rules: they will avoid triggers, put-down, interruptions and other language or behavior that will interfere with the negotiations.
2. Each side tells the story from his or her perspective
3. The disputants use active listening skills
4. The disputants identify the issues and interests.
5. They brainstorm possible solutions without judging them
6. They evaluate the options, using objective criteria.
7. They try to agree on a solution by discussing and revising the options.
8. Disputants put their agreement in writing, including what happens if the agreement is violated.

---

7. They try to agree on a solution by discussing and revising the options.

8. The disputants put their agreement in writing, including what happens if the agreement is violated.

You may want to use Student Handout/teacher Overhead #15: "Steps in Negotiations," to review the steps with your class. While negotiating is a process that involves steps, this does not mean that there must be rigid compliance with these steps, but rather that the steps can help the disputants to come to a resolution.

Studies of professional negotiators show that they: ask questions, seek information and test for understanding. This is all part of active listening. They provide reasons to substantiate their statements (reference to objective criteria) and preface their remarks with constructive phrases (active listening). They avoid making irritating remarks, aggressive behavior or defend/attack spirals (avoid triggers). See Student Handout/Teacher Overhead #16.

You may want to refer to the steps or the tips from professional negotiators to point out both positive and negative or missed efforts by your students in their negotiation of the problem with the cleaners. If you had assigned observers to watch each pair of negotiators, they can help you. If you have time and feel that your students could use more practice negotiating, a list of additional sources of roleplays can be found on the DVD.

Now let's negotiate, using the scenario "Going to the Cleaners." This activity involves a problem that you perhaps have experienced: You bring an item of clothing to the cleaners and it is returned to you with a burn hole, a stain, a rip or some other damage that did not exist when you brought the item to the cleaners. In the hypothetical facts in handout #17 below, Ken Jones brought his fairly new, fairly expensive jacket to Ace Dry Cleaners and it has been returned to him with a burn hole that he believes was not there when it brought it to the cleaners.

Student Handout/Teacher Overhead #16:
What can we learn from professional negotiators?

Professional negotiators:
- ✓ Ask questions (active listening)
- ✓ Seek information (active listening)
- ✓ Test for understanding (recapitulation)(active listening)
- ✓ Provide reasons to substantiate their statements (objective criteria)
- ✓ Preface with constructive phrases

And Avoid:
- ✓ Making irritating remarks (triggers)
- ✓ Aggressive Behavior (triggers)
- ✓ Defend-Attack Spirals

---

[23] This summary is based on remarks made by Linda Stamato, co-director of the Rutgers Center for Negotiation and Conflict Resolution at our July 1996 Summer Institute on Conflict Resolution and United States History.

This fact pattern can be used simply to identify the interests; to identify the underlying interests and brainstorm the possible solutions; to identify interests, brainstorm and evaluate them; or to go through the entire negotiation process and come to a resolution. Students playing the role of Ace Dry Cleaning ("Ace") will invariably start with the assertion that the burn hole is not their fault and they should not have to pay for it (their position). They may elaborate that there is a company policy prohibiting smoking and/or that none of the employees at Ace Dry Cleaners smoke. Since the students are roleplaying rather than following a set script or simulation, they are free to make reasonable assertions. Students playing the role of Ken will take the position that Ace Dry Cleaners is

---

Student Handout/teacher Overhead #17: "*Going to the Cleaners*"

The Facts:

Ken Jones had bought a $250 sports coat last year. This was a lot of money for him. He had worn it several times, but it was still relatively new. It was his favorite sports coat. He brought it to Ace Dry Cleaners to have it cleaned. When Ken picked up the jacket at the Ace Dry Cleaners, he found a fairly noticeable cigarette burn that hadn't been there when he brought the coat to the cleaners and he does not smoke. Ken asked the cleaners to pay him $250 for the ruined sports coat. Ace denied that he was responsible for the burn because there was a no smoking policy at work and no one smoked. He refused to pay. Ace also argued that the coat was used and was no longer worth $250. Ken countered that he would have to pay at least $250 to buy a similar coat.

Directions:

1. Divide into pairs (or add a third person as an observer)
2. Assign or select roles as Ken or Ace.
3. Play your roles as Ken (whose jacket has a burn hole in it) and Ace (the owner of the dry cleaner). The observer takes notes on the process and results.
4. Use active listening skills.
5. Identify the underlying interests of Ken and Ace.
6. Brainstorm at least three possible solutions
7. Identify objective standards and evaluate the possible solutions.
8. Try to come to a resolution that meets the most important interests of both parties.

Debriefing:

1. What is the issue?
2. What are the interests?
3. What are the possible solutions?
4. What are some objective sources for evaluating the possible solutions?
5. Who was able to resolve the dispute?
6. For those unable to resolve the dispute, what were the impediments?
7. For those who resolved it, what were your solutions?
8. Do these solutions look workable? Evaluate them one at a time.
9. Can they be enforced without the help of outside person?
10. What is the benefit of working out solution themselves rather than going to the police, a judge?
11. Could an outside person help to resolve the dispute?

responsible for the burn and should replace the jacket because there was no hole in the jacket when it was brought to the cleaners. Ace may respond that the jacket was not new when it was brought to the cleaners. Ken may contend that it was his favorite jacket, that it cost $250 and that it has been ruined.

Review the directions from handout #17: "Going to the Cleaners". Ask your students in their pairs as Ace and Ken to identify the underlying interests. Ace may appreciate that while it is important for Ace Dry Cleaners not to pay for burn holes when there is no real proof that the damage happened at the cleaners, it is also important to maintain good customer relations with Ken and other customers ("preserve the relationship"). Ken may appreciate that there are only a few convenient dry cleaners in the neighborhood, that Ace has done a good job in the past and that it is unlikely that he will be able to replace a jacket that is several years old with the same jacket. In short, they may both see that there is a value in continuing their relationship.

Then have your students in pairs brainstorm possible solutions without judging them. They may consider having Ace repair or pay for repairing the jacket. They might also consider having Ace pay for part but not all of the cost of a replacement jacket because there is no proof that the burn hole happened at the cleaners and the jacket was not new anyway. Pairs of students might agree that Ace can offer Ken a certain amount of free dry cleaning since this costs him little but has a benefit to Ken. Other pairs of students might decide that they cannot come to an agreement. Ace may decide that he was not at fault and may refuse to pay for or repair the jacket. Ken may decide that he will accept nothing less than full cost of the jacket and will no longer use Ace Dry Cleaners. The observer should be taking notes about the process and the results. Since you may have more than a dozen pairs of students negotiating simultaneously, the observer will help you follow what happened in each group.

Once the parties have come to an agreement, or even if they have not, stop the negotiations after 10-15 minutes. Ask the observers from each group to summarize the process: what did the parties identify as their interests and possible solutions; what did they use as objective sources for evaluating the possible solution; were they able to come to a resolution; if not, what were the impediments to finding a resolution. Continue the debriefing by having the class consider whether the agreements that the parties have concluded are workable and whether they can be carried out without the help of an outside person. Consider whether an outside person could help resolve the dispute. When is it necessary to call a police officer and what would be his or her role? When is it necessary to go to court and what would be the role of a judge? What is the value of working out a solution without the help of a third party?

Students should understand that the police should be called if one of the disputants becomes violent. The role of the police officer is essentially to keep the peace, not to resolve the dispute (however some officers are trained to help mediate conflicts). They might need a third-party to intervene if the parties are too emotional or cannot come to an agreement. They can go to court, where a judge will decide the case, and one side will one win and the other will lose. They can go to a mediator, who will help them come to a resolution (see mediation, lesson 10 below).

Negotiation Evaluation Form

You may want to use the attached "Negotiation Evaluation Form" (Student Handout/Teacher Overhead #18) to help you assess your students' progress or develop your own. The Evaluation form can be used by you or by the observer. You can assign numeric amounts to each category, which would form the basis for a participation grade. It asks questions about each of the specific skills involved in negotiating: the identification of interests, the use of active listening skills, brainstorming solution, evaluating solutions, missed opportunities. The alternative chart is focused on more generic categories: evidence of persuasion, quality of information, group cooperation, understanding of the issue and delivery and presentation. It also provides criteria for grading each rubric.

RUBRICS/SCORES	Excellent-4	Good-3	Fair-2	Poor-1
Separating emotions and issues	Emotions identified. Minimal triggers used and/or interruption made.	Emotions identified. Minimal triggers used and/or interruption made.	Emotions identified. Triggers used frequently and/or interrupts often.	Emotions not identified. Triggers used frequently. Interrupts often.
Identification of issues and interests	Issues clearly identified. Underlying interests of both sides clearly understood.	Issues and own interests identified but no effort to understand interests of other side.	Effort to identify issues. Positions repeated. Interests of self or other side not identified.	No effort to identify issues or interests. Positions repeated or no solid position taken.
Active listening- providing feedback	Pays attention. Asks clarifying questions, paraphrases, makes his understanding clear, and shares relevant information.	Pays attention. Seeks information by questioning, paraphrasing or restating and shares some relevant information. Tries to communicate understanding.	Eye contact. Seeks but does not share information. Irrelevant comments made. Understanding of issues not clearly communicated.	No eye contact. No effort to seek or offer additional information. Not paying attention. Understanding of issue not clearly communicated.
Brainstroming possible solutions	Seeks a wide variety of possible solutions and withholds judging them until after a full list has been developed.	Seeks a limited number of alternative solutions and immediately eliminates some of them	Seeks a limited number of alternative solitions and immediately judges and discards most	Little or no effort to brainstorm a variety of possible solutions to the conflict. Monopolizes the discussion.
Evaluating possible solutions	Considers pros and cons of possible solutions by reference to objective criteria and interests of the parties.	Considers the pros and cons of possible solutions with reference to the interests of the parties but no objective criteria.	Considers the possible solutions but without reference to the interests of the parties or objective criteria.	Little or no consideration of the merits of the possible solutions.
Delivery and presentation	Speaker uses facts, bacground and references to similar situations or analogies; is articulate and convincing.	Speaker refers to facts or background; (makes analogies) is clear but unconvincing.	Speaker includes a few references to facts or background; (analogies) is awkward or unconvincing.	Speaker includes no reference to facts or background (no analogies); speaks in generalizations.
Cooperation	Offers suggestions; considers ideas of others; tries to find a resolution.	Offers suggestions and considers ideas of others.	Offers suggestions but does not cooperate with other side.	Makes no effort to work with others to try to find a solution.

Student handout/Teacher Overhead #18: *Negotiation Evaluation Form*

Lesson Ten: Mediation

Mediation involves a third-party, with no interest in the dispute, who helps the disputants to come to a resolution. It allows the conflict to surface and be managed and directed toward resolution. The role of the mediator is not to decide what the best solution is but to help the disputants come to a resolution. It still enables the parties to frame their own agreements. It can produce creative, value-added solutions that are durable and may "enlarge the pie" and assist in continuing relationships.

When is a mediator necessary? If direct negotiations do not work, a mediator might help to focus the discussion on interests, options and criteria. A mediator may be necessary when the parties are unable to separate their emotions from the problem, when the issue is highly controversial, when the parties have uneven bargaining power, and when the parties are unable to identify the issues or their interests. Where parties are willing to talk with each other and situation is sufficiently calm, negotiation is more likely. Where issues are complex, parties are unwilling to talk or situation is hot or emotional, mediation is probably necessary. For example, mediation is sometimes used in divorce proceedings because the parties are sometimes very emotional. Mediation is also used in complex environmental cases that require a great deal of expertise on the part of the mediator. Mediation may help to even the playing field when one party has a great deal of bargaining power. You may want to use Student Handout/teacher Overhead #19: "What is Mediation" with your students to summarize the value and nature of mediation.

Student Handout/Teacher Overhead #19: ***What is Mediation?***

- Involves a third-party with no interest in the dispute helps the disputants to come to a resolution

- Establishes trust and a fair process

- Allows conflict to surface, to be managed and directed toward resolution

- Helps disputants to understand the problem and to identify solutions

- Allows the disputing parties to frame their own agreements (the agreements are NOT decided by third-party)

- Can produce creative, value-added solution that are durable and may "enlarge the pie"

- Assists continuing relationships

At the meetings at Camp David with Egyptian President Anwar Sadat and Israeli Prime Minister Menachem Begin in 1978, U.S. President Jimmy Carter helped to broker an agreement that ended three decades of warfare between Israel and Egypt. President Carter treated the two leaders equally and with dignity and respect to avoid any suspicion of favoritism. He helped the two parties to focus on their vital interests rather than their years of animosity and their opposing positions. This eventually enabled them to agree to Israeli withdrawal from Sinai (which met President Sadat's need for sovereignty over the Sinai peninsula) and to Egyptian recognition of Israel and the stationing of U.S. and other troops in a demilitarized zone (which met Prime Minister Begin's need for security). President Carter had a unique position as a mediator (he was able to offer both sides economic aid, unlike most mediators, although this was not an overt part of the mediation process). The two Middle Eastern leaders still were unable to resolve other issues, but without Carter's intervention and persistence, Sadat and Begin probably would not have been able to overcome their suspicions and reach the land for peace agreement in the justly celebrated Camp David Accord which ended decades of warfare between the two countries.[24]

You may want to use Student Handout/Teacher Overhead #20: "Steps in Mediation" to summarize the steps involved in mediation. While the steps in mediation and negotiation are basically the same (set the ground rules, each side tells story, try to clarify issues, brainstorm and evaluate solutions and come to an agreement), in mediation there is a disinterested third-party—the mediator—to help the disputants resolve their conflict. The major difference between mediation and negotiation is that the mediator states the rules, asks questions and paraphrases to help the parties come to a resolution. This does not mean that the disputants are free to aggravate each other and to avoid trying to seek a resolution. The mediator must have the disputants' trust and must maintain his or her neutrality.

In addition, the mediator has an important tool to use. He or she can "caucus" or meet separately with each of the disputants. Caucusing is a good way for the mediator to discover the disputants' real interests, as opposed to their stated positions. The disputants may not want to share this information directly with the other side. Caucusing is also a good way to elicit possible solutions from each disputant and to test out responses to solutions that have been suggested. Again, the disputants may not want to reveal this to the whole group. It is critical for the mediator to meet with each disputant or each side of a dispute so that there is no appearance of favoritism. The mediator must maintain the trust of all of the disputants and meeting with only one side would end this trust. A mediator cannot be effective unless the disputants believe that he or she is neutral.

Student Handout/Teacher Overhead #20: ***Steps in Mediation***

1. Mediator introduces himself and the disputants and sets the ground rules—no triggers, no interruptions, respect each other, and agree to work together on resolving the issue.
2. Each side tells story
3. Mediator helps disputants to identify facts and issues through questions, paraphrasing and reframing
4. Mediator summarizes and the parties agree on issues and interests
5. Mediator helps disputants brainstorm alternative solutions
6. Mediator helps disputants to evaluate, discuss and revise solutions
7. Optional Caucus: sometimes the mediator may speak separately with each of the disputants
8. Mediator helps disputants agree on a solution
9. Mediator writes down the agreement, including what to do if the conflict recurs.

---

[24] Dayle E. Powell, conflict resolution specialist at the Carter Center, Emory University, graciously provided insight into Carter's conflict resolution techniques to co-author, John Whiteclay Chambers II, at a two-day seminar on "The Interconnections Between Domestic Dispute Resolution and International Conflict Resolution," sponsored by Rutgers University and the U.S. Institute for Peace, at Rutgers University, New Brunswick, New Jersey, in February 1990. See also, Dayle Powell, "Fundamental Issues in Conflict Resolution: Differences and Parallels in the Domestic and Global Fields," paper presented at the seminar. Anwar el-Sadat paid a high price for his statesmanship. He was assassinated by an Egyptian Muslim fundamentalist in 1981.

In mediation, the mediator is doing the active listening to help the disputant hear each other better. See the chart below comparing mediation and negotiation (Student Handout/Teacher Overhead #21). Although the mediator sets the ground rules and keeps the process moving, he or she is not in total control of the process but must respond to the needs (e.g., one or more disputants may have some emotions interfering with the process and may need to vent a bit) and interests of the disputants.

Selecting students to be mediators

Although your initial impulse may be to select as mediators those students who exhibit the best leadership skills or are the most articulate, this may not always be the best idea. Optimally, you would provide an opportunity for every student to practice mediating. With twenty historical activities and six or more conflict resolution scenarios, this might be possible. It also might be possible for every student to have the opportunity to mediate since many of the activities involve small groups of three to five and several groups of students can mediate at the same time. However, if you do not have enough time for every student to play the role of mediator, you might

---

Student Handout/Teacher Overhead #21: *Comparison of Negotiation and Mediation*

NEGOTIATION	MEDIATION
Parties agree to ground rules	Mediator states ground rules and parties agree
Each disputant presents facts, feelings and issues	Each disputant states facts, feelings and issues
Other disputant(s) restate and question	Mediator and other disputant(s) restate and question
Disputants agree on issues and interests	Mediator summarizes issues and interests and parties agree
Disputants brainstorm solution	Mediator helps disputants brainstorm solutions, may offer suggestions
Disputants evaluate solution	Mediator helps parties evaluate solutions
Disputants agree on a solution	Mediator helps parties to agree on a solution
Disputants agree on what to do if conflict recurs	Mediator helps parties to determine what to do if conflict recurs
Disputants prepare a written agreement	Mediator prepares a written agreement
	***Possible additional step: CAUCUS— mediator meets separately with disputants

consider providing opportunities for those students most in need of developing their interpersonal skills. In addition, a shy, retiring or quiet student may be an excellent mediator since the key skill is active listening, not assertiveness. We have been amazed at how, when given the opportunity, ordinarily shy students are able to exert quiet but effective control over the mediation process. Teachers also have reported that some of their special education students have turned out to be patient, empathetic listeners and very good mediators.

Mock Mediation activity: "Downtown"

There are many possible scenarios to use with your students to practice mediation skills. The activity below, "Downtown"[25] is adapted from "We Can Work it Out!" which includes several other mediation scenarios that might interest your students (most of them can also be used alternatively as negotiations). Divide your class into groups of three: the teen (whom we have named "Pat" because the name is gender neutral), the store owner, and the mediator. Students playing the role of the teen should read handout #22: "Downtown," and the teen roleplay part (handout #23 on the CD). The store owner should read handout #22: "Downtown," and the store owner roleplay part (handout #24 on the CD). The mediator should review the facts (handout #22: "Downtown") and the steps in mediation (handout #20). You may want to add an observer as a fourth person to each group. The observer does not participate in the mediation but rather takes notes about the process and the results to share with the class as part of the debriefing. The value of the role of an observer is to give you additional eyes to follow what is going on in each group. It also forces students to practice listening (not active listening with feedback-just listening), an underrated but critical skill.

Instead of "Downtown," you may prefer to use "Not in my Store," a more complex mediation activity, which has an underlying history of racial and ethnic antagonism in the community (See Student Handout/Teacher Overhead #25 below).

After your students have tried to mediate an agreement to the problem in "Downtown" or "Not in My Store" for approximately 20 minutes (or however much time you have allotted or you think your students will need for at least some of them to come to a resolution), debrief the process and the results. If you are short on time, keep the time for the mediation fairly short. It is more important for the students to get a taste of how the process works than to come to a resolution. It is critical, however, that you provide time to debrief the process. Students may be frustrated or uncomfortable with their roles, and you will need to discuss these feelings.

The more objective debriefing involves asking the observers from each group the following questions, writing the responses for each group on a board or chart and discussing them as a class: What did the parties identify as the issues? What did they identify as their interests? Were the parties able to acknowledge any emotions involved and work towards a resolution? Which groups were able to resolve the dispute? For those unable to resolve it, what were the impediments? For those who resolved it, what were your solutions? Do these solutions look workable? Did the mediator help to resolve the dispute? How? What is the value of having a mediator help disputants resolve their conflict? When do you need the help of a mediator? What would probably happen if the disputants were unable to resolve their conflict (this is the BATNA or WATNA)? You may want to use the Mediation Evaluation Form (Student Handout/Teacher Overhead #26) to help you assess your students' understanding and progress.

---

[25] This activity is hypothetical.

Student Handout/Teacher Overhead #22: *"Downtown"*

The Facts

Pat likes to go into town and look around the stores. Pat's parents do not like the idea of him/her going into town alone, although he/she is 16 years old. However, he/she is allowed to go into town if he/she is with friends because his/her parents believe that he/she is safe in a group. Everyone goes into town. It's a way to pass time. Recently a number of stores downtown have experienced some shoplifting and vandalism. As a result, the stores have made a policy that no one under sixteen can enter a store without a parent or guardian. The policy also limits the number of kids aged 16-18 that can enter a store to two. Other kids have to wait outside until the pair inside leave. Stores have threatened to call the police if the kids give them any trouble about the new policy. This policy makes Pat and his/her friends angry. They feel that it is unfair. They do not want to disobey their parents' rules and they do not want to get in trouble with the law either. The head of the downtown merchants association offers to convene a meeting between the teens and the store owners.

Directions

1. Divide into groups of THREE:
   - Teen (Use Student Handout/Teacher Overhead #23)
   - Store owner (Use Student handout/Teacher Overhead #24)
   - Mediator (Use Student Handout/Teacher Overhead #20)
2. Assign or choose roles
3. Mediator introduces parties and sets rules
4. Acknowledge any emotions
5. Identify the issues and interests
6. Brainstorm possible solutions
7. Evaluate each solution
8. Mediator helps the parties to find a resolution agreeable to all
9. Observer takes notes on the process and results

Debriefing

1. Did the mediator introduce everyone and set the ground rules?
2. Did the mediator help the disputants to acknowledge their emotions? Did they avoid triggers?
3. Did the mediator help the disputants to identify interests and issues? What were they?
4. Did the mediator help the disputants to generate options? What options were generated?
5. What objective criteria were used to evaluate these options?
6. Which groups were able to resolve the dispute?
7. For those unable to resolve it, what were the impediments?
8. For those who resolved it, what were your solutions?
9. Do these solutions look workable?
10. Did the mediator help to resolve the dispute? How?
11. What is the value of having a mediator help disputants resolve their conflict?
12. What would probably happen if these disputants were unable to resolve their conflict?

Student Handout/Teacher Overhead #25: *"Not in My Store"*

The Facts

Ali Mobarrak is a recent immigrant from Pakistan. He has taken all of his savings and opened a small convenience store on a busy street in downtown Jersey City, New Jersey. The neighborhood is mostly populated by poor Latino and African-American families, many single parent families.The store is near a middle school and a high school. Recent immigrants from Korea, Pakistan, Afghanistan, and other middle eastern countries now run all of the small stores in the neighborhood. There is a great deal of antagonism between the long-term residents and the shopkeepers. The African-American and Latino residents feel that they are not being treated with respect by the Middle Eastern or Asian shopkeepers. The shopkeepers think that the young people are rude and the parents exercise no authority over them.

Lately there has been an increase in the amaount of vandalism and shoplifting in the neighborhood and this has been affecting Mr. Mobarrak's slim profits. Juan Sanchez and Albert Carter are students at Snyder High School. One day after school, they entered Mobarrak's store to buy some pens and notebooks for school, but discovered that they did not have enough money. Since Mr. Mobarrak was busy with another customer and not watching them, they put the pens and pads in their backpacks and started to walk out of the store. However, Mr. Mobarrak happened to have a mirror in the corner that enabled him to see what the two boys were doing. Mr. Mobarrak followed the two boys out of the store and alerted Officer Conroy, who was walking down the street, about the shoplifting. Officer Conroy has been trained as a community mediator and asked the two boys to call their parents. He asked the parents to meet him, their boys and Mr. Mobarrak at the police station.

Directions

1. Divide into groups of six or seven: Mr. Mobarrak, Albert Carter, his father, Mr. Carter, Juan Sanchez, his mother, Mrs. Sanchez, an observer and Officer Conroy as the mediator
2. Assign or choose roles
3. Mediator introduces parties and sets rules
4. Acknowledge any emotions
5. Identify the issues and interests
6. Brainstorm possible solutions
7. Evaluate each solution
8. Mediator helps the parties to find a resolution agreeable to all

Debriefing

1. Did the mediator introduce everyone and set the ground rules?
2. Did the mediator help the disputants to acknowledge their emotions? Did they avoid triggers?
3. Did the mediator help the disputants to identify interests and issues? What were they?
4. Did the mediator help the disputants to generate options? What options were generated?
5. What objective criteria were used to evaluate these options?
6. Which groups were able to resolve the dispute?
7. For those unable to resolve it, what were the impediments?
8. For those who resolved it, what were your solutions?
9. Do these solutions look workable?
10. Did the mediator help to resolve the dispute? How?
11. What is the value of having a mediator help disputants resolve their conflict?
12. What would probably happen if these disputants were unable to resolve their conflict?

Student handout/Teacher Overhead #26: *Mediation Evaluation Form*				
RUBRICS/SCORES	Excellent-4	Good-3	Fair-2	Poor-1
Did the mediator: Set the ground rules	Very clearly	Fairly clearly	Some ambiguity	No rules set
Create an atmosphere of trust	Definitely	Mostly	Somewhat	No
Treat the parties fairly	Yes	Mostly	Somewhat	No
Caucus	Effectively	Somewhat effectively	Not effectively	No
Help parties to: Acknowledge emotions	Emotions identified and separated from the issues; no triggers	Emotions identified. Minimal triggers.	Emotions identified. Triggers used.	Emotions not identified. Triggers used frequently.
Identify issues and interests	Issues clearly identified. Underlying interests of both sides clearly understood.	Issues and own interests identified but no effort to understand interests of other side.	Effort to identify issues. Positions repeated. Interests of self or other side not identified.	No effort to identify issues or interests. Positions repeated or no solid position taken.
Active listening-providing feedback	Asks questions, paraphrases, summarizes and helps disputants to understand the issues and interests.	Seeks information by questioning, paraphrasing or restating and shares limited amount of information	Eye contact. Summarizes what the disputants have said but does not seek additional information.	No eye contact. No effort to seek or offer additional information. Understanding of issue not clearly communicated.
Brainstorming possible solutions	Seeks a wide variety of possible solutions and withholds judging them until after a full list has been developed.	Seeks a limited number of alternative solutions and immediately eliminates some of them	Seeks a limited number of alternative solitions and immediately judges and discards most	Little or no effort to brainstorm a variety of possible solutions to the conflict. Monopolizes the discussion.
Evaluate possible solutions	Helps disputants evaluate possible solutions by reference to objective criteria and their interests.	Helps disputants evaluate possible solutions with reference to their interests but no objective criteria.	Considers the possible solutions but without reference to the interests of the parties or objective criteria.	Does not help the parties to evaluate the merits of the possible solutions.
Encourage cooperation among disputants	Offers and seeks suggestions; considers ideas of others; tries to find a resolution.	Offers suggestions and considers ideas of others.	Offers suggestions but does not consider ideas of others.	Imposes own view rather than encouraging cooperation among disputants.

Mediation Evaluation Form

You may want to use the attached negotiation mediation form (Student Handout/Teacher Overhead #26) to help you assess your students' progress or develop your own form. The Evaluation Form may be used by you and/or by the observer. You can assign numeric amounts to each category, which would form the basis for a participation grade. It asks questions about each of the specific skills involved in negotiating: the identification of interests, the use of active listening skills, brainstorming solution, evaluating solutions, missed opportunities. The alternative chart is focused on more generic categories: evidence of persuasion, quality of information, group cooperation, understanding of the issue and delivery and presentation. It also provides criteria for grading each rubric.

Lesson Eleven: Mediation or Negotiation?

To conclude, you may want to compare mediation and negotiation by having some of your student try to reach a solution through negotiation and some through mediation, using the scenario below, "The Noisy Neighbor"[24] (Student Handout/Teacher Overhead #27). As the title suggests, this activity involves an immediate dispute and an underlying issue involving noise by a teenage boy, Louis, that bothers Cora, the neighbor in a duplex apartment. Students should identify the issues: both the immediate issue of what to do about the shattered window in Cora's door and the long-term issue about the noise in the apartment. Then they should identify the interests. What common interests do the parties (Cora, Louis, and his father, George) have? Probably no one wants to move out of their apartment so there is a common interest in resolving the dispute. Students should brainstorm possible solutions. After all of the groups have come to a resolution or you have run out of the time allotted, compare the processes and the results of the mediations and the negotiations as a whole class.

Ask the observers if those groups without mediators were able to resolve the dispute themselves? Ask the other observers if the groups with mediators were able to resolve the dispute? Did the mediator help to resolve the dispute? How?

Ask the whole class: What would probably happen if these disputants were unable to resolve their conflict? The most likely result would be avoidance and continued bad relations between the neighbors. The BATNA would be that they could appeal to the landlord for help resolving the dispute or go to court for a decision. The WATNA would be a decision that either Cora or George and his children cannot abide and will perhaps force one of them to move. What is the value of having a mediator help disputants resolve their conflict? What is the value of having the disputants resolve their conflict by themselves? Mediation and negotiation help the disputants to maintain control over their dispute, help to preserve the relationship, and offer opportunities for creative solutions.

Help your students to conclude that if only a few people are involved and the parties to the dispute can acknowledge their emotions and put them aside, then negotiation is possible. If there is a large group of people involved, or there is very uneven bargaining power or the parties are too emotional, then mediation may be more effective. You may want to use the Negotiation Evaluation Form (handout #18) or Mediation Evaluation Form (handout #26) to assess your students' understanding and progress. For additional scenarios to practice negotiating or mediation, see *We Can Work it Out! Problem Solving Through Mediation* by Street Law, Inc., published and distributed by Social Studies School Service.

---

[24] This scenario is from *Community Works: Smart Teens Make Safer Communities*, 2nd ed., 2004.

Student Handout/Teacher Overhead #27: *The Noisy Neighbor*

The Facts:

Cora lives in a duplex on a quiet street in Shortville. She has enjoyed living there for several years. The house is on a bus line and close to a grocery store. Several months ago, George, a father with two teenagers, Louis and Ana, moved into the upstairs apartment. Now there is a lot more noise in Cora's building. Some evenings the noise makes it impossible for Cora to get to sleep. Cora wants to get along with her new neighbors, but several times she has had to talk to George about the noise. George considers Cora to be a complainer. He knows that the kids should be quieter, but he does not like to keep after them about it. Last night Louis came home with a friend from a party around 3:00 a.m. and made a lot of noise in the hallway. Cora was so frustrated that she opened the door and started yelling at the kids. Her yelling triggered Louis' anger and without thinking, he picked up a broom that was in the corner of the hallway and shook it at her. The broom hit one of the little windows in Cora's door and shattered it. Cora called Louis a juvenile delinquent and vowed to call the police.

Directions:

1. Divide into groups of four (Cora, George, Louis, and an observer); or five (Cora, George, Louis, a mediator and an observer).
2. Assign or choose roles
3. Acknowledge any emotions
4. Identify the issues and interests
5. Brainstorm possible solutions
6. Evaluate each solution
7. (Mediator helps) the parties to find a resolution agreeable to all
8. Observer takes notes on the process and results

Debriefing

1. Did the mediator introduce everyone and set the ground rules?
2. Did the mediator help the disputants to acknowledge their emotions? Did they avoid triggers?
3. Did the mediator help the disputants to identify interests and issues? What were they?
4. Did the mediator help the disputants to generate options? What options were generated?
5. What objective criteria were used to evaluate these options?
6. Which groups were able to resolve the dispute?
7. For those unable to resolve it, what were the impediments?
8. For those who resolved it, what were your solutions?
9. Do these solutions look workable?
10. Did the mediator help to resolve the dispute? How?
11. What is the value of having a mediator help disputants resolve their conflict?
12. What is the value of having the disputants resolve their conflict by themselves?
13. What would probably happen if these disputants were unable to resolve their conflict?

Lesson Twelve: Teachable Moments

Teachers involved in our Conflict Resolution and United States History workshops have shared with us many instances where they have taken opportunities provided by fights, disputes, or violence in the classroom, in the hallway or involving students in their classroom as "teachable moments." For example, when a teacher returned to her classroom after lunch to find two young women fighting over a boy in the class, instead of sending them to the principal, she had the class conduct a hearing to establish the facts and had the class help the two disputing girls come to a resolution. Although this was a school district were fighting is not usual, this teacher reported that there were no further incidents in her classroom for the remainder of the year, unlike prior years. Even more strikingly, a teacher in another urban school district used the instance of a mistaken shooting by the police of one of the students in the school to fully explore the value of negotiating rather than escalating a conflict. (There had been a background of hostile police-community relations based on mistrust and misunderstanding that had been allowed to simmer and then exploded into violence).

Many teachers have commented that by helping their students to better understand how to deal with conflicts in their lives, they also learned how to better deal with everyday conflict that accompanies a classroom of 25, 30 or more students. These teacher have taken the conflict resolution lessons as a way to better manage their classrooms by first better understanding conflict and the skills involved in managing it and then by enabling their students to become part of the management of the classroom rather than part of the problem.

Such teachable moments may or may not arise. The main purpose of providing this background in conflict resolution skills is to have your students use them in their lives and to better understand American history. Chapter Three provides suggestions on how to use these skills in a variety of historical roleplaying activities.

TEACHER OVERHEADS/STUDENT HANDOUTS ON CD

1. Pre-Post Test about Attitudes regarding conflict

2. Conflict Resolution Bingo

3. What is Conflict?

4. "The Bloody Conflict"

5. Fact sheet for Dr. Runcible

6. Fact sheet for Dr. Quarg

7. The Sources of Conflict

8. Responses to Conflict

9. Advantages and disadvantages of different responses to conflict

10. Steps in Conflict Resolution

11. Positions and Interests

12. "Triggers"

13. "Do I Understand You?"

14. "John and Matt at the Locker "

15. Steps in Negotiation

16. What can we learn from professional negotiators?

17. "Going to the Cleaners"

18. Negotiation Evaluation form

19. What is Mediation?

20. Steps in Mediation

21. Comparison of Negotiation and Mediation

22. "Downtown"

23. Facts for Teen

24. Facts for Store Owner

25. "Not in My Store"

26. Mediation Evaluation form

Sources and Credits for Illustrations

p. 29:   "Prehistoric Firing Squad" cartoon, *www.CartoonStock.com*

p. 30:   "Fastest Gun in the West" cartoon, *Nevada Historical Society*

CHAPTER THREE

HOW TO USE THE CURRICULUM PACKAGE

This chapter provides suggestions on how to use the materials in the historical case studies, how to integrate the conflict resolution concepts from Chapter Two, how to set up the historical roleplaying activities, how to debrief them and how to assess your students' understanding of conflict resolution and U.S. history.

The *Conflict Resolution and United States History* curriculum package includes two volumes of historical case studies. In addition to these written materials, the curriculum package includes a CD and DVD. The CD, "*Conflict Resolution and US History* Resource Materials" includes timelines and outlines in Microsoft Word and Microsoft PowerPoint that can be used as student handouts or teacher overheads for each chapter in the accompanying volume. The CD also includes relevant primary source documents—maps, speeches, letters, diary entries, newspaper articles, legislation—for each case study in the volume as well as forms to use in debriefing and assessing your students. The DVD, "Historical Roleplaying Using Conflict Resolution Skills," includes videotaped demonstrations of actual classroom use of some of the case studies by teachers and their middle and high school students. Watching the DVD may provide you and your students with a better idea of how to apply the conflict resolution skills and the historical background to each case study to do historical roleplaying activities.

The purpose of this chapter is to facilitate the use of the printed historical case studies, the student handouts and teacher overheads and primary source documents on the CD and the DVD. The chapter includes suggestions based on our experiences and those of teachers who have used these materials in their classrooms.

The Structure of the Case Studies

Each case study begins with a list of objectives and correlations with the National Standards for United States History. Although only the National History Standards are included, many of the case studies also meet National Standards for Economics, Geography and Civics and Government. Each case study then provides a brief overview of the conflict and then a systematic review of the historical background, including both the long-term and proximate causes of the specific conflict to be examined. Each case study then provides short biographies of the historical participants in the conflict, the positions and interests of the participants, and directions for the teacher to use to establish both the immediate context for the historical role play and the individuals and groups to be involved. Most of the case studies recommend stopping at a particular point in the evolution of the conflict, at a moment when the situation might be still fluid enough so that escalation to violence has not yet occurred. It is at that point that students are invited to try to resolve the conflict by playing the roles of historical figures using interest-based negotiation or mediation skills. After doing the historical role play, each case study provides a framework for the teacher to use in debriefing both the process and the results of the historical roleplaying. The case studies then resume with what really happened in history (what we have called "the facts continued"), the costs and consequences. Each case study concludes with questions for discussion and a listing of additional resources.

While the majority of the case studies involve a single historical roleplaying activity, some include parallel or paired historical conflicts or multiple historical roleplaying activities for the same case study. For example, the chapter about the Native Americans and European Colonists (Volume One, Chapter Four) includes two parallel studies: one about the Puritans and the Wampanoags in New England and the other about the Quakers and the Lenni Lenape in Pennsylvania. By doing fairly parallel negotiations/mediations in both instances and comparing the history of violence in Puritan New England with the relatively peaceful coexistence of colonists and Indians in Quaker Pennsylvania, students not only learn about the specific history that unfolded in both places but also appreciate that while conflict between differing cultures was probably unavoidable, escalation to war was not necessarily the inevitable result. These paired case studies might also enable your students to appreciate the impact that religious or secular attitudes or ideologies, and political leadership can have in escalating or de-escalating conflict.

Labor strife during industrial development also offers two parallel case studies: one about the Pullman Strike and Boycott in 1894 and the other about the Paterson Silk Strike in 1913 (Volume Two, Chapter Four). The two paired studies can be used to reinforce each other so that your students not only learn the historical facts behind both instances of industrial violence but also appreciate that workers at that time had no legal right to withhold their labor by striking and few legal protections, and that owners and managers of corporations and other businesses had comparatively few incentives to negotiate with their workers. One of the results was that there was considerable violence in labor-management relations in the years between the 1870s and 1930s.

Other case studies involve more than one point in history where we suggest stopping to do a mock exercise in conflict resolution, or several options or alternative activities. For example, The American Revolution case study (Volume One, Chapter Five) first includes a mock mediation by selected members of the First Continental Congress in 1774 and subsequently a mock negotiation between the American colonies and Britain in 1775. Similarly, the case study concerning the United States and the war in Vietnam (Volume Two, Chapter Eleven) includes several alternative or cumulative activities: a mock mediation in 1966 as well as a mock negotiation in 1969, both of which address the question of whether the Vietnam War might have been resolved at an earlier date than it was.

The curriculum package offers a variety of options so that you can decide what best fits within your class schedule, which activities best illustrate the points that you seek to emphasize about particular periods or events, and also what might be of particular interest to you or your students. For example, your students might be more interested in roleplaying the First Continental Congress or they may prefer to negotiate as Benjamin Franklin or Lord North. You might allow some students to negotiate an activity and others to mediate it to see if there are any differences in the outcomes and, if so, what they might be. You may want to try one activity one year and a different option another year and see which one works better for you and your students. You may want your students to use the documents included on the CD as the starting point for a case study or you may want to select certain documents as supplementary materials for your students to evaluate, or to use in their mock negotiations or mediations or other activities.

Some of the mock negotiations involve only two participants (such as Lord North and Benjamin Franklin in London in 1775 or John Slidell and Manuel de la Peña y Peña in Mexico in 1845), plus a nonparticipating observer/recorder/reporter. Other negotiations may include numerous participants such as the Quakers and Lenni Lenape (Volume One, Chapter Four), or the Cuban Missile Crisis (Volume Two, Chapter Ten). The mock mediations involve anywhere from three to twelve participants, plus nonparticipating observer/recorder/reporters. For example, the Mexican War mediation would include three participants plus an observer/reporter/recorder, while the Reconstruction activity involves more than a dozen active participants. For activities involving a small number of participants, you may want to have several different "teams" or groups of students simultaneously roleplaying the same historical conflict. Although this may create quite a bit of noise in your classroom, having several concurrent mock mediations or negotiations allows the students the independence and creativity to arrive at differing results. Even more importantly, analyzing the different results in the debriefing and comparing them with what really happened offers excellent openings for discussion. Such a comparison also may be helpful for understanding the complexities of each case study and the opportunities and limitations that existed at the time. (See the section on "Debriefing" below.) Where the negotiations or mediations involve 10-20 participants, you may want to form two groups or involve your entire class as one group. For example, Slavery and the Constitution (Volume One, Chapter Six), the Compromise of 1850 (Volume One, Chapter Nine), the mock congressional hearing before the Joint Committee on Reconstruction in 1866 (Volume One, Chapter Eleven), the Montgomery Bus Boycott (Volume Two, Chapter Nine), and the Los Angeles Riots (Volume Two, Chapter Twelve) all involve multiple participants and a mediator. You may want to add several "newspaper reporters" to observe, record and report what happened, and hold one activity involving your entire class.

Historical Background

Each case study includes a rich historical background prepared with the help of one or more prominent historians. In addition, the CD includes a timeline of historical events that can be used as an overhead or as a student handout. For example, the case study about the American Revolution reviews the history of relations between the North American colonies and Britain at the end of the French and Indian War and continuing through 1776, including specific instances which exacerbated the growing sense of grievances on both sides of the Atlantic. The flow of history is interrupted at two points in time: at the First Continental Congress in September 1774 where students are asked to mediate a response to Britain after the Coercive Acts and in January 1775 when students are asked to negotiate as a representative from the American colonies (Benjamin Franklin) and a representative for the British crown (Lord North) to try to find a peaceful resolution to the growing conflict. The Vietnam War activity (Volume Two, Chapter Eleven) begins during World War II and the flow of history is stopped in 1966 for a mock mediation then continues until 1969 when another historical roleplaying activity, this time a negotiation, takes place.

Each case study includes much more detailed historical background than what you would find in a typical American history textbook. Teachers involved in the development of the curriculum package have uniformly told us to include more rather than less information. Depending on the age and ability level of your students, you may wish to use all of the background provided, simplify it by primarily using the student handouts on the CD, or enhance it with the primary source documents on the CD or with additional student research. Although each chapter provides one or more specific activities for you to use with your class, you may wish instead to improvise your own activity based upon the background that we have provided. Creatively is always encouraged!

Directions for Historical Roleplaying

The "flow" of history comes to an abrupt halt in each case study and a specific date and place is identified for the participants to try to find a resolution to the growing conflict at hand. The setup for each activity is placed in the present tense so that the students can put themselves into the historical situation as if they were there at the time. This helps to make the roleplaying both more historical and more immediate.

In the case study of the American Revolution, for example, our march of history stops temporarily on September 28, 1774 while the delegates to the First Continental Congress are meeting at Carpenter's Hall in Philadelphia. At this point in time, the radical Suffolk Resolves confronting British policy have been delivered by express rider Paul Revere from Massachusetts for the Congress to consider. Pennsylvania delegate Joseph Galloway has just proposed a compromise "Plan of Union" to the Congress to correct the defects in the current British system of governance with its American colonies but still maintain the relationship. The directions set out a small, informal meeting of some of the delegates at the Congress, a "congressional caucus," to be mediated by Peyton Randolph, president of the Continental Congress. You would review the positions and interests of the historical participants and place the students in groups with instructions to use conflict resolution skills, especially active listening skills, to try to agree on an appropriate response to the "Coercive Acts" which Britain has imposed on her North American (and particularly Massachusetts) colonies.

As part of the instructions to your students before they engage in the historical role play, you will probably want to review the steps in either negotiation or mediation with your class as a whole. Historical roleplaying is not the same as historical reenactments, where the goal is to "replay" history as close as possible to what actually happened. In historical roleplaying, you are giving your students a role to play—the role of an actual historical person—but the student may "play" that role a number of different ways. He or she might focus primarily on using the conflict resolution skills or, alternatively, might try to adhere closely to the position that was taken in history and make little effort to try to find a resolution to the conflict. Students should understand from your instructions that they are free to creatively diverge from what actually happened in history, so long as they try to stay within the scope of their participant's interests and make suggestions that might have been within the realm of possibility given the particular historical setting and circumstances. Most importantly, the students should be instructed to carefully listen to each other.

You may want to show your class the DVD which demonstrates how middle and high school students have done historical roleplaying activities to help your students to better understand the process and the possibilities offered by historical roleplaying.

Finally, if you think that any of the historical roles may be uncomfortable for your students, you may want to explicitly mention this to the class to help reduce any possible discomfort. For example, students may feel uncomfortable playing the roles of slaveholders or segregationists.

Historical Participants

The case studies all involve actual historical conflicts. The participants in the historical role plays (with the exception of composite World War II veterans in the Women in the Workforce After World War II case study (Volume Two, Chapter Eight) were actual historical individuals. We have identified real historical individuals who represented particular groups, viewpoints, and interests in the conflict. Similarly, most of the meetings we describe in the directions to the historical roleplaying activities actually took place.

While the vast majority of our case studies involve students in roleplaying meetings that actually took place in history, a few of the case studies envision meetings that did not occur but for which there had been efforts to meet or such meetings were historically plausible. For example, in an effort to avoid war, John Easton met with Metacom (King Philip) of the Wampanoags in 1675, although the governors from the Massachusetts Bay and Plymouth Colonies were not at the meeting. Benjamin Franklin was an American envoy in London representing and lobbying for a number of colonies, who spoke with members of Parliament and certainly tried to talk with Lord North in 1775. Although in actuality, Lord North refused to meet with Franklin, such a meeting was not beyond the realm of possibility. John Slidell did travel to Mexico in 1845 in order to meet with the Mexican Foreign Minister Manuel de la Peña y Peña; however, the political situation in Mexico and Mexican national honor did not allow the Mexican government to receive him once the scope of his mission became public. Although Spain, Cuba and the United States did not sit down together in 1898, it is not beyond the realm of possibility for a meeting of representatives from these countries to have taken place. In all cases, the historical situations are real and the meetings might plausibly have occurred.

The role of the mediator/facilitator

While many of the case studies involve direct negotiations between representatives of two groups or among three or more groups, in a number of cases we have suggested the use of a mediator either because there is an imbalance of power or because a large number of participants is involved. The role of the mediator (or facilitator, if a less formal situation is envisioned) is to help the disputing parties to understand the issues and the available options and bring them to a resolution that they find mutually acceptable. The mediator should be a disinterested third party, that is, someone without an interest in the outcome of the mediation who is respected by the disputants. The mediator or facilitator does not tell the disputing parties what to do, although he or she might make suggestions for them to consider. Nor does the presence of a mediator absolve the disputing parties from using conflict resolution skills or give them the license to try to make the mediator's job more difficult. Rather, the disputing parties, who may be delegates to Congress, members of different interest groups, or representatives of various countries, still have an obligation to try to identify the issues and their interests and to seek options that might be mutually acceptable. The mediator helps to keep the rhetoric down and to focus the parties on the issues, their interests and the available options (See Chapter Two for more details about mediators).

Sometimes the mediators are simply unnamed, disinterested third-parties. In other case studies, where an actual historical figure did or could have played the role of the mediator, the individual is identified for the role. For example, Peyton Randolph, as the president of the First Continental Congress, is in a good position to mediate with his colleagues and is identified for the role of mediator. Although not a totally disinterested third party, he is respected by his colleagues for his judgment and wisdom and was a moderating influence as the First Continental Congress debated how to respond to the growing distrust and despair with British colonial policies in September 1774. In the Pullman Strike, we have suggested Jane Addams as a mediator because she is a well-respected member of the Chicago Civic Federation and had offered to mediate the dispute between the Pullman Palace Car Company and its workers. In the Immigration debate we suggested Jeremiah Jenks, an economist and mediator who was not actually involved in the debate but who was respected for his background and experience. In the Montgomery Bus Boycott, we suggest the vice-president of the National City Lines, which ran the buses in Montgomery, as the mediator, because he had experience with desegregating buses and because he was not part of the local struggle in Montgomery.

The role of the observer/recorder/reporter

Having one or more students act as an observer/recorder/reporter serves a number of useful purposes. The first purpose is to observe the negotiation or mediation process. During the process, the observer/recorder/ reporter listens carefully to what is being said and done (body language), without actually speaking with the participants. The value of observing is greatly undervalued and infrequently practiced. We rarely spend time developing our observation skills, yet everyone would agree that they are very important. This provides students an opportunity to practice their observation skills.

The second purpose is to record both the process and the results of the negotiations or mediation. You may want the observer/recorder/reporter to use the generic observer's form to take notes about the process, using specific rubrics, and to memorialize any agreements that the parties have reached. Alternatively, you may want to tailor the form to fit the specific historical conflict under examination.

The third, and perhaps most important, purpose for the observer/recorder/reporter is to report on what happened during the negotiation or mediation process and any resulting agreements to the rest of the class, as part of the debriefing. Especially when there are numerous groups negotiating or mediation simultaneously, the observer/recorder/reporter provides extra eyes and ears to help the teacher follow the process and the results.

The observer/recorder/reporter might be an actual historical person or simply an individual given the role of observing, recording and reporting on the negotiations or mediation, without directly participating in the negotiation or mediation process (which may take the form of a Congressional hearing or caucus or other format that best fits the historical situation). For example, in the Mock Congressional Caucus in the American Revolution case study, we have identified Charles Thomson, who is the secretary of the First Continental Congress, to serve as the observer/recorder/reporter since his role historically was essentially that of a recorder. However, in the Benjamin Franklin/Lord North negotiation we have identified only the role of generic "observer/recorder/reporter".

If you only want to involve a small number of students as active participants in an historical roleplaying activity for purposes of demonstration or other reasons, you might want to have a large number of observer/ recorder/reporters. You might assign the students who are the observer/recorder/reporters different tasks, different questions or different emphasis (e.g., observe one historical participant only). You might also use the observer/ recorder/reporters as a "reporter" to take notes about the negotiation or mediation and to write a newspaper article from a particular perspective (e.g., have Susan B. Anthony, Lucy Stone and Catharine Beecher, who had very different views about the roles of women in the mid-nineteenth century and none of whom participated in the Seneca Falls Women's Rights Convention in 1848, write articles about the convention from their perspective). Alternatively, you may want to have one student serve as the observer/recorder and another student as the reporter for the group.

Selecting students for roles

Teachers using these case studies have suggested that while their initial inclination was to select their best, brightest or most outspoken or outgoing students as the mediators, it was sometimes the shy student who turns out to be an excellent listener and mediator. Sometimes the very strong or assertive students tend to try to take too much control of the situation rather than creating a nonthreatening environment, listening carefully to different points of view and encouraging the other students to participate in the mediation process. In addition, pushing students to take roles outside of their normal comfort level may be a good way to help them build self-confidence in their abilities. In order to encourage all students to see conflicts and solutions from different perspectives, it is a good idea to have students experiment with roles that are contrary to their natural inclinations and to rotate the role of mediator and observer/recorder/reporter so that each student has the opportunity to experience history from these different perspectives.

Positions and Interests

Identifying and separating the positions (that is, the stated goals and desires) from the interests (that is, the underlying material, attitudinal, or emotional needs or fears or reasons behind the positions) is a key element in interest-based negotiation and mediation and in applying interest-based conflict resolution skills to learning and understanding history. Each case study includes an outline of the positions and interests of the participants. In order to visualize these more effectively, the positions and interests are also set forth as overheads or handouts on the CD.

Using the example of the American Revolution, the "radicals," such as Samuel Adams from Massachusetts, Christopher Gadsden from South Carolina and Richard Henry Lee from Virginia, all argued for outright resistance to Britain. That was their position. Their interests were primarily ideological, but also economic. More than anything else, they wanted to preserve their fundamental right to govern themselves. They greatly feared that Britain was trying to repress the colonies as it had repressed Ireland. In addition, New England merchants were involved in smuggling items that were supposed to be taxed or purchased only from Britain or her other colonies, and Southern planters were in debt to Scottish tobacco brokers. The "moderates," such as William Livingston from New Jersey and George Read from Delaware, urged restraint and further attempts at reconciliation. That was their position. Although they were also concerned about their liberty, their interests were focused more on commerce and prosperity than ideology. They had more faith that Britain would treat the colonies fairly. The "conservatives," such as Joseph Galloway from Pennsylvania and James Duane from New York, wanted to continue the relationship with Britain and the protection of the British royal navy. Their interests were to maintain stability (avoiding lawlessness and mob action by the colonists) and, therefore, they were more interested in a peaceful resolution to the conflict with Britain. They were more fearful of anarchy in the colonies than restrictions imposed by Britain. Clearly, there were areas of overlapping interests and a certain amount of flexibility in the positions. The "compromise" solution that the First Continental Congress developed was an economic boycott of commerce with Britain through an agree-upon ban on importation and exportation.

In many conflicts, the positions are much less flexible. The alternative American Revolution negotiating activity, involving Lord North and Benjamin Franklin in 1775, is a good example of growing inflexibility. Instead of focusing on the many mutual interests that the American colonies and the British Crown shared—maintaining mutually profitable trade relations, continued good will and peace—the British took the position that Parliament had the right as the supreme legislative body to determine and lay taxes on the colonies. With the conflict framed as an issue of sovereignty, the colonists took the position that taxation without representation was tyranny. There was little room to satisfy both of these positions (James Galloway's "Plan of Union" between Great Britain and the Colonies was one possibility) although there were many ways that the interests (primarily economic) of Britain and her American colonies might have been met.

In some but not all cases, the positions taken reflect the underlying interests. Identifying what the disputing parties are saying (their positions) as well as their economic, social, political or ideological interests, fears, concerns or needs (their interests) helps students to see the many interests involved. Another value is that the process of separating interests from positions helps to identify potential areas where some, or at least the most important, interests of the parties might be satisfied. Thus, a basis for coming to an agreement might be identified, which would be impossible if each party simply continued in an unmovable position that precluded the opposing position, viewing the situation like a zero sum game. Instead, the aim of interest-based conflict resolution is to think creatively, reframe the issues and the conflict, and to seek ways in which at least some of the underlying interests of the parties can be achieved. Finally, this approach to learning history helps students to appreciate that there is almost always more than one perspective on the same set of facts.

Use of the CD with handouts/overheads and documents

The CD includes large-print pages with the roles, positions and interests, and short biographies of the participants, as well as relevant maps and documents, for each historical case study. You may want to use these visual aids either as overheads to share with the entire class or as handouts to share selectively with the students who are playing particular roles. Also available on the CD for classroom use are timelines of events leading up to the conflict; a summary of "the facts continued," that is, what really happened after the point in time when the case study stopped for the roleplaying exercise; and the costs of the actual resolution to the conflict (frequently, the resolution has been war), primarily in terms of lives and property damage. You may want to use the relevant primary source documents (excerpts from speeches, diaries, letters, laws, court cases, and treaties) on the CD as a basis for your students to research the positions and interest of the individuals and groups involved in the historical role play or as an extension once your class has concluded the historical roleplaying activity.

Debriefing the historical roleplaying activity

After your students have finished playing the roles of the historical figures in the historical conflict, you need to lead them through a "debriefing." In the debriefing, you will ask your students a series of questions to obtain useful information about what happened in their historical role plays in terms of process and results, to compare the process and results of the mediations or negotiations by the various teams of students and to review what really happened in history and to compare the results of your students' efforts to resolve the conflict with what actually happened in history whether war, compromise or avoidance.

The debriefing is probably the *most* important part of the historical roleplaying activity. This is true for several reasons. Most immediately, the debriefing enables you to bring your students out of their roles and to help your class to analyze the situation objectively. Equally important, by bringing everyone out of the roles that they have just played, you can explicitly raise and discuss any emotional discomfort that any students may have experienced in playing their roles. For example, it might be uncomfortable for your students to play the roles of the European colonists in New England in the late 1600s in conflict with the Native Americans, or the slave owners in the Compromise of 1850, or the white southern segregationists in the Montgomery Bus Boycott. Any such discomfort needs to be discussed.

Debriefing the historical roleplaying activity also enables your students to appreciate that there were several different perspectives regarding the factual context. It is in the debriefing of the historical roleplaying activity and the comparison to what actually happened in history that students obtain a rich understanding of the complexity, opportunities and implications of the historical conflict and the way it was actually resolved. It is critical that your students come away from the historical roleplaying activity understanding what really happened and why, and not to confuse what might have happened with the actual events. Clearly, your own assessments of your students and standardized examinations such as the SATs require that students know the actual course of historical events. However, the richer understanding that students obtain from the fuller exploration offered in our case studies should help your students to remember not only the facts but also the causation and consequences of historical decisions.

After concluding the role play, the teacher should begin the debriefing by asking the observer/recorder/reporter(s) from each group to first explain how the process of negotiation or mediation worked or failed to work in the group and secondly if the group was able to agree on a solution and, if so, what it was. The reporter could use either the generic forms provided on the CD or a form that you may want to develop to specifically address the issues raised in the case study. If there are several groups, you may want to summarize the process and the results from each group on a chalk board or white board and, after all of the groups have reported, note any similarities and differences among the groups.

The student reporters should be able to explain if and how the parties used active listening skills, if and how they brainstormed and evaluated possible solutions (see the observer's evaluation forms for mediation and negotiation). Ideally, the student reporters will be able to outline the strengths and weaknesses of the mediator or the negotiators with sufficient sensitivity to avoid upsetting the student whom they are discussing. What do you do, however, if an observer/recorder/reporter just bluntly states that the mediator or one or more of the negotiators has done a terrible job? To some extent, the rubrics on the generic form take some of the sting out of what might otherwise be too personal. The teacher can also soften any comments that are too extreme by emphasizing the difficulty of the task. In most of the case studies, the actual participants in history were *not* able to find an amicable resolution to their conflict without resorting to violence, so the student negotiators or mediators should not be made to think of themselves as failures. We are not trying to cast blame or failure, but rather to note missed opportunities and to emphasize creative, plausible solutions. For example, students roleplaying the Federal Convention of 1787 frequently have been unable to come to any agreement about slavery in 1787 and the result is that the fledgling United States of America breaks into several countries. Appreciating this possibility enables students to understand how fragile the unity of the country was in 1787 and why an irrational, and to many an obnoxious, compromise of counting slaves as three-fifths of a person for purposes of representation and taxation was agreed upon.

Distinguishing the results of the historical role plays and what actually happened in history

The next and **absolutely crucial** step is to conclude the debriefing by comparing and contrasting what really happened in history with the results of the historical roleplaying activity. Distinguishing the results of the historical roleplaying activity that your students did from the actual resolution of the conflict is imperative so that students remember the actual historical facts and simply use the historical roleplaying activity as a way to more fully appreciate the historical context and the individuals involved as well as the opportunities that were available at the time. Each case study continues with what really happened ("the facts continued" section). Obviously, your students need to learn what actually happened in history. You don't want them thinking that history happened according to their roleplaying (unless it actually did!). But, now that your students have personally involved themselves in trying to resolve the issue, they should be very interested in learning the details of what happened. They will also have a much richer understanding of the causation of the historical conflict, the limitations on what was possible at that point in time, and the consequences of the actions that were taken.

In many cases, those students who chose to focus on using conflict resolution skills and trying to resolve the conflict peacefully will end up with a result that may be far removed from what happened in history (unless, it is the unusual situation where the disputing parties actually resolve their differences peacefully, as in the Cuban Missile Crisis). For example, students playing the roles of Lord North and Benjamin Franklin often find a rational solution other than war in 1775. The same is true for students negotiating the differences between Mexico and the United States in 1845. Alternatively, some students might play their roles with great historical accuracy and the results may be the same or fairly similar to what actually happened in history. While the students negotiating as Lord North and Benjamin Franklin on the DVD were very rational and open-minded, other students have played the role of Lord North much more rigidly and a mutually agreeable solution was not possible. In one instance, the student playing the role of Thaddeus Stevens in the Reconstruction role play was so rigidly adamant about his position that he brought the entire process to a standstill. Clearly, this result bears a certain relationship to what actually happened in history: the Radical Republicans in Congress insisted on their vision of Reconstruction and were not willing to make accommodations, which ultimately aided the enemies of Reconstruction. So, even though the students in this group were unable to come to a resolution that met the interests of other members to the Reconstruction mediation, the result of their role play showed how the intransigence of even one person can have a impact (positive or negative) on history. Neither of these results is right or wrong. Both of these responses to the directions for roleplaying an historical conflict serve an instructive purpose.

You and your students then should analyze whether the ahistorical results of the mock activity were within the realm of historical plausibility or possibility, that is, could the solution have possibly happened given the historical circumstances? Although the issue of plausibility is conjectural, comparing the resolutions the students arrived at in their role plays with what really happened allows them to appreciate that there were lost opportunities for better alternatives to what actually happened (usually a war) or that the options were limited because of national pride or other emotional or extremely powerful forces. It may be that your students have discovered alternative resolutions that the actual historical participants overlooked because they were focused on their positions, their pride or their passions rather than their real interests (perhaps the Spanish government could have negotiated with the United States and Cuba in 1898 rather than fighting a war that it knew it couldn't win?)

Sometimes your students may negotiate a very creative solution that is ahead of its times historically. A quick-thinking student negotiator for Mexico proposed that the United State and Mexico jointly develop the region that was comprised of Mexico's northern provinces and has become the southwest U.S., a very forward-looking concept for 1845, but perhaps not for the twenty-first century (much like our "Free Trade Zones"). Or, they may find a way to alter power imbalances, such as existed in the case study regarding Cherokee Removal. One group of clever students playing the role of the Cherokees proposed a farsighted alliance with the railroads to build on Cherokee lands to get to the gold fields that had been discovered. The Cherokees were not strong enough by themselves to reverse the ideas held by most early nineteenth century Americans that the Native Americans were not fully utilizing their land and should be moved out of the way. By building a mutually beneficial economic alliance with early capitalists seeking to build railroads and to develop natural resources, the Cherokees could strengthen their position vis-à-vis the state and national government.

One test of the plausibility of a particular solution is whether it would have been acceptable to the constituent groups in that particular historical period. Not only are the negotiators acting within the confines of their own positions and interests, they also must consider the pressure of their constituencies, whether they are the voters, a particular political party or the members of a labor union or a Nativist organization other interests group. Would it have been plausible for the Paterson Silk manufacturing owners or the Pullman Palace Car Company to accept demands from striking workers that would reduce their profits or managerial flexibility when strikes were outlawed and there were no processes in place for resolving labor disputes? Would it have been within the realm of possibility for Mexico to have avoided war with the United States in 1846 or Spain to have avoided war with the United States in 1898 without having the government fall? Would the Mexican or Spanish governments have had the support of powerful groups in their societies if they had ceded land (e.g., Mexico's northern provinces or Spain's Cuba) for money or for other tangible benefits to the country without a fight or was this too much of an affront to the country's national pride? Note that the governments in Mexico in 1846 and Spain in 1898 both fell anyway after fighting and losing a war with the Unites States.

Why was it possible for John F. Kennedy and Nikita Khrushchev to avoid nuclear confrontation in the Cuban Missile Crisis? Was it simply that the stakes were higher once war became nuclear so that fear played a larger role? Or were both President Kennedy and Premier Khrushchev able to put aside their emotions and exercise leadership, despite fears that their constituencies might see them as "weak". Note that Khrushchev's role in the Cuban Missile Crisis did help to lead to his downfall.

Students have negotiated rational resolutions to conflicts that were in reality clouded by vanity, fear, arrogance, prejudice or other emotions. The solutions obtained by the students negotiating as Lord North and Benjamin Franklin on the DVD ignore the passion and pride involved in the situation but otherwise meet the underlying interests of both parties in continuing commercial relations and stability. The students are respectful of each other, carefully listen to each other's views and try to brainstorm and discuss possible options that might reduce the growing hostilities between Britain and her North American colonies. By putting aside the need to ensure Parliament's "right" to tax the American colonies without their consent, and focusing instead on the underlying interests, the students playing the roles of Lord North and Benjamin Franklin were able to find common ground: the colonies would send representatives to the Parliament to help determine issues of national concern (Britain would continue to determine all issues relating to foreign countries), the local governments of the colonies could continue to determine issues of solely local concern, and the British would build garrisons for the soldiers so that the colonists did not have to house and feed the British soldiers. Would these solutions have been acceptable to the American colonists and the British Crown in 1775? Not likely as long as the King and the majority of Parliament insisted on "punishing" the colonists, but certainly possible if they followed their national interests. While these solutions differ greatly from the bloody war that Britain and the American colonies fought between 1776 and 1783, such agreements were not beyond the realm of possibility in 1775 before blood was shed. Edmund Burke's contemporary analysis of the situation was: "The retention of America was worth far more to the mother country economically, politically and even morally than any sum which might be raised by taxation, or even than any principle so-called of the Constitution."[1]

By comparing the mock mediation/negotiations with what really happened in history, the debriefing should result in a rich understanding of history. While students need to learn what actually happened in history, by first using the historical background to role play alternative possibilities, the comparison makes them appreciate

---

[1] Edmund Burke, "The Retention of America", a speech given in 1790.

the lost opportunities that were due to personalities, entrenched positions or limitations imposed by prevailing societal values. It also enables students to understand the difficulties faced by decision-makers and to understand that every conflict, in the past and present, can be perceived from more than one perspective. Finally, the debriefing should help your students to appreciate that decisions have consequences and that history did not just "happen" as it did but rather that it was the result of decisions that were made.

Questions for Discussion

Each chapter concludes with suggested questions for discussion, or you may want to prepare your own questions. The questions presented at the end of each chapter are primarily designed to raise large issues about the conflict, to help students to think creatively about it and to enable students to appreciate both the opportunities and limitations that existed at the specific historical juncture under examination. The questions will help you to conclude the debriefing and to bring all of the alternative thinking together into a full understanding of the causes of the conflict, the historical framework for its resolution and the consequences of the resolution. The questions may be used for classroom discussion, written homework assignment or as essay questions on a formal assessment (See Section on Assessment below).

Additional resources

Each case study offers a list of sources for obtaining further information or analyses. The lists include books, articles, websites and other materials that have provided information for the case study and which you may want to consult. In addition, the accompanying CD includes for each chapter excerpts from primary source documents, or entire documents, maps, speeches, and other helpful images. You and/or your students may want to further investigate a particular historical conflict, or you may want your students to use the primary source documents in their negotiations. Alternatively, you may want to use these primary source documents as part of your assessment by asking your students to comment on what is said in the documents or by comparing and contrasting what is said in several documents.

Assessment of Students' Knowledge and Performance

Although there are plenty of materials available for testing students' understanding of U.S. history, there are few such instruments for assessing knowledge of conflict resolution skills or mastery in their use. Therefore, with the help of teachers who have used our curricular materials, we have included on the accompanying CD several instruments that may be of use in assessing your students' understanding, appreciation and use of conflict resolution skills. The first is a "Conflict Resolution Form," which you might want to use with your students as a pre-post test (Student Handout/Teacher Overhead #1). It is designed to assess student appreciation of when and how conflict resolution skills might be employed. You would have your students take the test before you begin any conflict resolution lessons to determine what their attitudes were and then have your students take the same test again after you have completed the conflict resolution lessons as well as one or more of the historical roleplaying activities. This will allow you to determine how effective the lessons have been in making any attitudinal changes, recognizing that it is difficult to change attitudes. The second instrument is designed to help teachers to evaluate individual student use of conflict resolution skills as they do the historical roleplaying activities. It includes a series of rubrics (Student Handout/Teacher Overhead #28). The third instrument is merely a simplified version of the previous instrument (Student Handout/Teacher Overhead #29). You may want to use whatever test of American history content you currently use with your students with the students using the

Conflict Resolution and United State History materials and to compare the results with students not using the Conflict Resolution and United State History curriculum. Finally, you may want to use some of the questions posed at the end of each of the historical case studies as essay questions and grade the students' written answers as part of your assessment of their knowledge of content-based history.

Conclusions

As long as there are competing needs or differing interests, there will be conflict. What can we learn by carefully examining the causes of conflicts and possible peaceful solutions over the course of American history? As you prepare your students for the historical roleplaying activities, the specifics of each situation may ultimately lead to an understanding of the differences between material interests and psychological needs and how both may provide a basis for resolving a conflict. The historical roleplaying activities will demonstrate that there are many different ways to look at the same set of facts. And, the debriefings may help your students to see that alternative solutions are almost always possible, although viable solutions are limited to some extent by individual and societal attitudes. By involving your students in understanding different perspectives and the underlying causes of specific conflicts in American history, they may begin to see patterns and to draw some conclusions about the nature and the causes of conflict. What conclusions can we draw from history about the interactions of human beings and groups on an individual, state and international level?

We learn that individuals can make a difference. Certainly, if William Pitt (Lord Chatham) had been British Prime Minister rather than Lord North in the 1770s, his government would have responded differently to the colonists, as he indicated in his speeches to Parliament at the time. If Henry Clay had won the presidential election in 1844, war with Mexico certainly would have been less likely because the Whig policy was for gradual, peaceful expansion rather than conquest by war.

We learn that organized groups are often more effective than individuals and that building coalitions can also help in negotiations. A small, dedicated group that thinks insightfully and acts strategically can sometimes have a huge impact. Among the American colonists, the "radicals" (such as Adams, Gadsden and Lee) formed a tight-knit group across the various colonies through Committees of Correspondence and they gained the upper hand at the meetings of the Continental Congress. Ultimately, their view prevailed. In another instance more than half a century later, the Cherokees might have gained more support for remaining on their land in Georgia if they had tried to build a coalition with business interests, such as the railroads which were interested in running trains across their land, or with abolitionists or women who were concerned about the denial of rights to slaves, women and abolitionists, themselves, in the 1830s. In the 1840s, Mexico tried to gain the support of other nations (Britain and France) in its growing conflict with the United States but London and Paris, while happy to limit U.S. expansion, had their own interests and were unwilling to jeopardize them by unduly antagonizing the United States. In the post-World War II era, civil rights leaders, much like the abolitionists a century earlier, seized the high moral ground and brought together a wide range of individuals with similar values regarding the rights of African Americans. With a broad liberal alliance reaching across racial and geographical lines, these coalitions were effective in moving forward their agenda for ending racial segregation and trying to build a multiracial democracy in America.

The failure of conflict resolution sometimes is simply due to the fact that concessions are offered too late. For example, in the dispute with the American colonies, Lord North's government offered major concessions only in 1778 after a British army had been defeated and France had entered the war as an ally of the United States. While the concessions offered by the British Carlisle Commission—for what became known later as commonwealth status—were too late in 1778. However, they might have provided the basis for a working agreement in 1776. Similarly, the concessions offered by the Spanish to the Cubans in 1898 might have averted war if they had been offered in the 1880s, but by 1898, the concessions were too late. They only further convinced the Cuban insurrectionists that Madrid was weak and that Cuban independence was within reach. In both cases, there was a failure to consider the WATNA (the worst alternative to a negotiated agreement), which was, in both instances, the loss of a valuable colony.

We also learn to appreciate that once started, hostilities are difficult to de-escalate. That is one of the basic lessons of the war in Vietnam and of the American invasion of Iraq. Too often, combat only ends when one side demonstrates overwhelming force or one or both sides are depleted by casualties, economic (supplies or infrastructure) inadequacies or loss or change of moral resolve.

Finally, the historical roleplaying helps us to appreciate that those with power—whether political or economic—are not usually willing to share their power unless they are forced or otherwise induced to do so. The Civil War might have been averted by the gradual emancipation of slaves (an idea that was discussed in many circles, especially in Virginia). Daniel Webster had suggested in 1850 that the proceeds from the sale of the land that Virginia ceded to the Union in 1787 that became the Northwest Territory be used to reimburse slave owners for the gradual emancipation of their slaves. But there was no legal incentive for the South to consider such possibilities because slavery was protected by state and federal laws and was seen as economically and culturally beneficial to the slaveholders. The Southern politicians needed to see the larger public interest: that the Southern whites—slaveholding and non-slave holding alike—might actually benefit from contract wage labor rather than the slave labor system and certainly by continued union with the North. The Northern Republican politicians needed to see that, as eager as they were to end slavery and as difficult as it would be to increase taxes, generating funds for the elimination of slavery might be a workable solution that would end slavery and keep the Union together.

Similarly, in looking at industrial relations at the turn of the twentieth century, the Pullman Palace Car Company might have averted a strike in 1894 had it agreed to meet and speak with its workers and their representatives. But, there was no legal incentive for Pullman to do this: the law was on the side of capital, management and the new corporations. Strikes were forbidden, and no law required recognition of a union or negotiations with a labor union. Until the 1930s, the courts supported the right of owners and managers of a corporation to the labor of their employees based on the idea that "freedom of contract" allowed individual laborers to accept or not accept labor conditions. When individuals organized as a labor group staged a strike by withholding their labor, their efforts were viewed by the courts as an unreasonable restraint of trade that violated that Sherman Antitrust Act. George Pullman, and recalcitrant "robber barons" like John D. Rockefeller, Cornelius Vanderbilt, Andrew Carnegie, Henry Clark Frick and Henry Ford, needed to see the larger public interest involved in recognizing legitimate unions, avoiding disruptive strikes and having a stable and effective work force. This view led to a coalition of moderate labor leaders, enlightened corporate leaders and reformist political leaders who saw the value of replacing industrial warfare with joint efforts to increase economic growth.

Engaging students in historical roleplaying and looking at plausible alternatives in the past not only motivates young people to learn history but also enables them to appreciate that there is more than one perspective regarding any conflict, and that it is the decisions and responses made by leaders and groups that determines whether a conflict is resolved by violence or by negotiation. Rather than seeing history as an inevitable flow of events over which they have no control and, therefore, little incentive to act to change anything, students using conflict resolution skills in historical roleplaying learn to appreciate that history is the result of the skills and leadership of individuals and groups. Understanding that the efforts of individuals or groups can have positive (or negative) results may give your students a sense of empowerment. This knowledge may provide them with a better understanding of history and encourage them to act more effectively as informed and responsible citizens in American democracy.

Chapter Four

Native Americans and European Colonists

Objectives

- To understand the underlying sources of conflict between European colonists and Native Americans in the late 1600s.

- To examine the impact of changes in trading and the pressure for more land in New England and Pennsylvania in the late 1600s and early 1700s.

- To analyze the impact of Puritan and Quaker religion and ideology on their relations with Native Americans

- To examine the consequences of King Philip's War in New England.

- To compare the responses by European colonists in New England and Pennsylvania to conflicts with Native Americans.

Correlations with National History Standards

Era One
Standard 1D

Differences and similarities among Africans, Europeans and Native Americans

- Compare political systems

- Compare social organizations

- Compare economic systems

- Compare dominant ideas and values

Era Two
Standard 1B

European struggle for control of North America

- Analyze relationships between Native Americans and European settlers.

- Compare how English settlers interacted with Native Americans in New England, mid-Atlantic, Chesapeake, and lower South colonies.

Standard 2B

Religious diversity in the colonies

- Explain how Puritanism shaped New England communities and how it changed during the 17th century.

OVERVIEW

*W*hile violent war erupted between the Puritans and the Wampanoags in New England (King Philip's War, 1675–76), peaceful relations existed between the Quakers and the Lenni Lenape along the Delaware River basin in New Jersey, New York and Pennsylvania. Was this pure accident? The result of the more peaceful nature of the Lenni Lenape? The result of William Penn's efforts to establish a "firm league of peace" with the Native Americans? Economic factors? What role did the religious beliefs of the European settlers play? What role did leaders' personalities play? Was the bloody war avoidable? What conclusions can be drawn about the nature of conflict, the differences among European settlers' views towards the Native Americans, and the impact that an individual and groups can have?

This lesson consists of two case studies:

Part One: The Puritans and King Philip's War, 1675-76

Part Two: The Quakers and the Lenni Lenape, Delaware Indians, 1682–84.

PART ONE: THE PURITANS AND KING PHILIP'S WAR, 1675–76

HISTORICAL BACKGROUND

*T*he area that became New England had long been settled by a variety of Algonquian-speaking peoples: Massachusetts, Narragansetts, Mohegan-Pequots, and Wampanoags, as well as the Abnaki in northern New England (Maine and New Hampshire). They hunted and farmed the land, raising primarily corn, beans and squash, and fished in the many waterways. Farming was semi-migratory. New fields were opened by burning trees and underbrush and were fertilized with fish and cornstalks. Farming was done mostly by women. Men grew tobacco, hunted, traded, negotiated alliances, and defended their people and crops. Individual kinship bands, often confined to a single village or river valley, were the effective units of organization. Land was held in common by the kinship bands and used as needed. The "sachems," or chiefs, helped to negotiate for their people and to pursue the seasonal and often vengeful conflicts with other neighboring native tribes. Although influential and often charismatic individuals, sachems held no absolute political or religious authority nor did they have the ability to coerce others to follow them. Culture was passed orally from elders to the younger generation.

Into this world came 100 people from Plymouth, England on the *Mayflower* in 1620. About 40 of them were "Separatists" who sought to completely separate themselves from the Church of England. These Separatists (called

Native American Village, 1590

Pilgrims) came to America searching for a place to practice their religion free from repression and interference from the outside world. They also hoped to prosper financially in their new life, along with their non-Separatist travelers. The charter they had was for land in Virginia; however, they landed at a good harbor in Massachusetts Bay. The land had been cleared, but no one was in sight. The Pilgrims believed that this was a sign from God that the Almighty had cleared the land for their use. They named their new home "Plymouth" in honor of the town from which they had sailed. In reality, the Pilgrims established their colony on land that had been the Indian village of Patuxet. A smallpox epidemic in 1616–1618, brought by earlier European traders and fishermen, had decimated whole villages and reduced the native population in New England from more than 100,000 to less than 70,000.

It was the good fortune of the Pilgrims to encounter Squanto, a native of Patuxet who had survived the epidemic because he had been kidnapped in 1614 by English traders. His captors had intended to sell him into slavery in Spain, but somehow he managed to escape and reach England, where a London merchant sent him to Newfoundland. He finally made his way home only to find that his entire tribe had perished, so he joined the nearby Wampanoags. Squanto provided critical assistance to the English settlers, serving as their interpreter, guide, and teacher. Despite the distrust that the English and Native American had for each other, in 1621 Massasoit, sachem of the Wampanoag tribe, and John Carver, the Pilgrims' Governor, concluded a treaty that formed the basis for trade and mutual assistance. The local Wampanoags needed a military ally to help them in their struggle with their more numerous neighbors, the Narragansetts.

Plymouth was still a small colony of only about 300 settlers when a second and much larger group of English colonists, led by John Winthrop, arrived under the auspices of the Massachusetts Bay Company in 1630. These were the people now generally referred to as "Puritans." They wanted to purify the Church of England rather than separate from it like the Pilgrims, and they later became known as "Congregationalists."

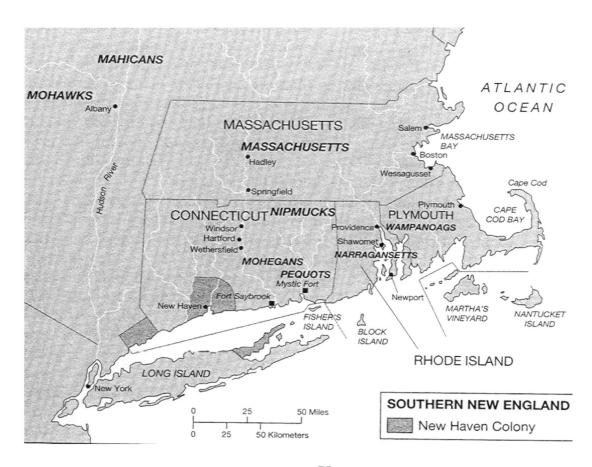

During the 1630s, the native population was further reduced by another smallpox epidemic. The English saw this as the divine hand of God intervening on their behalf. Meanwhile, during the "Great Migration" between 1630 and 1641, some 20,000 Puritans arrived in New England and established towns farther and farther into the region's interior. For a while, the Puritans and neighboring Indians got along peaceably. Tensions began to mount in the mid-1630s when the English started to move into the Connecticut River Valley, an attractive site because of the fertile soil and game lands and a river that provided ready access to the ocean. This land, however, was controlled by the Pequot Indians, an aggressive tribe that dominated several others and served as middlemen in the trade between the New England Indians and the Dutch in New Netherlands. The Puritans claimed the land by "right of discovery," because as John Winthrop wrote:

> As for the Natives in New England, they inclose noe Land, neither have any settled habitation, nor any tame Cattle to improve the Land, and soe have noe other but a Natural Right to those Countries, soe as if we leave them sufficient for their use, we may lawfully take the rest, there being more than enough for them and use (*Winthrop Papers,* Massachusetts Historical Society, 1929).

In 1631, Roger Williams, a Separatist, emigrated from England to the Massachusetts Bay Colony. He was welcomed at first as a "godly minister," but his criticism of the Puritan system of government soon made him enemies. Williams insisted that the king of England had no right to give away land belonging to the Indians; that church and state should be kept separate; and that the Puritans had no right to force their beliefs on others. The Puritan leaders banished Williams from Massachusetts in 1635 for propagating "new and dangerous opinions." He sought refuge with Massasoit and the Wampanoags. The nearby Narragansett tribe gave Williams land on the western shores of the Seekonk River, where he founded a town that he called "Providence" in 1636, the earliest Rhode Island settlement—a place of religious tolerance and a haven for religious dissenters. Williams later wrote about the language and culture of the Indians in New England. (See Document 1: Roger Williams on the Language and Culture of the Indians of New England, 1643.)

Although some Puritans continued to purchase land from local tribes, the English settlers often used alcohol, livestock trespassing and fines for minor offenses of English law as ways to reduce the prices. Rather than convert the "savages" of New England, many Puritans attempted to make them accountable to their ordinances. The real issues involved disputes over land, fur trade and political control of the region. During the summer of 1636, some Block Island Indians, a tribe subordinate to the Narragansetts, killed a Massachusetts Bay trader. Although the Pequots had not been directly involved, Boston authorities believed that the Pequots were harboring two of the perpetrators. The English raided Indian towns on Block Island, then laid waste to a Pequot village. In retaliation, the Pequots attacked the new English town of Wethersfield in April 1637, killing

Woodcut of Massacre of Pequots (1637)

nine colonists. Several weeks later, a Massachusetts force and a Connecticut contingent (Plymouth avoided this war for the most part) attacked a Pequot stronghold near the Mystic River and burned it to the ground. The English killed 500–800 people, primarily women and children, to the astonishment of their Narragansett allies. The few survivors were enslaved. It took another three months to subdue the remaining Pequots. With the close of the Pequot War in 1637, English sovereignty was established over all of the native peoples of southeastern New England except the Narragansetts, and colonial settlements quickly spread throughout the Connecticut Valley.

During the next several years, the English and Indians became increasingly tied to one another through trade and commerce. The essential products were furs, much in demand in Europe, and wampum, beads of white and purple-black seashells that were signs of prestige among the Natives and served as an official medium of exchange with colonial leaders. The Indians exchanged wampum and furs for English goods, such as muskets, iron pots, fishhooks, cloth, other tools and household goods, and liquor. The commercial ties between the English and the natives helped to foster peace between the two groups but also transformed Indian culture from communal hunters and growers to one dependent upon European trade.

The reduction in the number of English migrating to the New World and the diplomatic efforts of the United Colonies of New England (Massachusetts Bay, Plymouth, Rhode Island and Connecticut) from 1643 to 1662 served to restrain aggression on the part of individual colonies between 1645 and 1675. The English population in New England had grown to well over 20,000 by 1642. Although natural increases continued at a fast pace, the "Great Migration" had come to an end during England's civil war in the 1640s. The Puritan population, pushing southward and westward, was 25,000 by 1650 and 60,000 by 1675. The colonists were able to purchase additional land at reasonable prices through accommodating sachems, such as the Mohegan/Pequot's Uncas and the Wampanoag's Massasoit.

After 1660, however, these restraining conditions began to collapse. The fur trade started to decline due to changes in English fashion, which also caused the value of wampum to plummet. As commercial agriculture came to dominate the economy, the Indians found it difficult to compete; yet they had become dependent upon English trade goods. The only thing of value they had left to trade was land and, although this was a commodity the English definitely wanted, the Indians were reluctant to part with it. In truth, the Indians did not feel that they *could* part with it—the idea of land as a commodity was utterly foreign to them. The Wampanoags also became trapped in the middle of land and power disputes between Rhode Island and Plymouth. Both the Wampanoag leader Massasoit, and the Pilgrim elders who had originally negotiated with him in 1620, were dead by 1661. Many of the old agreements, such as the treaty between the Pilgrims and Massasoit's people, had lapsed.

Meanwhile, many Indians were becoming increasingly resentful of Puritan missionary activities aimed at changing their traditional way of life. Originally, Indians who had converted to Christianity had returned to their villages where missionaries had hoped they would convert others. However, they tended to move back to their old beliefs. In 1651, Reverend John Eliot, the Puritan minister of the Boston-area town of Roxbury, had established the first village for Indians who had converted to Christianity. By 1675, there were fourteen so-called "praying towns" in Massachusetts and Connecticut. The converts lived in English-style houses, wore English clothes and spoke the English language. These requirements broke the bonds that held Indian societies together. The non-Christian Indians particularly objected to the Puritan expectations that even non-converts would adhere to strict Christian regulations. They were forced to obey religious sanctions regarding the Sabbath, blasphemy, adultery, and drunkenness. There also were increasing complaints by Indians that the colonists' stray horses and pigs were damaging their crops. The restoration of the Stuart monarchy in England in 1660 created great uncertainty about the Massachusetts Bay charter and the lack of a charter by Plymouth. The United Colonies had ceased functioning.

During these years of rising tensions and political uncertainties, there was a dramatic change in the leadership of the southeastern coastal Indians. After the death of Massasoit in 1661, his eldest son, Wamsutta, became chief. A year later, Major Josiah Winslow, Plymouth's military commander and later governor of the

"Phillip [sic] alias Metacomet of Pokanoket"

colony, arrested Wamsutta and forced him to travel at gunpoint to meet with colonial leaders. The Puritan leaders demanded that he answer charges that he was conspiring to attack English settlements. Wamsutta denied the accusations and was sent on his way, but at some point during the trip he had become ill and died before returning home. Many Wampanoags believed that the colonists were responsible for his death, either by poisoning him or by subjecting him to terror and humiliation that killed him. Massasoit's second son, Metacom (or "King Philip" as the English called him), took over leadership of the Wampanoags. He blamed the colonists for the death of his brother and deeply resented the fact that the English treated the Indians as a conquered people rather than as a free and sovereign community. For their part, the English viewed Metacom with suspicion; rumors were circulating that he, like his brother before him, was plotting an attack. Still, in 1664, Metacom and Plymouth agreed to a new pact, in which the Wampanoags accepted that they were subjects of the English crown and agreed not to sell land to anyone without approval from the colony. In return, Plymouth promised that all settlers would treat the Indians as friends.

In 1667, Plymouth authorized the establishment of the town of Swansea within four miles of Metacom's home village at Mt. Hope (now Bristol, Rhode Island). Metacom's unwillingness to sell land had been ignored and relations became strained. He met frequently with the Narragansett sachem, Canonchet, and obtained a great number of weapons. In 1671, Metacom was brought to Plymouth to answer charges that he was plotting an attack against the colonists. Connecticut Governor John Winthrop, Jr. was present at a meeting called between Metacom and various colonial governors. He listened to Metacom's complaints and offered to assist in settling the dispute between the Wampanoags and Plymouth Colony. Winthrop joined the other colonists in deciding that Metacom was completely at fault. Metacom was forced to sign a statement agreeing to surrender to the colonists "all my English armes to be kept by them for their security, so long as they shall see reason." Five months later when Metacom had failed to deliver more weapons, the Governor of Plymouth accused Metacom of defying the 1671 agreement to surrender his tribe's guns to authorities. Although he confessed to no crimes, Metacom was forced to sign a document agreeing to pay a fine of 100 pounds over a five-year period and to make an annual tribute of five wolves' heads as a show of loyalty. During the early 1670s, Plymouth called upon Metacom to yield to its authority, but he resisted time and again. Metacom came to believe that the relentless push for land and control by the English settlers was a threat to the existence of the New England Indians, and he sought to unite the rival Indian tribes.

Tensions flared in January, 1675, after John Sassamon, a Wampanoag who was a Christian convert, informed Plymouth Colony's Governor Winslow that Metacom was preparing for a full-scale attack on the town of Swansea. Soon after, Sassamon's body, bruised and with a broken neck, was found beneath a frozen lake. The English presumed Metacom had ordered the murder in revenge for Sassamon's treachery in divulging the Wampanoag plans to the enemy. Plymouth officials quickly rounded up three conspirators, including Metacom's counselor Tobias, tried them before a jury of twelve colonists and six non-voting Indians, and found them guilty. They were sentenced to death by hanging. Metacom was not included because there was no evidence linking him to the murders—or, possibly, because Plymouth was wary of pursuing him. To Metacom, the trial was yet another miscarriage of justice, in which whites could testify against Indians, but Indian witnesses were not heard.

Three days after the executions in June, 1675, word of Wampanoags arming near Swansea and Plymouth reached colonial authorities. Metacom summarized his concerns in June 1675 to John Easton, a Quaker who was deputy governor of Rhode Island:

> [T]hey [the Indians] said they had been the first in doing Good to the English, and the English the first in doing wrong, said when the English first Came their king's father was as a great man and the English as a little Child. He Constrained other Indians from wronging the English and gave them Corn and showed them how to plant and was free to do them any good and had let them have a 100 times more land than now the king had for his own people. But their king's brother when he was king Came miserably to die by being forced to Court as they judged poisoned. And another grievance was if 20 of their honest Indians testified that a Englishman had done them wrong, it was as nothing; and if but one of their worst Indians testified against any Indian or their king when it pleased the English that was sufficient. Another grievance was when their kings sold land the English would say it was more than they agreed to and a writing must be proved against all them, and some of their kings had done wrong to sell so much, he left his people none. And some being given to drunkenness the English made them drunk and then cheated them in bargains, but now their kings were forewarned not for to part with the land for nothing in Comparison to the value thereof. . . . Another grievance, the English Cattle and horses still increased that when they removed 30 miles from where English had anything to do, they Could not keep their corn from being spoiled, they never being used to fences, and thought when the English bought land of them that they would have kept their Cattle upon their own land. (Although this speech has been included in many historical works, questions have been recently raised as to whether Metacom said this. See Document 2: Metacom on the "Injustice of the English" and the accompanying explanation and compare with Document 3: "A Relation of the Indian War" by Mr. Easton, of Rhode Island, 1675.)

At this point Metacom seemed to believe that he had no choice but to go war. John Easton proposed that the issue of native and colonial relations be considered by a panel of mediators.

MOCK MEDIATION: NATIVE AMERICANS AND EUROPEAN COLONISTS IN NEW ENGLAND

Although in reality Easton's efforts were overtaken by events, we will imagine that his proposal for mediation was accepted. Plymouth Governor Winslow, Connecticut Governor Winthrop and Reverend Increase Mather select John Easton as a mediator. Metacom, his trusted advisor Annawon, and the Narragansett Chief Canochet select the female sachem, Weetamoo, as a mediator. All of them meet in June 1675 at the home of Roger Williams, who will observe and record what happens at the mediation session.

THE PARTICIPANTS

Josiah Winslow, Governor of Plymouth Colony

Born in 1629 in Plymouth, Winslow was the first native-born governor in America. He grew up among Pilgrim leaders who gave him a thorough education. He studied at Harvard, although he never received a degree. He served as Plymouth Commissioner for the United Colonies from 1658 until 1672, and in 1659 he succeeded Myles Standish as commander-in-chief of the colony. In 1673, Winslow became governor of Plymouth Colony.

When hostilities broke out at Swansea, Winslow signed the declaration of war against the Wampanoags and issued a statement denying any legitimate grievances by the Indians because the colonists had honestly purchased their land. As commander-in-chief of the United Colonies' forces, he led the attack against the Narragansetts in December 1675 that brought them into the war against the colonists. He retired as commander in the spring of 1676, due to illness, and died in 1680.

John Winthrop, Jr., Governor of Connecticut

Born in Suffolk, England in 1605, Winthrop was the son of the Puritan leader John Winthrop, Sr., who organized the initial segment of the Puritan migration to New England in the early 1630s and served as the governor of the Massachusetts Bay Colony for almost all the years between 1630 and his death in 1649. The younger Winthrop moved to Boston in 1631 and lived in various New England towns, including Ipswich, which he helped found, and Salem. He encouraged the establishment of manufacturing in America by securing a grant of 3,000 acres of land to be used for iron making. After his father's death, he settled permanently in Connecticut, where he was elected an assistant in 1651, chief executive in 1657, lieutenant-governor in 1658, and governor in 1659. He was re-elected continually to this last post until his death in 1676. His most important achievement as governor was obtaining a charter from England for the colony in 1663, the most liberal one granted up to that time.

Reverend Increase Mather, influential Puritan minister

Born in Dorchester, Massachusetts in 1639, Mather was brought up in the strict Puritanism of his father, Reverend Richard Mather. He was educated at home and at a free school in Boston, graduating from Harvard in 1656 and Trinity College, Dublin in 1658. After serving as a chaplain in England, he returned to Boston where he became a teacher at the Second Church in 1664. The Mather family occupied a prestigious place in Puritan society. After John Sassamon reported to Governor Winslow that Metacom was forging an Indian alliance against the colonists, Governor Winslow conferred with Reverend Mather and other Boston authorities. Reverend Mather suggested that "This information has come from an Indian source, and we cannot believe the Indians even when they speak the truth." Mather became acting president of Harvard in 1685 and helped secure a new charter for Massachusetts from England. In the two books about the conflicts between the colonists and the New England Indians that he wrote, he saw the Puritan victories as the result of divine providence against the heathens.

Annawon, Advisor to Wampanoag chiefs

Annawaon had served as counsel to Chief Massasoit, and continued as adviser to his son, Metacom. Metacom relied heavily on Annawon's diplomatic skills in attempting to create a confederacy among the New England tribes. Annawon believed that the Wampanoags must take a hard line against the English if they were to survive as a people. He reminded Metacom how they had lost much of their land and also how their pride had been destroyed by the English. He believed that the Pequots were no longer a free people. They were always breaking the white man's law and being punished for it. Annawon is credited with providing the military leadership that made possible early Wampanoag military successes in the war.

Canonchet, Narragansett chief

Born in 1630, Canonchet was leader of the mighty Narragansett Nation, the most powerful tribe in Southern New England, during King Philip's War. He was the son of Miantonomo, whom the Mohegans had killed in 1643 at the request of the colonists. At the beginning of the war, he was unsure of which side to support and initially remained neutral, perhaps biding his time to see who would gain the upper hand in the war. In 1675, he agreed to turn over to the English any of Metacom's people who might flee to Narragansett territory, but he reneged on this promise and sheltered fugitives. After the colonists attacked the Wampanoags in December, 1675, Canonchet supported Metacom and the Wampanoags and led his warriors in attacks on white settlements.

Metacom, Leader of the Wampanoags

Known as **King Philip** to the English settlers, Metacom was the younger son of Massasoit, the Wampanoag leader who had established peace with the Pilgrims in 1621. He was born around 1639. His older brother, Wamsutta, had been arrested and questioned in 1661 by the Plymouth leaders about rumors that the Wampanoags were planning an attack on English settlements. When Wamsutta died while returning from this meeting, Metacom assumed leadership of the tribe. In succeeding years, he became increasingly concerned about the European encroachment on the Wampanoags' ancestral lands and the effects of European culture and Christianity on his people. Yet Metacom made many concessions to Plymouth: he recognized the authority of the English crown, agreed to obtain the colonists' approval before selling land to outsiders, and even consented to surrender his tribe's weapons. However, he did not see the Wampanoags as subsidiary to the Plymouth Colony.

Although it does not seem that Metacom was prepared for war in 1675, he believed the verdict and death penalty against three Wampanoags for the death of John Sassamon left him little choice but to fight. Metacom was caught and killed by colonial forces in August 1676 at the end of the war.

Mediator: John Easton, Deputy Governor of Rhode Island

Born in Wales to a Quaker family, Easton emigrated as a boy with his brother and father to Massachusetts in 1634. They were among the first settlers of Newport and became prominent in the colony of Rhode Island. John's father, Nicholas Easton, was deputy governor 1666-1671 and governor of Rhode Island from 1672 to 1674. John Easton was elected attorney general for the colony 1653-63, when he became assistant under the charter of 1663, and in 1674 was elected deputy-governor of Rhode Island, serving until 1676. He served as governor of the colony from 1690 to 1695. Easton became an extensive landowner in Rhode Island. He wrote a *Narrative of the Causes which led to Philip's Indian War*, which was not published until 1858. He had suggested mediation to avoid war.

Mediator: Weetamoo, Female sachem of the Pocasset tribe and Metcom's sister-in-law

Weetamoo grew up in the vicinity of Tiverton, Rhode Island, close to the Plymouth Colony border. She inherited the position of sachem from her father, who had no son. She married Metacom's brother, Wamsutta. She was also Metacom's sister-in-law through her sister, who was one of his wives. Weetamoo believed that her husband had been poisoned by the English and became hostile to the white settlers. Metacom sought Weetamoo as an ally against the English, and she gave permission for her Pocasset warriors to join the Wampanoags. Weetamoo helped Metacom escape the English through the Pocasset swamps. Her superior knowledge of the land enabled them to find a safe way through the swamp and to elude the English. During the Great Swamp Fight in December 1675, Weetamoo helped build canoes and rafts for escape. At the height of her power, she commanded 300 warriors. She was respected as a capable leader and fighter. Mary Rowlandson, an English captive during King Philip's War, was very impressed with Weetamoo, whom she described as "a severe and proud dame. . . in dressing herself neat . . . powdering her hair and painting her face, going with necklaces, with jewels in the ears, and bracelets upon her hands."

Observer/Recorder/Reporter: Roger Williams, Founder of Rhode Island

Born in London around 1603, Williams was the son of a well-to-do businessman. He graduated from Cambridge in 1627 and took his religious orders in 1629. In late 1630, he set sail for Massachusetts to pursue his religious beliefs. At his church in Salem, Massachusetts, Williams worked for a more democratic church system. His public declarations that civil governments had no power to enforce religious injunctions and that land claims under the royal charter violated Indian rights soon made him unpopular with the Puritan religious and civil leaders, and in 1635, they banished him from the colony. Williams gathered his followers and fled to Narragansett Bay, where he founded Providence in 1636, Rhode Island's first settlement. In 1644, he wrote *The Bloody Tenent of Persecution,* claiming that all individuals and religious bodies are entitled to religious liberty as a natural right. That same year while in England, Williams secured a charter for Rhode Island. He served as president of the colony during the 1650s. Under his leadership, Rhode Island pursued democratic policies, religious liberty, and separation of church and state, offering Quakers and Jews a safe haven despite protests by Massachusetts. Williams worked to get along with the neighboring Narragansett Indians and successfully defended their claims against attempts by Europeans to defraud them of their land. King Philip's War darkened his later years. He died in 1705.

POSITIONS AND INTERESTS

The Colonists

Positions

- The natives had disobeyed the 1671 agreement not to bear arms, thus defying the political authority of the English colonists.

- The natives did not farm the land they used; they merely hunted over it. (The English did not view the farming that was done by the female natives as agriculture.)

- It was difficult to understand the natives or accept their primitive, heathen lifestyle, and attempts to convert and civilize them often proved futile. The Indians had little respect for Christian principles or English law.

- The natives were not trustworthy or honorable. They were constantly plotting attacks on colonial settlements, which sometimes made repressive measures, such as disarming them, necessary. The murder of John Sassamon was just one example of their disreputable and barbaric behavior.

Interests

- *Religious:* The Puritans were motivated by deep religious convictions to settle New England in a way that was pleasing to God. Perceiving His hand in all events, they were convinced that He had sent plagues upon the Indians in order to make way for Puritan settlements and had given them victory in the Pequot War of 1637.

- *Economic:* Many of the prominent colonial leaders in King Philip's War also had substantial financial interests in New England property, and despite the fact that the colonists did often purchase land from the Indians, they actually believed that English patents and charters gave them all the legal claim they needed. The Puritans also had commercial interests in the fur trade with the Indians, and, as long as that trade flourished, they were willing to recognize native rights and concerns to some extent. When that trade declined, however, the English saw little reason to accommodate the Indians. It was the land itself that became vitally important, and the colonists were determined to have that land.

- *Security.* The settlers needed to assure themselves that the natives, whom they perceived as savages, would not threaten their towns and villages. However, they believed they were militarily superior to the natives.

- *Cultural.* Although the original group of Pilgrims was small, vulnerable, and dependent on native assistance, the English always believed themselves to be culturally superior to the Indians. They were never seriously prepared to meet them as equals because they did not respect the Indian way of life. The strict Puritan view of the world saw the natives as heathens and savages. Their only hope was to be converted to Christianity and to follow all of the Puritan restrictions.

- *Conflict among colonists:* Both before and after the war, the colonies squabbled over territory and boundaries. Massachusetts and Rhode Island leaders thought that Plymouth was partially to blame for their problems with the Wampanoags.

The Indians

Positions

- The Indians had willingly helped the first small group of English settlers, and Massasoit had negotiated in good faith with them. However, instead of being grateful for the help they had extended, the colonists harassed and abused the Indians.

- The English expected the natives to convert to Christianity and to obey the Puritan code of behavior. The Indians resented having the settlers impose their religion and culture on them.

- Some of the Indians had willingly "sold" land to the colonists, but they did not understand why they could not continue to hunt and fish on it. Others had been pressured to sell land, and they wanted the colonists to stop pressuring them to sell any more.

- The colonists provided liquor to the Indians even though the natives were physically ill-equipped to handle it.

- The colonists let their animals wander and destroy Indian crops.

- The Englishmen had no respect for the Indians, treating them as a subordinate and conquered people. The Indians resented this humiliating treatment.

Interests

- *Economic.* While they profited from the fur and wampum trade for several years, before long they had grown dependent on English goods and commerce. After the collapse of the fur trade in the 1660s, the Indians were unable to compete in the English economy and were no longer proud and self-sufficient.

- *Cultural.* Equally devastating to the Indians as the loss of their land was the destruction of their way of life by Europeans. Missionaries attempted to convert the natives to Christianity while colonial officials forced them to obey English laws. Indians were tried in English courts with all-English juries. They were even forced to obey religious sanctions regarding the Sabbath, blasphemy, adultery, and drunkenness.

- *Lack of respect.* The Puritans seemed to have no respect for the Indian way of life.

- *Survival.* When the Pilgrims arrived in 1620, the Wampanoags were a weak and vulnerable people, decimated by disease and bordered by the powerful Narragansetts. Most welcomed a peaceful alliance with the English to provide some protection against their traditional enemies. Now, many were concerned about the rapidly growing English population.

- *Intertribal conflicts.* The Wampanoags had no place to go because the hostile Mohegans in the west made retreat impossible. Like the colonists, the various Indian tribes were far from united in their positions. Some were willing to go to great lengths to preserve alliances with the English, while others were much more hostile. Some tribes, such as the Mohegans, were more willing to fight with the colonists against the other New England Indians.

TEACHER INSTRUCTIONS

Preparation

1. Share the historical background with the class. Encourage students to focus on the people involved and their positions and interests, in order to gain as thorough an understanding as possible of the events, characters, and historical context. See student Handout #1: "Timeline".

2. Distribute Student Handout #2: "Positions and Interests" for students to read.

3. Give out the brief biographies (Student Handouts #3-10) for students to review.

Directions

1. Divide the class into groups of nine, as follows:

    Representatives for the English Settlers:

    Josiah Winslow (Governor of Plymouth Colony, for the Pilgrims)

    John Winthrop, Jr. (Governor of Connecticut, for the Puritans)

    Reverend Increase Mather (Puritan minister from Massachusetts Bay Colony)

    Representatives for the Indians:

    Metacom [King Philip] (Leader of the Wampanoags)

    Annawon (Metacom's trusted counselor, for the Wampanoags)

    Canonchet (Leader of the Narragansetts)

    Mediators: John Easton (Quaker English settler) and Weetamoo (female Indian chief)

    Observer/Recorder/Reporter: Roger Williams

2. Distribute Student Handout: The Mock Mediation.

3. Review the setting and the directions with the students. Instruct the participants to imagine they have been invited to a meeting to resolve the crisis between King Philip's Wampanoags and Plymouth Colony. Each participant should act in a manner consistent with his/her assigned role and interests.

Debriefing

1. Conduct a classroom discussion about the mock mediations. Have each observer describe how the process worked in their group. Summarize and compare the results each group obtained.

2. Either have the students read "The Facts Continued" or share it with the class as a lecture. Compare the results of the mock mediation with what actually happened in history.

3. Use the "Questions for Discussion" for essay topics or in-class discussion.

THE FACTS CONTINUED

$\mathcal{T}$he peaceful solution that John Easton hoped for was not to be. Within days, he received the news that Metacom's warriors were burning and ransacking houses at the English village of Swansea. For Metacom, the fighting had probably come sooner than he had expected or wanted. He was short on men, had no confirmed allies, and was up against three English colonies with a large combined militia. Nevertheless, Metacom, with the assistance of his leading strategist Annawon, initially conducted several successful raids against Plymouth towns in 1675. These successes brought him valuable allies—the Nipmucks of Massachusetts and the Connecticut River Indians, including the support of the Saconnet's squaw sachem, Awashonks, and the Pocasset's squaw sachem, Weetamoo. The Plymouth and Massachusetts militia attempted to capture Metacom by chasing him into the Pocasset Swamp, but they became bogged down in the thick undergrowth. They decided to build a fort with the idea of starving Metacom out of the swamp, but Metacom and his followers escaped, with the help of Weetamoo, who was familiar with the land. While these events played out in Southern New England, the Abnaki tribes in the North attacked English settlements in areas that later became Maine and New Hampshire.

In 1675, the European population in all of the New England colonies was about 55,000. The population of all of the native tribes was around 16,000. In September 1675, Massachusetts Bay Colony, Plymouth, Rhode Island, and Connecticut, acting in concert as the United Colonies, formally declared war, mustered an army of several thousand, and sought alliances with other Indian tribes, such as the Mohegans and the Mohawks. The United Colonies attacked the winter camp of the still-neutral Narragansetts in December 1675 when they refused to cooperate in surrendering some of Metacom's followers. Since the war was not going well for the colonists at this point, the attack on the powerful Narragansetts was a bold and risky move. The colonists killed several hundred Indians, and the outraged survivors, under the leadership of Canonchet, quickly fled to aid Metacom and strengthened the anti-English alliance among the Wampanoags, the Nipmucks and the Narragansetts.

"Goffe rallying the men of Hadley in defense of Indian attack during King Philip's War, Hadley, Mass., 1675-76"

The Mohawks and Mohegans joined the English as allies. In February, 1676, the Narragansetts launched an attack on Lancaster, Massachusetts, setting fire to the town and killing more than 50 people. Indians raided and destroyed several other towns in Massachusetts Bay, Plymouth, Connecticut, and Rhode Island. Eventually, frontier towns were simply abandoned by their terrified citizens.

Although many of the English had previously scorned the Indians as unworthy opponents, the natives seemed destined for victory in the winter of 1675–76. Their guerrilla war tactics were much more effective than the colonists' conventional military strategies. The Puritans thought that God was angry with them, perhaps because of their avarice, their wearing of wigs, or the tolerance shown to Quakers. (One historian has suggested that it was ironic that the Puritans never considered that God might be angry with them for fighting the Indians.) Boston declared a "Day of Humiliation" with fasting and prayer in an attempt to appease the Almighty. In March 1676, frustrated colonists turned against friendly, Christianized Indians in their midst. To protect these Indians from mobs, colonial leaders sought to build them shelters but ultimately they moved them to barren, bitter-cold islands in Boston Harbor, where about 400 nearly starved to death.

In the spring of 1676, Metacom's offensive suddenly collapsed, as a result of shortages of food, warriors, and munitions, and a view of warfare that concluded before total annihilation of the enemy The victories for the natives had come at great cost; they often lost at least half as many fighters as they killed. Disease and the rigors of winter had also taken their toll. Having been driven from their cornfields and forced to hunt in unfamiliar territory, the Indians eventually found themselves without an adequate supply of food. The loss of the powerful Narragansett leader Canonchet, who was captured and killed in April, 1676, was devastating. In addition, the weapons often used by the Indians were European muskets and gunpowder, and the colonists were not about to replenish their supply of guns or ammunition. This dependence on European arms was a crucial, if unavoidable, weakness for the Indians. In the long run, the colonists had much greater resources in terms of men and supplies than their native adversaries did. Or perhaps, the Indians were simply not prepared to continue the struggle indefinitely. They were used to contests in which one side conceded defeat before total annihilation, but the English seemed determined to fight until they could fight no more.

The Mohegans, still allies of the English, sent Canonchet's head to Hartford as a show of loyalty to the colony of Connecticut. In late spring and summer of 1676, the colonists attacked Indian encampments and supply bases, killing hundreds, and forcing the natives to surrender in droves. In June, the Massachusetts authorities offered amnesty to Indians who surrendered. Captain Benjamin Church convinced his longtime friend Awashonks, the squaw sachem of the Saconnets who had been Metacom's ally, to help the English. Many warring Indians started to think that their cause was lost. On August 6, 1676, English forces surrounded Weetamoo's camp in Massachusetts. She headed down the Taunton River by canoe. The soldiers fired at it, causing it to sink. Weetamoo tried to swim ashore but drowned in the strong current. The colonists cut off her head and displayed it on a pole at Taunton.

In mid-August, Metacom, who previously had cleverly eluded the clutches of Captain Church several times, was killed when he was betrayed by a Wampanoag who had a personal grudge against him. In Plymouth, a "solemn day of Thanksgiving to Almighty God" was declared on August 17, 1676, and Metacom's head was paraded through the streets. After the ceremony, the Pilgrims placed the head upon a pole in the center of town, a warning to all those who passed by. After the death of Metacom, his aged advisor Annawon assumed control of his forces and managed to elude capture for several days, eventually surrendering on August 26, 1676. Although colonial officials ordered him put to death, Church, who had come to respect his enemy, argued for his life. Annawon's life was temporarily spared, but while Church was away, a mob seized the Wampanoag leader and beheaded him.

The costs of the war

Although the colonists emerged from King Philip's War as victors, their triumph was achieved at a tremendous cost. In proportion to the population, this conflict inflicted greater casualties than any other war in American history. Out of a total population of less than 80,000, at least 6,000 people perished (one-third Europeans; two-thirds natives). Fully eight percent of Plymouth's adult males were killed in the war. Twelve of the ninety New England towns were completely destroyed; at least forty others were partially destroyed or burned. The economy was severely disrupted as the war consumed all available manpower and interrupted trade. The United Colonies claimed the war cost them a total of 100,000–150,000 pounds (the equivalent of seven million dollars today), a burden to be borne by all the people through a heavy taxation. The Wampanoags' land, and that of their allies, was awarded to Plymouth Colony and promptly sold to outside speculators to help surviving towns with the crushing war costs. Massachusetts also had to continue battling the Abnaki Indians along the Maine coast. The war in northeastern New England would not officially end until April 1678.

The effect of the war for the Indians was devastating: Wampanoag society was all but decimated, a few survivors preserved their tribal identity on the isolated island of Martha's Vineyard. All captured Indians, and many who surrendered, whether Wampanoag, Nipmuck, or Narragansett, were indiscriminately sold into slavery, including Metacom's widow and son. After the hostilities ended, few Indians had much trust in the intentions of Puritan missionaries, and the "praying towns" of Indian converts gradually withered away. After the war, the Wampanoags and their allies lived in small clusters, often working as servants or sailors. The colonial powers put those Indians who remained in the area under severe restrictions to prevent the possibility of future uprisings. Many were assigned to reservations that were supervised by the colonial governments or by church-sponsored missionaries. Often guardians—white men who represented the Indians in dealings with the colonists—were appointed to manage the land, money and other assets for the Indians. The New England natives were now totally subjugated to the white settlers. (Compare Document 3: "A Relation of the Indian War" by John Easton and Document 4: from *A Brief History of the War with the Indians in New England* by Increase Mather, for two opposing views of the causes of the war.)

Costs of the War

✓ Out of a total population of less than 80,000 at least 6,000 people perished (one-third Europeans and two-thirds natives).

✓ 12 of New England's 90 towns were completely destroyed and 40 others partially destroyed or burned.

✓ The colonial economy in New England was totally disrupted.

✓ The Wampanoag's land was awarded to Plymouth Colony

✓ The war cost the United Colonies an equivalent of $7 million.

✓ The Wampanoag's land was awarded to Plymouth Colony.

✓ Wampanoag society was all but wiped out.

✓ The New England natives were totally subjugated: captured Indians were sold into slavery; others lived on supervised reservations.

QUESTIONS FOR DISCUSSION

1. What might have satisfied the colonists?

    *   More Indian land for settlements and commercial expansion.

    *   Security that the Indians would not attack their villages.

    *   A continuation of profitable trade.

    *   Indians adhering to Puritan codes of behavior.

2. What might have satisfied the Indians?

    *   No more pressure for land concessions and the right to continue to hunt and fish on land sold or ceded to the colonists.

    *   Protection for their crops from destruction by the colonists' animals.

    *   Indians accused of wrongdoing tried by their own people or given a fair trial with Indians represented on colonial juries.

    *   Freedom to practice their own religious practices without being forced to follow Christian law.

    *   Full and equal participation in the growing English economy.

    *   To be treated with respect, as a free and independent people.

3. Could King Philip's War have been avoided?

4. Would a mediation of the issues causing tensions between the Indians and the colonists have been historically feasible in New England in 1675?

5. What might have been some possible peaceful resolutions?

6. How might history have differed if all the various Indian tribes in New England had united to fight against the English colonists in King Philip's War?

7. How might the history of New England have differed if the Indians had won King Philip's War?

ADDITIONAL RESOURCES

Bourne, Russell. *The Red King's Rebellion: Racial Politics in New England, 1675–1678.* New York: Oxford University Press, 1990.

Drake, James D. *King Philip's War: Civil War in New England, 1675–76.* University of Massachusetts Press, 1999.

Jennings, Francis. *The Invasion of America: Indians, Colonialism, and the Cant of Conquest.* Chapel Hill: University of North Carolina Press, 1975.

Kawashima, Yasuhide. *Igniting King Philip's War: The John Sassamon Murder Trial.* Lawrence: University Press of Kansas, 2001.

Leach, Douglas Edward. *Flintlock and Tomahawk: New England in King Philip's War.* New York: W.W. Norton, 1958.

Lepore, Jill. *Encounters in the New World: A History in Documents.* New York: Oxford University Press, 2000.

_____ . *The Name of War: King Philip's War and the Origins of American Identity.* New York: Random House, 1999.

Mandel, Daniel R. *Behind the Frontier: Indians in Eighteenth Century Eastern Massachusetts.* Lincoln: University of Nebraska Press, 1996.

Mather, Increase. *A Brief History of the War with the Indians in New England.* Boston: John Foster, 1676.

Nash, Gary B. *Red, White and Black: The Peoples of Early North America.* 4th ed. Upper Saddle River, NJ: Prentice Hall, 2000.

O'Brien, Jean. *Dispossession by Degrees: Indian Land and Identity in Natick, Massachusetts.* New York: Cambridge University Press, 1997.

O'Connell, Barry. *On Our Own Ground.* Amherst: University of Massachusetts Press, 1992.

Philbrick, Nathaniel. *Mayflower: A Story of Courage, Community and War.* New York: Viking, 2006.

Salisbury, Neil. *Manitou and Providence: Indians, Europeans and the Making of New England, 1500-1643.* New York: Oxford University Press, 1982.

Segal, Charles M. and David C. Stineback. *Puritans, Indians, and Manifest Destiny.* New York: Putnam's, 1977.

Steele, Ian K. *Warpaths: Invasions of North America.* New York: Oxford University Press, 1994.

Vaughan, Alden T. *New England Frontier: Puritans and Indians, 1620-1675.* Boston: Little & Brown, 1965.

PART TWO: THE QUAKERS AND THE LENNI LENAPE INDIANS, 1682–84

HISTORICAL BACKGROUND

*T*he Lenni Lenape ("original people"), Indians of the Delaware Nation, lived on lands from the headwaters of the Delaware River south to the Delaware Bay and east to the Atlantic Ocean, including all of today's New Jersey, Delaware and eastern Pennsylvania. They were part of the Algonquian-speaking Indians who populated the eastern woodlands from the Carolinas to New England. The Delawares included several loosely connected bands, including the Unami along the western banks of the Delaware River. The Lenni Lenape did not have a centralized authority or a confederation as their Iroquois neighbors to the north did. Although Lenni Lenape communities were sometimes raided by the Susquehannas from the west and the Iroquois from the north, they were known as mediators and peacemakers. The Lenni Lenape moved seasonally, hunting, fishing and farming. Their view of land use and ownership was different from that of English common law regarding private property. The idea of an individual exclusively owning life-giving land was alien to their way of thinking. Instead, the kin-group collectively possessed land which families used as they needed.

The Delaware River basin of present-day southeastern Pennsylvania, western New Jersey and northern Delaware had been settled by scattered Dutch, Swedes and Finns since at least the 1630s. They were involved in fur-trading and farming on lands which they purchased from the Indians. The early colonial settlers recognized that they were greatly outnumbered and in potential danger, and they supplemented their land purchases by building stockades and blockhouses. In exchange for furs from the Indians, the European traders had given the Lenni Lenape guns and strong drink. In spite of land agreements, cultural differences, petty frictions, stray animals, thefts and alcohol all led to a series of conflicts and bloodshed between the Europeans and the Indians that continued through the 1660s.

The Lenni Lenape came to view the Europeans with both attraction and mistrust. They were attracted by the desirable goods that the colonists had to trade and their help against other tribes. But their experiences with violence also made them wary of Europeans. Decades of contact with European traders, fisherman and farmers had led to

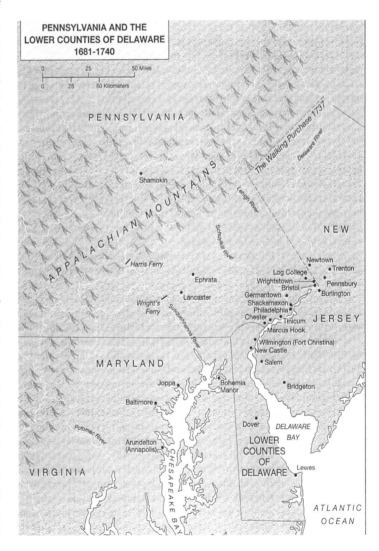

PENNSYLVANIA AND THE
LOWER COUNTIES OF DELAWARE
1681-1740

devastating epidemics and reduced the Lenni Lenape to a remnant of their former size. By 1680, the Lenni Lenape in the Delaware River basin numbered under 8,000.

The Delaware Valley came under English control after the English won the third Anglo-Dutch War (1672–78). There were fewer than 2,000 European settlers in the area at the time. In 1681, King Charles II granted a charter to William Penn for a proprietary colony in what was to be called "Pennsylvania," or "Penn's Woods." Penn had petitioned for a charter to the lands of Pennsylvania in lieu of the king's payment of an old debt to Penn's father. Except for the scattered Swedish and Dutch settlements, this was one of the last areas on the Eastern seaboard not yet fully colonized by Europeans. Eleven of the thirteen original colonies had already been founded. Most of the land in what was to become Philadelphia had already been purchased by the Swedish and Dutch from the Lenni Lenape. The remainder continued to be used by the various Delaware kin-groups.

The Quakers were part of the radical, anticlerical Protestant reformation in England. The Religious Society of Friends or Quakers began during the English Civil War in the 1640s. Led by George Fox and Margaret Fell, the Quakers had their greatest success in converting yeoman farmers and artisans in northern England. Quakers held that God's "saving light" enlightens all people and rejected Calvinist predestination and emphasis on human depravity. Worship was held in silence without ordained clergy. Those who felt inspired by God to speak offered their own spontaneous messages. Friends recognized everyone, regardless of race, creed or gender, as children of God, and sought consensus, or a "sense of the Meeting," to make decisions, a process that recognized each person as equal and a vehicle for God's truth. Quakers recognized God alone as holding authority over individuals in matters of conscience and refused to take off their hats to anyone except God, addressed "superiors" without the use of honorific titles. They refused to swear an oath, support the established church, observe the outward sacraments, participate in war or serve in the military. The Church of England and the English monarchy saw the Quakers as potential anarchists and troublemakers because they would not bow to authority, and Quakers were often persecuted for their views.

William Penn's father was a wealthy man and had been an admiral in the Royal Navy. Rebelling against his father's Anglicanism and his military profession, Penn, as a young man, had become a Quaker and a pacifist. He had been imprisoned several times for his beliefs, in spite of the fact that he was a personal friend of the king. After years of pressure by Penn, King Charles II, seeing an opportunity to rid himself of a large number of dissenters (Quakers) from England and to eliminate a long-standing debt to Penn's father, granted Penn a charter for a colony in March 1681. The King's Charter granted William Penn the proprietorship of all "the lands and dominions" bounded on the east by the Delaware River, 12 miles north of New Castle to 43 degrees latitude or the head of the river. Penn was given the power to govern and, with an assembly, to make laws, appoint magistrates, and establish a judicial system. The Charter urged that the English settlers ". . . reduce the savage natives, by gentle and just measures, to the love of civil society and Christian religion," but also provided that given the "many barbarous nations, the incursions, as well as the savages themselves, we have given . . . power . . . to levy, muster and train all sorts of men. . . to make war."

Quaker immigration was focused during the 1670s on East and West Jersey, formerly part of New Netherland. As one of the founders and promoters of the Quaker province of West Jersey, settled in 1677, Penn was aware of the necessity of winning the goodwill of the Indians. Before coming to his colony, Penn sent a letter to the "Indian Kings" in October 1681:

> My Friends:
>
> There is one great God and power that hath made the world and all things therein, to whom you and I and all people owe their being and well-being, and to whom you and I must one day give an account for all that we do in this world. This great God hath written His law in our hearts, by which we are taught and commanded to love and help and do good to one another, and not to do harm or mischief to another.

Now this great God hath been pleased to make me concerned in your parts of the world, and the King of the country where I live hath given unto me a great province therein, but I desire to enjoy it with your love and consent, that we may always live together as neighbors and friends, else what would the great God say to us Who hath made us not to devour and destroy one another but [to] live soberly and kindly together in the world?

Now I would have [you] well to observe that I am very sensible of the unkindness and injustice that hath been too much exercised towards you by the people of these parts of the world, who have sought themselves and to make great advantages by you rather than [to] be examples of justice and goodness unto you, which I hear hath been a matter of trouble to you and caused great grudgings and animosities, sometimes to the shedding of blood, which hath made the great God angry. But I am not such a man, as is well known in my country. I have great love and regard towards you, and *I desire to win and gain your love and friendship by a kind, just, and peaceable life, and the people I send are of the same mind and shall in all things behave themselves accordingly; and if in anything any shall offend you or your people, you shall have a full and speedy satisfaction for the same by an equal number of honest men on both sides, that by no means you may have just occasion of being offended against them* [emphasis added]. (See Document 5: Penn's Letter to the Delawares, 1681.)

Thus, Penn recognized the Indians as the rightful owners of the territory and gave notice that he allowed settlers to establish farms within the boundaries of his charter only with the consent of the Indians there. Penn concluded his letter promising to send commissioners to deal with the Indians about purchasing land and making a league of peace. Penn's agent, William Markham, was sent to the new colony ahead of Penn's arrival and empowered to settle boundaries and make land purchases. Arriving in April 1681, he negotiated through local interpreters with the sachems of the Delaware people for several months before Penn's arrival in present-day Philadelphia. The sachems were basically heads of families with the authority to enter into treaties and bind the members of the family. Every valley and stream had to be acquired from particular bands of Lenni Lenape whose rights were recognized by neighboring Indians. The process was long and expensive. The total Indian purchase price was much greater than the debt that King Charles had discharged by his grant.

In 1682–83, 589 individuals signed up to purchase land as part of Penn's "holy experiment." The majority (88 percent) was from the British Isles, including Ireland, Scotland and Wales, however, some purchasers were from Holland, France and Germany. They were not all Quakers. Penn's "holy experiment" was to include people of different religious persuasions living together in an atmosphere of tolerance and peace. Penn also thought that he could help the Indians through his examples of tolerance, peace and loving kindness. (See Document 6: Penn's Conditions or Concessions to the First Purchasers, July 1681.) Penn's ship, *the Welcome*, arrived at his colony along the banks of the Delaware River (New Castle, Delaware) in October 1682.

The landing of William Penn from the Welcome

Mock Treaty Negotiations: Native Americans and Quakers

*T*he 38-year-old Proprietor, William Penn, arrived in October 1682 on the ship *Welcome* at his colony along the banks of the Delaware River (New Castle, Delaware). His reputation and his representatives had preceded him. He and William Markham are alleged to have met with the sachems of the local Unami bands under the spreading elm tree at the Indian village of Shackamaxon (the present Kensington section of Philadelphia, just north of center city, along the Delaware River), long a gathering place for the Delawares, to confirm treaties of peace, land transfer and trade with the Indians. Both the Indian sachems and the European leaders were aware of the bloody conflicts which had recently occurred in New England (King Philip's War between the Puritans and the Wampanoag Indians and their allies in 1675–76) and in Virginia (Bacon's Rebellion in 1676) and were interested in avoiding such bloodshed in the Delaware Valley. Since Markham and Penn were as yet unfamiliar with the language and customs of the Lenni Lenape on their initial arrival, they engaged a prominent local Swede, Captain Laurence Cox as their interpreter and messenger to the Indians.

While William Penn and Captain Markham did, indeed, meet with members of the Delaware Nation to purchase land and establish a system for resolving disputes, we have included Swedish and Mennonite settlers in a hypothetical negotiation so that their views may be heard also. It is late 1683. The purpose of the negotiations is to provide security and mutual benefit for the colonists and the Indians by establishing mechanisms for resolving conflicts arising from differing interests and customs.

The Participants

William Penn, Founder and proprietor of Pennsylvania

Penn was born in London in 1644 to relative privilege as the son of a soon-to-be admiral in the British Navy. Penn attended an elite school and enrolled in Oxford University, but was dismissed in 1661 for religious "nonconformity" (criticizing the ceremonies of the Anglican Church). His father attempted to "reform" him by sending him on "the grand tour" of Europe and later dispatching him to oversee his Irish estate. While in Ireland, Penn heard a Quaker preacher, Thomas Loe, and became a convert to the dissident faith in 1667. Penn saw the proprietary colony of Pennsylvania as a laboratory for working out a "holy experiment" of religious toleration and peace. In 1672, Penn married Gulielma Springett, whose father was a rich London Puritan. They had three children. Gulielma was pregnant in 1682 when Penn sailed to North America to set up his colony. After Gulielma's death in 1694, at age 51, Penn married Hannah Callowhill, the 25 year-old only child of a wealthy merchant. Although the Society of Friends preached simplicity as one of its spiritual goals, Penn never abandoned his upper-class status and always appreciated the "good life," often living beyond his means. Penn exerted strong personal leadership in America, but he did not profit from the colony. In fact, as an absentee landlord from his estates in Ireland and his colony in Pennsylvania, he did not always receive his rents and ended up in debt. Penn had in stroke in 1712 and died in 1718.

William Penn in later life

Captain William Markham, Adviser and deputy governor to William Penn

Markham was born in England in 1635. He was not a Quaker but rather a member of the Church of England and an English officer. As a first cousin to Penn and trusted adviser, Markham was dispatched to the new colony in July 1681 as deputy governor, with instructions to appoint a council, commission sheriffs and justices of the peace, lay out and plan for the new town of Philadelphia and settle border disputes. He landed near present-day Chester, Pennsylvania, among the Dutch, Swedish and Finnish settlers on the lower Delaware River. He was one of the first purchasers, buying 5,000 acres of land from the Indians, which became the site for Pennsbury Manor. Markham was shrewd and practical and not spiritually idealistic like Penn. Other Quaker colonists complained that he could not accommodate himself to the Quaker point of view. He was more concerned about practical concerns about how to ensure Pennsylvania's survival.

John Printz, A prominent Swedish settler hostile to the Indians

Printz was governor of "New Sweden" in 1644 (an area which later became part of Penn's grant) and believed that the solution to "the Indian problem" was extermination. Swedish settlers had been killed in the 1640s and 1650s by Indians. Printz advocated that a force of soldiers should "break the neck of every Indian in the Delaware River basin," believing that one had not only to purchase the land but also to "win it with the sword." Printz was no longer alive by 1683. We will have his son, John Printz, Jr., representing his view that force was the way to deal with the Indians and that stockades, garrisons and militias must be provided as insurance against future Indian uprisings.

Mierka Dilbeck, A German Mennonite pacifist

Mierka and her family had left Holland because of persecution to settle in Germany in the early 1600s. In October 1683, she was part of a group of thirteen Mennonite families that emigrated from Germany to the Pennsylvania area, forming the so-called "Germantown" settlement in northern Philadelphia. Heirs to a deep tradition that emphasized a restored, pure Christianity, the German Mennonites joined the Quakers in observing the clear constraints of the gospel: do unto others as you would have them do unto you. However, unlike the Quakers who took their pacifism from the teachings of Jesus, the Mennonites believed in the literal truth of the Ten Commandments. The Mennonites were conservative, traditional farmers who wanted to stay more removed from worldly matters than the liberal Quakers engaged in social justice. In 1688, the Germantown settlement produced the first protest by Europeans in North America against slavery as inconsistent with Christian principles.

Tomackhickon, One of the leaders (or "sachems") of a tribe of the Delaware Indian Nation

Typical of most Delaware, Tomackhickon was tall, straight, well-built and strong. The colonists found him to be of "equable temperament," and speculated that this was because he enjoyed a simple way of life that left him free from the tensions of "civilized" life. Tomackhickon had experienced both the appeal and the danger of the white man's weapons. He recognized that accommodation of some sort by the Unami tribe of the Delaware Nation with the European settlers was unavoidable because of the superior technology that the Europeans had.

Tamany [Tamene, Tamanee, or Tamanend], A Sachem leader of a tribe of the Delaware Indian Nation

Tamany's kin-group lived in the region that became Bucks County, Pennsylvania (north of Philadelphia). He is recorded in the 1694 Pennsylvania Provincial Council minutes as professing strong friendship with the European settlers. Although his Indian name "Tamany" supposedly meant "amiable," he was not an amiable man. His strength, bold attitude and tenacity became the stuff of legend in the ensuing years. He was one of the "sachems" who negotiated a treaty with William Markham and William Penn.

Captain Laurence Cox [*anglicized from Lasse Cock*], A Swede who served as host and interpreter (The observer/recorder/reporter)

Cox was born in 1646, one of several sons of early Swedish immigrants to the Delaware Valley. He learned the language and customs of the Lenni Lenape, was well regarded by them and acted as an interpreter and messenger between the Indians and the Swedes, the Dutch, and later the English. He lived at Shackamaxon, along the Delaware River, on land which he had purchased earlier. He was the interpreter for most of Penn's negotiations with the sachems from the Lenni Lenape. In addition to actually translating the English and Indian languages, he also housed, fed and entertained the Indians at his home as well as buying presents for the Indians during the negotiations. Cox died in 1699.

POSITIONS AND INTERESTS

The Quakers

Positions

- Quakers viewed all people as children of God. Penn stated that the Indians were the rightful owners of the land, since they occupied it. The Quakers or "Friends" wanted to create a "holy experiment" in Pennsylvania where everyone could live in peace and harmony. The Quakers' benevolent view of the Indians is best expressed in Penn's 1683 "Letter to the Free Society of Traders": But in Liberality they excel; nothing is too good for their friend. Give them a fine Gun, Coat, or other thing, it may pass twenty hands before it sticks: light of Heart, strong Affections, but soon spent; the most merry Creatures that live, Feast and dance perpetually; they never have much or want much; Wealth circulateth like the Blood; all parts partake: and though none shall want what another hath, yet [they are] exact Observers of Property. (See Document 7: Penn's Letter to the Free Society of Traders, August 1683.)

- Penn was less impressed by the spiritual life of the Native Americans ("These poor people are under a dark night in things relating to religion, to be sure the tradition of it; yet they believe in God and immortality, without the help of metaphysics. . .") and he hoped that the encouragement of the "arts of civilization" would make the Indians more receptive to the teachings of the gospel.

Interests

- *Religious:* The Quakers believed in and lived the precepts of equality which they espoused. They were truly interested in creating a peaceful society. The first generation of Quaker settlers hoped that their civilizing influence would enhance the spiritual life of the Indians and encourage them to accept the gospel.

- *Economic:* The Quakers were also practical: they recognized that they needed to attract additional European settlers to their colony and that they needed to be able to sell clear land titles to new settlers.

- *Survival:* They were also concerned about their survival, and saw peaceful relations and trade, encouraged by fair dealings, as critical to the economic viability of the colony. They recognized that as pacifists they would need means other than force to provide security and were interested in convincing the Indians that they were not a threat but rather could be trustworthy and beneficial friends.

- Representative of Quaker notions of fair dealing is Penn's *Concessions and Agreements of West New Jersey, 1675–76*, whereby the "proprietors freeholders and inhabitants of the said province and the Indian Natives thereof . . . concluded and agreed" that if Europeans or Natives did any injury to the other "Justice may be done and satisfaction made to the Person or persons" through a "tryall [trial] to be by six of the neighborhood and six of the said Indian Natives to be indifferently and impartially Chosen. . . ."

The Swedish and Dutch Settlers

Positions

- The Swedes were Calvinistic and Lutheran; the Dutch Calvinistic. They had purchased land from the Indians more to try to avoid wars than because of a belief in peace. They did not hold the Indians in high esteem.

Interests

- The Swedes and Dutch were interested in physical and financial survival. They did not really trust each other and saw the English as threats to their control, land and trading. They had long been involved in trade with the Indians and did not want to be excluded. They watched with a wary eye as Penn's colony began.

- They saw Quaker pacifism as a threat to security, and anti-clericalism as a threat to good order and proper authority. They saw the Indians as an impediment to the establishment of their colonial community. They did not trust the Indians and believed that taking measures to ensure their safety, such as building stockaded forts, were necessary, and that military actions against the Indians were justified because of past raids by Indians on Swedish and Dutch settlements.

The Dutch/German Mennonites

Positions

- Having left Europe because of threats of violence against them, the religious, pacifist Mennonites wanted to live in peace and harmony.

- They also wanted to create a "New Zion", a pure religious community in the New World. These settlers from the Rhine Valley of what is now Germany formed the basis of the continuing "Pennsylvania Dutch" (from "Deutsch" meaning German) community.

Interests

- As pacifists unwilling to defend themselves by force, the Mennonites wished for an accord with the Indians so that they could be left alone to live a secure as well as pure, simple religious life in the new world.

- The Mennonites had similar political views with the Quakers and supported the Quakers decisions in running the colony.

The Lenni Lenape

Positions

- The Lenni Lenape professed a "deep friendship" with the Europeans and a willingness to share their land with them and to trade with the European settlers to obtain iron implements and other commodities.

- Impressed with the power of the European settlers' technology—metal fish hooks, cloth, iron pots, muskets, gunpowder, shot and other implements which made their life easier—they concluded that the Europeans had powerful gods and wanted to befriend them.

Interests

- *Survival:* Concerned about physical and cultural survival, decimated by disease and weakened by European encroachment and trade, the Lenni Lenape recognized that some accommodation with Penn was necessary. Prior history with the Swedish and Dutch left them wary of promises by settlers.

- *Trade:* They wanted to maintain their land and their way of life but also to obtain the benefits of European technology by trading and making peace treaties.

- *Support:* They also sought to use their friendship with the colonists in case they were attacked by the Iroquois Confederation to their north.

TEACHER INSTRUCTIONS

Preparation

1. In order for the students to gain an understanding of the history, the people, their attitudes and interests, share the "Historical Background" with the class, either as a lecture or an individual reading.

2. Distribute student handout: "Positions and Interests" to prepare students for the mock negotiations.

3. Have students review the brief biographies.

Directions

1. Divide into groups of seven. Assign each member of the group one of the following seven roles:

   a. William Penn

   b. Captain William Markham

   c. Tomackhickon

   d. Tamany

   e. John Printz

   f. Mierka Dilbeck

   g. Captain Laurence Cox , observer/recorder/reporter

2. Distribute student handout: "The Mock Negotiations." Review the setting and directions with the students.

Debriefing

1. Discuss the negotiating process.

2. Compare the results in each group.

3. Compare the mock negotiations with what really happened.

Copyright, 1905, by John D. Morris & Company

Photograph of the famous Treaty Wampum belt presented to William Penn in Philadelphia by Chief Tamanend in 1682.

THE FACTS CONTINUED

*P*enn's agreement with the Indians, immortalized on canvas by Benjamin West in 1771 and further iconized in numerous renditions of "Peaceable Kingdoms" by primitive painter Edward Hicks in the 1800s, was described by Voltaire as the only treaty "never sworn to and never broken." Although there have been some doubts as to whether the "Treaty of Shackamaxon" ever actually existed, the substance of the accord that Penn made with the Indians was reverently remembered by succeeding generations of Indians and Quakers and formed the basis for land sales and fair trading. Wampum belts, made of sea shells turned into beads and woven together, depicting a Quaker with a broad-brimmed hat and an Indian holding or shaking hands circulated as far as the Midwest through the 1800s. Wampum belts were highly valued by the Indians as a currency of exchange for goods or presented as gifts symbolizing friendship and trust.

Penn's (1682) Treaty with the Indians
Painted by Benjamin West in 1771

Penn traveled extensively throughout the area of Pennsylvania in 1682-84, participating in Indian games, learning their language, and studying their beliefs and customs. Penn became convinced that the Native Indians in North America, because of their physical appearance, harvest festivals, lunar calendar, and language, were one of the ten lost Hebrew tribes. He returned to England and wrote glowingly of the goodness and lightheartedness of the Indians in an effort to attract additional Europeans to settle in his new colony. (See Document 7: Penn's Letter to the Free Society of Traders, 1683.) Over 700,000 acres of Pennsylvania land were sold by the Indians to members of Penn's colony between 1681 and 1685. (See Document 8: Declaration by William Penn protecting the Indians on the land they sell him, October 1683.) Ultimately about 4,000 people were persuaded to immigrate to Penn's colony. Penn returned to England in 1684. Due to a long court case in England against Lord Baltimore over Pennsylvania's border with Maryland, Penn only lived in Pennsylvania for a few years between 1682-1684 and again in 1699-1701.

On his second trip to Pennsylvania, Penn entered into a treaty of commerce and friendship in 1701 with the Susquehanna, Potomack and Shawnee Indians which established a commitment to peaceful relations between the English inhabitants of southern and western Pennsylvania and the area which became Ohio. Although no written documentation of the 1682 "Treaty of Shackamaxon" exists, a copy of the 1701 treaty was still displayed by Shawnee Indians in Ohio fifty years later. The 1701 treaty is the first treaty made by Penn for which the language of the text has been preserved in full. It was the last treaty personally negotiated by Penn rather than his agents. This treaty established a commitment to peaceful relations between the English inhabitants of Pennsylvania and the Indians and outlined guidelines for fair trade and land sales. We can assume that the provisions of the earlier Treaty at Shackamaxon (1682) were similar.

Such accords ushered in "The Quaker Peace" in Pennsylvania that lasted for nearly 75 years. It was marred by the non-Quaker heirs of Penn and the infamous "Walking Purchase" of 1737 perpetrated by Penn's sons who had left the Society of Friends. (See Document 9: The "Walking Purchase," August 1737.) It was further damaged by the shrewd land deals of Penn's secretary, James Logan, and by the large number of Scots-Irish Presbyterian immigrants who settled on the frontier in Pennsylvania where the Susquehanna Indians had retreated from pressure by the Iroquois to the north. However, the peace was not fully broken until the Quakers gave up control of the Pennsylvania Assembly in 1756 at the outset of the French and Indian War (see Chapter Five).

The Peaceable Kingdom by Edward Hicks in 1833

The "vision" which Penn put in motion with his letters and treaties, and most importantly through the example of tolerance and pacifism which he and many other Quakers actually lived, created a mythology which lived on long after Penn's death. Even during the French and Indian War in the 1750s, the Indians carefully avoided doingviolence to "the broad brims" (As the Indians called the Quakers), or the Children of "Onas" (as Penn was called by the Iroquois) or "Miquon" (as Penn was called by the Delawares), both meaning "feathers" for the goose quills used for writing with ink, punning the name "Penn".

Ultimately, after the Quaker governance of Pennsylvania ended, the Delawares, like other eastern Indian tribes, were pushed west, eventually ending up primarily in Oklahoma, where they divided and scattered to Wisconsin, Kansas, and Ontario, Canada too. TheDelawares no longer exist as a self-contained tribal group.

QUESTIONS FOR DISCUSSION

Why were the Quakers and Lenni Lenape Indians in the Delaware Valley able to avoid bloodshed from 1683 to 1756?

There were several areas of mutual interests:
- Trading their goods for other items;

- Need to spell out rules for fair trading and remedies for unfair trading;

- Avoiding violence;

- Need to spell out a peaceful procedure acceptable to all for settling disputes;

- An expanding economy.

Unlike the Puritans and other European colonists who saw their relations with the Indians as a zero-sum game, that is, either they or the Indians but not both could continue in the same area, the Quakers' attitude towards the Indians was one of respect, tolerance, and a desire to find a way to peacefully resolve differences for two culturally different people living in the same area.

The Quaker colony and the Lenni Lenape were able to avoid escalating minor frictions into major hostilities because of:
- Penn's vision of a peaceful society where everyone is tolerant of different religious and cultural beliefs.

- Quaker political control of the area through Penn's spiritual and legal authority and the deference of other groups, such as the Mennonites (but not the Scotch-Irish Presbyterians).

- Treaties which provided ways to resolve grievances through trials and joint committees which gave equal recognition to Indians and European settlers.

- The less war-like nature of the Lenni Lenape than some of the neighboring tribes, such as the Iroquois to the north.

- The existence of unsettled land to the west (the Susquehana Valley) for Indians and settlers to move to rather than fight.

- The recognition and existence of mutual economic benefits from sharing land and peaceful trading.

- The fact that the Quakers actually lived the life of tolerance which they professed, and did not provoke hostilities by being insensitive to religious and cultural differences.

There were other colonies where Quakers exerted considerable influence, and they also generally had more amicable relations with the Indians than those led by other religious denominations. However, in spite of the fact that Friends were a significant minority in the government of Rhode Island through the last quarter of the 17th century and into the next, that area experienced considerable bloodshed. Rhode Island Deputy Governor John Easton, a Quaker, was unable to prevent King Philip's War. John Archdale, a Quaker convert who became governor of the Carolinas in 1694, forbade the enslaving of Indians and drafted legislation to prevent the sale of liquor to the Indians, but he was also unable to avoid ongoing hostilities between the European settlers and the Indians. In Pennsylvania, the confluence of Penn's vision, the greater number of Quakers who provided a living example of pacifism, the more peaceable nature of the Lenni Lenape Indians and the existence of western lands with minimal populations which permitted both Indians and Europeans to move rather than fight allowed peaceful relations to hold for more than half a century. From the arrival of European settlers until 1756, the Lenni Lenape and the colonists, led by the Quakers, engaged in no major warfare.

ADDITIONAL RESOURCES

Bowden, Henry Warner. *American Indians and Christian Missions.* Chicago: The University of Chicago Press, 1981.

Bronner, Edwin B. *William Penn's "Holy Experiment.": The Founding of Pennsylvania, 1681-1701.* New York: Columbia University Press, 1962.

Dunn, Richard S. and Mary Maples, eds. *The World of William Penn.* Philadelphia, University of Pennsylvania Press, 1986.

Jennings, Francis. *The Ambiguous Iroquois Empire.* New York: Norton, 1984.

Johnson, Amadeus. *The Swedes on the Delaware 1638-1664.* Philadelphia: International Printing Co., 1927.

Juhnke, James C. and Carol M. Hunter. *The Missing Peace: The Search for Nonviolent Alternatives in United State History.* Ontario, CA: Pandora Press, 2001.

Kelsey, Rayner. *Friends and the Indians 1655-1917.* Philadelphia: The Associated Executive Committee of Friends on Indian Affairs, 1917.

Merrell, James H. *Into the American Woods: Negotiators on the Pennsylvania Frontier.* New York: Norton, 1999.

Moretta, John. *William Penn and the Quaker Legacy.* New York: Longman, 2006.

Myers, Albert Cook, ed. *William Penn's Own Account of the Lenni Lenape or Delaware Indians.* Wilmington: The Middle Atlantic Press, 1970.

Nash, Gary. *Red, White and Black: The Peoples of Early America.* 4th ed. Upper Saddle River, NJ: Prentice Hall, 2000.

Pencak, William A. and Daniel K. Richter, eds. *Friends and Enemies in Penn's Woods: Indians, Colonists, and the Racial Construction of Pennsylvania.* University Park: Pensylvania State University Press, 2004.

Pestana, Carla G. and Sharon Salingers, eds. *Inequality in Early America.* Hanover, NH: University Press of New England, 1999, pp. 267-291.

Soderlund, Jean, ed. *William Penn and the Founding of Pennsylvania.* Philadelphia: University of Pennsylvania, 1983.

Sugrue, Thomas J. "The Peopling and Depeopling of Early Pennsylvania: Indians and Colonists, 1680-1720." *Pennsylvania Magazine of History and Biography* 116 (1992): 3-31.

Weslager, C.A. *The Delaware Indians: A History.* New Brunswick, NJ: Rutgers University Press, 1972.

DOCUMENTS ON CD

Part One: King Philip's War, 1675-76

Document 1:   Roger Williams on the Language and Culture of the Indians of New England, 1643

Document 2:   Metacom (King Philip) on the Injustices of the English, 1675

Document 3:   A Relation of the Indian War, by Mr. Easton, of Rhode Island, 1675

Document 4:   Increase mather, Puritan Clergyman, on the Indians' Responsibility for the War, 1676

Part Two: The Quakers and the Lenni Lenape, Delaware Indians, 1682-84

Document 5:   William Penn's letter to the Delawares, October, 1681

Document 6:   Penn's Conditions or Concessions to the First Purchasers of Land, July, 1681

Document 7:   Penn's Letter to the Free Society of Traders, August, 1683

Document 8:   Declaration by William Penn to protect the Indians on the land they sell him, October, 1683

Document 9:   The "Walking Purchase", August, 1737

TEACHER OVERHEADS/STUDENT HANDOUTS ON CD

Part One: King Philip's War, 1675-76

1. Map of Southern New England

2. Timeline: Historical Background in New England

3. Timeline: Immediate Factors

4. Steps in Mediation

5. Positions and Interests

6. Directions for the Mock Mediation

7. Debriefing

8. What Actually Happened? The Facts Continued

9. Cost of King Philip's War

10. Questions for Discussion

Part Two: The Quakers and the Lenni Lenape, Delaware Indians, 1682-84

11. Historical Background

12. Images of William Penn

13. Positions and Interests

14. Directions for the Mock Treaty Negotiation

15. Debriefing

16. Images of William Penn's Treaty with the Indians

17. The Facts Continued

18. Questions for Discussion

Sources and Credits for Illustrations

p. 74: Native American Village, etching by Theodore de Bry, 1590, *Library of Congress (LC)*

p. 75: Map of Southern New England in 1600s, from *Red, White and Black: People of Early North America* by Gary B. Nash, reprinted with permission of Pearson Education, Inc.

p. 76: Woodcut of Massacre of Pequots, *1637, New York Public Library*

p. 78: "Phillip [sic] alias Metacomet of Pokanoket," *LC-USZ62-96234*

p. 85: "Goffe rallying the men of Hadley," *LC-USZ62-75122*

p. 90: Map of Pennsylvania and the Lower Counties of Delaware, 1681-1740, from *Red, White and Black: People of Early North America* by Gary B. Nash, reprinted with permission of Pearson Education, Inc.

p. 92: "The landing of William Penn from the Welcome," *Historical Society of Pennsylvania*

p. 93: William Penn, *LC-USZ62-12218*

p. 98: "The Belt of Wampum delivered by the Indians to William Penn," *LC-USZ62-96486*

p. 98: "Penn's Treaty with the Indians by Benjamin West," *Pennsylvania Academy of the Fine Arts*

p. 99: "The Peaceable Kingdom by Edward Hicks," *Pennsylvania Academy of the Fine Arts*

Chapter Five

Could the American Revolution Have Been Avoided?

Objectives

- To understand Britain's interest in economic and political centralization of its expanded empire after 1763.

- To contrast the rise of individualism and the development of representative government in the colonies in the seventhteen century with the class-based society in Britain.

- To appreciate missed opportunities for peaceful resolution to differences between Great Britain and her North American colonies during the period 1763–1776.

- To understand the influence of economic, political, ethnic and religious differences on the thinking of leaders in the various North American colonies regarding the relationship of the colonies and Britain.

Correlations with National History Standards

Era Two
Standard 2A

The student understands the roots of representative government and how political rights were defined.

- Explain the concept of the "rights of Englishmen" and the impact of the English Civil War and the Glorious Revolution on the colonies.

- Analyze how gender, property ownership, religion, and legal status affected political rights.

- Explain the social, economic and political tensions that led to violent conflicts between the colonists and their governments.

- Explain how the conflicts between legislative and executive branches contributed to the development of representative government.

Era Two
Standard 2B

The student understands religious diversity in the colonies and how ideas about religious freedom evolved.

- Explain the impact of the Great Awakening on colonial society.

Era Three
Standard 1A

The student understands the causes of the American Revolution.

- Explain the consequences of the Seven Years War and the overhaul of English imperial policy following the Treaty of Paris in 1763.

- Compare the arguments advanced by defenders and opponents of the new imperial policy in the traditional rights of English people and the legitimacy of asking the colonies to pay a share of the costs of empire.

- Reconstruct the chronology of the critical events leading to the outbreak of armed conflict between the American colonies and England.

- Analyze political, ideological, religious and economic origins of the Revolution.

- Reconstruct the arguments among patriots and loyalists about independence and draw conclusions about how the decision to declare independence was reached.

OVERVIEW

The origins of the American Revolution involved both internal and external areas of dispute. Externally the colonists differed with the British King, his ministers and the British Parliament over the extent of Parliament's authority in British North America. Internally, the various groups of colonists argued among themselves over how to respond to those acts of the British government that they saw as dangerous exertions of imperial power that seemed to threaten American interests and ideology. This case study examines the causes of the war and includes two historical role-plays. The first focuses on the divisions among the colonists at the First Continental Congress in the fall of 1774. The second focuses on the debate between the American colonies and the British Crown in 1775. The conflicting issues include economic, political, and ideological differences.

This lesson includes two activities:

- A Mock Mediation among colonists at the First Continental Congress in 1774

- A Mock Negotiation between Britain (Lord North) and the colonies (Benjamin Franklin) in 1775.

HISTORICAL BACKGROUND

Britain's North American colonies had grown dramatically in population and commerce during the first half of the 18th century. Boston, New York and Philadelphia blossomed from small villages into thriving commercial centers. As the cities grew, the view of society as functioning for the common good collided with the growing commercial ethic—individual pursuit of profit— as well as the search for additional land by farmers and speculators. The growing American emphasis on individualism derived from intellectual and religious trends as well as political developments in the colonies. A largely secular Enlightenment ideology rejected pessimistic notions of innate human depravity in favor of an emphasis on a human rationality and progress. The Great Awakening, a series of religious revivals that swept through the colonies from the backcountry to the cities between the 1720s and 1760s, challenged the authority of established ministers and emphasized the ability of individuals to achieve salvation through their own actions. The Great Awakening split many of the congregations and ultimately helped to promote religious pluralism among the multitude of religious denominations in America, particularly the Anglican, Congregational, Presbyterian, Methodist, Baptist, and Dutch Reformed churches. The growing American emphasis on individualism helped form the basis for political thinking and action in the colonies as the eighteenth century progressed.

Central authority was also facing growing challenges in the colonial governments, where locally elected legislatures bridled against royal governors and their appointed councils. By the 1730s, royal governments had replaced the proprietary governments in Virginia, Massachusetts, New York, New Jersey, South Carolina and North Carolina. Elected colonial assemblies or legislatures, originally thought of as advisory bodies, reflected the interests of their electorates and challenged the authority of the royal governors. Whig or "republican" ideology, inherited from dissidents in England and spread by colonial newspapers, emphasized the importance of locally elected legislatures to check executive authority.

The Treaty of Paris (1763), which ended the Seven Years War between England and France (known in the colonies as the French and Indian War), gave Britain title to French Canada, and France's other mainland North American possessions east of the Mississippi River, as well as Spanish Florida. The British victory was immense: it ended France's presence in North America and established a far-flung British empire that extended from North America to the Indian subcontinent.

The colonists in British America had participated in the war as adjunct soldiers and suppliers to British troops. They took enormous pride in Britain's triumph, but the war left them debt-ridden and weakened by the loss of lives. Boston alone lost almost 700 men out of a total population of less than 16,000. The members of the colonial assemblies, which by 1763 were handling a considerable portion of the colonies' internal affairs, assumed that Britain would allow them to determine and protect their constituents' interests after the war. Now that French Canada and Spanish Florida had passed into British hands, the colonists were less dependent on British military strength for protection against those traditional Continental European, Catholic enemies. In spite of the postwar economic recession, the elimination of hostile neighbors offered the British North American colonies unprecedented opportunities for economic growth and expansion.

The Seven Years War left England staggering under an immense war debt. In the spring of 1763, when George Grenville became chief minister to Britain's 25-year-old King George III, the British national debt stood at about 130 million pounds, twice what it had been before the war. Annual interest on the debt accounted for a large part of the burden on British taxpayers. Moreover, the costs of maintaining an empire were rising. After the war, the London government decided to establish a more consistent, centralized administration over its far-flung possessions. In addition to establishing and maintaining governments in its new colonies, Britain decided to keep an army to police Canada, keep peace over America's western frontier between the land-hungry colonists and the Indians and maintain British authority over the sometimes unruly residents of its older North American colonies. To reduce the debt, Grenville proposed new taxes in England and in the colonies. Since the colonists had been major beneficiaries of the war, Grenville argued that they could at least help shoulder the costs of the peacetime army.

Many colonists, however, were suspicious of a British standing army in the colonies in peacetime. It revived fears of military despots like Caesar in Rome and Cromwell in Britain. The colonists also questioned the use of the British Army to protect Indian territories. The Royal Proclamation of 1763 defined the area "beyond the Heads or Sources of any of the Rivers which fall into the Atlantic Ocean" as lands for Indian Nations or tribes. This prohibited the colonists from settling west of the Appalachian Mountains and and authorized the British Army to stay in the colonies to enforce it. (See Document 1: The Proclamation of 1763.) The colonists not only objected to the prohibition against moving west but also suspected that Britain intended to use the army to help collect taxes and customs duties and assure submission to the Mother Country.

Grenville pushed through Parliament several revenue-raising measures, including the Sugar Act. In the past, customs duties had been designed to regulate trade, and particularly to encourage colonists to trade primarily with Britain and other British colonies. The preamble to this act, however, stated that it was intended to raise revenues. The act reduced the tax on molasses imported from the non-British West Indies and increased enforcement against smuggling. The colonists argued that strict enforcement of the new tax would be costly to them and, by ending the complex exchanges based on molasses, would hurt the economic interests of both colonies and Mother Country. Many of the colonial legislatures protested the act, but only New York made a constitutional objection that, since the Sugar Act was designed to raise revenues, it was a tax that violated the rights of overseas English subjects who were not represented in the British House of Commons.

Proclamation Line of 1763

Grenville also announced his intention to extend to America stamp duties similar to those already imposed in England. He gave the colonies a year to suggest alternative ways of raising revenue. The colonies strenuously objected to the proposed stamp duties, which would be the first direct tax leveled by Parliament on the colonists. The House of Commons refused to receive the colonial petitions and, in 1765, Parliament passed the new Stamp Act, which required revenue stamps on every newspaper, pamphlet, almanac, legal document, liquor license, college diploma, pack of playing cards, and pair of dice. These new taxes fell particularly hard on the more articulate groups of colonial society—lawyers, publishers, and tavern owners (who were often at the social and political center of colonial life). Instead of trial by local jury, those accused of violating the Stamp Act would be tried in Vice-Admiralty Courts without juries.

Colonies Respond to the Stamp Act

The Virginia assembly, the House of Burgesses, was the first to react to the news of the Stamp Act in April 1765. Virginians were already distressed because of a severe decline in the price of tobacco, their main crop. Patrick Henry, a 29-year-old, fiery lawyer newly elected from a frontier county, asserted that the colonists held all of the rights and privileges of Englishmen and that Virginia's General Assembly had "the only and sole exclusive right and power to lay taxes and impositions upon the inhabitants of this Colony." In August, Bostonians found an effigy of Andrew Oliver, stamp distributor for the Massachusetts Bay Colony, hanging from a tree at the south end of town. The next day, the stamp distributor asked to be relieved of his commission. Another Boston "mob" attacked the homes of officials connected with the Admiralty Court and Customs Service, totally destroying the home of Lt. Governor Thomas Hutchinson. An uprising against the Stamp Act in Newport, Rhode Island, led to several days of uncontrolled rioting. Soon stamp distributors in one colony after another were resigning. This essentially nullified the Stamp Act, since if no one distributed stamps, no one could buy or use them.

The Colonists' View of the Stamp Act

In October 1765, nine colonies sent representatives to a Stamp Act Congress in New York in an effort to join forces in seeking repeal of the Stamp Act. Only once before, at the Albany Congress in 1754, had the colonies sent representatives to consult with each other on common concerns. The Congress expressed its strong sense of "affection and duty" to the King and his government, but stated that the colonists had all the rights of subjects who lived within Great Britain, including the right to be taxed only with their consent, which could only be given by their provincial legislatures since the colonists could not be represented in the House of Commons. (See Document 2: Declarations of the Stamp Act Congress.)

Formally organized resistance groups, called the "Sons of Liberty," threatened to prevent the British from using the royal army to enforce the Stamp Act. The Sons of Liberty were composed mostly of the "middling" orders of colonial society, including tradesmen, artisans and some ship captains, and some poorer orders. They argued that the Stamp Act was "unconstitutional," and, therefore, did not have to be obeyed. Public pressure forced many customs officers and court officials to open the ports and courts for business and printers to publish newspapers, and the Stamp Act never went into effect.

Meanwhile in Great Britain . . .

In 1766, the British Parliament debated the American colonists' reaction to the Stamp Act. Most of the members found the colonists views outrageous. They argued that the supremacy of Parliament, that is, the King, the House of Lords and the House of Commons acting together, was a governing principle of British politics since the Glorious Revolution of 1688, and that members of Parliament considered the interests of all British people everywhere, not just those of their constituents. Therefore, the colonists were "virtually represented" in Parliament and so could be rightfully taxed. The concept of virtual representation made little sense to the colonists who were used to a system of real or direct representation, under which representatives spoke for their local constituents and were sometimes even instructed by their constituents how to vote on certain issues.

Faced with vigorous opposition from the colonies, Parliament recognized that there was no point in trying to enforce the Stamp Act. Not only was American opposition virtually universal, but also colonial merchants had enforced non-importation agreements so successfully that American purchases of certain British goods had been substantially reduced. The North American colonies were Britain's major overseas market. The affected British manufacturers and their unemployed workers did not suffer in silence. In the spring of 1766, Parliament voted to repeal the Stamp Act, but first passed a Declaratory Act that asserted Parliament's power to enact laws that bound the colonies in "all cases whatsoever," thus maintaining the principle of Parliamentary supremacy. (See Document 3: The Declaratory Act, 1766.)

By then Grenville was out of office. In 1767, the new ministry introduced new revenue-raising import duties on paper, lead, painters' colors, and tea, known as the Townshend duties, after Charles Townshend, the King's Chancellor of the Exchequer (or Treasury). The funds raised were to be used to pay for the administration of justice, the support of civil government and for defense.

While in the colonies . . .

The colonies protested that the new law undermined the right of the provincial assemblies to tax colonists as well as the influence of the provincial assemblies over the administration of the provincial governments. Colonial assemblies had always paid the salaries of the royal governors, councils, judges and other Crown appointees, which helped keep them responsive to the needs and interests of the colonists. Parliament also passed a law suspending the New York Assembly until it conformed with the Quartering Act of 1765, which required provincial assemblies to provide supplies to royal troops within their borders. New York had argued that this was a tax law collected in goods, not money, and so was as objectionable as the Stamp Act. Given Parliament's interference with juries as well as provincial governments, some colonists began to suspect a plot to destroy those parts of government that spoke for the people, and to institute a government answerable only to the Crown.

A series of newspaper essays entitled, "Letters from a Farmer in Pennsylvania," written by Philadelphia lawyer John Dickinson and widely republished throughout the colonies in the winter of 1767-68, rallied colonial opposition to the New York Suspending Act and the Townshend duties. Since the duties were meant to raise revenue and not regulate trade, Dickinson argued, they were a tax that should be opposed as the Stamp Act had been. He contended that the attack on New York was a threat to all colonial legislatures and the colonists needed to unite in opposition. But he cautioned that hostility between Britain and the colonies should not be exacerbated because it might lead to separation, a fate he wanted to avoid. Dickinson recommended that the colonists petition the King and Parliament for redress. And if that failed, the colonists should cease buying British goods and rely instead upon their own "industry and frugality."

When petitions failed to bring a repeal of the Townshend duties, colonial merchants began organizing non-importation agreements, which were supported by agreements among consumers not to purchase British goods. First in Boston, and then in New York and Philadelphia, merchants and consumers pledged to neither import nor purchase British articles in the hope of bringing politically influential British merchants to their aid, for half of British shipping was engaged in commerce with the colonies, and a quarter of British exports went to the colonies. Local non-importation associations and committees enforced the agreements, and acted more and more like regular governments—inspecting merchants' papers and invoices, judging the guilt of suspected violators, imposing sanctions on those who broke the agreements. Merchants who violated the non-importation agreements might, for example, see their names published, and suffer social and economic boycotts that made life extremely unpleasant. Boycotts were more peaceful than visits from "mobs" but required careful organization and widespread participation.

Political cartoon depicting a tarred and feathered tax collector

In the summer of 1768, in response to the pleas of customs officers and other Crown officials who felt powerless as the non-importation committees took control and Boston crowds interfered with their efforts to enforce the trade laws, the British government dispatched two regiments of British troops to Boston. For the better part of the next two years, the "redcoats" were the source of persistent hostile confrontations with the Bostonians, who had a deep suspicion of "standing armies in times of peace," and were also upset by the soldiers' penchant for cursing, carousing, and taking part-time jobs at the docks at less than the usual wage. Tensions came to a head on March 5, 1770, when a contingent of British troops fired on an unruly crowd of harassing citizens, killing five people in what the Boston "patriots" publicized as "The Boston Massacre." Bowing to furious popular reaction recently appointed royal governor Thomas Hutchinson ordered the British troops removed to a fortress at Boston Harbor and arrested the commanding officer and the soldiers involved in the "Massacre."

Paul Revere's Engraving of the Boston Massacre, 1770
(You may want your students to consider the accuracy or propaganda
value of this image)

As a result of the colonial non-importation agreements, the Townshend duties failed miserably, bringing into the treasury less than 21,000 pounds by 1770 while costing British businesses 700,000 pounds in lost sales. After George III appointed Lord North as his chief minister (this was before the establishment of the office of Prime Minister) in 1770, the new government asked Parliament to repeal all of the Townshend duties except the one on tea, which was kept to show that Parliament had the right to tax the colonies.

From 1770 to 1772, relative quiet descended over colonial relations. But in 1772, the Crown created a new furor by announcing that it would pay the salaries of the royal governor and superior court judges in Massachusetts, removing that responsibility from the provincial legislature. Even though the measure would have saved the colony money, it was seen as a dangerous precedent because it undermined a right stated in the colony's charter and it made officials beholden to London. Boston's Town Meeting appointed a Committee of Correspondence "to state the rights of the colonists . . . and to communicate and publish the same to the several towns and to the world." By the end of 1772, eighty other Massachusetts towns had created committees of correspondence and other provincial assemblies began to appoint such committees to keep contact with each other.

In early 1773, Parliament enacted the Tea Act, which enabled the near-bankrupt East India Company to sell its surplus tea in America and Ireland at a reduced price through its own agents rather than through private merchants. Parliament refused to remove the remaining Townshend tax on tea, which would be collected directly by East India Company agents in America. Even with that tax, Parliament reasoned, the East Indian Company's tea could undersell smuggled Dutch tea, give the Americans cheaper tea, the crown a modest revenue, and the East India Company a new lease on life. Again, Parliament misjudged the American colonists, who interpreted the act as an effort to trick them into paying the remaining Townshend duty, and to accept implicitly Parliament's right to tax them. Colonial tea merchants, many of whom had been flagrantly smuggling tea from Holland, also denounced the new act for giving the East India Company a monopoly on the American tea market. They predicted that other monopolies would follow, squeezing American merchants from profitable lines of trade.

The colonists were able to mobilize effective resistance to the landing of tea at most major ports. In New York, a committee met the incoming tea ship and persuaded the captain to go back to England without unloading the tea and so preventing payment of the import tax. But in Boston, the tea ships were inadvertently allowed to enter the harbor, which meant that, unless they had official clearances, they could not leave without risking seizure by the Royal Navy for violating British customs laws. On December 16, 1773, the day before the tea became subject to seizure, 5,000 Bostonians packed the Old South Church and dispatched a final request to the governor, Thomas Hutchinson. But Hutchinson, whose sons were agents for the East India Company, would not be swayed. At nightfall, the meeting dissolved and a group of men, some of whom were dressed as Indians, boarded the tea ships, opened the 342 chests of tea and dumped 10,000 pounds worth of East India Company tea into the Boston Harbor. The event, remembered as "The Boston Tea Party," elicited enormous delight in otherwise cautious patriots like John Adams, in part because the violence was so successfully limited.

British response to the Boston Tea Party: The Coercive Acts

The Crown viewed the Boston Tea Party as a direct rebuke of British authority. Lord North called the Bostonians "fanatics" and stated that the dispute was no longer about taxes but about whether England had any authority over the colonies. "We must master them or totally leave them to themselves and treat them as aliens," King George III declared. The British Parliamentary system was in transition in the eighteenth century. The cabinet system with its prime minister was emerging. Yet the monarch still played an active role in government, choosing and dismissing government ministers as he wished, although sometimes Parliament could force action upon him. But he could dissolve Parliament, and he could and did use his considerable patronage power to secure a new Parliament more to his liking. Factionalism, differences over policies at home and abroad and relations with the crown contributed to a turnover of four different ministries between 1763 and 1770, when George III finally established under Frederick, Lord North, a ministry that could sustain itself in Parliament.

George III's outdated conception of the crown's role encouraged a movement among the factions (not yet a political party) in Parliament who called themselves Whigs to reduce the king's power and also to reform the corrupt and unrepresentative political system of election to Parliament. These Whig factions--foremost among them the earl of Rockingham, Edmund Burke, William Pitt, and the radical John Wilkes—opposed the King's

American Version of Boston Tea Party, engraved in 1784

British Version of Boston Tea Party, engraved in 1789

coercive policy toward the American colonies although they supported the idea of having the colonies pay for part of the cost of stationing British army units there to defend the empire. Pitt in particular was popular with the mercantile and manufacturing interests, political reformers and the supporters of the overseas empire in the Americas and Asia. Although they endorsed the idea of sovereignty of Parliament, these Whigs, like the colonists themselves, opposed direct taxation of the unrepresented colonists as a violation of a fundamental principle of the British constitution. While they had been opposed to the stamp tax, many had initially supported Townshend's duties on tea and other commodities, but most of them later abandoned these duties. Yet almost all of them supported the Declaratory Act that affirmed the supremacy of the British Parliament.

To varying degrees, the Whig factions sought reform at home, reduction of the king's patronage and expansion of the policy to include non-Anglicans, and they sought compromise and conciliation with the colonies in America. Ultimately some of them—with Burke and Pitt in the lead—were willing to accept the Continental Congress and the colonial legislatures as the legitimate bodies to tax the American colonists, including the colonies' share of mutual defense. In 1775, as war neared, Burke, for example, denounced the possible use of force and urged that the old imperial connection be restored on the basis of trust, consent and mutual self-interest. However, the Whig opposition, often divided among itself, remained a distinct minority in Parliament.

Lord North had the active support of the king and particularly of the conservative aristocracy and landed gentry and their supporters in the military, the professions, and the Anglican clergy, who would later form the Tory Party. Already concerned with growing threats to their privileges and authority in Britain, many members of these groups reacted vigorously to what they saw as challenges to law and order, property, and authority in America. Many who had served in military or civilian positions in America during the French and Indian War had little respect for the Americans, whom they considered greedy, rebellious, and ungrateful--seeking the benefits of belonging to the British empire without being willing to share its burdens. Thus, they supported a coercive policy against the Americans as they had against English radicals like John Wilkes. So great were the king's influence and the outrage among the propertied classes that the House of Commons adopted the Coercive Acts by overwhelming majorities.

Despite the opposition of William Pitt and Edmund Burke, both of whom were sympathetic to the Americans but were in the minority, Parliament passed the "Coercive Acts," a set of stern laws to punish the Massachusetts Bay Colony (See Document 4: The Coercive Acts, 1774):

1. The Boston Port Act, effectively closed the Port of Boston to commerce, forcing large numbers of Bostonians out of work, until the city agreed to pay for the destroyed tea.

2. The Massachusetts Government Act, annulled the colony's 1691 charter by allowing the Crown to appoint the colony's upper house, thus reducing popular participation.

3. The Administration of Justice Act, allowed Crown officers in Massachusetts who were accused of committing a capital offense in the course of putting down a riot or executing the revenue acts to be tried in British rather than colonial courts.

4. A new Quartering Act, allowed British troops to be quartered in homes, taverns or other private dwellings, first felt in Massachusetts where a heavy contingent of additional troops were brought back into Boston.

The King's ministers hoped that these measures would punish Massachusetts, divide the colonies, and send a warning to the other provinces to accept Parliament's power. Instead the "Coercive Acts" pushed the colonies together. The Americans called them the "Intolerable Acts," and included the Quebec Act, by which Parliament defined a permanent civil government for the formerly-French Canadian colony, extended Quebec's boundaries to include all territory west of the Appalachians and north of the Ohio River, and provided religious tolerance for Catholics, all to the outrage of the American colonists.

Colonial Reaction to the "Coercive/Intolerable Acts"—The First Continental Congress

When news of the Boston Port Act arrived in May 1774, Boston's town meeting dispatched a circular letter to all the colonies urging an immediate end to trade with England and the British West Indies. The proposal met resistance, particularly from merchants who had enough of non-importation agreements and thought that the Bostonians had gone too far by destroying the tea. But popular sentiment was stirred up as it had not been since the time of the Stamp Act. A call for a meeting of delegates from all of the colonies won ready and widespread support.

Fifty-five delegates from all of the colonies except Georgia came to Carpenters Hall (later Independence Hall) in Philadelphia from September 5 through October 26, 1774, to attend the (First) Continental Congress. The delegates had been elected by regular legislatures or by extra-legal assemblies, including conventions or congresses and, sometimes, county meetings. The provincial delegates were generally empowered "to consult and advise" with other delegates, as Connecticut instructed "on proper measures for advancing the best good of the colonies." (See Document 5: Instructions by the Virginia Convention to their Delegates, July 1774.)

Peyton Randolph, speaker of the Virginia House of Burgesses, was elected as the presiding officer or president. Charles Thomson, from Pennsylvania, was chosen to be secretary. Ignoring an eloquent plea by Patrick Henry of Virginia (one of the richest and most populous colonies) that votes be proportional to each colony's population and wealth, the delegates agreed that each colony would have one vote. If a delegation was evenly divided, the colony's vote would not count. The Congress voted to appoint a committee to state the rights of the colonies, the instances in which they had been violated, and the "means most proper...for obtaining a restoration to them" and another committee to examine Parliament's laws affecting colonial trade and manufacturing.

The Congress had no more than finished these preliminaries when it received a report that General Thomas Gage, British military commander and Massachusetts governor, had attempted to seize military supplies the colonists had stockpiled near Boston and, after being opposed, bombarded Boston from warships in the harbor. The story turned out to be untrue, but it affected the Congress's mood nonetheless.

A few days later, on September 16th, Paul Revere, an express rider from Massachusetts, delivered to the Congress the radical "resolves" of town representatives in Suffolk County, Massachusetts, which had met earlier that month to discuss the volatile situation with Britain. The so-called "Suffolk Resolves," drafted by Samuel Adams' lieutenant, Dr. Joseph Warren: 1) declared the Coercive Acts unconstitutional and therefore not to be obeyed; 2) urged the people to form their own government which would collect taxes and withhold taxes from the royal government until the Coercive Acts were repealed; 3) advised the people to arm and form their own militia; and 4) recommended strict economic sanctions against Britain. (see Document 6: Suffolk Resolves.) The Congress debated whether to support these resolves.

On September 28th, Joseph Galloway, a conservative delegate from Pennsylvania, suggested that the problem between Britain and the colonies arose because of defects in the current constitutional system. He proposed a new "Plan of Union" with Great Britain whereby the central administration would consist of a president-general appointed by the king, holding office at the king's pleasure, with a veto power over a Grand Council. The members of the Grand Council would be chosen for three-year terms by the assemblies of each province. The president-general and Council would constitute an "inferior and distinct" branch of the British Parliament. Measures dealing with America could originate with the Grand Council or with Parliament. Each would have a veto over the other. Galloway's Plan was an early version of the "Dominion System" which Britain would later establish with colonies such as Canada in the mid-19th century. (See Document 7: Joseph Galloway's "Plan of Union.")

ACTIVITY ONE: MOCK MEDIATION AT A CONGRESSIONAL CAUCUS

*T*he delegates to the First Continental Congress have been meeting for three weeks at Carpenter's Hall in Philadelphia to decide how to respond to the "Intolerable Acts." They have received the Suffolk Resolves from Massachusetts and a proposal for "A Plan of Union" with Britain from Joseph Galloway of Pennsylvania.

We are going to roleplay a hypothetical "caucus" or small group meeting of some of the delegates to the Congress, mediated by Peyton Randolph, president of the Continental Congress, with Charles Thomson, secretary of the Congress as the observer/recorder/reporter. It is September 28, 1774.

PARTICIPANTS

Samuel Adams (Massachusetts) was a short, stocky man, unconcerned with wealth, social rank or appearances. He was born in Boston in 1722, the son of a brewer. He graduated Harvard, and tried various business enterprises, which failed, probably because he was more interested in politics than profits. Elected to the Massachusetts House of Representatives in 1765, Adams soon became its clerk and one of its most ardent defenders of colonial rights. He supported resistance to the Stamp Act and the non-importation movement in opposition to the Townshend Acts. He bitterly opposed the use of standing armies, and served as spokesman for the town when it demanded the removal of royal troops after the Boston "Massacre." The Boston Committee of Correspondence was his creation. Although Adams helped organize Boston's resistance to the Tea Act, he was more a champion of resistance through petitions, correspondence networks, and public meetings. In the spring of 1774, Adams suggested that an American Bill of Rights might provide a basis for settling the Anglo-American conflict. Later he helped develop the strategy that led to the submission of the "Suffolk Resolves" to the Continental Congress for approval. In 1774, Adams favored

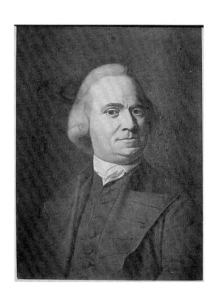

Samuel Adams

the immediate institution of a boycott on British imports. Only in mid-1776 did Adams advocate for separation from Britain. He later signed the Declaration of Independence. He continued to serve his state as lieutenant-governor from 1789-93 and governor from 1794-97. Adams died in 1803.

Christopher Gadsden

Christopher Gadsden (South Carolina) was born in Charleston, South Carolina in 1724. He was sent to a school in England and then to a counting-house in Philadelphia. In 1746 he returned to Charleston and became a leading merchant. In 1757, he entered the state Assembly, in which he served for nearly 30 years. At the Stamp Act Congress of 1765, Gadsden argued for colonial union and against recognition of the authority of Parliament. His political principles represented the liberal position of the South Carolina aristocracy—insistent on the rights of self-government under elite leadership. He became the acknowledged leader of "the radicals" in South Carolina. John Rutledge, another delegate from South Carolina, favored conciliation, leaving the South Carolina delegation to the First Continental Congress often split. Although a merchant himself, Gadsden was violently opposed to "allowing Parliament any Power of regulating Trade, or allowing [admitting] that they have any Thing to do with Us." He left the Second Continental Congress to take command of newly organized South Carolina forces, becoming a brigadier-general in the Continental Army the following year. In 1782, he refused the governorship offered him by the Assembly, but remained part of the Assembly until withdrawing from public life in 1784. Gadsden voted for ratification of the Federal Constitution in 1787 as part of the state convention. He worked for the reelection of his old friend John Adams to the presidency in 1800, and grieved over his defeat. Gadsden died in 1805.

Richard Henry Lee

Richard Henry Lee (Virginia) was born in Westmoreland County, Virginia in 1732, a fourth-generation Virginian and member of one of the Old Dominion's wealthiest land- and slave-owning families. Tall and spare, with red hair and a Roman profile, Lee was an admirer of New England and a close ally of John and Samuel Adams. Educated in England, Lee returned to Virginia and entered the House of Burgesses in 1758. He supported measures designed to appeal to a broad constituency, including a bill in 1762 to lower requirements for voting. Lee was part of the radical wing of the Virginia House of Burgesses, along with Patrick Henry and Thomas Jefferson, and assumed responsibilities for mobilizing the people as the revolutionary movement grew. He saw the colonists' cause as that of "Virtue and mankind." Elected to the First Continental Congress, he favored strong measures against England. He attempted unsuccessfully to attach to the petition to the King a statement in favor of arming and equipping the colonial militias. By the spring of 1776, Lee openly advocated independence. He favored a confederation of states, but refused to attend the Federal Convention in 1787 and led in Virginia's opposition to the new Constitution. He served in the U.S. Senate 1789-92, his chief aim being the passage of a Bill of Rights. Lee died in 1794.

William Livingston (New Jersey) was born in Albany, New York in 1723, to a wealthy, patrician family. He graduated from Yale, was admitted to the bar and became involved in New York politics as leader of a moderate liberal faction that opposed Parliamentary interference with colonial affairs. He tried to reconcile the Sons of Liberty and other radicals to his more moderate leadership. In 1769, Livingston was driven from power in the New York Assembly when the conservatives secured a majority in the Assembly. He retired to his country estate near Elizabethtown, New Jersey, and became a member of the Essex County Committee of Correspondence, quickly rising to a position of leadership. Livingston was a delegate from New Jersey to the First Continental Congress. He also served as a deputy at the Second Continental Congress. Livingston was elected governor of New Jersey under the newly-created state constitution, serving for fourteen tumultuous years. He attended the Federal Constitutional Convention in 1787 and worked for a compromise between the larger and smaller states. Largely through his influence, New Jersey quickly and unanimously ratified the federal Constitution. Livingston died in 1790.

William Livingston

George Read (Delaware) was born in Cecil County, Maryland, in 1733, but shortly thereafter moved with his family to New Castle, Delaware. He studied law, was admitted to the bar and developed a thriving practice in Delaware and Maryland. As attorney general for the lower counties in Delaware, he protested that the Stamp Act made "slaves" of the colonies. As a delegate to the First and Second Continental Congresses, he was a moderate, ready to uphold colonial rights but trying to avoid extreme measures. However, he often found himself carried away with the radical tide. Read played a prominent role at the Delaware constitutional convention in 1776 and led Delaware in defending itself against British attacks in 1777-78. At the Federal Convention in 1787, Read was concerned that the larger states would take advantage of the smaller ones and accepted the compromises that led to the Federal Constitution. Largely through his efforts, Delaware was the first state to ratify the Constitution. Read served as a U.S. Senator from Delaware and as chief justice of Delaware until his death in 1798.

George Read

Silas Deane

Silas Deane (Connecticut) was born in Groton, Connecticut in 1737. Son of a blacksmith, he graduated from Yale, taught school, studied law, and became a prosperous lawyer and merchant. In 1769, he was elected chairman of a local committee to enforce non-consumption in response to the Townshend Acts. Elected to the Connecticut General Assembly in 1772, he soon became one of its leaders. Although he supported colonial opposition to British policies, in 1774 he opposed hastily inaugurating a boycott of British goods, and argued that the colonies should consult with each other before instituting a plan of opposition to the Coercive Acts. He was a delegate to the First and Second Continental Congresses, actively involved in preparations for war with Britain. In 1776, Deane was selected as commissioner of a diplomatic mission to France to secure military supplies and arrange for European military leaders to assist the American cause. However, Arthur Lee, one of his fellow commissioners, accused Deane of attempting to personally profit from his diplomatic activities. Deane was never able to completely clear his name. He lost faith in the American cause and wrote letters to friends in America advising them to end the war for independence. He lived in exile after the war; financially bankrupt and physically unwell, he died in London in 1789.

James Duane (New York) was born in New York City in 1733, son of a prosperous merchant. Without formal university training, he studied law, was admitted to the bar and developed a thriving law practice. He attempted to quell a Stamp Act mob in 1765. Despite radical opposition, he was nominated as a delegate to the First Continental Congress, where he favored conciliation. He was a member of the committee that drew up the statement of rights for the colonists and worked to keep the tone moderate. Duane spoke for most American merchants who believed that, although the British trade regulations were burdensome in some respects, they were necessary for their "wealth, strength and safety." However, he wanted to exclude "every idea of taxation internal and external for raising a revenue on the subjects of America without their consent." Duane supported Galloway's Plan of Union. He signed the October 1774 non-importation agreement against Britain, although he considered it too extreme.

Duane sat in the Continental Congress almost continuously until 1783, and assisted in writing the final draft of the Articles of Confederation. He later served as mayor of New York, state senator, and federal district judge. He favored ratification of the Federal Constitution. Duane died suddenly in 1797.

Joseph Galloway (Pennsylvania) was born in Anne Arundel County, Maryland in 1731, to a prominent trading family. As a young man, he moved to Philadelphia, where he studied law, and became a popular attorney. He served in the Pennsylvania Assembly 1756-1776 (except for 1764-65) and as Speaker of the Assembly from 1766-1775. Galloway sympathized with the British desire to raise revenue in America but disagreed with Parliament's taxing the colonies and its restrictions on American commerce. He accepted the principle of Parliamentary supremacy, but argued that the colonists had a right to representation. He proposed a "Plan of Union" and argued that the Congress should draft a temperate petition that conceded Parliament's right to regulate trade and adopting an economic boycott only if the petition failed to win redress. After the Congress dissolved, Galloway openly criticized its proceedings, questioned its commitment to reconciliation, and explained his own position in a pamphlet, *A Candid Examination of the Mutual Claims of Great Britain, and the Colonies* (New York, February 1775). He refused to be a delegate to the Second Continental Congress. Although he had hoped to remain neutral in the impending conflict, Galloway eventually aided the British and fled to Britain in 1778 after the British forces left Philadelphia. Until the very close of the revolution, he attempted to bring about an accommodation between the mother country and the colonies. Galloway died in England in 1803.

The Mediator

Peyton Randolph (Virginia) was born in Williamsburg, Virginia in 1721, the son of wealthy John Randolph. He graduated from the College of William and Mary, attended the Middle Temple law school in London and began practicing law in 1744. In 1748, Randolph was appointed King's attorney for the province of Virginia. He saw himself as a spokesman for the rights of the Colony as well as those of the Crown, and was sometimes in sharp conflict with the royal governor. Randolph also became a member of the Virginia House of Burgesses beginning in 1748, and from 1759 to 1767 served on the Virginia committee of correspondence. In 1766, he resigned as King's attorney and was elected speaker of the Virginia House of Burgesses. Conservative in temperament, Randolph was representative of the point of view of the colonial aristocracy. Although he initially deplored the radicalism in Virginia and opposed Patrick Henry's resolutions against the Stamp Act, Randolph moved steadily with the current of revolutionary sentiment in Virginia. He was moderating in his influence and cautious in his leadership. Randolph was admired by his contemporaries for his judgment and wisdom. He was elected president of the Continental Congress in 1774 and again in 1775. Randolph died in 1775.

Peyton Randolph

The Observer/Recorder/Reporter

CHARLES THOMPSON ESQ.
Secretary to Congress.

Charles Thomson

Charles Thomson (Pennsylvania) was the secretary of the First Continental Congress. Born of a Protestant family in Ireland in 1729, he came to New Castle, Delaware, with his father and three brothers in 1740. He was sent to a academy in New London, Pennsylvania, where he advanced rapidly and became a Latin teacher. He met Benjamin Franklin and other influential Pennsylvanians, and became a Philadelphia merchant and politician, respected for his veracity by Native Americans, Quakers and others. Although Pennsylvania conservatives kept him from being elected a delegate to the Continental Congress, Thomson was unanimously chosen as its secretary in 1774, continuing in that position until the federal government came to power in 1789. Known for his fairness and integrity, the "perpetual secretary" provided the continuity and institutional memory to a Congress whose members were ever-changing. Thomson designed the Great Seal of the United States in 1782, and wrote on numerous subjects. He died in 1824.

POSITIONS AND INTERESTS

While most of the delegates to the First Continental Congress had never met before, the reputations of many preceded them from years of public debate that had been reported and reprinted in letters and newspaper articles. Everyone wanted to preserve their colonial institutions of local government. Most of the delegates were determined to present a united front to the world, no matter how sharply divided they might be in their closed-door sessions. Although there were ideological differences of opinion, and underlying regional and economic differences, the colonies shared a common heritage of language, ideas and political institutions and, most importantly, a determination to establish colonial rights firmly while remaining subjects of the British Crown. Although the positions held by many of the delegates to the First Continental Congress were often subject to change, there were basically three viewpoints: radical, moderate and conservative.

The Radicals

The "**radicals**," such as Samuel Adams from Massachusetts, Christopher Gadsden from South Carolina, and Richard Henry Lee from Virginia, argued for outright resistance to Britain. They supported the Suffolk Resolves. They agreed with the Pennsylvania jurist James Wilson and Thomas Jefferson of Virginia (who were not delegates to the Congress), who had concluded that Parliament had no right whatsoever to tax or pass laws over the American colonists. The colonists, Jefferson argued, had consented only to be subject to the King, who served as a link holding together the various parts of his kingdom, each of which had its own elected legislature. Friends of Jefferson had his ideas published in 1774 in "A Summary View of the Rights of British America." The radicals were focused primarily on ideology—they wanted more than anything else to preserve their fundamental rights to govern themselves. They saw the actions of the British King and Parliament as a demonstration of British determination to eliminate these rights. They noted that their petitions to the King and Parliament to redress complaints had been persistently ignored, and argued that resistance was necessary because acquiescence would establish a dangerous precedent for further violations of rights. They urged the delegates to support Massachusetts in its resistance to the Intolerable Acts because, if Massachusetts fell, the British would extend those policies to its neighbors. They feared that after destroying the assemblies' role in defending the colonies' economic and social interests, Britain would restrict colonial development, destroy them through taxation, and use the colonies only to enrich the Mother Country as was done with the Irish. The radicals had a greater distrust of British intentions and were more willing than the conservatives or moderates to accept the break in the social fabric that any significant change in the status quo would inevitably create.

The Moderates

The "**moderates**," such as William Livingston from New Jersey and George Read from Delaware, opposed Parliamentary interference with colonial affairs but urged restraint and further attempts at reconciliation. Their idea of liberty was closely tied to material prosperity, especially by the merchant class. They had supported the agreements for the non-importation and non-consumption of British goods during the Stamp Act crisis. The moderates were primarily focused on economic concerns. They did not want to push Britain to war. They urged the delegates to petition for a redress of grievances or, at most, to adopt a uniform plan for the non-importation of British goods, which they saw as a peaceable and effective method for recovering the colonists' liberty. More concerned about commerce and prosperity than ideology, the moderates were also more interested in stability and colonial unity than the radicals. The Suffolk Resolves were more inflammatory than they would have liked; however, rejecting them would have implied approval of objectionable British policies, so they supported them.

The Conservatives

The "**conservatives**," such as Joseph Galloway from Pennsylvania, and James Duane from New York, did not want to exacerbate the situation with Britain. They argued that colonial trade and the colonies in general needed the British markets and the protection of the royal navy; therefore, the colonies were obligated to accept Parliamentary regulation of trade. The conservatives wanted to continue as part of the British empire because they saw Britain as the freest country in the world. They suggested, however, that the political relationship between the American colonies and Britain needed to be restructured. The conservatives feared anarchy and social disorder more than they feared the intentions of the British government. They believed that the radicals were encouraging class divisions, lawlessness, disorder, and mob action. They also feared the capacity of Britain to destroy the colonies' economies by restricting their trade, and were thus concerned about implementing non-importation agreements. The conservatives stressed the cultural and economic bonds with Britain and the belief in the protection of liberty, and especially property, by the Magna Carta and British common law. However, even the conservatives were afraid to vote against the Suffolk Resolves because they did not want to appear to support coercive British policies, and because it seemed important to express support for beleaguered Massachusetts.

TEACHER INSTRUCTIONS FOR ACTIVITY ONE: MOCK CONGRESSIONAL CAUCUS

Preparation

1. Share the historical background with the class—either as a lecture and/or a reading assignment. Encourage students to try to gain as thorough an understanding as possible of the events, characters, and historical context. Use the overhead "Timeline" on the CD.

2. Distribute student handout: "Positions and Interests" for students to read.

3. Hand out the brief biographies for students to review.

4. Choose one (or both) of the activities for the class to use.

Directions

1. Divide the class into groups of ten (or, if there are insufficient numbers of students, reduce the number of radicals, moderates and conservatives equally):

    <u>The Radicals</u>

    Samuel Adams (Delegate from Massachusetts)

    Christopher Gadsden (Delegate from South Carolina)

    Richard Henry Lee (Delegate from Virginia)

    <u>The Moderates</u>

    William Livingston (Delegate from New Jersey)

    George Read (Delegate from Delaware)

    <u>The Conservatives</u>

    Silas Deane (Delegate from Connecticut)

    James Duane (Delegate from New York)

    Joseph Galloway (Delegate from Pennsylvania)

    <u>The Mediator</u>

    Peyton Randolph

    <u>The Observer/Recorder/Reporter</u>

    Charles Thomson

2. Distribute student handout: "Mock Congressional Caucus."

3. Review the setting and the directions with the students. Instruct the participants to imagine they have been attending the First Continental Congress meetings for over a month and that their group is meeting informally to try to find a solution that would satisfy the delegates and offer a basis for reconciliation with Britain. Each participant should act in a manner consistent with his/her assigned role and interests.

Debriefing

1. Once the negotiations are complete, conduct a classroom discussion about the mock Congressional caucus. Have the reporters describe how the process worked in their group. Summarize and compare the results each group obtained.

2. Either have the students read "The Facts Continued" or share the relevant portions with the class as a lecture. Compare the results and the process of the mock activities with what actually happened in history.

3. Use the "Questions for Discussion" for essay topics or in-class discussion.

THE FACTS CONTINUED

On September 17, 1774, the delegates at the First Continental Congress endorsed the Suffolk Resolves. On September 26th, Richard Henry Lee of Virginia moved that non-importation from Britain and Ireland begin on November 1st. The Massachusetts delegation demanded that non-importation, non-exportation and non-consumption should start at once. The instructions to the Virginia delegation forbade it to agree to non-importation before the 1774 tobacco crop was marketed in the spring of 1775. Gadsden proposed that Congress go ahead anyway, but the Maryland and North Carolina delegations declared that they would not agree to start non-importation without Virginia. The rest of the delegation from South Carolina opposed non-exportation because the bulk of its commerce was the sale of rice and indigo to Britain. After two days of debates, the delegates agreed to stop importation of all goods from Britain and Ireland on December 1st, and to stop the use and purchase of any goods brought in thereafter.

On September 28, Galloway, a conservative from Pennsylvania, offered his "Plan of Union," which would have enabled either the British Parliament or a colonial parliament to initiate legislation affecting the colonies but required both bodies to adopt such legislation before it could take effect, essentially giving the American parliament a veto over British legislation effecting America. Private letters indicate that several of the delegations were split. The Galloway Plan was defeated by a vote of 6-5. Because the radicals wanted it to appear that Congress was united, the Galloway Plan and the closely divided vote on it were subsequently expunged from the minutes of the Continental Congress.

The debate was interrupted by another "express" by Paul Revere on October 6th. He brought a letter from the Boston committee of correspondence that the British fortifications being built in Boston seemed to indicate "the town and country are to be treated by the soldiery as declared enemies." The committee asked the advice of Congress on whether the people of Boston should stay or abandon the town. While Lee wanted Congress to advise that Boston be evacuated and Gadsden moved that Gage be attacked, Galloway countered that Massachusetts do as it pleased. The delegates debated until October 11th when they prepared a relatively restrained letter to General Gage urging him to stop fortifying Boston and to stop irritating the people while Congress was peaceably trying to restore harmony with Britain. They also sent a message to the people of Boston, advising them to only use force defensively.

The Congress then turned to the debate over a declaration of rights. The crucial issue was the authority of Parliament to regulate trade. Christopher Gadsden denied that Parliament had any such power. James Duane replied that the right of regulating trade was grounded on "compact, acquiescence, necessity, protection, not merely on our consent." The Congress deadlocked: five colonies voted to concede the power to Parliament, five voted against it. The Rhode Island and Massachusetts delegations each split. John Adams provided a compromise that satisfied no one but was accepted to preserve unity. His resolution conceded that while Parliament should regulate trade, the Congress maintained that they had not conceded the right for Parliament to do so. Before the Congress adjourned in late October 1774, it agreed to a restrained "Declaration of Rights and Resolves"; to a plan of non-exportation, non-importation and non-consumption of British goods; and to reconvene in May 1775 if Britain had not redressed the colonists' grievances. (See Document 8: "Declaration and Resolves of the First Continental Congress," October 14, 1774.)

Beginning December 1, 1774, the colonies would stop the importation of all goods from Britain and its other colonies. Non-consumption would start March 1, 1775. Non-exportation (e.g., the tobacco crop) would begin on September 10, 1775. A Continental Association would enforce the ban on all imports and exports through the establishment of committees, elected by persons qualified to vote for members of their provincial assembly, in "every county, city and town" in America. (See Document 9: The Articles of Association, October 20, 1774.)

The Congress concluded with a petition to the king; an address to the people of Great Britain urging them to choose members of Parliament "of such wisdom, independence and public spirit, as may save the violated rights of the whole empire from the devices of wicked Ministers and evil Counsellors;" an address to the people of North America; and an address to the inhabitants of Quebec inviting them to join the "more numerous British colonies."

Britain Receives Suffolk Resolves and the Colonists Petition

The British government received the "Suffolk Resolves" first, even while Congress was still meeting. While the delegates to the Continental Congress saw these Resolves as supporting a moderate position, the King and his ministers viewed the colonists' claim that the Coercive Acts were unconstitutional as absurd; they viewed the call for disobedience, the formation of colonial governments to withhold taxes from the royal government, the formation of a colonial militia and an economic boycott against Britain as a declaration of independence—a treasonous action which required a harsh response. The appeals to the "affection of his majesty," other affirmations of loyalty and more conciliatory wording in the Declaration of Rights and Resolves, were viewed as mere rhetoric. Instead of encouraging Britain to recognize the rights that the American colonists thought were their due, their list of rights and grievances and the economic boycott was seen as provocation by provinces seeking independence.

The newly elected Parliament, which opened in November 1774, continued to endorse the King's efforts to quell resistance and disobedience in Massachusetts. From early December through the middle of March 1775, Benjamin Franklin, in London as an agent of the Continental Congress, sent messages through intermediaries to members of the British ministry. He insisted that the Tea Act and the Coercive Acts must be repealed and that Parliament renounce legislative authority over the internal affairs of the American colonies. He met with Lord Chatham (William Pitt), who proposed a commission to work out an agreement. On January 19, 1775, Chatham, who had seldom appeared in Parliament in recent years because of ill health, brought Franklin with him and introduced a motion to withdraw General Gage's troops from Boston. Lord Camden and others sympathetic to the colonies supported the motion, but to no avail: the motion failed. Ten days later Lord Chatham, with Franklin conspicuously present, introduced a bill in the House of Lords that would have limited Parliament's authority in America mainly to the regulation of trade. The bill was severely defeated.

ACTIVITY TWO: MOCK NEGOTIATION BETWEEN BRITAIN AND THE COLONIES

The British Parliament has been in session during the winter of 1774-1775, debating how to respond to the Suffolk Resolves as well as to the colonists' Declaration of Rights and Resolves. Benjamin Franklin has been in London since December 1774 as an agent of the Continental Congress. He has met with Lord Chatham and others sympathetic to the colonists' position. However, Lord North, the king's chief minister, has not been willing to meet with Franklin.

Let us hypothesize that Lord North has agreed to meet with Benjamin Franklin to discuss ways to resolve the growing conflict between Britain and her North American colonies. Roleplay a mock negotiation between Lord North, representing Britain, and Benjamin Franklin, representing the colonies, in London in January 1775.

PARTICIPANTS

Benjamin Franklin, for the colonies. Franklin was born in Boston in 1706. At age 17 he left for Philadelphia, where he obtained employment as a printer, eventually setting up his own shop. His thrift and industry won him prosperity. His good sense and charm won him many influential friends. He was a member of the Pennsylvania Assembly from 1736-1751 and deputy postmaster for Philadelphia from 1737-1753. From 1748-1754 Franklin turned to philosophical studies and conducted his many electrical experiments. In 1757, he sailed to England to present to Parliament the grievances of the Pennsylvania Assembly against the proprietors. When he returned, he was sent again to obtain recall of the Pennsylvania charter, an effort that submerged in the controversy over the Stamp Act. In 1766, Franklin became "ambassador extraordinaire" for the colonies. By 1770, he had rejected the supreme authority of Parliament and came to believe that good relations with Britain could only be reestablished with the repeal of the duty on tea. After passage of the Coercive Acts in 1774, Franklin began to despair of reconciliation and his ideas on American rights became more radical. He was sent by the First Continental Congress to meet with representatives of the British Crown and Parliament to try to find a resolution to the growing conflict. He later served as a delegate to the Second Continental Congress, where he was a member of the committee to draft the Declaration of Independence. He was one of three commissioners appointed to negotiate a treaty with France in 1776. In 1781, he, John Jay and John Adams negotiated a peace treaty with Britain. He served as president of the executive council of Pennsylvania from 1785-1786. At the age of 81, Franklin took his seat at the 1787 Federal Convention. He died in 1790.

Benjamin Franklin

Frederick, Lord North

Frederick, Lord North, for the British Crown and Parliament. Born in 1732, North was educated at Eton and Trinity College, Oxford. In 1754 he was elected to Parliament for the family borough of Banbury. Following the death of Charles Townshend in 1767, North accepted the post of Chancellor of the Exchequer and, in 1768, he became Leader of the House of Commons. In 1770, North became Chief Minister on the resignation of his cousin, the Duke of Grafton. He initially sought a conciliatory approach with the American colonies and repealed four of the five Townshend duties, retaining the tax on tea. Lord North intended to make a lesson of Massachusetts by punishing the colony, with the belief that the other colonies would not support Massachusetts. North's ministry passed the Coercive Acts in 1774. By December, North realized that Britain was on the verge of war with her colonies. In January 1775, he proposed a peace commission, offering to eliminate the tea tax so long as the colonies promised to pay the salaries of civil authorities regularly. But it was too late. North offered his resignation to George III, but the King refused to accept it. Lord North also faced problems in Ireland, and was forced to relax restrictions on Irish trade in 1779. North was threatened by the mob during the riots in 1780 and finally the king allowed him to resign in 1782. In 1790 Lord North succeeded his father in the House of Lords. He died in 1792.

POSITIONS AND INTERESTS

Lord North

Positions

- If the colonies would pay for their defense and civil government, Parliament would not tax them.

- The colonies are benefiting from being part of the British Empire and should share in the costs of their governance and protection.

- Parliament maintains its right to regulate the external trade of the colonies

- Parliament has supreme authority over its colonies.

Interests

- Ease the tax burden on the British for the costs of defense and civil government in the colonies.

- Make the trade within the Empire more profitable for British financial and mercantile interests.

- Limit or eliminate popular challenges to the ruling establishment.

- Maintain the prerogatives and power of the King and Parliament.

- Maintain a great and profitable colonial empire.

Benjamin Franklin

Positions

- Parliament has exceeded its authority by directly taxing the colonists in violation of their rights as British subjects.

- The colonial legislatures should have a certain amount of autonomy over internal issues.

- Recognition of the Continental Congress as the legitimate representative of the voice of the English North American colonies.

- Loyal to the King as sovereign.

Interests

- Fear that the British will suppress the colonists' liberties.

- Fear that the British will subordinate colonists' economic interests in favor of British economic elites.

- Need to maintain colonial unity to avoid having the colonies played off against each other.

- More concerned about commerce and prosperity than ideology--Britain is their main trading partner.

- Value in having British army and navy protect them against foreign powers.

Teacher Instructions For Activity Two: Mock Negotiation

Preparation

1. Share the historical background with the class—either as a lecture and/or a reading assignment. Encourage students to try to gain as thorough an understanding as possible of the events, characters, and historical context.

2. Distribute student handout: "Positions and Interests" for students to read.

3. Hand out the brief biographies for students to review.

Directions

1. Count by 1, 2, 3 and divide into groups of three with one 1, one 2 and one 3 in each group. In each group,

   1s are Benjamin Franklin

   2s are Lord North

   3s are Observers/Reporters

2. Distribute student handout: "Mock British-Colonist Negotiations."

3. Review the setting and the directions with the students.

4. Encourage students to stay within the limits of historical reality but also try to use conflict resolution skills: listen actively, brainstorm, evaluate options.

Debriefing

1. Ask the observer/recorder/reporters to explain briefly what happened in each group. Summarize and compare the results and processes in each group.

2. Distribute and discuss "The Facts Continued" and "The Historical Effects."

3. Compare the results of the mock mediation with what actually occurred.

Alternate Activity: Mock Parliamentary Debate

Lord North claimed that the British public vigorously supported the government's coercive policies, but recent research in petitions and town records indicates that outside of Parliament and the political elite, there was considerable sympathy for the Americans and their criticism of government restrictions on their liberties and livelihood. These sympathizers identified with the actions against the American colonists as similar to the political and economic discrimination, oppression, and infringements they faced at home. Sympathizers came from all levels of society, including manufacturers concerned with overseas markets, merchants in the American trade, artisans and skilled tradesman suffering under economic constraints, and emerging radical political groups in London and other cities, including the followers of radical John Wilkes, who had been denied a seat in Parliament despite his election. American sympathizers also included a sizable percentage of clergymen and laity in non-Anglican religions. These were the so-called "Dissenting" religions: Presbyterians, Congregationalists, Baptists, and Quakers, who, despite the Act of Toleration, still faced numerous economic, religious, and political constraints, including prohibition from holding political office. However, while sympathy for the American colonists appears to have been widespread among the British public, there was no mobilized movement on their behalf, and royal patronage and other forms of influence, particularly in unrepresentative districts with comparatively few voters, helped generate the sizable majorities in Parliament that sustained the coercive policies toward the American colonies (See Document 10: Petition of London Merchants for Reconciliation with America, January 23, 1775.)

Have students role-play the British King, his Ministers and Parliament, and discuss how they would respond to the colonists' proposal. Have the students research the background of the potential British participants, such as King George III, Lord North, William Pitt (Lord Chatham), Edmund Burke and Lord Dartmouth.

THE FACTS CONTINUED

Britain's Response

*I*n February 1775, Parliament declared that Massachusetts was in a state of rebellion supported by illegal combinations in other colonies, and supported the King's intention to take "the most effectual measures to endorse the due obedience to the laws and authority of the Supreme Legislature." The Parliament adopted the Prohibitory or New England Restraining Act, which denied New Englanders access to the North Atlantic fisheries and restricted their external trade.

During the winter and spring of 1775, no news arrived in the American colonies. Committees of correspondence and revolutionary committees began replacing the legal governing bodies in defiance of their charters and began raising active militias ("Minute Men"). General Gage brought 4,000 troops into Boston.

In a show of force to halt the emergence of new extralegal provincial governments, the British Ministry, in April 1775, ordered General Gage to arrest "the principal actors and abettors" of insurrection in Massachusetts. Gage sent 700 troops from Boston in an early morning raid on April 19, 1775 to seize colonial arms and ammunition in nearby Concord. The Americans learned of the plan and Paul Revere alerted the countryside. When troops reached Lexington, 70 American militiamen were on the village green. An exchange of fire killed eight colonists and wounded eighteen. When the British arrived at Concord, their advance was blocked by militiamen. The British marched back to Boston, harassed along the way by American militiamen. By the end of the day, 273 British and 95 Americans had been wounded or killed. War had begun.

The Second Continental Congress

On May 10, 1775, the Second Continental Congress convened in Philadelphia to news of fighting at Lexington and Concord. Massachusetts reported that it had taken steps to raise 13,600 soldiers from its people and to secure additional men from New Hampshire, Connecticut and Rhode Island because British reinforcements in Boston were "daily expected." This New England force began besieging the British troops in Boston. However, reconciliation was still the hope of the delegates. Even the Massachusetts delegates were instructed to take measures "best calculated for the recovery and establishment of American rights and Liberties, and for restoring harmony between Great-Britain and the Colonies." Although no one seemed to favor separation from Britain, the delegates differed on the likelihood of reconciliation, on how best to seek it, and on what terms would be minimally acceptable.

But events moved more rapidly than the deliberations. On May 9, the day before Congress assembled, provincial troops, led by Ethan Allen of Vermont and Benedict Arnold of Connecticut, seized the British-held Fort Ticonderoga and the nearby British post at Crown Point. The fort guarded a major waterway which had been critical in the French and Indian War. The Americans captured the cannons from Fort Ticonderoga for the New England troops to use against the British in Boston. It took a week before the news arrived in Philadelphia. The Continental Congress claimed it as an act of defense, based on "indubitable evidence" that the British were planning to invade the colonies from Quebec (this rumor turned out to be false). On May 29, the Continental

Congress renewed its invitation to Quebec to join the American Provinces in their struggle against British oppression. However, the Canadians did not trust the American colonists because of their anti-Catholic history. The British saw these actions as an effort by the Americans to conquer Canada, exacerbating doubts about the sincerity of American professions of loyalty, and making a peaceful reconciliation more unlikely.

On June 2, Congress received an official request from Massachusetts that Congress assume responsibility for the soldiers already besieging Boston. A Continental Army of 20,000 was authorized and, on June 15, George Washington, a Virginian, was chosen as commander-in-chief, making it clear that this was not a regional force but a genuinely Continental Army. Before Washington assumed command on June 17th, the colonial troops inflicted some of the heaviest losses of the entire war on the British forces who seized the earthworks at the Battle of Bunker Hill. Although the British nominally won battle, they lost 42 percent of the 2,500 men involved, a cost too heavy to dislodge the Americans from the other heights overlooking Boston that the Americans began to fortify with the artillery seized from Fort Ticonderoga.

The Continental Congress exercised legislative, executive and judicial responsibilities. It tried to raise revenue and troops to support the army, made moves to secure the neutrality of the interior Indian tribes, issued paper money, regulated trade including supervising non-importation and non-exportation, erected a postal system, and approved plans for a military hospital. It operated under a system of "labored coordination and mutual concession." Not all of the 65 delegates were ever present at any one time. Decisions often were delegated to local committees for execution.

Meanwhile in England, Lord North pushed his "Conciliatory Proposal" through the Parliament. The proposal promised that Parliament would desist from taxing any colony that granted sufficient, permanent funds for the defense and the support of civil government (See Document 11: The Conciliatory Proposal, February 21, 1775.) But by the time it was received in the colonies, battles had already been fought. Before leaving Virginia to attend the Second Continental Congress in Philadelphia, Thomas Jefferson had drafted a reply to the "Conciliatory Proposal," which the Virginia House of Burgesses adopted on June 10, 1775. Virginia's response stated that while it considered reconciliation with the Mother Country "the greatest of all human blessings" except for the possession of liberty, after careful consideration it concluded that the proposal "only changes the form of oppression, without lightening its burden." Jefferson carried Virginia's reply with him to Philadelphia and conveyed to Congress the first notice the delegates had of it.

The Continental Congress made one last attempt at reconciliation with the adoption of the "Olive Branch Petition" on July 5, 1775. Written by John Dickinson of Pennsylvania, it expressed hope for a restoration of harmony, asserted Americans' loyalty to the king, and urged him to prevent further military action until reconciliation could be achieved. (See Document 12: Olive Branch Petition.) In a "Declaration of the Causes and Necessities of Taking Up Arms," written by Dickinson and Thomas Jefferson and adopted on July 6, 1775, Congress rejected independence, but refused to be "enslaved" and ominously raised the possibility of obtaining foreign aid from Britain's old enemy, France.

On July 8, 1775, the Continental Congress approved an address "to the Inhabitants of Great-Britain" stating that the Americans were acting in defense of "glorious Privileges" for which their "gallant and virtuous Ancestors" had "fought, bled, and conquered." The charges that they were "aiming at Independence" were but "the Allegations of Your Ministers," disproven by their petitions for redress and failure to seek the aid of rival powers. On July 13th, the Congress approved a "speech" for presentation to the Iroquois Confederacy in New York, asserting that the Americans wanted to retain "the covenant chain" that bound their fathers with Britain, an effort to build an alliance with the Natives and to keep them from helping the British. An address to Ireland two weeks later insisted that the British government had denigrated the American "rebels" for merely asserting the rights of all British subjects. The American colonists hoped that they could engage other areas of the British empire in their quest for what they saw as rights due all British citizens. Finally, the Congress sent King George an "Olive Branch

Petition" requesting that he remove obstacles to reconciliation. As late as August 1775, Jefferson wrote in a private letter that he sincerely wished for reunion and "would rather be in dependence on Great Britain, properly limited, than on any nation on earth, or than on no nation."

By the end of 1775 news arrived that the king had rejected the Olive Branch Petition, had proclaimed the colonies in "open and avowed rebellion," and had dispatched an additional 20,000 troops to quell the American Insurrection.

In January 1776, Thomas Paine's pamphlet, *Common Sense,* was widely distributed throughout the colonies and credited with converting many, particularly in the South, to independence and rejecting loyalty to the Crown. Paine, a largely self-educated Englishman who had only arrived in the colonies in 1774, emphasized immediate political, economic and military expediency. Although he presented no argument that had not been made repeatedly before, the pamphlet was written in a manner and form that was accessible to the general public. It helped many colonists to conclude, after their decade-long fruitless search for redress within the empire and ultimate disillusionment with the British king and Parliament, that independence was necessary. It also helped moved the debate in the Second Continental Congress during the spring of 1776 from prospects for reconciliation to how an independent America should be governed and how it might seek financial assistance from France and the Netherlands.

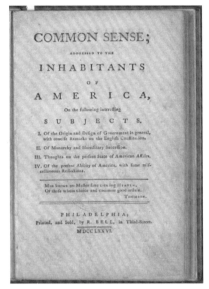

Common Sense, 1776

In June, a resolution was introduced by Richard Henry Lee of Virginia stating that the colonies ought to be free and independent of England. While this resolution was being considered, the Congress appointed a committee of five (Thomas Jefferson, John Adams, Benjamin Franklin, plus Roger Sherman of Connecticut and Robert Livingston of New York) to prepare a justification or statement of principles, a declaration of independence . On June 29th, Washington reported the arrival of some 50 British ships filled with troops at Sandy Hook near the entrance to New York harbor. Their number doubled within a few days as Washington prepared for the impending British attack on New York City. By July 1st, Congress also learned that another 53 British ships were outside of Charleston, South Carolina, and that an American army had been forced to retreat after an unsuccessful incursion into Canada. On July 2nd, 1776, twelve colonies voted in favor of independence, joined by New York a week later. The following day, the British landed on Staten Island and threatened New York City and the Jersey coast. While the British brought "the greatest fleet and the largest army ever assembled in North America into action against the Americans," the Continental Congress revised and finally adopted the Declaration of Independence on July 4, 1776.

The colonists were not well-prepared for war; however, they were fighting on their own land. After the Franco-American Alliance in 1778, British Peace Commissioners arrived in Philadelphia. The commissioners were willing to offer everything except independence, but by then the Americas believed they could win the war and would accept nothing less than independence. After British General Cornwallis surrendered to the American colonists at Yorktown on October 20, 1781, the war essentially came to an end, although minor battles between the British and the colonists continued for another two years. After several months of hard bargaining in 1782 by Benjamin Franklin, John Adams and John Jay, the British government of Lord Shelburne accepted American independence and a generous western boundary along the Mississippi River. A formal peace treaty was signed in Paris on September 3, 1783. The Peace Treaty was ratified by the Confederation of the United States of America on January 14, 1784. In addition to giving formal recognition to the United States, the treaty established the liberal boundaries for the United States, specified certain fishing rights, mandated creditors of each country to be paid, attempted to restore the rights and property of those colonists who had remained loyal to Britain, opened the Mississippi River to navigation by citizens of both nations and provided for the evacuation of all British forces. The new country began with an extensive expanse of land from the Atlantic Ocean to the Mississippi River.

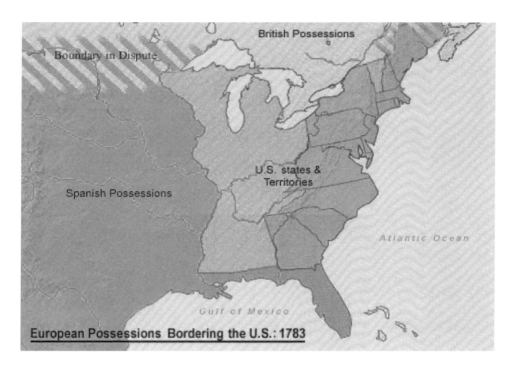

Boundaries of the United States as defined by the Treaty of Paris, 1783

QUESTIONS FOR DISCUSSION

1. What could the delegates at the First Continental Congress in 1774 have done to maintain a relationship with Britain?

2. Could a respected, influential voice of moderation, such as John Dickinson, have found a way to modify the support of the delegates at the First Continental Congress for the radical Suffolk resolves?

3. What role did timing play in limiting the effectiveness of concessions by the American colonists? By the British King and Parliament?

4. What could Parliament or King George have done to resolve the conflict with the colonies?

5. The taxes that Britain proposed to levy on the American colonies in the 1760s and 1770s were much lower than the taxes levied on the people in England. Why did Americans react so strongly against these taxes?

6. Do you think that the dispute between Britain and her American colonies was primarily economic or political? Support your opinion.

7. How important do you think the limitations established by the Proclamation Line were in worsening the relations between the American colonies and Britain? Compare the maps of the Proclamation Line of 1763 and the Treaty of Paris in 1783.

8. Identify the BATNAs (best alternative to a negotiated agreement) for the British and the Americans. Who had more to lose if they lost the war?

9. Why do you think that the British King and Parliament were insistent on maintaining British authority over the American colonies?

ADDITIONAL RESOURCES

Bailyn, Bernard. *Ideological Origins of the American Revolution.* Cambridge, MA: Harvard University Press, 1967.

Boyd, Julian P., ed. *The Papers of Thomas Jefferson*, Vol. 1 (1760-1776). Princeton: Princeton University Press, 1950.

Brown, Richard D., ed. *Major Problems in the Era of the American Revolution, 1760-1791.* Lexington, MA: D.C. Heath and Co., 1992.

Jensen, Merrill. *The Founding of a Nation: A History of the American Revolution, 1763-1776.* New York: Oxford University Press, 1968.

Journals of the Continental Congress, Vol. 1, 1774. Washington, D.C.: Government Printing Office, 1904.

Maier, Pauline. *American Scripture: Making the Declaration of Independence.* New York; Alfred A. Knopf, 1997.

_____. *From Resistance to Revolution: Colonial Radicals and the Development of American Opposition to Britain, 1765-1776.* New York: Alfred A. Knopf, 1972.

_____. *The Old Revolutionaries: Political Lives in the Age of Samuel Adams.* New York: Alfred A. Knopf, 1980.

Marston, Jerrilyn Greene. *King and Congress: The Transfer of Political Legitimacy, 1774-1776.* Princeton University Press, 1987.

McCullough, David. *1776.* New York: Simon and Schuster, 2005.

Messer, Peter C. *Stories of Independence: Identity, Ideology and History of Eighteenth-Century America.* DeKalb: Northern Illinois University Press, 2005.

Morgan, Edmund S. *Benjamin Franklin.* Yale University Press, 2002.

Morison, Samuel Eliot. *Sources and Documents illustrating the American Revolution, 1764-1788.* Oxford University Press, 1970.

Nash, Gary B. *Landmarks of the American Revolution.* New York: Oxford University Press, 2003.

_____. *The Unknown American Revolution: The Unruly Birth of Democracy and the Struggle to Create America.* New York: Viking, 2005.

Rakove, Jack N. *The Beginnings of National Politics: An Interpretive History of the Continental Congress.* New York, 1979.

Wood, Gordon. "Rhetoric and Reality in the American Revolution," *William and Mary Quarterly*, 3rd series 23 (1966): 3-32.

Documents on CD

Document 1:   The Proclamation of 1763

Document 2:   The Declaration of the Stamp Act Congress, 1765

Document 3:   The Declaratory Act, 1766

Document 4:   The Coercive Acts, 1774

Document 5:   Instructions by the Virginia Convention to Their Delegates in Congress, July, 1774

Document 6:   The Suffolk Resolves

Document 7:   Joseph Galloway's Plan of Union

Document 8:   Declaration and Resolves of the First Continental Congress, October 14, 1774

Document 9:   The Articles of Association, October 20, 1774

Document 10:   Petition of London Merchants for Reconciliation with America, January 23, 1775

Document 11:   Conciliatory Proposal, February 21, 1775

Document 12:   Olive Branch Petition, July 5, 1775

Teacher Overheads/Student Handouts on CD

1.   Map of the Proclamation Line of 1763

2.   Timeline, 1763-1783

3.   Steps in Mediation

4-13. Short biographies of Samuel Adams, Christopher Gadsen, Richard Henry Lee, William Livingston, George Reed, Silas Deane, James Duane, Joseph Galloway, Peyton Randolph and Charles Thomson.

14. Positions and Interests

15. Directions for the mock congressional caucus

16. What experiences led to the conflict?

17. Positions and interests of colonies and Britain

18. Directions for Negotiating, 1775

19. Short biography of Ben Franklin

20. Short biography of Lord North

21. What really happened?

22. The costs of the Revolutionary War

23. Map of the boundaries of the United States as defined by the Treaty of Paris in 1783

SOURCES AND CREDITS FOR ILLUSTRATIONS

p. 107: Map of the 1763 Proclamation Line, *The National Atlas of the United States*

p. 109: Colonists' View of the Stamp Act, *Library of Congress (LC) LC-USZ62242*

p. 110: Political Cartoon depicting a tarred and feathered tax collector, *LC-USZ62-43856*

p. 111: Paul Revere's Engraving of The Boston Massacre, *1770, The American Treasures of the Library of Congress*

p. 113: American Version of the Boston Tea Party, Reproduction based on engraving by D. Berger, 1784, *LC-USZC4-1582*

p. 113: British Version of the Boston Tea Party, Engraving by W.D. Cooper, London, 1789, *Library of Congress Rare Book Division*

p. 116: Samuel Adams, *NWDNS-148-CD-4-20*

p. 116: Christopher Gadsden, *The National Park Service*

p. 117: Richard Henry Lee, *NWDNS-148-CP-199*

p. 117: William Livingston, *The National Park Service*

p. 118: George Read, *Biographical Dictionary of the United States Congress*

p. 118: Silas Deane, *LC-USZ62-26779*

p. 119: Peyton Randolph, *NWDNS-148-GW-73 lb*

p. 120: Charles Thomson, *LC-USZ62-44786*

p. 125: Benjamin Franklin, *NWDNS-148-CD-14-20*

p. 125: Frederick, Lord North, *LC-USZ62-45299*

p. 130: Common Sense, *The American Treasures of the Library of Congress*

p. 131: Map of the 1783 Treaty of Paris, *University of Oregon*

CHAPTER SIX

ISSUES OF SLAVERY AT THE FEDERAL CONVENTION, 1787

OBJECTIVES

- To understand the interconnected issues regarding slavery, representation, commerce and union at the Federal Convention.

- To compare and contrast the positions and underlying interests of the delegates from various states at the Federal Convention.

- To understand what alternative solutions were available at the Federal Convention.

- To appreciate the long-term impact of decisions made about slavery in 1787.

CORRELATIONS WITH NATIONAL HISTORY STANDARDS

Era Two
Standard 3

The student understands how the values and institutions of European economic life took root in the colonies and how slavery shaped European and African life in the Americas.

- Explain the shift from indentured servitude to chattel slavery in the southern colonies.

Era Three
Standard 3A

The student understands the issues involved in the creation and ratification of the United States Constitution and the new government it established.

- Analyze the factors involved in calling the Constitutional Convention.

- Analyze the alternative plans considered by the delegates and the major compromises agreed upon to secure approval of the Constitution.

- Compare the arguments of Federalists and Anti-Federalists during the ratification debates and assess their relevance in late twentieth century politics.

OVERVIEW

*I*n the summer of 1787, delegates from twelve of the thirteen states met in Philadelphia to correct what they considered were the problems with the Articles of Confederation that had emerged since its ratification in 1781: Congress had no money and no power to get it from the states, no power to make state governments abide by international treaties or trade agreements, and no power to regulate trade among the states or to protect the property rights of individuals. While the delegates agreed that they needed a stronger national government, they feared too strong a central government and disagreed about how the states would be represented in a new and stronger national government, an issue that pitted large states against small states. They also divided over if and how slaves should be included in determining each state's representation in

Congress and whether or how long slave trade should continue, issues that generally set the southern slave states against the northern states, which had comparatively few slaves and were moving to end the institution of slavery. Although the delegates represented the various economic, political and ideological interests of their state and region, there were many areas of common concern: most importantly, the economic and national security problems of the new nation. While the delegates differed over the amount of power to give to the central government and also over slavery in a new republic based on individual liberty, they wanted to stay united and to avoid splitting into several small and weak republics. It was this desire to ensure that the new nation remain an enduring Union and one that could work effectively for the general welfare and the common defense that propelled the creation of the Constitution of the United States in 1787. While historians have traditionally focused on the debate over the degree of power for and within the new central government, the existence of black slavery was a powerful underlying and unresolved issue in 1787. It would rupture the Union seventy years later with a bloody Civil War.

HISTORICAL BACKGROUND

Slavery in the Colonies

Slavery played a significant role in the development of the American colonies. Slaves cleared forests, drained swamps, cultivated rice and tobacco and worked as domestic servants, artisans, skilled craftsmen or laborers. Slaves were common in most of the colonial seaboard cities as well as on farms and plantations. When the English seized the New Netherland colony in 1664, newly-named New York City had a higher percentage of slaves than Virginia. However, the southern states soon became the center of slavery.

The Spanish had brought African slaves to the Americas in the early sixteenth century, but the English were slow to adopt slavery. In 1619, a "Dutch Man-of-War" sold the Jamestown colony "20 and odd negroes." The Dutch probably considered these Africans slaves, but the English in Virginia most likely treated them as indentured servants since at least a few of the blacks who were sold in 1619 later showed up in records as free men and landowners. Indentured servants gained their freedom after serving their period of indenture (a contracted time of service), usually seven years. However, by 1660, Virginia had evolved into a society where slavery, that is, lifelong servitude which was also inherited by the children, was becoming increasingly common. Although both whites and blacks served as indentured servants, only blacks were slaves, and more and more Africans were being brought to the American colonies as slaves. By 1660, at least half of the 1,000 or so Africans in Virginia were slaves. By 1700, Virginia had at least 10,000 Africans, and almost all of them were slaves. Planters in Maryland, like Virginia, were using slaves to grow tobacco, and the institution of slavery became increasingly codified.

South Carolina, established in 1669, had slavery from the beginning, in part because many of its original leading settlers came from Barbados where slavery was already well established. The "Fundamental Constitution" of the colony, drafted in part by John Locke, explicitly provided for black slavery. By 1708, South Carolina had become the only colony with a black majority. Slaves were essential to the forest-products industry and the emerging rice and indigo plantations. By 1720, two-thirds of its population was slaves. In response to the bloody Stono Rebellion in 1739, South Carolina's white planter elites temporarily suspended the importation of slaves. By 1775, slaves were still about 60 percent of the population, but the Revolutionary War and the suspension of the African trade during and after the war, as well as immigration by whites into the Carolina backcountry, reduced the percentage of slaves to less than half the population by 1790.

Slavery grew less rapidly in the North. It was inconsistent with the Puritan, Quaker and Pietistic religious values and notions of community—although some members of all these faiths owned slaves. Rhode Island, which was not Puritan, was the only New England colony with a substantial slave population. It also became a center for the African slave trade, as its ships brought slaves from Africa to the West Indies and the South, often returning with Caribbean molasses which was converted into rum. Slavery was an important institution throughout the middle colonies, although objections were raised, mainly by Quakers and Mennonites (See Document 1: Resolutions of the German Mennonites, 1688.) In New York, slaves labored on farms, unloaded ships at wharves, provided skilled and unskilled urban labor, and everywhere provided domestic service. On the eve of the American Revolution, slaves were around 20 percent of the population in New Jersey and New York but probably no more than 10 percent of the population in Pennsylvania.

Between 1630 and 1775, approximately 340,000 slaves were imported to the mainland English colonies, mostly in the South. However, well before the Revolution, these colonies already had a self-sustaining slave population. Indeed, what became the United States was the only major slave society in the New World in which the slave population grew through natural increase. This was markedly different from the sugar colonies of the Caribbean, Brazil and Suriname, where the climate and conditions were so deadly that massive and continuous importations were necessary to maintain the slave populations. By the end of the eighteenth century, more than half a million black slaves labored in the thirteen colonies. The African slave trade proved highly profitable to many Europeans and Americans, and also to those in Africa who sold captives into the slave trade. Ship builders, merchants and seaman from New England and the mid-Atlantic colonies, as well as British investors and traders, all made money from human cargoes. By 1720, most of the slave ships headed for the North American mainland went to the Chesapeake or the Carolinas, where the worldwide demand for tobacco and rice made some planters very rich.

"Stowage of the British Slave Ship Brookes"
Caption reads "Plan of lower deck with the stowage of 292 slaves,
130 of these being stowed under the shelves...."

During the American Revolution, some free black men and African slaves enlisted in primarily northern units of the Continental Army, often with the encouragement of their masters, some of whom emancipated them for doing so. Massachusetts, Connecticut and Rhode Island organized some black battalions, but in these and other northern states, most blacks served in integrated units. Under southern influences, the Continental Congress and General Washington initially attempted to prohibit black enlistment. But, by early 1776, both the Congress and General Washington reversed their position. Similarly, Virginia, the largest state, initially prohibited blacks, slave or free, from serving in the military but later modified its position. These policy changes were not solely motivated by humanitarian or recruiting concerns. In late 1775, Lord Dunmore, the Royal Governor of Virginia, offered freedom to slaves willing to fight for the Crown. While this promoted southern fears of a race war, it also contributed to a re-evaluation of the initial ban on black soldiers. In 1779, the Continental Congress offered to compensate masters in South Carolina and Georgia who enlisted their slaves, but the legislatures in both states rejected this proposal.

Early Eighteenth Century Slave Trade

In 1775, slavery was legal in all thirteen colonies. However, during the Revolutionary period, opposition to slavery grew stronger. (See Document 2: Jefferson's Original Draft of the Declaration of Independence Indicting the British for Bringing Slavery to the Colonies, in 1776.) During and after the Revolutionary War, opponents of slavery formed abolitionist societies in all the northern states, usually led by local elites such as John Jay, Gouverneur Morris and Alexander Hamilton in New York and Benjamin Rush and Benjamin Franklin in Pennsylvania. The state constitutions of Massachusetts (1780) and New Hampshire (1784) were interpreted to prohibit slavery while Pennsylvania (1780), Connecticut (1783) and Rhode Island (1783) passed gradual emancipation acts. The Massachusetts' constitution declared that "all men were born free and equal," a provision interpreted by the courts to end slavery. Pennsylvania's gradual emancipation act provided that all children of slaves would be free but required to serve their mother's master as indentured servants until they turned twenty-eight. This balanced the master's property claims to the children against the goal of ending slavery. Efforts to pass gradual emancipation acts would not succeed in New York until 1799 and in New Jersey until 1804.

The American Revolution also influenced attitudes toward slavery in the South. Quakers in Virginia and North Carolina protested the institution, and small abolitionist societies formed in Virginia, Delaware, and Maryland. In 1782, Virginia allowed masters to manumit (free) slaves, leading to a significant number of private manumissions: between 1782 and 1810 the state's *free* black population grew from 2,000 to about 30,000. Although Maryland and Delaware were committed to the institution of slavery, there was a great deal of private manumission, and the slave population was beginning to decline in both states. The Revolution also had a profound effect on black communities, especially in the North. Serving with skill, honor and courage, black soldiers challenged existing beliefs about race. The dislocations from the Revolutionary War allowed many slaves to escape to freedom. During and after the war, free blacks organized churches, schools and other institutions. In 1786, Richard Allen began preaching to free blacks in Philadelphia. He helped organize the Free African Society in 1787 and, in 1794, organized the African Methodist Episcopal Church. Meanwhile, Phillis Wheatley, a young, free black woman in Boston, began publishing poems and essays. Wheatley's poetry went through numerous editions in England and America before her death in 1784. Although few in number, these black leaders in arts, religion and culture were living refutation of the predominant views of slaveowners regarding the inferiority of blacks.

In 1787, blacks were about 4 percent of the population in the northern states, and less than a quarter of them were slaves. By contrast, about 43 percent of the population in South Carolina and 40 percent of Virginia's population were slaves. The first national census in 1790 showed a total population of 3,900,000, of which 757,000 were "negroes." (See the 1790 Census: Total and Slave Populations by State, on page 149 and as a

Slaves hoeing tobacco

Slaves clearing a field to plant

handout on the CD.) Slaves were critical to the maintenance of the wealth and lifestyle of southern economic elites and political leaders. In addition, many white Southerners, including Thomas Jefferson, were very concerned about the idea of a large number of free blacks living among them.

During the Revolution, all the states banned the African slave trade, (in the case of the Carolinas and Georgia, it was simply suspended) and on the eve of the Federal Convention in 1787, the foreign slave trade was still closed throughout the nation. Virginia and Maryland had more slaves than they needed for their plantations, but the leaders of South Carolina and Georgia expected to import more slaves from abroad in the future. Slavery itself was illegal in Massachusetts and New Hampshire and being gradually abolished in Pennsylvania, Rhode Island and Connecticut. Slavery was legal and vigorous in Georgia, South Carolina, North Carolina, Virginia, Maryland, Delaware, New Jersey and New York. Despite its founding ideology of individual liberty and self-government, the United States was a slaveowning republic.

Slave advertisement, 1780

Background to the Federal Convention of 1787

The Federal Convention of 1787 grew out of the perception on the part of many leading Americans that the nation needed a stronger national government. Since the American Revolution had been, in part, a revolt against the abuse of power by the central government in London, the Second Continental Congress had created a relatively weak and decentralized government, without a single executive or a judiciary in the Articles of Confederation in 1781. (See Document 3: The Articles of Confederation.) The states were sovereign. The limited national power rested with the Congress, which consisted of a single house. Each state could send three to five delegates to the Congress, but no matter how many delegates the state had, each state had only one vote in Congress. This meant that tiny Rhode Island had as much political power as highly-populated Virginia.

Under the Articles of Confederation, Congress had no power to tax, only to request funds from the states. During the war, the national government teetered on the verge of bankruptcy, and the army often went unpaid. After the war, Congress was unable to pay off its debts, while the states ignored the agreements that Congress had made with foreign nations, including key provisions of the peace treaty with England. There was no national currency, and trade and tariff policies were basically in the hands of the states. Nationalists, such as George Washington, James Madison, Alexander Hamilton and John Jay, wanted a stronger central government empowered to regulate commerce, enforce treaty obligations, collect taxes and maintain an effective defense.

After a series of failed attempts to amend the Articles of Confederation (including the Annapolis Convention in 1786), the Congress authorized the thirteen states to send delegates to meet in Philadelphia in May 1787. In order for a state delegation to vote, it had to have at least two members present. Eventually, a total of fifty-five delegates from twelve states came to the Convention, but no more than eleven delegations were present at any one time: the delegation from New Hampshire did not arrive until mid-July, and the delegation from New York left in early July. Some of the same individuals were also serving as delegates to the Continental Congress, which was meeting at the same time in New York City. Rhode Island never sent a delegation to Philadelphia. Most delegates were politically experienced, and many were wealthy. At least twenty-six owned slaves, and more than half had legal training. To avoid public speculation and lobbying, the delegates met behind the sealed doors of the Pennsylvania statehouse (later known as "Independence Hall") and were sworn to secrecy. The Convention chose George Washington as its president.

The Convention and Issues Affected by Slavery

Most of the delegates shared a nationalist perspective, instilled through their extensive involvement with the national government. Thirty-nine had sat in Congress, where they had seen the defects of the Articles of Confederation firsthand. Although the purpose of the Convention was to propose "revisions" to the Articles of Confederation, it was clear from the start that many of the leaders of the Convention had more in mind. Madison and the delegation from Virginia arrived early in Philadelphia and worked with the Pennsylvania delegation to develop the "Virginia Plan," which was introduced by Edmond Randolph, the young governor of Virginia. The plan called for a radical restructuring of the government, from a federation of states into a national government, to provide for "common defence, security of liberty and general welfare." Thus, on May 29, began nearly four months of debates. During these debates, the delegates did not merely suggest revisions to the Articles of Confederation; they completely scrapped it for a whole new system of government.

Independence Hall, Philadelphia

Nevertheless, the Convention intended to create a government of limited powers. No one thought that the national government should, or could, regulate local affairs. The main issues were about the structure of the new government. Although slavery was not directly at issue, the delegates understood that slavery would affect national issues, such as representation in Congress, national taxation, domestic and foreign commerce, foreign affairs and military policy. No delegate thought that the Convention would empower Congress to end slavery, regulate the treatment of slaves or provide for the manumission of slaves. Slavery was seen as an institution controlled by each state.

Representation and Slavery

The issue of representation in the new government began with the Virginia Plan, which proposed a bicameral legislature and fixed representation in both houses proportional to each state's population and/or wealth. The Virginia Plan's call for "rights of suffrage in the National Legislature . . . proportioned to the Quotas of contributions, or to the number of free inhabitants..." aroused immediate opposition (Farrand, *Records of the Federal Convention of 1787*, Volume 1, 20–22). On May 30, James Madison moved to delete the term "free inhabitants" because he understood the potential for slavery to "divert" attention "from the general question whether the principle of representation should be changed" from states to population. George Read declared that the deputies from Delaware could not assent to "any change in the rule of suffrage..." (Farrand I, 35-37). The Convention adjourned.

On June 15, William Paterson proposed the "New Jersey Plan" as a substitute for the Virginia Plan. His plan would have continued a single chamber with equal representation for each state but would have revised the Articles of Confederation to enlarge the powers of the national government and to enable the Congress to requisition (or tax) each state "in proportion to the whole number of white & other free citizens & inhabitants of every age sex and condition including those bound to servitude for a term of years & three-fifths of all other persons not comprehended in the foregoing description, except Indians not paying taxes" (Farrand I, 243). The three-fifths ratio for counting black slaves was not a new idea. It had originated with a 1783 amendment proposed to change the basis for determining the wealth of each state from real estate to population in the Articles of Confederation. This would have increased the financial obligations of the southern states to the national government. In 1783, the North proposed counting all slaves and the South insisted that slaves were not as productive as white males. On June 18, 1787, Alexander Hamilton from New York opposed the New Jersey Plan because it did not create a sufficiently strong federal government. He argued that the problems with the existing structure of government were too great to be solved by Paterson's plan, which was rejected 7-3 on June 19th.

By June 30, the Convention was at a standstill over the issue of representation in the Congress, and Madison noted "that the States were divided into different interests not by their difference of size, but by other circumstances; the most material of which resulted partly from climate, but principally from their having or not having slaves. These two causes concurred in forming the great division of interests in the States. It did not lie between the large and small States: it lay between the northern and southern, and if any defensive power were necessary, it ought to be mutually given to these two interests" (Farrand I, 486). The question of representation was sent to a committee composed of one delegate from each state, and the Convention adjourned until July 5th. The Committee proposed an upper house with each state having equal votes and a lower house based on population, with slaves to be counted as three-fifths of other persons for purposes of determining representation (Farrand I, 524). A five-man committee was appointed to redraft the clause on July 6th (Farrand I, 538). William Paterson protested against the three-fifths clause for purposes of representation, and a four-day debate over slavery and representation continued (Farrand I, 561). This debate was necessitated by the need to establish the size of the first House of Representatives before a census would be taken in 1790.

Rufus King, from Massachusetts, warned that the South would not unite with the rest of the country "unless some respect were paid to their superior wealth" (Farrand, I, 562). He also reminded his northern colleagues that if they expected "preferential distinction in Commerce," they should be willing to give up something. On July 10, without the benefit of a census, the delegates allocated thirty-five seats in the new Congress to the northern states and thirty to the southern states. Charles Pinckney, from South Carolina, asserted that the South only wanted "equality" so that Congress would not pass commercial regulation favorable to the North. The Convention adopted an apportionment scheme for representation in the first Congress and on July 11 debated the provision for a census to determine future representation in Congress. Pierce Butler, also from South Carolina, and General Pinckney moved that "blacks be included in the rule of representation, equally with whites" (Farrand I, 575). Nathaniel Gorham of Massachusetts protested that when the three-fifths ratio was originally proposed in 1783 as part of a plan to raise revenues, the delegates from the states having slaves argued that slaves were inferior to freemen and should not be counted equally. Butler insisted that:

> the labour of a slave in South Carolina was as productive and valuable as that of a freeman in Massachusetts, that as wealth was the great means of defence and utility to the Nation they were equally valuable to it with freeman; and that consequently an equal representation ought to be allowed for them in a Government which was instituted principally for the protection of property, and was itself to be supported by property (Farrand I, 580).

Responding for Virginia, George Mason said that he "could not agree with the motion for equal representation of blacks, notwithstanding that it was favorable to Virginia, because he thought it was unjust" (Farrand I, 581). Butler's motion was defeated, and the debate continued. Rufus King suggested that the inclusion of blacks along with whites would excite great discontent among the states having no slaves. James Wilson of Pennsylvania did not see on what principle the inclusion of blacks in the proportion of three-fifths could be explained. "Are they admitted as Citizens? Then why are they not admitted on an equality with white citizens? Are they admitted as property? Then why is not other property admitted into the computation?" These difficulties, however, he thought "must be overruled by the necessity of compromise" (Farrand I, 587). Gouverneur Morris was equally unhappy with the idea of including slaves as three-fifths for purposes of representation. He declared that he was "reduced to the dilemma of doing injustice to the Southern States or to human nature," and he chose the former, asserting that he "could never agree to give such encouragement to the slave trade" by allowing the slave states "a representation of their negroes;" and he "did not believe those States would ever confederate on terms that would deprive them of that trade" (Farrand I, 588). A motion for counting blacks in the proportion of three-fifths for purposes of representation was defeated, and the debate continued.

Meanwhile the Continental Congress, which has been at a standstill for lack of a quorum for most of June, gained sufficient delegates to return to its discussion about the land ordinance regarding the northwestern territory. (Two delegates from North Carolina and two from Georgia were serving as delegates to both the Federal Convention in Philadelphia and the Continental Congress in New York.) On July 9th, the Congress agreed to include a provision in the ordinance to prohibit slavery north of the Ohio River and provide for the return of fugitive slaves. Article 6 of the Northwest Ordinance, as passed by the Continental Congress on July 13, 1787, banned slavery in the Northwest Territory. (See Document 4: Article 6 of the Northwest Ordinance.) This provision was supported by the delegates from Virginia, North Carolina, South Carolina and Georgia, as well as Massachusetts, New York, New Jersey and Delaware.

Back at the Federal Convention in Philadelphia, after heated debate on July 12, the three-fifths clause was provisionally approved as part of the Connecticut Compromise, which proposed representation in the House by population and representation in the Senate by state. However, the basis for representation in the House was redebated and reconsidered repeatedly over the next two months before final adoption. Although South Carolina's delegates were willing to accept full taxation for slaves if they also were fully counted for representation, Gouverneur Morris, from Pennsylvania, argued there would never be direct taxes because it was "idle to suppose that the General Government can stretch its hand directly into the pockets of the people scattered over so vast a Country." At one point, Morris suggested that "the Southern Gentlemen will not be satisfied unless they see the way open to their gaining a majority in the public Councils." Pierce Butler responded, "The security the Southern States want is that their negroes may not be taken from them which some gentlemen within or without doors, [inside or outside of the Convention] have a very good mind to do." Six southern states demanded substantial representation for their slave population or they would oppose the Constitution. Morris was prepared to call their bluff, but no other northern delegate was willing to join him (Farrand I, 597-604).

Map showing the Mason-Dixon Line

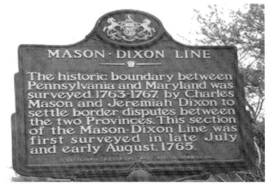

Mason-Dixon Line Marker

All of the delegates understood that although there were moral implications to the debate over counting slaves for representation, the debate was really about political power. If the Constitution did *not* count slaves for representation, then the five states south of the Mason-Dixon Line expected to have about 41 percent of the representatives in the Congress. If slaves were counted fully, the five states believed they would have about half of the seats in Congress. Under the three-fifths clause, these states expected to have about 47 percent of the seats in Congress.

Commerce and Slave Trade

The northern delegations wanted a constitution that would authorize Congress to regulate commerce by a simple majority vote. The southern delegations stated that they wanted no national regulation of commerce; however, they understood that some regulation was necessary. Some Southerners argued for regulation of commerce by a two-thirds majority in Congress and demanded an absolute ban on export taxes by the states or the federal government. In addition to southern concerns about taxing their agricultural exports, South Carolina and Georgia feared Congress would use the commerce clause to end the African slave trade. Even though their states were not currently importing slaves from Africa, they wanted to preserve the right to reopen the trade if they deemed it necessary. But the delegates from southern states were split on the issue: all the delegates from Virginia and some from Maryland opposed the slave trade on moral, economic and prudential grounds. Both states had a surplus of slaves which they could sell to the Deep South. The northern states were also split: Pennsylvania, New Jersey and Delaware opposed the slave trade on moral grounds; the delegates from Connecticut argued that the North should not force its morality on another section of the country.

During the debate on August 22, Roger Sherman declared that he disapproved of slave trading, but that "as the States were now possessed of the right to import slaves, as the public good did not require it to be taken from them, and as it was expedient to have as few objections as possible to the proposed scheme of government," he thought it best to "leave the matter as we find it" and noted that the abolition of slavery seemed to be proceeding anyway. George Mason complained that the "infernal traffic originated in the avarice of British merchants," and suggested that the express prohibitions against the importation of slaves by the states of Maryland, Virginia and North Carolina would be in vain if South Carolina and Georgia were at liberty to import slaves. (See Document 5: Excerpts from the Debate and Vote on the Slave Trade, Farrand II, 370.)

Charles Pinckney declared that "If slavery be wrong, it is justified by the example of all the world," and cited Greece, Rome, other ancient states, and modern states like France, England and Holland, all of which sanctioned slavery. He also suggested that if the southern states were left alone, they would probably stop importing slaves. However, attempts to take away the right would produce serious objections to the Constitution. General Pinckney insisted that South Carolina and Georgia could not do without slaves; that Virginia would gain by stopping importation and that the importation of slaves was for the interest of the whole Union—the more slaves, the more agricultural goods to be carried by northern ships, the more consumption, the more revenue for the common treasury. Since Virginia had a surplus of slaves, an end to foreign importation of slaves would enhance the value of the slaves that Virginia could sell to other southern states. Rutledge aggressively declared: "If the Convention thinks that North Carolina, South Carolina and Georgia will ever agree to the plan unless their right to import slaves be untouched, the expectation is in vain. The people of those States will never be such fools as to give up so important an interest." (See Document 6: Excerpts from the Debate and Vote on the Fugitive Slaves, Farrand II, 371- 373.) The issue was referred to the Committee of Detail which reported on August 25.

Fugitive Slaves

On August 28, Pierce Butler and Charles Pinckney moved "to require fugitive slaves and servants to be delivered up like criminals" (Farrand II, 443). They were mocked for this suggestion. Pennsylvania's James Wilson complained that this "would oblige the Executive of the State to do it at public expense." Roger Sherman saw "no more propriety in the public seizing and surrendering a slave or servant, than a horse." Butler withdrew the proposal. However, the next day Butler introduced a provision that "if a person bound to service or labor in the U-[United] States shall escape into another State, he or she shall be...delivered up to the person justly claiming their service or labor (Farrand II, 454). This clause was inserted after the extradition clause for discussion by the delegates.

Mock Mediation: Delegate Caucus in 1787

A After a long, hot summer of negotiation and renegotiation, the delegates to the Federal Convention were at loggerheads about the slave trade and the commerce clause; whether the national government should enforce the return of fugitive slaves; and whether and how slaves should be included in the population count for determining representation in the federal legislature.

Have your students conduct a mock caucus of selected delegates at the Federal Convention in Philadelphia. It is August 1787. As they often did in reality, we will have a hypothetical break where some delegates have retired to the City Tavern for dinner and to caucus about these three highly charged issues relating to slavery. Either Benjamin Franklin or George Washington, both highly respected by the other delegates, will help to mediate the discussion and to bring the delegates to a resolution on these issues.

The Participants

Pierce Butler (South Carolina: 1744–1822) Pierce Butler was born in Ireland and settled in South Carolina in 1771. A wealthy planter with more than 100 slaves, he served in the South Carolina legislature from 1778–82 and 1784–89. At the Convention, Butler argued that "the labour of a slave in South Carolina was as productive and valuable as that of a freeman in Massachusetts," and since the national government "was instituted principally for the protection of property," slaves should be counted fully for representation. In a heated debate with Gouverneur Morris, Butler declared that "The security the Southern States want is that their negroes may not be taken from them which some gentlemen within or without doors, have a very good mind to do." He strongly opposed ending the slave trade and introduced the fugitive slave clause requiring states to return runaways to their masters. Fearful of any actions that would threaten slavery, he was zealously committed to protecting the institution. He later served in the U.S. Senate (1789–96, 1802–06).

Pierce Butler

John Dickinson

John Dickinson (Delaware: 1732–1808) John Dickinson was born in Maryland but grew up in Delaware. He practiced law and held numerous public offices in both Pennsylvania and Delaware. In *The Letters from a Pennsylvania Farmer* (1768), he denied Parliament had any power to tax the colonies. He served in the Stamp Act Congress and the Continental Congress, where he advocated keeping open the chance for reconciliation with Britain and also chaired the committee which drafted the Articles of Confederation. Although Dickinson opposed British measures such as the Stamp Act, he disapproved of violent resistance and hoped for reconciliation between the colonies and England. He refused to sign the Declaration of Independence but then enlisted in the Continental Army. Dickinson owned slaves but fiercely opposed the continuation of the slave trade, a practice which he felt was "inadmissible on every principle of honor and safety." He also believed that the representatives of the Deep South were bluffing when they said that they would reject the Constitution if they did not get their way on the slave trade.

Rufus King

Rufus King (Massachusetts: 1755–1827) Rufus King was the eldest son of a successful merchant. He graduated from Harvard in 1777, was admitted to the bar in 1780 and opened an office in Newburyport. He was a delegate to Congress from 1784–86. Although he originally opposed any radical alteration of the Articles of Confederation, in the Convention he argued for a strong central government. After the Convention, King moved to New York City. He was elected to the New York Assembly and as a U.S. Senator from that state. In 1791, he also was elected as director of the Bank of the United States. He served as minister to Great Britain under Washington from 1796–1803. King was the Federalist candidate for vice-president in 1804 and 1808. King opposed the War of 1812. In his last term in the Senate, he opposed admitting Missouri as a slave state during the Missouri Compromise debates in 1820.

James Madison

James Madison (Virginia: 1751–1836) James Madison was educated at the College of New Jersey (Princeton University) and served on the committee which framed Virginia's constitution and Declaration of Rights in 1776. As a delegate to the Continental Congress, he suggested that state contributions to the federal government be based on population and incorporate the three-fifths rule for counting slaves. This "federal ratio" was the model for the three-fifths compromise at the Constitutional Convention. At the Convention, Madison argued strongly for a powerful central government with representation based on population rather than the states themselves, a plan which would benefit more populous states such as Virginia. He feared that giving equal representation to the states would result in a northern majority, although he assumed, like many Southerners, that the development of the trans-Appalachian west would bring the South more into population parity with the North. Like other Virginians, he was opposed to the slave trade. Unlike most other Southerners, Madison favored giving the federal government authority to regulate commerce. Madison took extensive notes of the proceedings of the Convention, and spoke out strongly for ratification of the Constitution. Madison served in Congress, as Secretary of State, and in 1809 became the fourth president.

George Mason

George Mason (Virginia: 1724/5–1792) George Mason was a wealthy, slaveholding planter who held numerous positions in local government and served with George Washington in the Virginia House of Burgesses in 1759. During the revolutionary period, he helped draft the Virginia state constitution and Declaration of Rights which influenced the Declaration of Independence and the Bill of Rights of the U.S. Constitution. Mason denounced slavery as an evil system that produced "the most pernicious effect on manners," and "would bring the judgment of heaven on the Country." Yet, he only argued that the national government should have the power to end the African slave trade (an action which would have benefited Virginia planters who had a surplus of slaves in 1783), not slavery itself. Mason played an active part in the Federal Convention but finally refused to sign the Constitution and campaigned against its ratification because he saw it as creating too strong a central government.

Gouverneur Morris

Gouverneur Morris (Pennsylvania: 1752–1816) Gouverneur Morris was born in the manor house at Morrisania, New York. His grandfather, Lewis Morris, served as Chief Justice of New York and governor of New Jersey. Morris graduated King's College (now Columbia University) in 1768 and was admitted to the bar in 1771. When the war began, Morris became an ardent supporter of the Revolution. In 1777, along with John Jay and Robert Livingston, Morris helped draft the New York State Constitution. After service in the Continental Congress, Morris moved to Philadelphia where he practiced law. As a delegate from Pennsylvania to the Convention of 1787, Morris favored a strong, centralized government. He strenuously opposed equal representation in the Senate, the concessions to slavery in the three-fifths clause and the compromise over the slave trade. He declared that the three-fifths clause and the compromise over the slave trade "when fairly explained comes to this: that the inhabitant of Georgia and South Carolina who goes to the Coast of Africa, and in defiance of the most sacred laws of humanity tears away his fellow creatures from their dearest connections and damns them to the most cruel bondages, shall have more votes in a Government instituted for protection of the rights of mankind, than the Citizen of Pennsylvania or New Jersey who views with a laudable horror, so nefarious a practice." In spite of these concerns, he was a firm supporter of the final Constitution. In 1789 he replaced Jefferson as minister to France until he was expelled by the Revolutionary French government. He was U.S. Senator from New York from 1800 to 1802 before retiring to the family mansion.

William Paterson (New Jersey: 1745–1806) William Paterson was born in Ireland and raised in New Jersey. He graduated from the College of New Jersey (Princeton University) in 1763 and practiced law until 1775, when he entered politics. He helped write New Jersey's constitution and was elected state attorney general. He later served as governor of New Jersey, U.S. Senator, and as associate justice of the U.S. Supreme Court. Although a slave owner, Paterson opposed the three-fifths compromise, stating that he regarded "negroe slaves in no light but as property. They are not free agents, have no personal liberty, no faculty of acquiring property, but on the contrary are themselves property, and like other property entirely at the will of their master."

William Paterson

Charles Cotesworth Pinckney

General Charles Cotesworth Pinckney (South Carolina: 1746–1825) General Pinckney studied law in England and began practice in his native South Carolina in 1770. He entered the Continental Army in 1775 as a colonel and was a general before his discharge. Like his younger cousin, Charles Pinckney who was also a delegate from South Carolina, General Pinckney was deeply committed to protecting his state's interests and was a tenacious defender of slavery at the Convention. He threatened to vote against the plan "if the Committee should fail to insert some security to the Southern States against an emancipation of slaves." He urged that "blacks be included in the rule of Representation, equally with whites," and was unhappy with the three-fifths compromise. He argued strongly against ending the slave trade and was a supporter of the fugitive slave clause. In the end, he was very satisfied that the new Constitution protected slavery. He was an unsuccessful candidate for U.S. president in 1804 and 1808.

Roger Sherman (Connecticut: 1721/22–1793) Roger Sherman was born in Newport, Massachusetts. He received no formal education beyond the common schools, but throughout his life he read widely. At age 20, Sherman moved to Connecticut where he became the surveyor for New Haven County. This position was unusually lucrative, and Sherman became a considerable landowner. In 1754, he was admitted to the Litchfield bar and was elected to the General Assembly in 1755. At age forty, he moved to New Haven and opened various businesses. He served in the Connecticut state legislature from 1764 to 1785. Frustrated with the limitations of the Confederation, Sherman drew up a series of amendments designed to strengthen it. He entered the Federal Convention still "disposed to patch up the old scheme of Government," but soon saw the need for creating a new system. Sherman actively campaigned for ratification of the Constitution. He was elected to the U.S. Congress in 1789 and to the U.S. Senate in 1791.

Roger Sherman

James Wilson

James Wilson (Pennsylvania: 1742–1798) James Wilson moved from his native Scotland in 1765, settled in Philadelphia, studied law with John Dickinson, and by 1774 was a successful attorney and a committed opponent of English rule. In an essay written in 1774, he set out a number of arguments challenging Parliamentary authority over the American colonies. He signed the Declaration of Independence as a delegate to the Second Continental Congress. A firm believer in popular sovereignty, Wilson favored the direct election of the president and members of both houses of Congress, rejecting the idea of equal representation for each state in the Senate. He vigorously supported the three-fifths clause and the compromise over the slave trade, but he expressed concern that the fugitive slave clause would cost the northern states money by requiring them to track down runaway slaves. While Wilson was personally opposed to slavery, he believed that compromise was necessary. He later served on the U.S. Supreme Court but died in disgrace, fleeing creditors.

POSITIONS AND INTERESTS

Not every member of each state delegation uniformly supported every position. For example, Madison fully supported the Commerce Clause, while the Virginia delegation as a whole did not. Similarly, James Wilson supported the slave trade compromise, while the Pennsylvania delegation as a whole did not. Nevertheless, there were positions and interests.

The South

Positions

- Slave trade was necessary for the economies and prosperity of the southern states.

- South Carolina threatened to walk out of the union if slaves were not included in representation. Virginia believed it was morally entitled to the most delegates in Congress because it was the most populous state.

- Slaves constituted an interest in the political economy of the society and that interest should be represented according to the population of slaves.

- Slaveowners' considerable property investments in their slaves should be recognized.

- Slavery was not immoral. It was a legitimate institution found in all the successful republics of the ancient world.

- Slavery was the best system of race relations for controlling the dangerous impulses of the blacks.

Interests

Economic

- South Carolina delegates admitted that slavery was highly profitable for slaveowners and for the country.

- Virginia and Maryland had more slaves than they needed—it was to their economic benefit to end the international slave trade which was bringing in additional slaves, and thus diluting the value of their excess slaves at the auction block. South Carolina and Georgia could get additional slaves at a lower price from foreign slave trade than if they bought slaves from Virginia or Maryland.

- Southern slaveowners did not want to lose their significant investment in their slaves.

- Southern delegates wanted to make sure that the new Congress would not eliminate slave trade or pass commercial regulations favoring the northern states at the expense of southern agricultural exports.

Political

- Counting slaves as three-fifths or equal with whites would give slaveowning states more political clout in the new Congress than if slaves were not counted for purposes of representation.

- Southern states wanted to form a stronger national government for defense and economic benefits, but with limited powers.

Security

- Southern whites feared the social impact of large numbers of freed slaves (never publicly stated).

The North

Positions

Delaware, Pennsylvania and New Jersey argued that:

- Slavery was immoral and should not be supported in a government of free people.

- Slaves were not citizens and did not vote; therefore they should not be counted for representation.

- The African slave trade was particularly immoral, so Congress should have the power to end it.

- Slavery weakened the national government, especially in times of war (Ten of thousands of slaves responded to British offers of freedom and fled to British lines during the American Revolution)

Massachusetts and Connecticut argued that:

- The United States needed a Union of all the states to form a national marketplace.

- The North wanted stronger central regulation of commerce to protect property and to prevent states from being played off against each other by foreign powers.

- Southern property interests in slaves must be respected.

Interests

Economic

- The North wanted a national commerce clause to protect their mercantile and shipping interests.

- They had a commercial interest in brokering and transporting the agricultural products of slavery.

- The northern states wanted to form a stronger union for defense and economy.

Political

- The northern states were concerned about the allocation of political power—counting slaves as part of population for purposes of determining representation in Congress gave the South more political power.

- Having one vote per state was important for both smaller states and those which could not expand westward, such as Delaware, New Jersey and the states of New England.

- The fugitive slave clause would involve all states in supporting the institution of slavery; hunting people who have taken great risks to achieve their freedom was particularly immoral.

- Northern states wanted the southern states to agree to a stronger national government.

State	Total Population	Slave Population	Percentage Slave Population
Connecticut	237,946	2,764	1.2
Delaware	59,096	8,887	15
Georgia	82,548	29,264	35.3
Kentucky	73,667	12,430	16.9
Maryland	319,728	103,036	32.2
Massachusetts	378,787	0	0
New Hampshire	141,885	158	0.1
New Jersey	184,139	11,423	6.2
New York	340,120	21,324	6.3
North Carolina	393,751	100,783	25.6
Pennsylvania	434,373	3,737	0.9
Rhode Island	68,825	958	1.4
South Carolina	249,073	107,094	43
Tennessee	35,691	3,417	9.6
Vermont	85,425	0	0
Virginia	691,737	292,627	42.3
Totals	3,776,791	697,902	18.5

1790 Census: Total and Slave Populations by State

DIRECTIONS FOR THE MOCK MEDIATION

Preparation

1. Share the historical background with the class. Focus on the people involved and their positions and interests in order to gain a thorough understanding of the events, characters and historical context.

2. Summarize what has already taken place at the Convention. For example, the Connecticut Compromise has already been accepted but can be reopened for further discussion by the delegates and the mediator.

3. Distribute Student Handout: "Positions and Interests" for students to read.

4. Distribute the brief biographies for students to review.

Directions

1. Divide the class into groups of seven or eleven, as follows (make sure that there is an historically accurate representation of states and views):

    Delegates:

    Rufus King (Massachusetts) and/or Roger Sherman (Connecticut)

    James Wilson and/or Gouverneur Morris (Pennsylvania)

    William Paterson (New Jersey) and/or John Dickinson (Delaware)

    George Mason and/or James Madison (Virginia)

    Pierce Butler and/or General Charles Cotesworth Pinckney (South Carolina)

    Mediator: Benjamin Franklin OR George Washington

    Observer/Recorder/Reporter: Mark Anthony, a fictitious slave, OR Reverend Richard Allen

    Optional Delegates: You may wish to add some of the following as additional or alternate delegates: Elbridge Gerry (Massachusetts), Oliver Ellsworth (Connecticut), George Read (Delaware), Luther Martin (Maryland), Alexander Hamilton (New York), Hugh Williamson (North Carolina), Charles Pinckney (South Carolina) and Abraham Baldwin (Georgia). If you use one or more of the optional delegates, have your students research their historical backgrounds.

2. Distribute Student Handout: "The Mock Mediation" and review the roles for the facilitator, the delegates and the observer/recorder/reporters.

3. Review the setting and roles, positions and interests with the students and have them proceed with their mock caucuses.

Debriefing

1. Once the groups have finished, bring the class back together for a discussion. Have each observer/ reporter/recorder describe how the process worked in their group.

2. Summarize and compare the results from each group.

3. Review "The Facts Continued." Compare the results of the mock caucus with what actually happened at the Constitutional Convention. Discuss why the results did or did not differ from the historical reality.

4. Use the "Questions for Discussion" for essay topics or for further in-class discussion.

THE FACTS CONTINUED

The Constitution that the framers completed in September 1787 resulted from a four-month negotiation and debate in which possibilities were tested, rejected, and then revised and adjusted according to the changing perspectives of the various delegates. Although leaving much authority to the states, the new Constitution established a national government clearly superior to the states. It totally abandoned the notion of a federation of virtually independent states. It vested Congress with the authority to levy and collect taxes, to regulate interstate commerce, to conduct diplomacy, declare war and raise an army. States could no longer coin money, interfere with contracts and debts or tax interstate commerce. The acts and treaties of the United States became "the supreme law of the land." The inability to fully resolve the issue of power between the federal and state governments led to federalism: a system of shared power and dual lawmaking. Slavery was treated as a political, not a moral, issue at the convention and many compromises were made.

Representation

The framers agreed that: "Representation and direct Taxes shall be apportioned among the several States which may be included within this Union, according to their respective Numbers, which shall be determined by adding to the whole Number of free Persons, including those bound to Service for a Term of Years, and excluding Indians not taxed, *three-fifths of all other persons [emphasis added]*." (See Document 7: United States Constitution, Article I, section 2.)

The vote was:

YES: Connecticut, Pennsylvania, Maryland, Virginia, Georgia

NO: New Jersey, Delaware

Divided: Massachusetts, South Carolina

The Result: Slaves would be counted as three-fifths for representation in the lower house of Congress, for taxes and for the makeup of the electoral college which was based on representation in Congress. The proportionate share of the population by the southern states turned out to be only 44.8 percent based on the 1790 census rather than the 47 percent which had been expected at the convention. Thereafter, the southern share declined. Ironically, while most of the delegates at the convention expected the Senate to protect the northern states, in fact, it has more frequently protected the southern states. Article 1, section 2 was changed by the Fourteeneth Amendment in 1868.

The Slave Trade

The framers agreed that: "The migration or importation of *such persons* as the several States now existing shall think proper to admit, shall not be prohibited by the Legislature prior to the year 1808, but a Tax or duty may be imposed on such importation, not exceeding ten dollars for each Person." (Article I, section 9) "No Amendment which may be made prior to the Year 1808 shall in any Manner affect the first and fourth clauses in the Ninth Section of the first Article... [emphasis added]" (See Document 8: United States Constitution, Article V.)

The vote was:

YES: New Hampshire, Massachusetts, Connecticut, Maryland, North Carolina, South Carolina and Georgia

NO: New Jersey, Pennsylvania, Delaware, and Virginia

Result: The African slave trade would continue until 1808 and any import tax on slaves would not be more than $10 a person.

Fugitive Slaves

The agreement reached by the framers regarding fugitive slaves was: "No Person held to Service or Labour in one State, under the Laws thereof, escaping into another, shall, in Consequence of any Law or Regulation therein, be discharged from such Service or Labour but shall be delivered up on Claim of the Party to whom such Services or Labour may be due." (See Document 9: United States Constitution, Article IV, section 2.)

The vote: Agreed to without a formal vote being taken and without dissent.

The Result: Fugitive slaves would be returned to their owners.

Clearly the slave states had obtained significant concessions at the Convention. The fugitive slave clause was added with little debate and without any *quid pro quo* for the North.

Ratification

At the close of the convention, Eldridge Gerry of Massachusetts, Edmond Randolph and George Mason of Virginia, explained that they could not sign the document that they had helped to create because they had political and practical objections to many provisions. Gerry thought the three-fifths compromise gave too much political power to the South at the expense of New England. Mason opposed allowing the slave trade to continue because it made the United States weaker and more vulnerable.

Having strengthened national authority, the convention had to face the issue of ratification. Article VII of the new Constitution provided for its ratification when passed by the Conventions of nine states. It seemed unwise to submit the Constitution to ratification by state legislatures because they would probably reject it. Therefore, the framers provided for ratification by special state conventions composed of delegates elected by the people. Ratification by state conventions satisfied their concern that the Constitution be approved by the consent of the people in order to become a higher law beyond the reach of future legislators. The framers expected the nation's "natural aristocracy" to continue to exercise political leadership. As part of the campaign for ratification, those in support called themselves Federalists, a term that implied that the Constitution balanced the relationship between the national and state governments and lessened the opposition of those hostile to a centralization of national authority. *The Federalist Papers* were part of a massive effort to persuade public

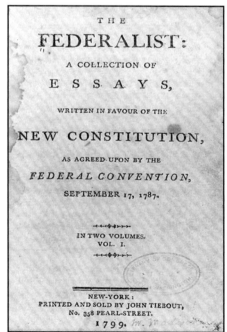

*The Federalist Papers, 1787-1788
Collected Edition, ca. 1799*

opinion in support of the new Constitution. The opponents became known as Anti-Federalists, a term which probably hurt them. The Anti-Federalists reflected a deep-seated American suspicion of concentrated power and strong central government.

Federalist delegates prevailed in eight conventions between December 1787 and May 1788, sometimes ramming through approval. Rhode Island and North Carolina rejected the Constitution and refused to join the new Union until several years later. The Constitution became the law of the land on June 21, 1788, when the ninth state, New Hampshire, ratified it. Ratification barely squeaked through in the big states of Massachusetts, Virginia, and New York. Some Northerners opposed the Constitution because of the concessions to slavery. Many were concerned about the centralization of power and threats to liberty. In South Carolina, Charles Cotesworth Pinckney reassured the state legislature: "We have a security that the general government can never emancipate them, for no such authority is granted and it is admitted, on all hands, that the general government has no powers but what are expressly granted by the Constitution, and that all rights not expressed were reserved by the several states."

The Legacy

At the time of the Convention, slavery was a profitable and healthy institution. However, the declining value of tobacco and slaves in the Upper South led some to wonder whether the institution would be permanent. This led Sherman, Wilson and other Northerners to claim that slavery might end soon. However, the invention of the cotton gin in 1793 made slavery even more profitable by making the widespread production of cotton possible. There was a rapid push westward into additional lands for cotton growing in Alabama, Mississippi and Louisiana. Although South Carolina imported no new slaves from 1787 through 1803, there were 80,000 new slaves imported from abroad to other states from 1803 to 1808. In 1808, Congress banned the importation of foreign slaves, but an illegal trade continued in South Carolina, Georgia and Florida until the Civil War. The national government, dominated by the slaveowning South, winked at this trade. In 1793, Congress passed a fugitive slave law, but because of northern opposition it was weak and did little to help masters recover their runaway slaves.

The unresolved controversy over the future of slavery underlay the struggle for sectional advantage that took place as the country expanded west, and slavery steadily marched into the old Southwest. Before 1820, five additional slave states (Kentucky, Tennessee, Louisiana, Mississippi and Alabama) had been admitted to the Union, increasing the total to eleven, which were balanced by eleven free states. The resulting political equilibrium in the Senate was threatened, however, when the territory of Missouri, settled mostly by farmers and planters from Kentucky and Tennessee, petitioned for admission as a slave state in 1819. Congress finally agreed to admit Missouri as a slave state in 1820, but it preserved the balance by admitting Maine as a free state. The Missouri Compromise again postponed the basic issue regarding slavery. Most importantly, it banned slavery north of 36 degrees, 30 minutes latitude—the southern border of Missouri. (See Document 10: Missouri Compromise, 1820.)

However, the vast territorial acquisition from Mexico following the Mexican War (See Chapter Eight: War between the United States and Mexico) forced Congress to reconsider the problem of slavery in the West. The Compromise of 1850 (See Chapter Nine: The Compromise of 1850) has been described as an "armistice." Under the Compromise, California was admitted as a free state; Utah and New Mexico territories were created with the question of slavery in each to be determined by popular sovereignty; the slave trade in Washington, D.C. was ended and a new Fugitive Slave Act made it easier for southerners to recover their fugitive slaves.

In 1861, President Abraham Lincoln called slavery "an unqualified evil to the negro, the white man, and the State" but declared in his first inaugural address that he had "no purpose, directly or indirectly, to interfere with slavery in the States where it exists." Nevertheless, the South seceded and the Civil War began. By 1862, most Republicans had become convinced that the war against a slaveholders' rebellion must become a war against slavery itself. The Constitution, however, gave Congress no power to touch slavery in the existing states. In the

Emancipation Proclamation (1863), Lincoln avoided this constitutional problem by making emancipation a war measure under his constitutional powers as commander-in-chief. Ironically, had the eleven slave states remained in the Union, they would still have been able to block a constitutional amendment ending slavery. After the defeat of the Confederacy, the Thirteenth Amendment, ratified on December 18, 1865, removed any doubts about the constitutionality of Lincoln's action. The Thirteenth Amendment simply asserted that "neither slavery nor involuntary servitude...shall exist within the United States." (See Document 11: United States Constitution, Thirteenth Amendment.)

QUESTIONS FOR DISCUSSION

1. Why were the delegates at the Constitutional Convention unable or unwilling to address the issue of slavery directly?

2. What alternatives to the compromises reached might have been possible at the Federal Convention in 1787?

3. Although little has been said in the letters of the delegates to the Federal Convention, some scholars have hypothesized that the "Great Compromise" at the Federal Convention included Article 6 of the Northwest Ordinance that precluded slavery north of the Ohio River and let it continue south of the Ohio River. Consider the dates of the two historic discussions that were taking place almost simultaneously during the summer of 1787 at the Continental Congress in New York and the Federal Convention in Philadelphia (see page 142). Do you believe that this hypothesis might be correct? Why or why not?

4. How would the history of the United States have differed if the gradual abolition of slavery had been included in the Constitution in 1787?

ADDITIONAL RESOURCES

Bailyn, Bernard. *To Begin the World Anew: The Genius and Ambiguities of the American Founders*. New York: Knopf, 2003.

Berlin, Ira. *Generations of Captivity: A History of African-American Slaves*. Cambridge, MA: Harvard University Press, 2003.

Bernstein, Richard B. *Are We to be a Nation?* Cambridge, MA: Harvard University Press, 1987.

Blumrosen, Alfred W. and Ruth G. *Slave Nation: How Slavery United the Colonies and Sparked the American Revolution*. Naperville, IL: Sourcebook, Inc, 2005.

Brown, Christopher Leslie. *Moral Capital: Foundations of British Abolitionism*. Chapel Hill: University of North Carolina Press, 2006.

Cornell, Saul. *The Other Founders: Anti-Federalism and the Dissenting Tradition in America, 1788-1828*. Chapel Hill: University of North Carolina Press, 1999.

Dain. Bruce. *A Hideous Monster of the Mind: American Race Theory in the Early Republic*. Cambridge, MA: Harvard University Press, 2002.

Davis, David Brion. *The Problem of Slavery in the Age of Revolution, 1770-1823.* Ithaca, NY: Cornell University Press, 1975.

Elliot, Jonathan. *The Debates in the Several State Conventions on the Adoption of the Federal Constitution.* 1888.

Farrand, Max, ed. *The Records of the Federal Convention of 1787,* Vol. I-IV. New Haven, CT: Yale University Press, 1966.

Fehrenbacher, Don E. with Ward M. McAfee. *The Slaveholding Republic: An Account of the United States Government Relations to Slavery.* New York: Oxford University Press, 2001.

Finkelman, Paul. *Slavery and the Founders: Race and Liberty in the Age of Jefferson.* Armonk, NY: M.E. Sharpe, 1996.

"The Founders' Constitution" at http://press-pubs.uchicago.edu/founders.

Franklin, John Hope and Alfred A . Moss, Jr. *From Slavery to Freedom: A History of African Americans.* 7th ed. New York: Alfred A. Knopf, 1994.

Freehling, William W. "The Founding Fathers and Slavery." *American Historical Review 77* (1972): 81–93.

_____. *Road to Disunion, Volume I, 1776-1854.* New York: Oxford University Press, 1990.

Kaminski, John. *A Necessary Evil: Slavery in the Debate over the Constitution.* Madison, WI: Madison House, 1995.

Lynd, Straughton. *Class Conflict, Slavery and the U.S. Constitution,* 1980.

Nash, Gary. *Race and Revolution.* New York: Madison House Publishers, 1990.

Rakove, Jack. *James Madison and the Creation of the American Republic.* Addison Wesley Longman, 2001.

_____. *Original Meanings: Politics and Ideas in the Making of the Constitution.* New York: Vintage Books, 1997.

Richards, Leonard L. *The Slave Power: The Free North and Southern Domination, 1780-1860.* Baton Rouge, Louisiana State University Press, 2000.

Robinson, Donald. *Slavery in the Structure of American Politics, 1765–1820.* New York: Harcourt Brace Jovanovich, Inc. 1971.

Wiecek, William M. *The Sources of Antislavery Constitutionalism in America.* Ithaca, NY: Cornell University Press, 1977.

Wills, Gary. *Negro President: Jefferson and the Slave Power.* New York: Houghton Mifflin, 2003.

Wood, Betty. *The Origins of American Slavery.* New York: Hill and Wang, 1997.

DOCUMENTS ON CD

Document 1:   Resolutions of the German Mennonites, 1688

Document 2:   Jefferson's original draft of the Declaration of Independence indicting the British for bringing slavery to the colonies, 1776

Document 3:   The Articles of Confederation, 1781

Document 4:   Northwest Ordinance, July 13, 1787

Document 5:   Excerpts from the Debate and vote on the slave trade, from Farrand, *The Records of the Federal Convention of 1787*

Document 6:   Excerpts from the Debate and vote on fugitive slaves, from Farrand, *The Records of the Federal Convention of 1787*

Document 7:   United States Constitution, Article I, section 2

Document 8:   United States Constitution, Article V

Document 9:   United States Constitution, Article IV, section 2

Document 10:   Missouri Compromise, 1820

Document 11:   United States Constitution, Thirteenth Amendment, ratified December 18, 1865

TEACHER OVERHEADS/STUDENT HANDOUTS ON CD

1. Timeline

2. What experiences led to the Federal Convention in 1787

3. Who was at the Federal Convention?

4. Slavery issues at the Federal Convention

5. Short biographies of Pierce Butler, John Dickinson, Rufus King, James Madison, George Mason, Gouverneur Morris, William Paterson, General Pinckney, Roger Sherman and James Wilson

6. Southern Positions and Interests

7. 1790 Census: Total and Slave Populations by State

8. Directions for a mock mediation

9. What really happened?

10. What were the costs?

SOURCES AND CREDITS FOR ILLUSTRATIONS

p. 137: "Stowage of the British Slave Ship *Brookes*," *Library of Congress (LC) USZ62-44000*

p. 138: "Slaves hoeing tobacco," *Jamestown National Historic Park*

p. 138: "Slaves clearing and planting a field," *Special Collections- University of Virginia Library*

p. 139: "Slave advertisement, 1780," *Rare Books Division, Library of Congress*

p. 140: Independence Hall, Philadelphia, *National Archives-NWDNS-66-G-IE-6*

p. 142: The Mason Dixon Line Map and Marker, *Carroll County, Maryland*

p. 144: Pierce Butler, *Soldier-Statesmen of the Constitution series, U.S. Army, Center of Military History*

p. 144: John Dickinson, *Soldier-Statesmen of the Constitution series, U.S. Army, Center of Military History*

p. 145: Rufus King, *LC-USZ62-6061*

p. 145: James Madison, *LC-USZ62-13004*

p. 145: George Mason, *National Archives-NWDNS-148-CP-121*

p. 146: Gouverneur Morris, *LC-USZ62-45482*

p. 146: William Paterson, *Soldier-Statesmen of the Constitution series, U.S. Army, Center of Military History*

p. 146: Charles Cotesworth Pinckney, *National Archives-NWDNS-148-CC-13-9*

p. 147: Roger Sherman, *LC-USZ62-111793*

p. 147: James Wilson, *LC-USZ62-6065*

p. 149: 1790 Census: Total and Slave Populations by State (U.S. Census)

p. 152: *The Federalist Papers, LC Rare Book Division*

Chapter Seven

The Cherokee Indian Removal

Objectives

- To understand the political, cultural and economic development of the Cherokee Nation in the early 1800s.

- To analyze the political, economic and ideological reasons pushing the idea of Cherokee Removal.

- To understand the positions and interests of the leading individuals involved in the conflict over the land of the Cherokee Nation in Georgia.

- To consider what alternative resolutions might have been possible.

- To recognize the suffering by the Cherokees on their forced westward march, known as the "Trail of Tears."

Correlations with National History Standards

Era Four
Standard 1B

The student understands federal and state Indian policy and the strategies for survival forged by Native Americans.

- Compare the policies toward Native Americans pursued by presidential administrations through the Jacksonian era.

- Compare federal and state Indian policy and explain Whig opposition to the removal of Native Americans.

- Analyze the impact of removal and resettlement on the Cherokee, Creek, Chickasaw, Choctaw and Seminole.

- Explain and evaluate the various strategies of Native Americans such as accommodation, revitalization and resistance.

Overview

From the beginning, the American settlers had pushed the Indians westward. The Europeans brought with them new diseases, new goods, new cultures and a desire for land, all of which threatened the traditions and often the very existence of the various Indian peoples. When several European nations had vied for influence in North America, the Indians could try to play them against each other. But with the emergence of the United States, and the decline of British, French and Spanish power in North America, the eastern Indians were confronted with a single, aggressive, expansionist nation with little to restrain it. Sometimes the pressure for Indian land turned into bloodshed, leaving the names King Philip, Pontiac, Tecumseh, Sitting Bull and Crazy Horse, and the battle sites at Fallen Timbers, Horseshoe Bend, Little Big Horn and Wounded Knee to haunt the American memory. More often, the battleground has been less bloody, though in many ways no less violent and no less important to the course of American history. In the late 1820s and the 1830s, the era named after President Andrew Jackson, there was a great debate among Americans and Native Americans over Jackson's official policy of Indian Removal—the removal of Native Americans from the Eastern coastal areas to west of the Mississippi River. The debate raged from the Georgia frontier to New England churches, from Indian councils to the floor of the United States Senate, from newspapers to petitions. Indian Removal captured the attention of the American people because it lay at the intersection of a number of issues that were central to the nation's life at the time: relations between the federal government and the states, between the Northeast (which tended to oppose removal) and the South (which tended to support it), and between the executive (which favored removal) and the judiciary (which did not). It also brought out rhetoric about national honor and racial ideologies as well as true concern and compassion for the Native Americans. At the center of this debate was one of the most powerful and acculturated Indian nations—the Cherokees, who lived in the Great Smokey Mountains of the southeastern United States.

HISTORICAL BACKGROUND

At the beginning of the American Revolution, the Cherokees inhabited a vast area in the southeastern United States, including much of northwestern present-day Georgia. After more than two centuries of contact with European explorers and settlers, they found themselves bound with European colonists by trade and diplomacy, but there were also times of strife. During the Revolution, the Cherokees had sided with the British, a decision that earned them the enmity of the colonists. After the war with Britain ended in 1783, the new American nation began an expansionist program that was met with verbal and armed resistance by the Native Americans. The 1785 Treaty of Hopewell brought a brief respite when the United States established peace with the Cherokees, proclaimed its sovereignty over them and recognized tribal claims to most of their lands. Unfortunately, the treaty did little to prevent continuing pressures by whites for Cherokee lands in Georgia, North Carolina, and the growing frontier communities west of the Appalachian Mountains.

Beginning in the late 1780s, President Washington and his Secretary of War Henry Knox fashioned what they believed was a more enlightened, more humane, and less costly policy, but one that would allow for the continued expansion of white settlement. Instead of driving the Cherokees out, the federal government would respect Indian sovereignty and land rights, would negotiate land sales freely and fairly, and would "civilize" the natives by sending missionaries to educate and convert them along with agricultural experts and equipment to help them adopt white ways. The aim was to get the Native American men to give up hunting in favor of farming, to move Native American women from farming into the home, to corral Native American children into school and to entice all of them into Christianity.

The Treaty of Holston in 1791 was the first of many treaties that emphasized the new "civilizing" policy while conceding to the Cherokees a degree of sovereignty and recognizing certain tribal laws and customs. This "sovereignty" was always qualified and mostly reflected expediency. Cherokee delegations were received with all the pomp given to diplomats of foreign nations, but their requests were mostly ignored. Through the Federal Trade and Intercourse Acts of 1790, 1802 and 1834, the new nation sought to prevent the exploitation and corruption of the Indians by vicious and unscrupulous traders through a strict system of licenses. These Acts also appropriated federal funds to be used for the education of Indians and for agents who would reside among the Indians and to supply them with "useful domestic animals and implements of husbandry."

Federal policy toward the Native Americans included the twin threads of "civilizing" them so that they would live more like the whites and trying to obtain the Indian lands for use by white settlers. Thomas Jefferson stated that these two policies were complementary: if the Indians were assimilated to the life-style of white Americans, they would farm rather than hunt and therefore, make more land available for white settlement. As presidents, Jefferson, Madison and Monroe had all seriously considered the feasibility of transferring Indians to land west of the Mississippi River. In the early 1800s, the federal government was sponsoring attempts to civilize

160

Land Occupied by Southeastern Tribes, 1820s

and assimilate such southeastern tribes as the Cherokees, Chickasaws, Choctaws and Creeks, while at the same time attempting to open Indian land east of the Mississippi River to white settlement. This was based both on a humanitarian desire to bring the "benefits" of white society to the Indians and to absorb them into white society as well as the need to put American expansion and dispossession of the Indians on firmer moral ground. Although some Cherokees migrated across the Mississippi River in 1808–1810, most stayed on their eastern lands. In 1813–14, the Cherokees fought alongside General Andrew Jackson's forces against the "Red Stick" Creeks.

In the treaties of 1817 and 1819, the Cherokees ceded territory in the east in exchange for western lands, asserting that it would be their last land sale. The U.S. allowed Cherokees who wanted to become citizens of the U.S. and who they considered capable of managing their own property to receive 640 acres of land and to remain on Cherokee lands in Georgia and other southeastern states. Starting in 1817, the American Board of Commissioners for the Foreign [religious] Missions maintained a significant presence in the Cherokee Nation. In 1819, lobbied by the missionaries, Congress appropriated $10,000 annually for the "civilization of the tribes adjoining the frontier settlements." Protestant missionaries administered the "civilizing fund" and established mission schools. Some Cherokee men, women and children learned well the lessons of literacy, artisan skills and the governmental techniques their agents and missionaries taught them. Many wanted to learn English so that the white men could no longer cheat them. Gradually, some became converted Christians.

The Cherokee Nation, composed of some 16,000 people, experienced a burst of economic and political energy as well as enhanced tribal pride during the decade of the 1820s. Between 1819 and 1829, the Cherokee Nation became economically self-sufficient and politically self-governing. While many Cherokees lived in rough-hewn cabins, at least twenty men registered claims for real property exceeding $10,000 (a very large amount in 1820) in assessed valuation. This included stores, taverns, mills, ferries and large plantations worked by some 1, 500 black slaves owned by the Cherokee economic elite. This economic elite, which consisted mostly of mixed bloods, the offspring of primarily white fathers and Cherokee mothers, was also the political elite. They were educated at white missionary schools, fully conversant in both Indian and white worlds and became wealthy by shifting to white forms of agriculture, including cotton plantations worked by slaves, and commerce, including mills, crops, taverns, ferries and roads. By 1830s, some Cherokee wore frock coats, pantaloons, stiff collars and top hats.

Sequoyah
Inventor of the Cherokee Alphabet

A Cherokee alphabet was developed by the Cherokee Sequoyah in 1822. In 1828, the Cherokee Nation began publication of a national newspaper, *The Cherokee Phoenix*. The Cherokee Nation adopted a constitution in 1827 that was modeled after that of the southern states and the United States. It provided for a bicameral legislature, an executive and a judiciary. The first written laws punished theft and murder. Cherokee property law was more egalitarian than comparable legislation among whites. Land was held as common property by the Nation. Unoccupied land could be used by any member but could not be sold. Improvements belonged to those who made them, purchased them or inherited them.

The "civilizing" program was probably more successful with the Cherokees than with any other native tribe, and, in fact, probably more successful than either its authors or its beneficiaries had anticipated. The "remarkable progress" of the Cherokees was the subject of considerable public notice and discussion. However, contrary to the aims of the federal government, this period of Cherokee renaissance under federal auspices (1819–29) strengthened rather than weakened the Cherokee's determination to retain their own separate identity and destiny on their ancient lands. The well-educated Cherokees were not only more difficult to trick or intimidate, they also understood the productive value of their land and had a strong sense of pride in their ancestry. For example, John Ross, who became president to the Cherokee's National Committee (the tribe's legislature) and later its first chief, was a wealthy, slaveowning planter with two hundred acres of choice farmland in Rome, Georgia, where he built a gracious two-storied home in 1827.

Home of John Ross in Rome, Georgia

The Immediate Facts

Despite the numerous treaties guaranteeing the sovereignty of the Native Americans over their land and in spite of (or perhaps because of) the educational, economic and political advances of the Cherokees, Georgia settlers continued to encroach upon the Cherokee land as well as that of the neighboring Creeks. Mississippi and Alabama also violated federal treaties in annexing Choctaw and Chickasaw land. (Mississippi became a state in 1817; Alabama in 1819.) In 1824, the Cherokees presented a memorial to Congress declaring their policy against removal. In 1826–27, the last of the Creek land was forcibly ceded in Georgia. By a law signed December 1828, the state of Georgia asserted sovereignty over Cherokee land, pronouncing the laws of the Cherokee Nation null and void after June 1, 1830.

Andrew Jackson was elected president of the United States in 1828. He came to the presidency after a long career as a Tennessee lawyer, slaveowning planter, and war hero. A man of steely determination, quick temper and iron will, he was passionately, if somewhat paradoxically, devoted both to states' rights and to the security and expansion of the American nation. Jackson was born in South Carolina in 1767. His father died soon after he was born, and his mother died while he was still a child. Jackson lacked the education and polish of the political leaders of the founding generation. While he lacked gentility, he made up for this in his ability to lead and his determination to succeed. Heavily involved in land speculation—some of it Indian lands—from an early date, Jackson pushed for extensive land cessions from the Southern tribes between 1814 and 1820. His view towards the native tribes was as paradoxical as his views on states' rights and federal expansion. He had Indians friends but he was also celebrated on the frontier mainly as an Indian fighter. He did not believe that the native tribes were sovereign entities entitled to self-government. Early in his administration, Jackson made it clear that attempts by "the Indians inhabiting parts of Georgia and Alabama…to establish an independent government would not be countenanced by the Executive of the United States" and "advised them to emigrate beyond the Mississippi or submit to the laws of those states." (See Document 1: President Andrew Jackson's Case for the Removal Act: First Annual Message to Congress, December 8, 1829.)

Heroic Portrait of Andrew Jackson
at the Battle of New Orleans, 1815

"King Andrew The First"
Hostile Political Cartoon

Jackson pursued his removal policy, winning congressional approval by narrow margins in May 1830 for "An Act to Provide for an Exchange of Lands with the Indians Residing in any of the States or Territories, and for their Removal West of the Mississippi River." (See Document 2: Indian Removal Act, May 28, 1830.) The law made removal voluntary. "It would be as cruel as unjust," Jackson wrote, "to compel the aborigines to abandon the graves of their fathers and seek a home in a distant land." However, Jackson insisted, natives "should be distinctly informed that if they remain within the limits of the States they must be subject to the state's law."

The Cherokees, however, were determined to stay on their land. In 1829, they passed a law making it a capital crime for anyone to sell any of the Nation's land. They campaigned in Congress, in the press and in the courts. After gold was discovered on the Cherokee lands in northwestern Georgia in July 1829, there was a land stampede. The state of Georgia attempted to exert its authority over the Cherokee land by requiring all white people going into Cherokee country to secure a permit from the state. Several missionaries, including Samuel Worcester, who refused to secure a permit and justify Georgia's policy, were arrested and tried. The case was ultimately appealed to the United States Supreme Court.

Chief Justice John Marshall, a Federalist and ardent nationalist, writing for the majority, held in *Worcester v. Georgia* in 1832 that the Georgia acts were void. He recognized the Cherokee Nation as a "domestic dependent nation" rather than as a sovereign nation as the Cherokees had wanted. Marshall concluded that "the Cherokee nation, then, is a distinct community, occupying its own territory, with boundaries accurately described, in which the laws of Georgia have no force, and which the citizens of Georgia have no right to enter, but with the assent of the Cherokees themselves, or in conformity with the treaties and with the acts of Congress." (See Document 3: U.S. Supreme Court: *Worcester v. Georgia*, January 1832.) This meant that the Cherokees were subject to the laws and treaties of the federal government, but not the states.

These were grand, bold words, but they neither released the missionaries nor helped the Cherokees. President Jackson is alleged to have said: "John Marshall has made his decision; now let him enforce it." Whether he uttered these words or not, his policy was, indeed, to ignore the court's decision. So, too, did Georgia. In 1832, Georgians surveyed the lands of the Cherokee Nation in preparation for distributing the land to Georgia citizens in a land lottery. By 1835, there were some 15,000 whites living on lands the Cherokees insisted still belonged to the Cherokee Nation. During the period 1830–36, the United States ratified almost seventy treaties, acquiring 100 million acres of Indian land and moving to the west 46,000 Indians (including the Choctaws, Chickasaws and Creeks). In 1834, Congress created a special Indian territory in what later became Oklahoma.

In the presidential election of 1832, the issue of Cherokee Removal became a major national issue used by the anti-Jacksonian Whig Party to mobilize sympathetic northern voters. After Jackson's re-election in 1832, many missionaries began to change course and lapse into silence or to counsel removal rather than supporting the Cherokees in their resistance. At the same time a "treaty" or "removal" party emerged in the Cherokee Nation. Led by Major Ridge, a prominent Cherokee leader, his son John Ridge, and his nephew Elias Boudinot, this group believed that the only road to the salvation of their people lay in moving to the west. Without authorization from the legislative council of the Cherokee Nation, this small group which represented only a tiny faction of the Cherokee Nation signed the Treaty of New Echota in December 1835. The agreement provided for the surrender of all Cherokee lands in the east, new lands in the area that is now Oklahoma, and federal removal and subsistence for a year at federal expense from an appropriation of $5 million. (See Document 4: The Treaty of Echota, 1835.) Although the "treaty" was ratified by the U.S. Senate in 1836, John Ross and his followers remained steadfast in their refusal to vacate their lands in Georgia.

THE MOCK NEGOTIATIONS

O   On February 22, 1837, John Ross sent a final memorial and petition to the United States Senate and House of Representatives. He received no reply.

We will instead imagine that President Jackson (lame duck president through March 1837 when Martin Van Buren, his former vice president who would be sworn in as his successor) confers with the Democratic leadership of the United States Senate and House of Representatives and they agree to have Secretary of War, Lewis Cass, as well as Senators Theodore Frelinghuysen and George Troup, Georgia Governor Wilson Lumpkin and Reverend Jones meet with Cherokee leaders John Ross, Nancy Ward and Elias Boudinot to try to negotiate a peaceful resolution to the controversy over Cherokee lands and Cherokee sovereignty.

THE PARTICIPANTS

John Ross

John Ross, Anti-Removal Cherokee Chief

John Ross was born in 1791 to a Scottish father and a one-quarter Cherokee mother. He grew up in a prosperous Anglo-Indian world where his father provided his children tutors and other educational advantages. His Cherokee mother instilled in him pride in his Indian ancestry. He established Ross Landing (now Chattanooga, Tennessee) for trading traffic on the Tennessee River, gained lucrative government contracts to supply the Indians and soldiers, and expanded his agricultural holdings and his slaves. Ross began his political career as an occasional clerk to the Cherokee chiefs, became a delegate to Washington in 1816, and in 1819 became president of the National Committee, the Cherokee legislature. After service in the Creek War, he married Elizabeth (Quatie) Brown-Henley, a full-blooded Cherokee, and moved to Coosa (now Rome), Georgia, in 1827, where he built a two-storied house, and became quite wealthy with his fields and ferry. He oversaw the development of the first constitutional government of an American Indian tribe, which placed premier importance on maintaining the Cherokees' homelands. In 1828, Ross was elected the first chief under the new constitution. By the time of Removal, Ross was one of the five wealthiest men in the Cherokee Nation. He opposed Removal. Ross's wife died a victim of Removal in 1839. In Oklahoma, Ross married a young Quaker from Delaware. (See Document 5: John Ross, Petitions and Memorials to Congress.)

Nancy Ward, Anti-Removal Cherokee

Nancy Ward was called a "War Woman," a title traditionally awarded to women who distinguished themselves while accompanying war parties to cook food, carry water and perform other gender specific tasks, and later a "Beloved Woman." After her husband's death in battle in 1755, Ward had rallied the warriors. She also had aided the patriot cause during the American Revolution. In 1817, 1818, and later in 1831, an elderly Nancy Ward and other women prepared petitions to the National Council, first arguing against the ceding of more land, then against the allotment of land to individuals, and finally against removal (See Document 6: Nancy Ward, Petition, 1821.)

Nancy Ward

Theodore Frelinghuysen

Senator Theodore Frelinghuysen, Anti-Removal U.S. Senator (Whig)

Senator Theodore Frelinghuysen was a devoutly religious, anti–Jacksonian freshman senator from New Jersey, who had been president of the religious American Board of Commissioners for Foreign Missions. In 1830, he argued for six hours over a period of three days against the removal bill. He based his arguments on the equality of all men, natural law, the United States Constitution, prior treaties, fairness and justice. "Do the obligations of justice change with the color of the skin?" he asked. He became known as the "Christian statesman." Frelinghuysen and other northern congressmen tried to add provisions guaranteeing Indians rights provided by treaties. Frelinghuysen went on to become president of the American Bible Society, chancellor of New York University, vice-presidential candidate for the Whigs in 1844, and president of Rutgers College. (See Document 7: Theodore Frelinghuysen, speech before the Senate, 1830.)

Reverend Evan Jones, Anti-Removal Missionary

Reverend Evan Jones was a Baptist minister. Born in Wales and educated in London, Jones emigrated to Philadelphia at the age of 33. He had no sympathy for slavery and even less for the white frontier people of the South who kept trying to drive the Cherokees to the west. A man of great energy and a domineering personality, Jones headed the Baptist mission to the Cherokees for forty years. By 1827, he had concluded that the Cherokees had made great advances toward civilization and shifted his principal effort from farming and education towards evangelism. He collected an every-expanding team of Cherokee converts and exhorters to assist him in spreading Christianity among the Cherokees in North Carolina, a large part of northern Georgia and a small area in Tennessee, competing with the Methodists and Moravians. He was perhaps the only white missionary to learn to speak with sufficient confidence to preach as well as to write in Sequoyan. Even after many of the other missionaries stopped their resistance to Cherokee removal after 1832, Jones continued wholeheartedly in support of Cherokee Chief John Ross. He was chosen to draft a response to Boudinot's 1937 pamphlet defending the actions of the Removal Party. (See Document 8: Excerpt from "William Penn" essays in Defense of Cherokees, prepared by Jeremiah Evarts for the American Board of Commissioners for Foreign Missions, 1829.)

Reverend Evan Jones

Lewis Cass, Secretary of War (Pro-Removal)

Lewis Cass

Lewis Cass was President Jackson's Secretary of War during the period 1831–1836. His responsibilities included the management of Indian affairs. He had previously been Governor of the Michigan Territory, 1813–31, where he gained a great deal of experience working with Indian tribes since the office of territorial governor included that of superintendent of Indian affairs. By the mid-1820s, Cass had become widely regarded as one of the best informed, most experienced and thoughtful experts in the country on Indian policy. He was reputed to be a hardheaded, tough, but fair, negotiator. By 1830, he believed that, as a practical necessity, the Indians must all be removed west of the Mississippi but advanced humane ideals for organizing the new Indian territory. He published several articles explaining that the land could not be held by the Indians solely for hunting but must give way to the needs of "providence" in using the land for production. Although he was not a racist, his writings were used by the government to rationalize highly discriminatory policies. (See Document 9: Lewis Cass, Removal of Indians, *North American Review.*, 1830)

George Troup

George M. Troup, U.S. Senator from Georgia (Pro-Removal Democrat)

George M. Troup was born in the part of Georgia that later became Alabama. He was educated at Princeton University. During the 1820s, while governor of Georgia, Troup orchestrated a campaign of bluster, threat and audacity that enabled him to acquire the rich lands of the Creek Indians for the state of Georgia and earned him great political popularity. He believed that the Indians were an inferior race to the white man, one step above the African slaves, and feared that the North would deal with the Indians in a way that would set a precedent for dealing with the slaves. In the early 1830s, Troup was the U.S. Senator from Georgia. He wanted the Cherokees removed. Responding to the *Worcester v. Georgia* decision, Senator Troup said: "The people of Georgia will receive with indignant feelings, as they ought, the decisions of the Supreme Court, so flagrantly violative of their sovereign state…The jurisdiction claimed over one portion of our population (the Indians) may very soon be extended to another (the Africans), and in both cases they may be sustained by fanatics of the north." Troup was supported by wealthy coastal planters and merchants. Although both Troup and Lumpkin favored Indian removal, they were political rivals. (See Document 10: George M. Troup, letter to the *Georgia Journal*.)

Wilson Lumpkin, Governor of Georgia (Pro-Removal Democrat)

Wilson Lumpkin grew up on the Georgia frontier. He was U.S. Commissioner among the Creek and Cherokee Indians 1818–21. Lumpkin was Congressman from Georgia 1824–31, Governor of Georgia 1831–35 and U.S. Senator from Georgia 1837–1841. He was a devout Baptist and often had the missionaries as well as the traders and smaller planters behind him. Lumpkin had participated in a survey of the northwest corner of Georgia which was claimed by the Cherokees and became an enthusiast for the construction of a railroad link from the agricultural heartland of the state to the state's river network in the northwest. He strongly favored removal of the Cherokees. (See Document 11: Wilson Lumpkin, Message to Georgia Legislature, 1832.)

Wilson Lumpkin

Elias Boudinot

Elias Boudinot, Pro-Removal Cherokee leader

Elias Boudinot was a full-blooded Cherokee who had studied as an adolescent at the missionary boarding school in Cornwall, Connecticut. In 1826, he married Harriet Gould, one of the daughters of a white employee at the school. The managers of the school disavowed these actions, but adverse public opinion forced the school to close. Boudinot was the editor of the *Cherokee Phoenix* from 1828 to 1832. By 1832, Boudinot and his cousin, John Ridge, had concluded that removal was inevitable and that delaying the inevitable might destroy the wealth and moral fiber of the Cherokee Nation. They tried to persuade John Ross to make a treaty. After 1832, Boudinot argued for removal, and became a leader of the "Treaty or Removal Party." He agreed to the Treaty of New Echota in 1835 (See Document 4: The Treaty of New Echota.)

167

POSITIONS AND INTERESTS

Pro-Removal

Georgians (Lumpkin and Troup)

Positions

- The northerners are being unfair and hypocritical because most of the Natives in northeastern areas have already been either killed or removed.

- The federal government has promised that it would remove the Indians from Georgia since 1802.

- The Cherokees are not a sovereign entity because you cannot have a sovereign state within a sovereign state. They were subject to the laws of Georgia if they chose to reside in Georgia.

- State officials in Georgia have long considered the Indians as "dependent tenants" subject to the will of the state.

Interests

- Maintain states rights

- Fear of setting a precedent regarding the African slaves

- Economic development in western Georgia being prevented by the presence of the Indians

- Believe that the Indian is by nature savage and not subject to civilization

- Have no love for Indians because they have often been victims of Indians attacks (forgetting the causes of the conflicts or that the Indians, too had suffered terrible attacks from whites)

- Are determined to acquire more land (The Creek word for Georgians was "Eccanunuxulgee," which means "people greedily grasping after the lands of the red people")

The Federal Government (Cass)

Positions/Interests

- Cass believes that Indian removal is not only legally, economically and morally justified but also morally necessary, because only by emigration can the Native Americans survive as a race and become civilized.

- Indians need hunting grounds (ignoring the fact that their staples are supplied by agriculture).

He is representing the views of President Jackson, who:

- Is motivated by concern for the nation's growth, unity and security

- Wants limited federal power but is a fervent nationalist in regard to territorial expansion

- Believes the federal government is offering extremely generous terms to the Indians

- Argues that removal is the only way to safeguard tribal integrity from rapacious whites.

The Treaty, or "Removal" Party (after 1832) (Boudinot)

Positions

- The time to resist has passed because removal is going to happen.

- It is better to work with rather than against the federal government in order to preserve the Cherokee Nation.

Interests

- Competing for leadership of the Cherokee nation

- Underlying motives for some might be to make the best deal they can for their holdings in Georgia.

Anti-Removal

The Anti-Removal Missionaries/Congressmen (Sen. Frelinghuysen and Evan Jones)

Positions

- The Cherokees are being won to Christianity and as Christians are worthy of benevolent treatment

- It is unfair to rob the Cherokees of the land of their forefathers

- The Constitution as interpreted by the Supreme Court and prior treaties support the claims of the Cherokees to remain of their land

- Jackson's argument that this is for the protection of the Cherokees is hypocritical

Interests *(Evan Jones)*

- Desire to continue their lucrative and successful missionary activities with the southeastern Indians through the existing "civilizing" fund

- Long personal connections with the Cherokees

Interests *(Sen. Frelinghuysen)*

- Politics—Whigs want to gain voters sympathetic to the plight of the Cherokees by attacking Jackson and the Democratic Party

- Geopolitical interest in NOT allowing southern settlers to expand in western lands reserved for Indians

John Ross/Majority of Cherokee Indians

Positions

- Cherokees have resided on and used the lands in Georgia long before the white man arrived.

- The federal government has made repeated promises that it would help the Indians, not move them to other lands.

- The series of treaties with the federal government recognizes their sovereignty

- The Cherokees have become the most "civilized" Indian Nation as the federal government as white society had required.

Interests/Fears

- If they cannot sustain their legal rights in Georgia supported by the U.S. Supreme Court, they will not be able to sustain themselves as a Nation anywhere.

- Bribes, intimidation and fraud will be involved in removal as it had been in the expropriation of Creek and Cherokee lands in 1814–17.

- Some Cherokees welcome the offers to travel the white man's road; others feared that they would become assimilated because they can only maintain their traditional culture in their native woodlands in the Great Smokey Mountains.

TEACHER INSTRUCTIONS

Preparation

1. Either assign the "Historical Background" to be read as homework or present the material to the class as a lecture.

2. Each student should review the positions and interests of all participants.

3. Hand out: The Participants. Students should review all of the brief biographies.

Directions

1. Divide the class into groups of nine or ten.

2. Assign each person a role:

   a.   Chief John Ross

   b.   Nancy Ward

   c.   Senator Frelinghuysen

   d.   Evan Jones

   e.   Lewis Cass

   f.   George Troup

   g.   Wilson Lumpkin

   h.   Elias Boudinot.

   i.   Assign one or two observer/recorder/reporters per group. These may simply be anonymous "observers," or hypothesize that Frances Trolloppe, a British novelist, and Alexis De Tocqueville, a liberal French aristocrat, both of whom traveled through the United States in 1830 and wrote about what they saw, are invited to observe the negotiations and to write about them. (In fact, neither was in the United States in 1837.)

3.   Distribute Handout: The Mock Negotiation.

4.   Review the setting and the instructions for the negotiation with the students. Explain to the students that in response to a final petition from the Cherokee Chief, John Ross, they are to imagine that President Jackson has agreed to negotiate with a Cherokee delegation. The mock negotiation should last 30-60 minutes.

Debriefing

1.   Once the groups finish their mock negotiations, debrief the activity. Conduct a classroom discussion, beginning with each observer describing how the process worked in their group.

2.   Discuss the problem of a great power imbalance between the forces pressing for removal, which included President Jackson, the Georgia government and most of the white southern community. What could be done to try to equalize this imbalance? Note that this is the reason why we have included a mediator—to try to help the Cherokees. See "Questions for Discussion," numbers 2-5 for some ideas.

3.   Discuss "The Historical Effects," "The Facts Continued," and "The Cherokees Today," comparing the results of the mock negotiations with what actually occurred in history.

Alternative Activity—Mock Congressional Debate

Research and identify those members of Congress who were involved in the debate about the Cherokees and create a mock congressional debate with a mediator or facilitator.

Depiction of the
"Trail of Tears"

THE FACTS CONTINUED

The efforts by Chief John Ross to overturn the removal Treaty of New Echota failed, but he continued to work to soften its impact, to ensure Cherokee control of the actual removal process, and to obtain a two-year extension of the final deadline for removal. Initially, civilian contractors were hired to organize voluntary traveling parties of Cherokees, but they proved so corrupt that the military was assigned to relocate the Cherokees. By May of 1838—the deadline for removal—only 2000 of the 16,000 Cherokees had been moved west. Consequently, U.S. soldiers and state militiamen built stockade forts at various points in the nation. In the summer of 1838, thousands of Cherokees were forced often at the point of a bayonet, with no more than the clothes on their backs, into stockades, herded into camps and onto steamboats from which hundreds still managed to escape. The federal government wanted to demonstrate that removal would not be a big burden on the government and limited the amount of funds, resulting in inadequate provisions, a situation which was compounded by the Cherokees' refusal to do any planning about leaving. By fall, Ross and other leaders had convinced the military to permit the Cherokees to conduct their own removal. Ross divided the remaining Cherokees into thirteen parties to leave for the west in October. Although the original plan had been for the Cherokees to move over the summer months, the majority left in the fall and made the 800-mile trip during the fall and winter. The last party arrived in March 1839.

No one knows exactly how many Cherokees perished in the ordeal, called by the Cherokees, the "Trail of Tears." The estimate usually cited is more than 4,000 deaths (one-fifth to one-fourth of the entire Cherokee population). The ordeal was especially hard for babies, children and the elderly. One Georgian involved in the removal of the Cherokees commented: "I fought through the Civil War and have seen men shot to pieces and slaughtered by thousands, but the Cherokee Removal was the cruelest work I ever knew." (See Document 12: Evan Jones, letters about removal, May–December 1838.)

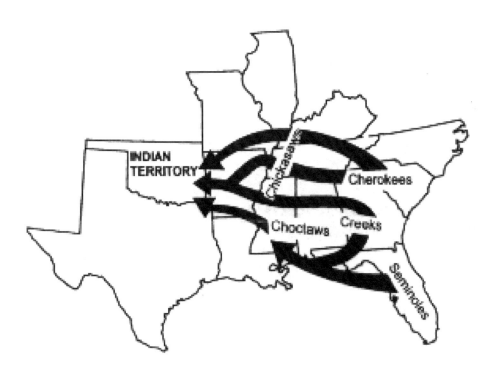

Removal of Cherokees (and other southeastern Indian Nations)
to Indian Territory (Oklahoma)

Life in their new home was not easy for the Cherokees. Political strife continued. The Treaty of Echota was viewed by many as treason and was handled in terms of an older tradition of clan revenge. According to a journal kept by a missionary who traveled west with the Cherokees, members of the clans to which John Ridge, Major Ridge and Elias Boudinot belonged agreed among themselves to kill the leading members of the Treaty Party and carried out their intention in the Cherokee Nation West in June 1839. There was no recognized official authority at the time to enforce the law. Federal officials had undermined any remaining tribal sovereignty.

Half a dozen years after removal, there was still civil strife among the Ross party, the Treaty Party and the earlier settlers (Cherokees who had voluntarily moved west before the 1830s). The Treaty of 1846 was aimed at ending the factionalism. The decade of the 1850s was prosperous and tranquil for the Cherokees in the west. A new national newspaper and a new school system were started. The tranquility was broken by the Civil War. Afterwards, although the Cherokees negotiated a fairly lenient treaty with President Johnson during Reconstruction, they never attained the economic or political stability that they had had during the period prior to Removal.

The Historical Effects

The Cherokee Removal—and the removal of other eastern tribes—Creeks, Choctaws, Chickasaws, and later the Seminoles—ended all hopes for Indian sovereignty and deepened Indian mistrust of the federal government, if not all white men. By forcibly removing the Cherokees and others from their ancestral lands in the east to lands set aside for a number of different native tribes in the west, the federal government established a precedent for creating Indians reservations in areas unrelated to their native lands. A negotiated settlement might have saved the lives of thousands of Cherokees and the pride of the Cherokee Nation. The Cherokee Nation might have served as a positive example of what the supposedly "savage" Indian was capable of accomplishing. By remaining in Georgia, the Cherokees might have become an alternative example of Indian integrity within an existing state or of peaceful Indian assimilation within the larger white society.

The Cherokees Today

The Cherokee culture did not die with removal. It evolved during the latter part of the 19th and 20th century. An identifiable culture remains today. The Cherokees are by far the largest group of American Indians. The 2000 census indicated that more than 875,000 individuals identified themselves as having some Cherokee blood, out of approximately 4.3 million people with Native American ancestry in the United States. There are a large number of Native American tribes and bands recognized and eligible to receive services from the United States Bureau of Indian Affairs. Three of the federally-recognized Cherokee groups include the large Cherokee Nation of Oklahoma, as well as the United Keetoowah Band of Cherokee Indians in Oklahoma and the Eastern Band of Cherokees in North Carolina. Although three groups have no political connection with each other, they have a shared cultural background. The remainder of the Cherokees are widely distributed geographically in more than 32 states.

At the start of the 21st century, the Cherokees are doing better economically than other Native American groups. Cherokees tend to be older and have fewer children, are better educated, more often employed, have more income and are more likely to live in metropolitan areas than American Indians in general. However, the Cherokee population as a whole is economically below that of the median for the U.S. population as a whole. Although many Cherokees are totally assimilated, most take pride in their heritage and Indian identity. The Cherokee language is still spoken by 15,000–25,000 tribal members, mostly from the western tribes. Some experts predict that Cherokees will assimilate further and be more like the total United States population. Others believe that, given the resurgence of Indian identity and a renewed demand for their rights as sovereign people, the Cherokees will continue as a separate nation long into the future. The primary concern of the Cherokee Nation as a whole is to find a way to define their identity as Indians within the context of also being modern Americans.

Questions for Discussion

1. What were the most influential factors—racial, economic, political, cultural—behind the Indian Removal Policy?

2. Were there alternative strategies that the Cherokees might have been pursued that could have enabled them to maintain their lands in the East?

3. Could the Cherokees have created a broader and more influential coalition of allies to support them? If so, which groups might have joined? (E.g., Railroad interests? The churches? The anti-Jacksonian politicians, such as the Whigs? The anti-Lumpkin faction in Georgia politics?)

4. Are there any ways in asymmetrical power relationships that groups with less power, such as the Cherokee, can enhance their power and make the relationship more symmetrical or even reverse the subordinate/dominant power relationship?

5. Were removal, assimilation, or eradication the only alternatives for the Cherokees? For Native Americans in general? Have there been instances in the United States or other countries in which indigenous populations have maintained their lands, their cultures, and their communities?

6. At what point and why did the Cherokees lose their struggles to maintain their lands?

7. Do you think that it was unavoidable that the Cherokees would be forced out of their ancestral lands? Why or why not?

Additional Resources

Anderson, William L. *Cherokee Removal: Before and After.* Athens, GA: University of Georgia Press, 1991.

Conley, Robert J. *The Cherokee Nation: A History.* Albuquerque, NM: University of New Mexico Press, 2005.

Denson, Andrew. *Demanding the Cherokee Nation: Indian Autonomy and American Culture, 1830-1900.* Lincoln: University of Nebraska Press, 2004.

Ehle, John. *Trail of Tears: The Rise and Fall of the Cherokee Nation.* New York: Anchor Books/Doubleday, 1988.

Filler, Louis and Allen Guttmann. *The Removal of the Cherokee Nation: Manifest Destiny or National Dishonor?* New York: Krieger Publishing Company, 1977.

Finger, John R. *The Eastern Band of Cherokees, 1819–1900.* Knoxville, TN: University of Tennessee Press, 1984.

Fixico, Donald L. *The American Indian Mind in a Linear World: American Indian Studies and Traditional Knowledge.* New York: Routledge, 2003.

McLoughlin, William G. *After the Trail of Tears: The Cherokees' Struggle for Sovereignty, 1839-1880.* Chapel Hill: University of North Carolina Press, 1993.

_____. *Cherokee Renascence in the New Republic.* Princeton, NJ: Princeton University Press, 1986.

_____. *Cherokees and Missionaries*, 1787–1839. New Haven, CT: Yale University Press, 1984.

Moulton, Gary E., ed. *The Papers of Chief John Ross*. Norman, OK: University of Oklahoma Press, 1985.

Perdue, Theda. "Cherokee Women and the Trail of Tears," *Journal of Women's History* 1 (1989): 14–30.

Perdue, Theda and Michael Green, eds. *The Cherokee Removal: A Brief History with Documents*. New York: St. Martin's Press, 1995.

Prucha, Francis P. "Andrew Jackson's Indian Policy: A Reassessment," *Journal of American History* 56 (1969): 527–39.

Remini, Robert. *The Legacy of Andrew Jackson: Essays on Democracy, Indian Removal and Slavery*. Baton Rouge: Louisiana State University, 1988.

Satz, Ronald. *American Indian Policy in the Jacksonian Era*. Lincoln: University of Nebraska Press, 1975.

Thornton, Russell. *The Cherokees: A Population History*. Lincoln: University of Nebraska Press, 1990.

Wallace, Anthony F.C. *The Long Bitter Trail: Andrew Jackson and the Indians*. New York: Hill and Wang, 1993.

Young, Mary. "The Cherokee Nation: Mirror of the Republic," *American Quarterly* 33 (1981): 502–504.

DOCUMENTS ON CD

Document 1:	President Andrew Jackson's Case for the Removal Act: First Annual Message to Congress, December 8, 1829
Document 2:	United States Congress: *Indian Removal Act*, May 28, 1830
Document 3:	U.S. Supreme Court: *Worcester v. Georgia,* January Term, 1832
Document 4:	Treaty of New Echota, December 29, 1835
Document 5:	Nancy Ward Petition, 1821
Document 6:	John Ross Petition to Congress, 1836
Document 7:	Senator Theodore Frelinghuysen speech before Senate, April 30, 1830
Document 8:	Excerpt from "William Penn" essays in Defense of Cherokees, prepared by Jeremiah Evarts for the American Board of Commissioners for Foreign Missions, 1829
Document 9:	Lewis Cass "Removal of Indians" in *North Atlantic Review*, 1830
Document 10:	George Troup letter to the *Georgia Journal*, March 5, 1832
Document 11:	Wilson Lumpkin Message to Georgia Legislature, November 24, 1832
Document 12:	Evan Jones, Letters, 1838

Teacher Overheads/Student Handouts On CD

1. Objectives

2. Historical Background, 1787-1820

3. Historical Background: Treaties

4. Historical Background: Civilizing Policy

5. Map of Major Southeastern Tribes, 1820's

6. Cherokee Renaissance, 1819-1829

7. Cherokee Renaissance: Sequoyah

8. Home of John Ross

9. Cherokee Resistance

10. Andrew Jackson is elected president

11. Timeline: Historical Background

12. Decision for Indian Removal ignored the U.S. Supreme Court

13. Split in Cherokee Resistance: The Treaty of New Echota

14. Directions for Mock Negotiations, March 1837

15-22. Biographies of the Participants

23-27. Positions and Interests

28. The roles

29. Debriefing

30. What Really Happened?

31. The Trail of Tears

32. Trail of Tears Map

33. The Legacy

34. Cherokees today

35. Questions for Discussion

Sources and Credits for Illustrations

p. 161: Map of Southeastern Tribes c.1820, *National Park Service*

p. 161: Sequoyah, Inventor of the Cherokee Alphabet, *LC-USZC4-3156*

p. 162: Home of John Ross, *National Park Service*

p. 164: Andrew Jackson as Indian Fighter, *LC-USZC4-4084*

p. 164: Andrew Jackson as "King Andrew," *LC-USZ62-1562*

p. 165: John Ross, Cherokee Chief, *LC-USZC4-3156*

p. 165: Nancy Ward, *The Tennessee Overhill Experience*

p. 165: Theodore Frelinghuysen, *LC-BH82-4989C*

p. 166: Reverend Evan Jones, *Early Missionaries to the Cherokees*

p. 166: Lewis Cass, *LC-DIG-cwpbh-02843*

p. 167: George Troup, *Biographical Dictionary of the United States Congress*

p. 167: Wilson Lumpkin, Governor of Georgia, *LC-USZ62-15349*

p. 167: Elias Boudinot, *Oklahoma Historical Society*

p. 171: Trail of Tears Map, *National Park Service*

p. 172: "Trail of Tears," *Woolaroc Museum, Bartlesville, Oklahoma*

CHAPTER EIGHT

WAR BETWEEN MEXICO AND THE UNITED STATES

OBJECTIVES

- To explain the many forces encouraging U.S. westward expansion during the first half of the 19th century.

- To analyze the conflicting interests that led to war between Mexico and the United States in 1846.

- To understand the interplay of individual decisions and historical events in shaping history.

- To contrast the peaceful resolution of the boundary dispute with Great Britain regarding Oregon with the declaration of war with Mexico in 1846.

- To appreciate the influence of personal and national pride in conflicts.

- To appreciate the costs and consequences of the war between Mexico and the United States.

CORRELATION WITH NATIONAL HISTORY STANDARDS

Era Four: Expansion and Reform (1801–1861)
Standard 1C

The student understands the ideology of Manifest Destiny, the nation's expansion to the Northwest, and the Mexican-American War.

- Explain the economic, political, racial, and religious roots of Manifest Destiny and analyze how the concept influenced the westward expansion of the nation.

- Compare and explain the peaceful resolution of the Oregon dispute with Great Britain and the declaration of war with Mexico.

- Explain the causes of the Texas War for Independence and the Mexican-American War and evaluate the provisions and consequences of the Treaty of Guadalupe Hidalgo.

- Analyze different perspectives on the Mexican-American War.

OVERVIEW

Western expansion was hardly a new idea. Some of the original royal charters from Britain to the colonies in North America extended from coast to coast. Both the economic system and the social system of the United States were based in part on the opportunities that western lands offered for land speculation, settlement, farming and attracting immigrants. The idea of western expansion was an integral part of the culture and self-definition of the United States—a place for a fresh start where democracy and individualism prevailed. Politicians, editors, clergy and other influential persons pictured it as part of the nation's destiny to develop land that was sparsely populated or "inefficiently" used. Western expansion was at the expense of the Native Americans and later, the French, Spanish, and the Mexicans.

Protestant Americans claimed that Providence had ordained the spread of their unique and progressive civilization from ocean to ocean. Doubling the size of the country with the purchase of the Louisiana Territory from France in 1803, President Jefferson justified the expansion as creating "an empire of liberty." The surging popular sentiment for expansion and the growing conviction that it was the destiny of the United States to expand to the Pacific was at its peak in the 1840s, when journalist John L. O'Sullivan first used the phrase "manifest destiny" to describe it. This sense of manifest destiny was an underlying force behind the war between the United States and Mexico in 1846–48. Yet, there was also growing opposition in the North to the war and to westward expansion of the slave South.

Did the North Americans' drive westward make war with Mexico inevitable? What were the basic needs and interests of the United States and Mexico in the 1840s? Could the war between Mexico and the United States have been avoided through negotiation? Could it have been avoided through the use of international, third-party mediation? Why was the United States willing to agree to a boundary for Oregon at the 49th parallel with Great Britain but not able to negotiate with Mexico regarding a boundary for Texas?

This lesson includes the following alternative exercises:

•   A Mock Negotiation

•   A Mock Mediation

•   A Debate in the United States Congress

•   A Debate in the Mexican Congress.

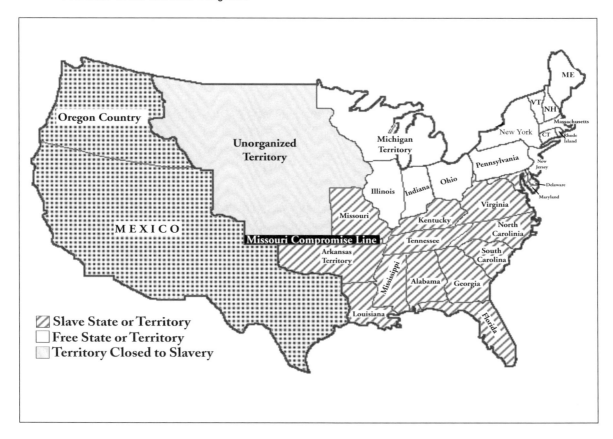

The United States after the Missouri Compromise of 1820

HISTORICAL BACKGROUND

*I*n 1819, a Spanish government weakened by the Napoleonic wars and revolts by her colonies, reluctantly signed the Adams-Onís Treaty with the United States, ceding Florida to the United States in return for U.S. assumption of $5 million in damage claims by U.S. citizens against Spain. The treaty defined the western boundary of the Louisiana Purchase as being from the mouth of the Sabine River proceeding in a broken northwesterly line along the Red River and the Arkansas River and the 42nd parallel, from which it went due west to the Pacific Ocean (see "Map of Disputed Territory, 1845-1846" on page 183). This surrendered Madrid's claims to the Pacific Northwest, but confirmed Spanish claims to the province of Texas west of the Sabine River in the Spanish colony of "New Spain" (as Mexico was known at the time). In 1821, after a decade of armed struggle, Mexico obtained its independence from Spain. The independent nation of Mexico, initially a monarchy, stretched from the Yucatan in the south to the northern provinces of Texas, New Mexico, and California.

Spanish authorities had encouraged immigration to its sparsely populated northern province (the future territory of Texas) through generous grants of land and the hiring of land agents, such as Stephen Austin. When the Republic of Mexico replaced the monarchy in 1824, it confirmed these land grants and issued others. Most of the North Americans moving into Texas were slaveholders seeking the fertile soil along the Gulf coast to grow cotton. The newcomers, who were required by law to become Roman Catholics and Mexican citizens, were predominantly Protestants who never ceased to think of themselves as North Americans. They quickly outnumbered the Hispanic residents. By 1836 there were 30,000 white Anglos, 5,000 black slaves and only 8,000 Hispanic Mexicans in Texas.

Soon after Mexico obtained independence in 1821, two U.S. envoys offered to purchase the Texas territory, but the Mexican authorities rebuffed their efforts. Concerned about the growing number of Anglo-Americans and their slaves in Texas, the Mexican government in 1829 abolished slavery in an attempt to discourage their future immigration, as Texas was the main area where slavery existed in Mexico. Local authorities in Texas, however, did not enforce the decree because they feared that it might provoke the settlers into rebelling. In 1834, the seeds for an uprising bore fruit when General Antonio Lopez de Santa Anna seized power in Mexico City and attempted to tighten the central government's control over outlying provinces. The Anglos in Texas regarded his actions as a violation of their rights under the 1824 Mexican constitution. Skirmishes began in 1835 between Texans and local Mexican soldiers. The Anglo-Texans set up a provisional government and their own army.

To suppress this emergent revolt, Santa Anna led a Mexican Army into Texas in 1836. His 5,000 soldiers besieged a group of 200 Texans and others in the old Alamo mission in San Antonio, and killed all of the defenders, including frontiersmen Davy Crockett and Jim Bowie. The slaughter infuriated many North Americans. Joined by hundreds of volunteers, the Texan army, under Sam Houston, defeated the Mexicans at San Jacinto, captured Santa Anna, and extracted a treaty from him that recognized the independence of Texas and set the southern and western boundary of Texas at the Rio Grande River instead of the Nueces River, which historically had been the boundary. Mexico immediately repudiated the agreement, as did Santa Anna after his release. Texas almost immediately sought annexation to the United States. Houston's friend, President Andrew Jackson, an

GENERAL D. ANTONIO LOPEZ DE SANTA-ANNA.

General Santa Anna

ardent expansionist, wanted Texas in the Union, but northern opposition to the expansion of slavery made annexation politically difficult, and Texas remained an independent republic for nine years.

In the meantime, other issues heightened tensions between the U.S. and Mexico. The claims that U.S. nationals had against the Mexican government from injuries or loss of property during the Mexican war of independence and subsequent internal conflicts remained unpaid. In 1840, an international claims commission settled this outstanding disagreement by requiring Mexico to pay U.S. nationals approximately $2 million, one-third of the original amount claimed. Many of these claims were contested by Mexico as flimsy and fraudulent. Although Mexico started to make payments, the country's fiscal problems forced the government to halt them in 1843. Mexican forays into Texas and the harsh treatment of Texan prisoners captured in border raids created additional friction, while U.S. naval incursion in Monterrey Bay renewed Mexican suspicions about U.S. expansionism.

U.S.-Mexican relations were tense in early 1845 when General José Joaquín de Herrera became president of Mexico. Herrera's position was made all the more difficult because of numerous economic, class, racial and political difficulties at home. In addition to a nearly empty treasury, Mexico had a highly stratified society that it had inherited from the Spanish. Those who had been born in Mexico of "pure Spanish blood"—the *criollos* or creoles—made up the upper class and held most public offices as well as most of the land. The *mestizos*, of mixed Spanish and Indian descent, composed the small laboring class, while the bottom was filled by the vast peasant class, which was primarily Indian and worked for the landowners. The Roman Catholic Church and the army remained firmly entrenched as the country's most powerful institutions. They had their own courts and privileges and any efforts by reformers to curb their power ignited political disputes. Indeed, the political situation in early republican Mexico was highly unstable. Four factions—radicals, moderates, conservatives and Santa Anna's followers— engendered much political disorder as they struggled over issues such as the relationship between the state, the church and the military, the extent of working class participation in public affairs and the form of government that Mexico should follow.

Mexican President Herrera's ability to govern such a deeply fragmented and unstable nation was severely compromised by a chain of events in the United States that set in motion the process for U.S. annexation of Texas.

U.S. President John Tyler (1841)

Near the end of his term, U.S. President John Tyler (Democrat from Virginia), trying to use Texas as an issue to obtain renomination by the Whigs, negotiated an annexation treaty and submitted it for Senate ratification in April 1844. He tried to get support for annexation by playing on fears of British seizure of Texas. Unable to win a two-thirds Senate majority for a treaty, Tyler, subsequently as a lame-duck president, suggested annexation by joint resolution requiring only simple majorities of both houses. His opponents—northern and western Whigs and northern Democrats—protested, but Congress annexed Texas by joint resolution in March 1845. (See Document 1: Joint Resolution of Congress, March 1, 1845.) Mexico protested and severed diplomatic relations with the United States.

In addition to the controversy over U.S. annexation of Texas, a major dispute existed over the Texas boundary. Mexico claimed that the southern and western boundary was the Nueces River, but the State of Texas and the U.S. Government claimed that it was the Rio Grande. Except for the 1836 treaty with Santa Anna, the Nueces River had been the accepted boundary. Since the Rio Grande ran 150 miles south of the Nueces River and much

Map of Disputed Territory, 1845-1846

farther to the north and west, the U.S. assertion of the Rio Grande as the boundary would double the size of the land it was claiming as Texas from Mexico.

After Mexican independence from Spain, Britain became the primary trading partner and main source of capital investment for Mexico. In the early 1840s, American expansionists viewed Mexican threats over U.S. annexation as being encouraged, even directed and supported, by Britain. Although London had encouraged Mexico to recognize an independent Texas Republic to prevent it from becoming part of the United States, and although there was friction between London and Washington over conflicting claims in the Northwest between the US and British Canada, London did not manipulate Mexico to block U.S. expansion. Indeed, in the Northwest, Britain proved willing to compromise Canadian expansion in light of larger British interests to avoid war or at least maintain harmonious relations with the United States.

After passage of the joint resolution for the annexation of Texas in March 1845, Mexico broke off diplomatic relations with the United States. Although furious with the U.S. and pressured by a bellicose Mexican press that was pushing for war with the U.S., President Herrera knew that he could ill afford a full-scale conflict— Mexico had neither the funds nor the army to fight the U.S. At the urging of France and Britain, Herrera belatedly sought to prevent U.S. annexation of Texas by recognizing the Republic of Texas with the stipulation that it remain independent. But this effort was too late.

In an attempt to salvage national pride, President Herrera in August 1845 dispatched a confidential note to the U.S. government indicating a willingness to receive a special emissary to negotiate the Texas boundary issue. Two months later, new U.S. President James K. Polk (an expansionist Democrat from Tennessee) sent John Slidell as a commissioner to Mexico, with instructions to negotiate the Texas boundary issue and the outstanding claims against Mexico by U.S. citizens, and a confidential authorization to offer $15 million for the purchase of the northern Mexican provinces of California and New Mexico (Polk later spoke of up to $40 million). (See Document 2: Excerpt from Biography of President Polk and Document 3: President Polk's Secret Instructions to John Slidell, November 10, 1845.)

MOCK NEGOTIATION OR MEDIATION

Mexican President Herrera had indicated a willingness to receive a special envoy from the United States. United States President Polk sent John Slidell as a special envoy on a secret mission to Mexico with instructions to negotiate the Texas boundary and the outstanding claims against Mexico by U.S. citizens and try to purchase the sparsely populated northern Mexico states of California and New Mexico.

It is now December 1845. Instead of his mission being revealed and rejected by the Mexican government as actually happened, let us take a step away from history and see if Mr. Slidell and Mexican Foreign Minister Manuel de la Peña y Peña can negotiate a resolution to the growing hostility between their countries. In fact, although the two men were in Mexico City in December 1845, such a meeting never really occurred.

THE PARTICIPANTS

Manuel Peña y Peña
Mexico

Manuel de la Peña y Peña, Negotiating for Mexico

Manuel de la Peña y Peña was President Herrera's Minister of Foreign Relations in 1845. He was a noted Mexican lawyer, jurist and public servant. He was moderate politically and recognized Mexico's economic and military inability to defeat the United States or even maintain effective control over its northern states. To encourage Mexican public opinion to allow negotiations with the United States and avoid war, he urged the U.S. consul in 1845 to make a peaceful gesture, such as withdrawing the U.S. naval force from off Vera Cruz. The central government was unwilling to take sole responsibility for a conciliatory policy, and Peña y Peña distributed letters to governors and state legislators soliciting their advice and support. In 1845, he believed that Mexico should be flexible and consider surrendering part of its territory that was sparsely populated and that it was unable to govern in any case. He was looking for a way to resolve the situation with the United States but also concerned about Mexico's national honor. Subsequently Peña y Peña was appointed head of the Supreme Court. In 1847, when Santa Anna fled after the fall of Mexico City, he named Peña y Peña as interim president and Peña y Peña opened negotiations with special U.S. envoy, Nicholas Trist, that led to the peace treaty.

John Slidell, Negotiating for the United States

John Slidell, a "manifest destiny" Democrat from Louisiana, was appointed by President Polk as a special envoy to Mexico late in 1845. He spoke fluent Spanish. His publicly stated role was to try to resolve the Texan boundary dispute and the claims against Mexico by U.S. nationals. He also had secret instructions from President Polk to offer $15 million to Mexico (later Polk expressed a willingness to pay up to $40 million) for the purchase of the provinces of New Mexico and California. Slidell was born in New York City, graduated Columbia College and went into a mercantile business. He later moved to New Orleans where he practiced law and became a member of Congress from 1843–45. His political ambition was to obtain a U.S. Senate seat, which he did in 1853–61. During the Civil War, he joined the Confederacy, and became its envoy to France.

John Slidell
United States

POSITIONS AND INTERESTS

Mexico

Positions

- Annexation of Texas was illegal
- Appalled at U.S. policy of pushing the Indians westward and U.S. support for slavery
- Angered by U.S. support of its citizens' claims against Mexico, many of which were seen as fraudulent
- Rejected U.S. claim to the land between the Nueces and the Rio Grande Rivers as without historical or legal basis
- Against U.S. sending troops into area disputed by the U.S. and Mexico

Interests

- Mexican honor, pride and self esteem hurt by the loss of Texas and high-handed way that the U.S. dealt with Mexico
- Mexico could ill-afford to lose trade revenues from North Americans as well as the economic loss of prosperous Texas
- Mexico *distrusted* the U.S. because of its history of expansion
- Mexico needed political and economic stability as the government was virtually bankrupt
- Fear that with Indian blood Mexicans would be seen as "racial inferiors" and treated by the North Americans like their Native Indian population (removed from their lands) or African population (enslaved)
- Needed to protect settlers in the northern provinces from raids by Indians (especially Apaches and Comanches).

The United States

Positions

- Mexico owed U.S. nationals more than $2 million of unpaid damages
- Mexico was not using or populating land in dispute
- U.S. supported the claim by Texas that the southern and western border of Texas was the Rio Grande rather than the Nueces River
- Mexico was standing in the way of America's "manifest destiny"

Interests

- *Economics:* U.S. wanted ports on California coast for trade with Far East (Polk), and for land speculation and settlement (historically)
- Fear that the British would help Mexico to retake Texas and abolish slavery
- *Politics:* Both parties looked to westward expansion. Most Democrats were willing to go to war. Most Whigs preferred peaceful annexation through settlement.
- *Race:* Anglo-American belief in their racial and political superiority to Mexicans
- *Ideology:* U.S. a "beacon to the world" for freedom and democracy; "manifest destiny" of U.S.
- *Religion:* Protestant North American image of Spanish Catholics as lazy and corrupt

TEACHER INSTRUCTIONS

Preparation

1. Share the "Historical Background" with the class as either a lecture or a handout. In addition, either distribute the map you may also wish to post a copy of the map in the classroom or display it as an overhead.

2. For all options, students should also read Student Handout: "Positions and Interests."

3. Have students read the brief biographies.

Directions

Option One—International Negotiation

1. Divide the class into groups of three, assigning each person one of the following roles:

    a. Manuel de la Peña y Peña, negotiating for Mexico

    b. John Slidell, negotiating for the United States

    c. Observer/Recorder/Reporter

2. All participants should read the directions for the negotiations and review the biography for their assigned role.

3. Give each negotiator the secret instructions from <u>his</u> president <u>only</u>.

Option Two—International Mediation

1. Divide the class into groups of four, assigning each person one of the following roles:

    a. Manuel de la Peña y Peña, Mexican Foreign Minister

    b. John Slidell, U.S. Commissioner to Mexico

    c. A mediator from an International Mediation Commission

    d. An observer/recorder/reporter for the Commission

2. All participants should read the directions for the mediation and review the biography for their assigned role.

3. Give each representative (roles a & b) the secret instructions from <u>his</u> president <u>only</u>.

Debriefing

1. Ask the Observers/Recorders/Reporters to explain briefly the results and the process of the negotiations or mediation in their group.

2. Share "The Facts Continued" with the class as a lecture and/or reading assignment and the map of the Mexican Cession, 1848.

3. Compare the results of the mock negotiations or mediation with what actually happened in history, including the details of Polk's secret instructions to Slidell to offer $15-40 million to

Mexico for the purchase of New Mexico and California and how this offer compared with what really happened.

4.   Use the "Questions for Discussion" for in-class discussion or essay topics.

Alternate Activities

Option One—Mock Debate in the United States Congress

War with Mexico was bitterly debated in the U.S. Congress in 1846. Have students conduct a mock congressional debate, including the war message by President James Polk (see Document 4: "Polk's War Message to Congress," May 1846); the speech in support of expansionism and war with Mexico by Thomas Hart Benton, Democratic Senator from Missouri, in *Congressional Globe*, May 28, 1846); and speeches by many northern Whigs who opposed the war. Students may wish to research additional members of the Congress that met in 1846.

Option Two—Mock Debate in the Mexican Congress

The Mexican Congress also debated whether war was a good idea. Have students conduct a mock congressional debate among the members of the Mexican Congress, which might include:

1.   José Fernando Ramirez, a member of the Mexican Congress during the war with the United States who chastised Mexicans for maintaining "ambitious and ignorant demagogues" in power.

2.   Antonio Lopez de Santa Anna, an influential and controversial military and political figure in Mexico who fought in the wars for Mexican independence from Spain, and later was president numerous times: 1829-30, 1832-36, 1841-44, 1846-47, and "perpetual dictator" from 1853-1855.

3.   José Joaquín de Herrera, who became president under pressure for war with the United States to recapture Texas.

4.   Mariano Paredes y Arrillaga, a Mexican general who, as a leader of the conservatives helped to put Santa Anna into the presidency in 1841and in December 1845, Paredes marched on Mexico City, overthrew Herrera and installed himself as president.

5.   Manuel Crescencio Rejón, a member of the first Congress after Mexican independence and a liberal and strong federalist who helped develop the federalist Constitution in 1824. A liberal, Rejón believed that "North America abominates us because almost all of us are descended from Indians. The Indian tribes, former owners of their land, have been thrust aside. Why should we expect anything different?"

THE FACTS CONTINUED

*O*fficials in Mexico were not certain as to the motives behind Slidell's mission. An emissary to resolve the Texas boundary had been invited, but a plenipotentiary minister, to solve broader issues, such as the Polk Administration's desire to purchase New Mexico and California, could not be tolerated. To accept Slidell in this capacity would have reopened diplomatic relations with the United States, which Mexico had severed in March of 1845 when the United States annexed Texas.

When Slidell reached Mexico City in early December 1845, the full nature of his mission had already become known publicly and caused an outcry in the Mexican press. Herrera was too politically vulnerable to receive him. Taking advantage of the situation, General Paredes, a favorite of conservatives, marched his army into Mexico City, overthrew Herrera, and installed himself as president. Joaquin Castillo Lanzas, a distinguished jurist believed to be well-disposed toward the U.S., became his Minister of Foreign Relations. Although President Paredes, much like his predecessor, wanted a peaceful solution to the Texas problem, he had tied his banner to nationalism to seize power. Given the highly partisan and inflammatory Mexican press, which demanded war to redeem the country's national pride, and the unstable political situation, Paredes found it impossible to publicly support negotiations with the United States.

The Polk administration and its emissaries believed in 1845 that Britain, having failed by diplomatic means to thwart annexation of Texas by the US, now intended to goad Mexico into a war with the United States to defeat annexation. But, far from encouraging Mexico to go to war, London had notified the Mexican leaders that they could expect no aid from Britain if they attempted an invasion of Texas, a warning the British repeated on several occasions as the crisis between the United States and Mexico heightened.

With Texas annexed, U.S. fears of British machination now shifted to the West Coast, where expansionists had long suspected London's interest in the harbors of California as part of its worldwide trading empire. There had been rumors since the early 1840s that Mexico might cede California to Britain in exchange for forgiveness of Mexico's debt obligations to British creditors. The expansionist press warned in 1845 that Britain was trying to encircle the United States by expanding its existing territory in Canada to include the Northwest territory, and possibly the entire West Coast and Texas as a British satellite.

Paredes did in fact urge London to side with Mexico in its dispute with the United States, but London continually refused. And, despite London's advice to end the crisis, Paredes refused to negotiate with Slidell, and with Slidell's departure in March 1846, efforts at a negotiated settlement between the US and Mexico ended.

Thus, when President Polk learned on January 13, 1846 that the Mexicans had refused to negotiate with John Slidell (building on Polk's fears of British instigation,) he responded by immediately ordering General Zachary Taylor to move south and occupy the disputed Texas territory up to the Rio Grande. It is unclear whether this action was initially due to fears that Mexico might invade Texas, or to pressure Mexico to negotiate, or to push that country into war. Taylor blockaded the port of Matamoros, at the mouth of the Rio Grande, itself an act of war under international law. With increased military activity in the disputed area and hostile movements elsewhere, Paredes declared on April 23, 1846 that a "defensive war" against the U.S. had begin, although neither he nor the Mexican legislature had declared war. He ordered the Mexican army to challenge Taylor's incursion into Mexican territory.

By the time Slidell returned to Washington and personally informed the president of the situation in Mexico, Polk's diary for May 9, 1846 shows that the president was already committed to asking Congress for a declaration of war, largely on the basis of Mexican recalcitrance on the border issue and the unpaid claims (See Document 4: Excerpt from Polk's diary). Later that day, a report arrived from General Taylor that Mexican cavalry had crossed the Rio Grande and in a skirmish two weeks earlier, killed or wounded 16 U.S. soldiers and captured nearly 50 others. General Taylor stated: "hostilities may now be considered as commenced."

Taking advantage of this incident, Polk sent a war message to the U.S. Congress on May 11, 1846, asserting that "Mexico has passed the boundary of the United States, has invaded our territory, and shed American blood on American soil." He asked Congress to recognize that a state of war existed and to appropriate $10 million to pursue hostilities with Mexico. Polk's war message detailed twenty years of accumulated grievances against Mexico, stressing that Slidell's offer to negotiate was rejected "upon the most frivolous pretexts." (See Document 5: Polk's Message on War with Mexico, compare with document 4, his diary excerpt.) The expansionist Democratic press supported his claims. Congress voted for war 174–11 in the House on May 11 and 40-2 in the Senate on May 12, 1846. There were, however, voices of dissent. Northern and Western Whigs criticized the war and some of them voted against the appropriations, but they limited their opposition to avoid being tarred as unpatriotic. In New England, Henry David Thoreau went to jail rather than pay the war taxes and wrote an essay on "Civil Disobedience" in support of nonviolent resistance against a war that he and many of the northern Whigs saw as being fought for the expansion of slavery.

Mexico's internal divisions hindered its war effort. Some Mexican officials complained of the apathy of many peasants and the lack of support for the central government. Others feared potential revolution and did not encourage popular mobilization for guerrilla warfare. In addition, Mexican regular army troops were underpaid, underfed, ill-clothed, badly equipped and often commanded by poorly-trained officers. The US army was equipped with the most modern artillery and other weaponry, and had many effective young officers, such as Robert E. Lee and Ulysses S. Grant. General Zachary Taylor defeated a Mexican army in early May 1846 and recklessly pursued it deep into northern Mexico, capturing the city of Monterrey in October. After a brief truce, in late February 1847, Taylor's forces came close to defeat at the Battle of Buena Vista but managed to hold the field. Although Mexico lost the regular army battles, it was more successful in some guerrilla actions.

Battle of Buena Vista, February 23, 1847 (U.S. view)

Major U.S. offensives, however, took place elsewhere as well. U.S. forces seized New Mexico and encouraged Anglo-American settlers in California to revolt, declare their independence from Mexico and establish a Republic of California ("The Bear Flag Republic"). A few members of the British Government argued vigorously for a military response to the U.S. seizure of California, but Prime Minister Robert Peel was reluctant to risk a war with the U.S. now that a resolution to the Oregon question was near. Britain was far more interested in ending the Oregon question. London responded to Congress's joint resolution on Oregon with a proposal that the British ambassador had rejected the previous year. The extreme American expansionists wanted to extend U.S. territory almost to present-day Juneau, Alaska (54 degrees, 40 minutes latitude, hence the slogan "54, 40 or fight"). The British were seeking to set the border deep into present-day Oregon. Instead of fighting, President Polk and the British government agreed to a compromise largely extending the 49th parallel as the border, which gave the Americans more than the Canadians received. The Senate quickly ratified the Oregon Treaty. Americans remained suspicious of British intentions, however, and the Polk administration politely but firmly rejected Lord Aberdeen's offer of British mediation to resolve the war with Mexico. President Polk decided to carry the war to Mexico's heartland in an attempt to pressure the Mexican government to cede territory to the U.S. (See Document 6: Letters of Jose Ramirez from Mexico City, 1847.) In March 1847, General Winfield Scott led another U.S. army in an amphibious landing near Vera Cruz, and an overland expedition to Mexico City. Scott's army outflanked the Mexican force under Santa Anna in several encounters and occupied the capital on September 13, 1847.

United States Occupation of Mexico City
September 14, 1847 (U.S. view)

Along with the invading army, President Polk had sent an executive agent, Nicholas Trist, chief clerk of the State Department, to negotiate with the Mexican government. Under southern pressure to demand all of northern Mexico, Polk recalled Trist in early October 1847. However, Trist ignored the president's directive and opened negotiations with the moderate Mexican faction, led by interim president Manuel de Peña y Peña that had recently come into power. Although the faction's hold on power was shaky, it was the only group with which an acceptable treaty could be made. Trist continued to negotiate until the terms of a treaty were agreed upon on February 2, 1848 at Guadalupe Hidalgo, near Mexico City. (See Document 7: Excerpts from letters from Nicholas Trist).

The Mexican Land Cession, 1848

According to the terms of the Treaty of Guadalupe Hidalgo, Mexico ceded its northern provinces of California and New Mexico (including the present day states of Arizona, New Mexico, Nevada, California, and Utah and parts of Colorado and Wyoming) to the United States and confirmed the annexation of Texas with the Rio Grande as the border. In return, the U.S. was to pay $15 million for California and New Mexico, and to assume the claims of American citizens totaling approximately $3 million. Under the signed treaty, the United States also guaranteed that Mexicans living in the area could continue to reside there and be secure in their land titles and the practice of their religion. Although the Mexican Congress included this provision in its ratification; it was deleted by the United States Senate. In practice, the U.S. Senate's action provided a means by which many Mexican landowners who remained in the annexed territories lost their land. The treaty, as signed and ratified by both countries, also stipulated that Mexican nationals who remained in the annexed territories would automatically acquire U.S. citizenship. The U.S. also pledged to prevent future raids by Apaches, Comanches, and other Indians upon settlers in these territories or across the border into northern Mexico and to obtain compensation for losses in such raids (the Mexican Army had been unable to prevent such raids, which had a devastating economic effect on the northern provinces of Mexico). (See Document 8: The Treaty of Guadalupe Hidalgo, 1848.)

Some Mexican statesmen, such as "radical" Manuel Rejón, urged the Mexican Congress to reject the treaty. Rejón blamed the United States for an uninterrupted series of aggressions. Since the United States had started the war, Rejón argued, there was no reason for Mexico to agree to cede it land. Other Mexicans, such as moderate Peña y Peña, contended that under the circumstances the treaty was the best that could be obtained. They emphasized that the treaty included political, economic, and religious guarantees for Mexicans residing in the ceded territory, a promise to suppress the incursions into Mexico being made by raiding Indians (who presented serious threats to life and property), a joint commission to determine the exact details of the boundary line, and a cash payment of $15 million at a time when the Mexican treasury was deeply in debt. (The Mexicans did not know that Polk had been prepared to pay $15-40 million for the territory in 1845-46.) Although the U.S. called this simply a payment, to preserve its national honor, Mexico called it an "indemnity." Peña y Peña feared that the continuation of war would bring anarchy and even greater loss to Mexico.

Although Polk was annoyed by Trist's actions, he realized that northern opposition to the war was growing in the country and in Congress (the Whigs had gained a majority in the House in the 1846 election) as was contrary sentiment among southern Democrats for conquest of *all* of Mexico. (See Document 9: Excerpts from Abraham Lincoln's speech in Congress protesting U.S. Aggression against Mexico, and Document 10: Excerpts from Henry David Thoreau's Essay on "Civil Disobedience," 1849.) Since Trist had generally conformed to his original instructions, Polk submitted the treaty to the U.S. Senate, which ratified it (38 to 14) on March 10, 1848 without the provision guaranteeing land titles and rights to the Mexicans who were currently living in the areas that were ceded to the United States by Mexico. The Mexican Congress ratified it two months later. The Mexican Cession expanded the size of the United States by one-third and extended it across the continent from sea to sea.

The Legacy

The war had profound effects on both countries. Some 1,700 U.S. soldiers had been killed in battle and another 11,500 died from other causes, mainly disease. Mexican fatalities numbered approximately 50,000. The war cost the United States approximately $100 million, at a time when U.S. government revenues were $36 million, expenditures were $45 million, and the U.S. national debt was $63 million, mostly because of the war with Mexico. The hostilities bankrupted the Mexican treasury. Mexico saw large amounts of property, agricultural goods, livestock and even art treasures destroyed by invading U.S. armies and was forced to relinquish half of its territory.

The war contributed to animosity between the two neighboring countries for decades to come. Adding to the animosity was Mexico's sense of betrayal by the U.S.'s refusal to recognize land ownership and other rights promised to Mexicans living in the land that was ceded by Article 20 of the treaty as originally negotiated. This article was deleted by the United States Senate when it approved the treaty. Furthermore, Mexico believed that it had gained some advantage from the United States pledge to restrain the Indians in the northern provinces of Mexico (south of the new international border between the two countries). However, restraining the Indians tribes from raiding the northern provinces of Mexico proved to be more difficult than the United States government had imagined. In 1854, the United States purchased 30,000 square miles of land from Mexico (the Gadsden Purchase) in what is now southern New Mexico and Arizona for a southern transcontinental railroad route. The land was populated primarily by Comanches and Apaches, and the purchase helped address Mexican claims that the United States was not meeting its agreement to control the Indians. In fact, it took the United States forty years to accomplish the goal of containing these western Indians.

Costs of the war

- 1,700 North Americans killed in battle and 11,500 died from disease

- 50,000 Mexican fatalities

- War cost U.S. approximately $100 million

- War left Mexico bankrupt

Treaty of Guadalupe Hidalgo, 1848

Most importantly, soon after the war between Mexico and the United States, both countries endured civil wars. California's admission to the Union in 1850 as a free state demonstrated to the slaveholding South that it would soon become a minority and that slavery might be eventually eliminated. Thus began the final path to disunion. (See Chapter 9: The Compromise of 1850.)

Although the heroic deaths of six young cadets ("los ninos') from the Mexican National Military Academy who chose to die rather than to surrender at the Battle of Chapultepec at Mexico City later became hallowed symbols of Mexican honor and patriotism, the country's politics, stormy since independence, grew even more tumultuous during the 1850s. U.S. troops left a country demoralized by defeat and open to uprisings, riots and continued political and economic instability. Santa Anna returned to power as "perpetual dictator" in 1853 but was overthrown two years later by a reform group, led by liberal Benito Juarez, who established the Constitution of 1857 which provided for the secularization of much church property and a reduction of the privileges of the army. Conservative opposition was so bitter, however, that a civil war, known as the War of Reform (1858-61), ensued. The liberals triumphed, and the conservatives sought foreign assistance. Responding to their pleas and his own imperial ambitions, Emperor Napoleon III of France sent French troops and a Hapsburg prince, Maximilian, to establish a brief (1864-67) and ill-fated empire in Mexico. By 1867, a combination of factors—primarily determined Mexican resistance, U.S. support for the insurgents' cause and the eventual withdrawal of support by Napoleon—

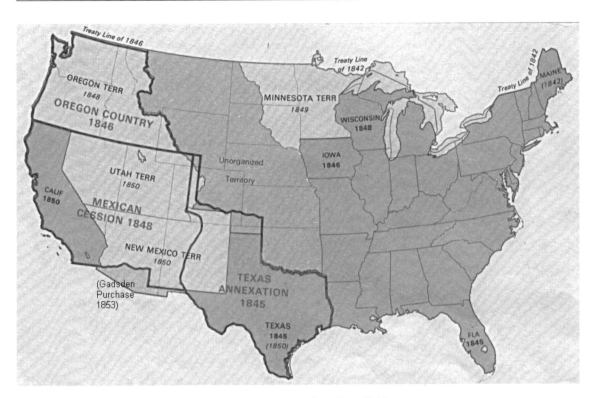

Map of Mexican Cession, 1848

enabled Benito Juarez to overthrow Emperor Maximilian and re-establish republican government in Mexico. But because of conservative opposition, neither Juarez nor his successor was able to implement the liberal reform programs. In 1876, General Porfiro Diaz led a successful armed revolt and, except for a brief period (1880–1884), held the reins of power until 1911. Diaz's dictatorial regime, while providing Mexico with political stability and considerable economic growth through outside investment, also brought increased social and economic inequity for the *mestizo* majority, and ultimately paved the way for the outbreak of revolution in 1910.

The Mexican Revolution evolved as a long and complex sequence of violent events lasting more than a decade. A moderate was elected president but his policies pleased no one and he was toppled in a coup in 1913 led by the army commander, who was deposed within a year. A new constitution was instituted in 1917 with promises of extensive land and labor reform. President Wilson twice sent troops into Mexico to protect American interests. After a series of coups and assassinations in the 1920s, the Institutional Revolutionary Party (PRI) was formed and controlled politics in Mexico for the next 70 years. During the Great Depression of the 1930s, Mexico nationalized the holdings of foreign oil companies. The possession of oil fields brought Mexico increasing prosperity after World War II. In 1976, vast new oil reserves were discovered, banks were nationalized and tight currency controls imposed. After the overborrowing and mismanagement of oil revenues led to inflation, the government defaulted on its debt in 1982, and the Mexican economy collapsed in 1994. The long-standing commitment to a centralized state economy began to be dismantled. The United States offered a rapid rescue package in 1994 and major economic reforms were instituted by Mexican President Ernesto Zedillo. The Mexican economy was able to quickly recover. Democratic reforms by Zedillo's administration caused the PRI to lose its absolute majority in Congress in 1997. In 2000, after 71 years of PRI control, Vincente Fox, of the opposition National Action Party (PAN) won the presidential election. By a razor-thin margin, the PAN candidate, Felipe Calderon, won the presidential election in 2006.

In trying to put the past behind us, it is clear that the people of the United States have been divided over the Mexican War from the beginning. The war was much more popular in the South and Southwest than in the North. In subsequent decades, the North continued to view it as an unjust war. In addition, the war and the area ceded by Mexico were blamed for leading to Southern secession and the Civil War. The brief flirtation by the United States with an overseas empire at the turn of the century led some to justify the Mexican War as an earlier example of the nation's Manifest Destiny to expand and bring democracy to other peoples. But a re-evaluation of unilateral U.S. intervention in Latin American countries under Presidents Theodore Roosevelt, William Howard Taft and Woodrow Wilson soon brought President James Polk's earlier intervention into disrepute again. The "Good Neighbor" policy begun in the late 1920s under President Herbert Hoover became a major aspect of U.S. policy toward Latin America under President Franklin D. Roosevelt. Although Polk's intervention of 1846-48 remained in disrepute, the threat of communism during the Cold War era was used to justify numerous direct or indirect U.S. military interventions in Latin America for fifty years after World War II.

Although the United States has never officially apologized to Mexico for its seizure by force of the northern provinces of Mexico in the nineteenth century, the private comments of Nicholas P. Trist, the U.S. negotiator at the peace Treaty of Guadalupe Hidalgo in 1848, demonstrate his recognition of the injustice of the war. As Trist told friends years later: "My object throughout was…to make the treaty as little exacting…upon Mexico as was compatible with its being accepted at home [by President Polk and the Democratic majority in the U.S. Congress]. In this I was governed by two considerations: One was the inequity of the war, as an abuse of power on our part. The other was the more disadvantageous the treaty was made to Mexico, the stronger would be the ground of opposition to it in the Mexican Congress by the party who had boasted of its ability to frustrate any peace measures." (See Document 7: Excerpts from Letters from Nicholas Trist). Thus, even the U.S. envoy who negotiated the peace treaty that ceded much of northern Mexico to the United States, was ashamed of what his country had done.

Mexico is now the United States' third largest trading partner. However, relations between Mexico and the United States remain strained primarily because of economic, cultural and immigration issues between the two countries. (See Volume Two, Chapter 7: Immigration Restrictions and the National Origins Act of 1924 for background and current information about immigration.) In recent years, both governments have been attempting to find ways to turn conflicting interests into policies of mutual benefit. The North American Free Trade Agreement (NAFTA), which phased out tariffs between Canada, the United States and Mexico over a fifteen year period beginning in 1994, was one such attempt. NAFTA has been supplemented by the North American Agreement on Environmental Cooperation and the North American Agreement on Labor Cooperation. As the economies of these three North American countries become more intertwined in an increasingly globalized world, there is even more reason for them to find ways to peacefully resolve continuing sources of conflict.

The belief in American exceptionalism and a manifest destiny, and a tradition of westward conquest and expansion across the continent, may have helped create a national image of Americans as providing in Jefferson's words, "an empire for liberty." But, however sincere, the rhetoric of liberty has often concealed some very grim realities. The story of the Mexican War, a war that might have been avoided—as war with Great Britain over the Oregon Territory was avoided by the very same president—carries with it a warning about the injustice that may be perpetrated by hubris and ambition as well as the unforeseen, tragic consequences that may result from war.

QUESTIONS FOR DISCUSSION

1. What were the causes of the war between the United States and Mexico in 1846?

2. Would it have been historically realistic for Mexico to have accepted a settlement to the dispute with the United States without having been forced by armed conflict and internal strife?

3. How might Mexico's national pride have permitted a settlement without violence?

4. What might have satisfied the interests of both countries while still maintaining national pride?

5. Could Mexico and the United States have accepted a resolution that acknowledged the annexation of Texas by the U.S. but with the southwestern boundary as the Nueces River rather than the Rio Grande?

6. How might subsequent history have been different if the conflict were resolved without a war?

    Some possibilities include:

•   A negotiated or mediated agreement without war could have avoided destruction of lives and property. It might have preserved Mexico's self esteem and helped Mexico avoid the next three decades of rebellion, civil war and foreign intervention which it had to endure, and also might have hastened economic and social development.

•   The war did not end the friction between the two countries. In fact, it probably intensified it. The invaders from the United States treated Mexicans as they did the Indians as racial inferiors. Mexicans were left with an even more bitter fear and hostility towards North Americans. This virulent xenophobia was disseminated and popularized in the traditional Mexican *corrido*, the folk song of the common people. "Yankeephobia" was given additional respectability by the intellectual community's tirades against U.S. imperialism. A mediated agreement might have avoided the worst of such sentiments and might have provided a basis for building a trustful and cooperative relationship between the two countries.

•   The Treaty of Guadalupe Hidalgo resulted in Mexico's loss of half of its territory. If there had been a mediated settlement based on law rather than force of arms, perhaps Mexico would have ceded or sold less land. Consequently much of the current southwestern United States might today still be part of Mexico. Mexico, rather than the United States, might have been the beneficiary of the California Gold Rush, which began a mere few months after the end of hostilities, and of the lucrative trade between the West Coast and Asia, great booms to its economic development.

ADDITIONAL RESOURCES

The Avalon Project at Yale Law School. http://www.yale.edu/lawweb/avalon.diplomacy/mexico/mxtreaty.htm

Bauer, Jack K. *The Mexican War, 1846–48*. New York: Macmillan, 1974.

Brack, Gene M. *Mexico Views Manifest Destiny, 1821–1846: Essays on the Origin of the Mexican War*. Albuquerque: University of New Mexico Press, 1975.

DeLay, Brian. "Independent Indians and the U.S.-Mexican War," *American Historical Review*. Vol. 112/1 (February 2007): 35-68.

Drexler, Robert W. *Guilty of Making Peace: A Biography of Nicholas P. Trist*. Lanham, MD.: University Press of America, 1991.

Eisenhower, John S.D. *So Far from God: The U.S. War with Mexico, 1846-48*. New York: Random House, 1989.

Francaviglia, Richard V. and Douglas W. Richmond, eds. *Dueling Eagles: Reinterpreting the U.S.-Mexican War, 1846-1848*. Fort Worth: Texas Christian University Press.

Frazier, Donald S., ed. *The United States and Mexico at War: Nineteenth Century Expansionism and Conflict.* New York: Macmillian, 1998.

Heidler, David S. and Jeanne T. Heidler. *The Mexican War.* Westport, CT: Greenwood Press, 2006.

Johannsen, Robert W. *To the Halls of the Montezuma: The Mexican War in the American Imagination.* New York: Oxford University Press, 1985.

Jones, Oakah L. *Santa Anna.* New York: Twayne, 1968.

Keller, Gary D. and Cordelia Candelaria, *The Legacy of the Mexican and Spanish-American Wars.* Tempe, AZ: Bilingual Press, 2000.

Levinson, Irving W. *Wars within War: Mexico Guerrillas, Domestic Elites and the United States of America, 1846-48.* Ft. Worth: Texas Christian University Press, 2005.

Mahin, Dean B. *Olive Branch and Sword: The United States and Mexico, 1845-48.* Jefferson, NC: McFarland & Co., 1997.

Meyer, Michael C. and William L. Sherman. *The Course of Mexican History.* 4th ed. New York: Oxford University Press, 1991.

Nugent, Walter. "The American Habit of Empire, and the Cases of Polk and Bush." *Western Historical Quarterly.* 38/1 (Spring 2007): 5-24.

Ohrt, Wallace. *Defiant Peacemaker: Nicholas Trist in the Mexican War.* College Station: Texas A&M University Press, 1997.

Pletcher, David M. *The Diplomacy of Annexation: Texas, Oregon, and the Mexican War.* Columbia: University of Missouri Press, 1973.

Ramirez, Jose Fernando (edited by Walter V. Scholes and translated by Elliott B. Scherr). *Mexico During the War with the United States.* Columbia, Mo.: University of Missouri, 1950.

Robinson, Cecil, ed. *The View from Chapultepec: Mexican Writers on the Mexican-American War.* Tucson, AZ: University of Arizona Press, 1989.

Ruiz, Ramon Eduardo, ed. *The Mexican War: Was It Manifest Destiny?* New York: Holt Rinehart & Winston, 1963.

Santoni, Pedro. *Mexicans at Arms: Puro Federalists and the Politics of War, 1845-1848.* Ft. Worth, TX: Texas Christian University Press, 1996.

Schroder, John H. *Mr. Polk's War: American Opposition and Dissent, 1846-48.* Madison: University of Wisconsin Press, 1973.

Silbey, Joel H. *Storm Over Texas: The Annexation Controversy and the Road to Civil War.* New York: Oxford University Press, 2005.

Vazquez, Josefina Zoraida and Lorenzo Meyer. *The United States and Mexico*. Chicago: University of Chicago Press, 1985.

Wasserman, Mark. *Everyday Life and Politics in Nineteenth Century Mexico: Men, Women and War.* Albuquerque: University of New Mexico Press, 2000.

DOCUMENTS ON CD

Document 1:   Joint Resolution of Congress, March 1, 1845

Document 2:   Excerpt from biography of James K. Polk, March 1845

Document 3:   Secret Instructions from President Polk to John Slidell, November 1845

Document 4:   Excerpt from the Diary of James K. Polk, May 1846

Document 5:   President Polk's Message on War with Mexico, May 11, 1846

Document 6:   Excerpts from Letters from Jose Ramirez in Mexico City, 1847

Document 7:   Excerpts from letters of Nicholas Trist

Document 8:   Treaty of Guadalupe Hidalgo, February 2, 1848

Document 9:   Excerpts from Lincoln's speech in Congress protesting U.S. aggression against Mexico, 1848

Document 10:   Excerpts from Henry David Thoreau's Essay on "Civil Disobedience," 1849.

TEACHER OVERHEADS/STUDENT HANDOUTS ON CD

1. Timeline 1819-1829

2. Map of the Missouri Compromise, 1820

3. Timeline, 1829-1836

4. Timeline 1836-1845

5. Map of the Disputed Territory, 1845

6. Positions and Interests of Mexico, 1845

7. Positions and Interests of the United States, 1845

8. Directions: Mock Negotiations

9. Biography: Manuel de la Peña y Peña

10. Biography: John Slidell

11. Alternative Mock Mediation

12. Debriefing

13. What really happened?

14. Treaty of Guadalupe Hidalgo

15. Map of the Mexican Cession, 1848

16. Costs of the war

17. Questions for Discussion

SOURCES AND CREDITS OF ILLUSTRATIONS

p. 180: Map of the Missouri Compromise of 1850, *University of Texas*

p. 181: General Santa Ana, *LC-USZ262-21276*

p. 182: President John Tyler, *Office of the White House*

p. 183: Map of Disputed Territory, 1845-1846, *The National Park Service*

p. 184: Manuel Pena y Pena, *University of Texas*

p. 184: John Slidell, *LC-USZC4-11108*

p. 189: Battle of Buena Vista, *Library of Congress Prints and Photographs Division*

p. 190: Scott's Grand Entry into Mexico City, *Library of Congress Prints and Photographs Division*

p. 191: Treaty of Guadalupe Hidalgo, *Library of Congress Special Exhibits*

p. 192: Map of the Mexican Cession, 1848, *University of Texas*

CHAPTER NINE

THE COMPROMISE OF 1850

OBJECTIVES

- To understand how the Mexican Cession reopened the issue of extending slavery to new territories.

- To understand how the Wilmot Proviso split the Whig and Democratic Parties and prepared the way for the creation of the Free Soil Party and, ultimately, the Republican Party.

- To compare the various plans for compromise from President Taylor and Senators Clay and Benton.

- To analyze the positions and political, economic and ideological issues of the various legislators involved in the Compromise of 1850.

- To appreciate what might have prevented a sectional split after 1850.

CORRELATIONS WITH NATIONAL HISTORY STANDARDS

Era Four
Standard 3

The student understands how the debates over slavery influenced politics and sectionalism.

- Explain the Missouri Compromise and evaluate its political consequences.

- Explain how tariff policy and issues of states' rights influenced party development and promoted sectional differences.

- Analyze how the debates over slavery strained national cohesiveness and fostered rising sectionalism.

OVERVIEW

From the founding of the Republic, there was a fundamental sectional divergence of interest between the North and South over slavery. While common interests in Union prevailed and resulted in the "three-fifths" and other compromises at the Constitutional Convention in 1787 (See Chapter Six: Issues of Slavery at the Federal Convention), the underlying sectional dispute regarding slavery and its expansion continued to simmer with periodic eruptions and consequent adjustments, such as the Missouri Compromise in 1820. The war with Mexico (1846-1848) resulted in the acquisition of a huge western expanse for settlement and reopened the contest between the two sections over slavery and political power. That struggle, rooted in the fundamental divergence of two societies—one with racial slavery and the other based on wage labor—was exacerbated by the increasing political influence of the North, whose population of immigrants and native-born Americans was growing more rapidly than the South. (See Chapter Eight: War between Mexico and the United States.) The Southern elites, dominated by slave-owning planters, saw themselves as an increasingly besieged minority section. Slavery ended in the North in the decades after the Revolution, but it grew in the South, where the overwhelming number of blacks lived, the vast majority in bondage. Southern whites, even the majority who did not own slaves, found their "peculiar institution" threatened by the South's shrinking political power. In the North, an increasingly vocal minority condemned the very existence of slavery in the Republic. A growing majority in the North, while accepting slavery in the South, came to perceive the planter "Slaveocracy" as possessing undue influence in national policies. That northern majority increasingly opposed the expansion of slavery into the West. The two main national political parties—the Whigs and the Democrats—began to fracture under the moral condemnation by northern abolitionists and the impassioned defense of slavery by Southern "fire-eaters." Was it possible in 1850 to achieve an equitable and lasting resolution to slavery's fundamental and continuing challenge to American democracy and the Union?

HISTORICAL BACKGROUND

The issue of the expansion of slavery first emerged when the new nation had to decide about the disposition of the unorganized lands east of the Mississippi River. The Northwest Ordinance of 1787 barred slavery in the area northwest of the Ohio River from which five new free (i.e., non-slave) states would eventually be carved. No law fixed the status of slavery south of the Ohio, but because those lands had once been claimed by slave states and slaveholders were already moving into them, it was assumed that slavery would exist there. The invention of the cotton gin by Eli Whitney in 1793 gave new life to a slave economy that otherwise might have died of its own accord. Thus, as cotton cultivation spread across the lower South, so did slavery.

The status of slavery in the remainder of the huge Louisiana Purchase (1803) Territory, however, ignited a sharp but brief sectional controversy. In 1819, the northern majority in the House of Representatives infuriated Southerners by refusing to allow Missouri's admission as a new slave state. The number of free and slave states was equal in 1819, but admitting Missouri as a slave state would upset the balance of sectional power in the Senate. Northerners protested that the South already had unfair representation in the House and the Electoral College because of the Constitution's "three-fifths clause," which counted slaves as 3/5 of a person for purposes of determining the number of representatives for each state. Southerners argued that it was intolerable that the northern majority in the House attempt to dictate what a new state's position on slavery might be. Not only did that stance violate what Southerners insisted was a state's sacrosanct right to determine its own institutions, but Southerners also feared that if Northerners could prohibit slavery from a new state, they might try to abolish it altogether.

In 1820, Congress resolved the immediate dispute by enacting the "Missouri Compromise." In exchange for admitting Missouri as a slave state, Maine became a new free state, thus preserving sectional parity in the Senate. More importantly, in the remainder of the Louisiana Territory, slavery would be allowed to spread south of the southern boundary line of Missouri at 36 degrees-30 minutes latitude westward to the Rocky Mountains, but slavery was to be "forever prohibited" north of that line.

After 1820, demand for cotton by textile mills in Britain and New England fueled the expansion of slavery in the South and the search for new land for growing cotton. The expansion of slavery reemerged as an issue in 1844-45 when the Republic of Texas sought annexation to the United States as a slave state. Annexation generated opposition in the North among those opposed to slavery or its extension. It was largely supported by white Southerners. Despite considerable opposition, annexation was achieved in 1845 through a joint resolution by a lame-duck Congress and outgoing President John Tyler. The annexation permitted up to four additional states to be created from the vast expanse of Texas, but the disputed southwestern border between Texas and Mexico was left unresolved. Mexico insisted that the historical line for the province of Texas was the Nueces River. Texas claimed land to the Rio Grande, which would have included most of New Mexico to the west.

When new President James K. Polk asked Congress for a declaration of war with Mexico in 1846, it generated a bitter debate in Congress and the country. Polk's Democratic Party, both northern and southern wings, primarily supported the war. The opposition party—the Whigs—vocally opposed the war (especially those in the North), but only a handful dared to vote against it. Soon after the war began, the prospect of acquiring territory from Mexico led to a far-reaching Congressional debate initiated by a provision introduced by Congressman David Wilmot, a freshman Democrat from Pennsylvania, that would have barred slavery from any territory obtained

Map of the Missouri Compromise, 1820

from Mexico as a result of the war. (See Document 1: The Wilmot Proviso.) Wilmot's Proviso shattered both Whigs and Democrats along sectional lines. All Southerners in the House opposed it, and with a few Democratic exceptions, all Northerners supported it. Wilmot's Proviso was adopted in the House but buried in the Senate.

The War with Mexico ended with the Treaty of Guadalupe Hidalgo in March 1848 and the U.S. acquisition from Mexico of a large stretch of land, including present day Arizona, Nevada, California, Utah, and parts of New Mexico, Colorado and Wyoming. Efforts to include the Wilmot Proviso in the treaty were defeated by more than two to one in Congress. While the Mexican Cession brought many benefits to the United States, including the unanticipated discovery of gold fields in California in 1848, it also brought forth with greater intensity than before the issue of the expansion of slavery. It became a key issue in the presidential election of 1848.

In the North, both Whigs and Democrats were pressed by antislavery elements. Consequently, neither party could stand unqualifiedly for or against the Wilmot Proviso without breaking apart. A third party, the "Free-Soil" Party, was formed from dissident New England Whigs, a few northern Democrats and remnants of the 1844 Liberty Party, the first antislavery party. These different groups coalesced in their support of the Wilmot Proviso— no slavery in the territories. The Free-Soil Party nominated former president Martin Van Buren, a New York Democrat as its presidential candidate. It condemned the alleged "aggressions of the slave power," pledged to bar slavery from the territories and promised free homesteads to western settlers. Meanwhile, the Whigs sought to unify behind their presidential nominee, General Zachary Taylor, a Mexican War hero and Louisiana planter with well over 100 slaves. southern Whigs argued that no large slaveholder like Taylor would ever betray his section by signing the Wilmot Proviso. In the North, the Whigs trumpeted Taylor as a professional soldier, victorious general and national hero, minimizing his potential opposition to the Wilmot Proviso and stressing their own hostility to any extension of slavery.

Democrats, also separated into northern and southern wings, emphasized two options. One, offered by lame-duck President Polk and others, was to extend the Missouri Compromise line westward through the new acquisition to the Pacific coast (where it would end about 100 miles south of San Francisco). Slavery would continue to be barred to the north and permitted south of that line. Another idea—"popular sovereignty"—was advocated by Democratic presidential candidate, former Senator Lewis Cass of Michigan. Popular sovereignty meant allowing voters in each territory to decide whether or not to legalize slavery. Most northern Democrats

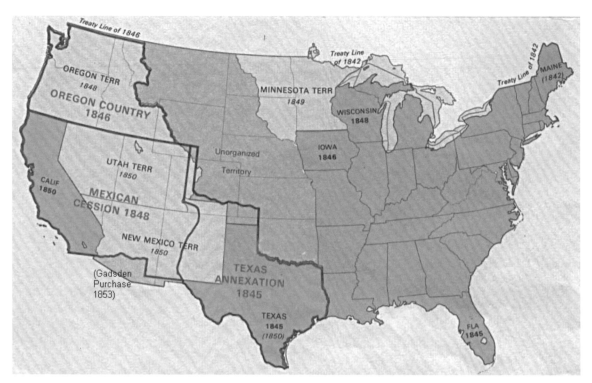

Map of Mexican Cession, 1848, with Polk's Texas Boundaries

hoped that popular sovereignty, by localizing the issue and removing it from national politics, might permit them to keep the southern wing within the party and enable them to win the presidency. Emphasizing popular sovereignty, Cass pledged to veto the Wilmot Proviso as president. So while southern Democratic politicians touted Cass's veto pledge as evidence that the party would not act against slavery, northern Democrats argued that popular sovereignty would stop the expansion of slavery and shouted that their candidate was a Yankee while Whigs had chosen a southern slaveholder.

The election of 1848 was extremely close. The victor, Taylor, obtained a popular majority in the South and a plurality (given the three way race) in the North. The Free-Soil Party obtained 14 percent of the popular vote in the North, a surprisingly strong showing for a new third party. Although Van Buren failed to win a single state, his candidacy proved instrumental in enabling Taylor to win the presidential election, because the Free-Soil Party split the Democratic vote in New York, causing Cass to lose that state and giving Taylor enough electoral votes to become president. Although the Whigs won the presidency, the Democrats had a majority in both houses of the new Congress, and both parties remained sectionally divided.

President Taylor and the new Congress with its fractured Democratic majorities took office in 1849 and were confronted with increasing pressure for action regarding the territories obtained from Mexico. Part of the pressure was the surge of a hundred thousand prospectors (later called the "49ers") to California in the rush to the newly discovered gold fields there. Outgoing president Polk added to the pressure by including with his announcement in December 1848 that gold had been discovered in California, a map of the Mexican Cession that showed the disputed Texas-New Mexico boundary line as the upper Rio Grande River.

Additional pressure for a decision about the extension or non-extension of slavery came from extremists in the North and the South, as well as from increasing numbers of moderates. In the North, abolitionists opposed the expansion of slavery because they saw slavery as inherently evil and a violation of an inalienable right to liberty. Some advocated extreme measures. David Walker, a black abolitionist, urged slaves to revolt. William Lloyd

Garrison, a white abolitionist, advocated nonviolent means to free the slaves. Garrison was willing to have the slave South secede and leave the United States smaller but "purer." Of greater influence was the spreading sentiment within the northern wings of the Whig and Democratic parties that, although slavery could continue to exist in the South, it should not be allowed to expand into new areas, particularly into lands from which it had been banned (the Republic of Mexico had abolished slavery in 1829). Part of this opposition was economic (fear of economic competition between slave and free labor), part was ideological, part political and part racist. Racism certainly existed in the North as indicated by restrictive laws against blacks in a number of northern states. By the late 1840s, many Northerners resented what they considered to be the disproportionate national political power of the South, especially since the North was the more populous section of the country. They sought to avert the growing influence of the "Slaveocracy" by preventing the creation of additional slave states. Many also were ideologically opposed to slavery as contrary to the nation's principles of individual rights and liberties.

William Lloyd Garrison

William Lloyd Garrison, Abolitionist

In the southern states, extremists proudly argued that the institution of slavery was a positive good. Partially in response to attacks by abolitionists, they claimed that slavery was beneficial to black slaves who were better cared for by their owners as valuable property than wage laborers who suffered periodic unemployment in the North. They gave religious and historic justification for slavery as well as arguing that it was an effective mechanism for labor as well as race control. To protect the South's "peculiar institution," secessionist "fire-eaters" called for the slave South to leave from the Union. While threatening rather than advocating secession, Senator John C. Calhoun (D-SC) took the lead in urging white Southerners of both political parties to act together to defend "Southern rights" against what he called in December 1848, "acts of aggression" committed by the North, acts which sought to limit the right of slaveowners to take their black slaves into federal territories. Increasingly, large numbers of southern whites came to see the northern attack on slavery and the extension of slavery as a denigration of southern white society and culture. Given the arid nature of much of the Mexican Cession (virtually no one in the United States realized how fertile the soil was in California), few southern slaveowners saw a future for slavery in the new territories. But they were angered by the attempts of Northerners to deny access to the territories to them for symbolic, if not economic, reasons. Many white Southerners feared also that the North's attempts to limit the expansion of slavery were preliminary to an effort to abolish slavery entirely.

Intensifying sectional attitudes and fears as well as partisan politics led moderates and conservatives in the congressional election year of 1850 to try to resolve or at least defuse the divisive issues presented by the Mexican Cession. President Zachary Taylor secretly urged California and New Mexico to apply immediately for statehood (expecting them to be free states) in order to avoid the sectional animosity created by the Wilmot Proviso in Congress. The president saw this as a fair sectional compromise since it would mollify the South by rendering the Wilmot Proviso irrelevant and satisfy the North by stopping the extension of slavery. He sought to remove the border dispute between Texas and New Mexico from Congress by turning it over to the U.S. Supreme Court, which had constitutional jurisdiction over disputes between states.

Not surprisingly, Taylor's plan proved extremely unpopular in Congress. Democrats North and South denounced it, although for different reasons. (See Document 2: Taylor's message to Congress, December 4, 1849.) The southern Democrats saw it as anti-slaveholder because it did not give them any opportunity to expand into the new lands they had helped to conquer. The northern Democrats saw it as inadequate to avoid Southern threats of secession over the "denial of their rights" and to keep the Southerners in the Democratic Party. Taylor's fellow southern Whigs responded with frosty silence, as his plan obviously sought to limit slavery. Only the northern

Whigs praised it, because it would prevent slavery in the area gained from Mexico. At the same time, Senators Henry Foote (D-MS) and Thomas Hart Benton (D-MO) introduced contradictory bills for establishing the boundary between Texas and New Mexico. (See maps of proposals by Benton and others for dividing Texas on page 205.)

Also in January 1850, Senator James Mason (D-VA) introduced a bill for a fugitive slave law to provide for effective federal enforcement of the return of slaves who escaped across state lines. The issue of runway slaves was important to slaveowners. Although the Fugitive Slave Act of 1793 required the federal government to help recapture slaves who ran away across state lines, it had not been effectively enforced. With the end of slavery in the North and growing antislavery sentiment there, including the creation of an "underground railroad" to help southern slaves escape, a number of northern states had passed "personal liberty" laws, prohibiting forcible seizure and removal of "fugitives" without formal extradition proceedings and forbidding state authorities from helping to return fugitive slaves. Slaveholders in the Upper South in particular wanted a stronger federal fugitive slave law to help recapture runaway slaves in the North.

In addition, the existence of slavery and the slave trade in the nation's capital became a sectionally divisive issue. northern antislavery advocates were especially appalled at public slave auctions in the capital, Washington, D.C., and some even sought the elimination of slavery itself in the District of Columbia. In December 1848, a majority of Northerners in the House endorsed a northern Whig request for a positive committee report on abolishing the slave trade in the capital. Only after forceful southern protests made clear the intensity of the South's outrage at the suggestion did a few northern Whigs and more northern Democrats join southern Representatives in tabling the resolution.

The aging and ailing but still prominent Henry Clay (Whig-KY), recently returned to the Senate after a long absence, attempted a compromise by offering eight resolutions that he hoped might resolve the issue of the Wilmot Proviso and mute the sectional differences (he especially hoped to reunite the two wings of his own Whig Party). Clay's proposals included the following (see Document 3: Clay's Proposals):

1. Admission of California as a free state

2. Prohibition of the slave trade in the District of Columbia

3. Noninterference with slavery or private sales of slaves in the District of Columbia

4. Declaration that Congress had no authority to interfere with interstate slave trade

5. More effective provisions for return of fugitive slaves from free states and territories

6. Organization, without restriction on slavery, of the remainder of the Mexican Cession

7. Adjustment of the Texas-New Mexico boundary (splitting a large Texas in half and awarding southern half below El Paso, including Austin to Texas, and the northern half, including Dallas/Fort Worth and Santa Fe to New Mexico)

8. U.S. Government assumption of the still unpaid $10 million public debt of the Republic of Texas before it had become a state

Clay saw the first two as benefiting those advocating free states, the next three as benefiting the slave states and the last three items as benefiting both sides.

Although in the Senate the Democrats had an extremely slim majority over the Whigs and although North and South were equally represented (15 free states and 15 slave states), the reaction to Clay's proposed compromise generally followed sectional and also party lines. southern Whigs and northern Democrats tended to support Clay's resolutions, while southern Democrats and northern Whigs tended to oppose them, but for

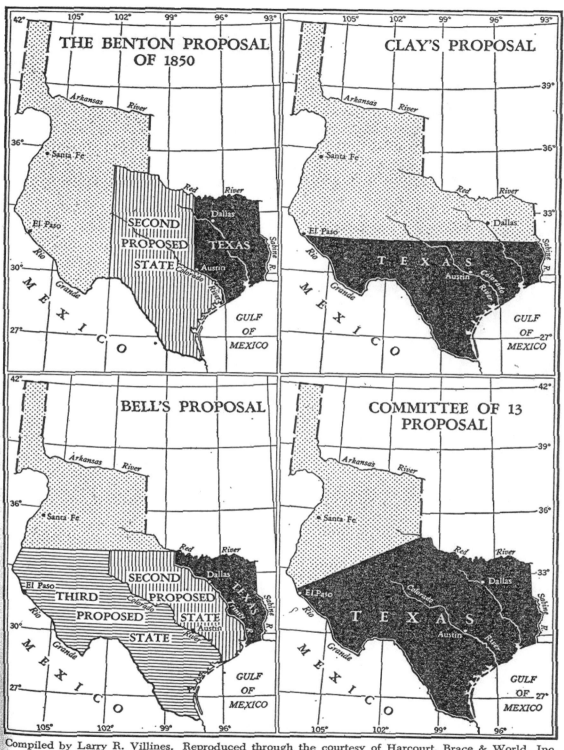

Compiled by Larry R. Villines. Reproduced through the courtesy of Harcourt, Brace & World, Inc.

FOUR PROPOSALS FOR DIVIDING TEXAS SOIL

Four Proposals for Dividing Texas

entirely different reasons. Clay's proposed compromise produced one of the greatest debates in the history of the U.S. Senate. It also marked the last meeting of three leading, aged senators who had represented their respective regions for more than three decades: Henry Clay, Whig from Kentucky; John C. Calhoun, Democrat from South Carolina; and Daniel Webster, Whig from Massachusetts. In his speech of February 5-6, 1850, the 72-year-old Henry Clay championed his resolutions, appealed to each side to make concessions and warned that secession from the Union was not a proper option for the South.

On March 4th, John C. Calhoun, 67 years old and suffering from a terminal illness (he would die on March 31st), sat in silence and wrapped in blankets in the Senate while his speech was read for him (see Document 5: Floor remarks of Senator Hart Benton, 1850.) He took an extreme position even for a southern Democrat. Supporting the purpose of the act, he, nonetheless opposed the compromise because it did not provide adequate guarantees for the slave-owning South. Calhoun insisted that if California were admitted as a free state, all the southern slave states should secede, because California would give the North a majority (16-15 states) in the Senate and the North already had a majority in the House. Disunion could only be prevented, Calhoun argued, by recognizing that slaveholders had equal right of access to the newly acquired territories, by ending Northern agitation against slavery, and by a constitutional amendment to restore the South's power to protect itself. The amendment he had in mind would provide dual executives (one from the North and one from the South), each with veto power, under the doctrine of what Calhoun called a "concurrent majority."

On March 7th, 68-year-old Daniel Webster, spoke in favor of Clay's resolutions. "I wish to speak today, not as a Massachusetts man, not as a northern man, but as an American...," Webster began. "I speak today for the preservation of the Union. Hear me for my cause." Although a New England Whig, Webster argued that the Wilmot Proviso was unnecessary (he still had presidential ambitions and sought national support). There was no need for Congress to act on slavery in the territories, he declared, because the hostile soil and climate in the Mexican Cession would preclude slavery. He also was willing to support a more rigorous fugitive slave law, and he took a pragmatic partisan approach in regard to the border and thus the size of Texas and New Mexico. But in calling for such a compromise, Webster alienated many of his fellow northern Whigs.

In contrast to Webster's support for the compromise, most northern Whigs and all Free Soilers vigorously opposed Clay's proposal. They demanded enactment of the Wilmot Proviso and congressional prohibition of slavery from the new territories. They argued against the expansive territorial claims of slaveholding Texas. Senator William Henry Seward (Whig-NY) took an extreme position against Clay's resolutions in his speech of March 11th, holding "all legislative compromises radically wrong and essentially vicious," and appealing to a "higher law" than the Constitution in justifying the refusal of constitutional protection of slavery. Similarly, newly elected Salmon P. Chase, a Free Soiler from Ohio, denounced slavery as immoral and claimed it was the duty of Congress to prohibit slavery in the Mexican Cession. Northern Whigs and Free Soilers opposed Clay's compromise. They supported President Taylor's plan to bring the Mexican Cession in as free states.

The Immediate Historical Context

On April 18, 1850, Clay's resolutions were referred to a specially appointed Senate Select Committee of Thirteen, headed by Clay. The committee consisted of 7 Whigs and 6 Democrats representing 7 slave and 6 free states. Its mission, pressed by Democratic Senator Henry Foote (D-MS), was to consider all matters related to slavery simultaneously. In contrast to the individual resolutions, it would produce an "Omnibus Bill" that would seek to resolve the issue as a package of compromises upon which senators would vote yes or no.

On May 8, 1850, the Senate Select Committee of Thirteen reported out three bills. One, the "Omnibus Bill," combined into a single measure the bills for organizing California, New Mexico, and Utah through popular sovereignty. It also proposed a new Texas-New Mexico boundary that gave Texas far more land than northern Whigs and Free Soilers could tolerate and far less than southern Democrats demanded. The second bill prohibited slave auctions in the District of Columbia. The third bill was James Mason's (D-VA) new fugitive slave law.

But President Zachary Taylor continued to pursue his own plan, rally northern Whig congressmen against compromise, and stop any concessions on the Texas-New Mexico boundary dispute. He fervently denied that any part of the former Mexican province of New Mexico east of the Rio Grande belong to Texas, and his private intimations that he would send federal troops to block any attempt by armed Texans to seize Santa Fe only made it clearer that no compromise could pass Congress while Taylor remained president.

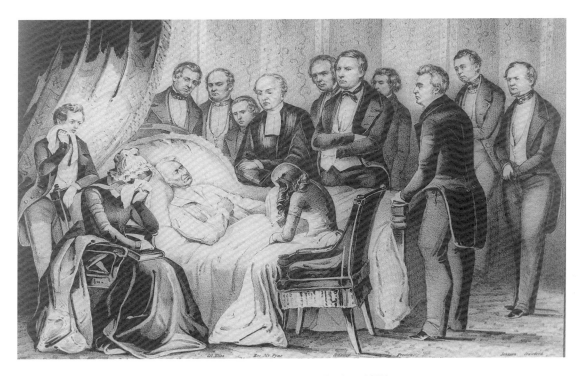

The Death of President Taylor, 1850

At the Fourth of July celebration in 1850, President Taylor sat out in the hot sun for the lengthy ceremonies, then ate large quantities of cherries and iced milk. Five days later he was dead of acute gastroenteritis. Fifty-year-old Vice President Millard Fillmore from Buffalo, New York, a former Whig leader of the House of Representatives, succeeded Taylor as president and changed the political equation. Unlike Taylor, Fillmore favored some congressional compromise. Consequently, the new president began pressuring northern Whigs to change their position and support the Compromise. On August 6th, President Fillmore sent a message urging Congress to immediately settle the boundary dispute between Texas and New Mexico in order to stop Texas extremists from sending the state militia to seize Santa Fe, the result of which would be a shooting war. (See Document 9: President Fillmore's message to Congress, August 6, 1850.) Nevertheless, the unusual coalition of northern Whigs and southern Democrats that opposed the Compromise held together for a while, and the Omnibus Bill died. Now, Stephen A. Douglas (D-IL), who succeeded Clay as floor manager and chair of the Committee on Territories, sought to have the Senate enact the measures individually rather than as a package. Douglas was a champion of sectional compromise, and he advocated "popular sovereignty" that would allow initial settlers in a territory to determine whether the state would be slave or free.

MOCK CAUCUS

I It is late August 1850. The Congress has been in session since early December 1849—the longest session ever held to date—and there is increasing pressure to find a solution to the logjam about the intertwined issues of the expansion of slavery in the area obtained from Mexico, the border of Texas and New Mexico, Texas bonds, fugitive slaves, and slavery in the District of Columbia. In 1850, and indeed until 1913, U.S. Senators are selected by the state legislatures, whereas members of the House of Representatives stand every two years for public election.

We are hypothesizing a mock caucus of selected U.S. Senators with contending perspectives about how to resolve the issues relating to the expansion of slavery in the Mexican Cession. Senator William R. King, Democrat from Alabama and the Senate president *pro tempore* will try to mediate a resolution among the many competing proposals for resolving these issues.

THE PARTICIPANTS

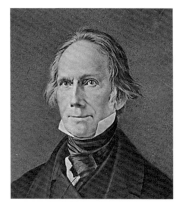

Henry Clay

Senator Henry Clay, Whig from Kentucky

Born in Virginia, Clay moved to Kentucky, where he served almost continuously as Speaker of the U.S. House of Representatives (1810-1824), as Secretary of State (1825-1829), and as a Senator from Kentucky (1831-1842). He ran unsuccessfully for president in 1824 and 1832, and after taking a lead in founding the Whig Party in the winter of 1833-34, as the Whig presidential nominee in 1844. Though himself a slaveholder, Clay long championed the eventual end of slavery through gradual emancipation and the foreign colonization of freed slaves. For many years, he served as president of the American Colonization Society. In 1844 Clay opposed the immediate annexation of Texas, in part because he knew Northerners resented the spread of slavery. In late 1847, while in retirement from office, he made a widely publicized speech in Lexington, Kentucky, avowing his opposition to any territorial acquisition from Mexico and to any further spread of slavery. A week after Taylor presented his proposal to Congress in January 1850, Clay presented an alternative plan for the Mexican Cession. Unlike Taylor, who urged Congress to do nothing other than admitting California and New Mexico as states, Clay insisted that Congress must draw a new boundary between Texas and New Mexico and organize territorial governments, without the Wilmot Proviso, in the remainder of the Cession outside of California. He also insisted that Mexico's antislavery statutes continue in force in the Cession, thus barring slavery without the need for the Proviso. For the next six months, Clay led the pro-compromise forces in the Senate. (See Document 4: Senator Henry Clay's Resolutions, 1850.)

Senator Daniel Webster, Whig from Massachusetts

Initially a Federalist from New Hampshire, Webster moved to Boston and became a successful lawyer and Whig political leader from Massachusetts. He was the most formidable orator of his time. Long an intra-party rival of Clay, he unsuccessfully sought the Whig presidential nomination in 1836, 1840 and 1848. In 1844–45 he led Massachusetts Whigs' opposition to Texas annexation because he opposed slavery extension, yet as a Senator in 1850 he championed congressional compromise rather than the Taylor plan. While Webster, like

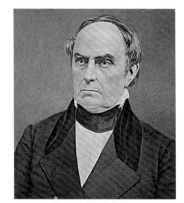

Daniel Webster

Clay, argued that the Wilmot Proviso was unnecessary since the arid climate would stop slavery from entering any territories organized in the Cession, he was prepared to make far more concessions to the South than was Clay initially. He reminded his colleagues that they were pledged to admit more slave states from Texas, which might balance the admission of California, and he urged the passage of a more rigorous fugitive slave law that would facilitate the recapture of runaway slaves in the North (see Document 6: Speech by Daniel Webster.) President Fillmore would appoint Webster as his new Secretary of State, and from that post Webster led the administration's efforts to pressure northern Whigs to support pro-southern concessions. Once the Fugitive Slave Act of 1850 became law, Webster also led the efforts to enforce it in the North. (See Document 6: Speech by Senator Webster, 1850.)

Senator William H. Seward, Whig from New York

William H. Seward

A lawyer in upstate New York, Seward helped found that state's Whig Party in 1834 and served two terms as a Whig governor between 1838 and 1842. Elected to the United States Senate in 1849, Seward was a leader of the antislavery wing of the New York Whig Party and arch-rival of fellow New York Whig, Vice President Millard Fillmore, who became president upon Zachary Taylor's death. During 1850, Seward was the foremost leader of northern Whig opponents of congressional compromise. He demanded California's immediate admission as a free state "directly, without conditions, without qualifications, and without compromise." Should territories be organized in the Cession, the Wilmot Proviso must be written into the legislation because the Constitution devoted the national domain "to liberty." Indeed, there was "a higher law than the Constitution, which regulates our authority over the domain, and devotes it to the same noble purposes." God intended the territories to be free, and legislators as "his stewards" must heed God's will. Seward refused to endorse Taylor's proposal and, in fact, by broaching imposition of the Proviso, Seward flouted Taylor's pleas that Congress avoid the Proviso to preserve sectional comity. (See Document 7: Speech by William Seward, 1850.) Reelected in 1854, Seward continued his strong antislavery stand as he bid for the leadership of the new Republican Party, declaring in 1858 that the slavery struggle was "an irrepressible conflict" between North and South and that the nation must eventually become either "entirely a slaveholding or entirely a free-labor nation." In part because of his antislavery radicalism, Seward lost the Republican presidential nomination to Abraham Lincoln in 1860 but served as Secretary of State for the next eight years.

Senator Jefferson Davis, Democrat from Mississippi

Jefferson Davis

Born in Kentucky in 1808 and educated at West Point, Davis served in the army between 1828 and 1835, before launching a career as a large slaveholding planter and politician in Mississippi. Davis established what he considered a model plantation, with slave tribunals in which slaves could testify before slave judges in cases involving other black slaves. Davis in 1850 inherited Calhoun's role as leader of southern Democratic opponents of any compromise that admitted California, let alone New Mexico, as a new free state. He denounced Taylor's plan as the Wilmot Proviso in disguise since it would admit California and perhaps New Mexico as free states before slaveholders had a chance to exercise their equal rights to move into commonly held American territories for which southern soldiers had shed blood. Nor could Davis tolerate Clay's plan, which also advocated California's admission and the continuing operation of Mexico's prohibition of slavery in the Mexican Cession. Davis and most of his fellow southern Democrats had an alternative plan for the Mexican Cession: extend the Missouri Compromise line to the Pacific Coast (where it would have reached the Pacific Ocean close to the modern town of Carmel, California), barring slavery north of that line but recognizing it south of that line in the Cession. (See Document 8: Speech by Jefferson Davis, 1850.) In June 1850, a convention of southern politicians in Nashville would adopt this formula. (See Document 10: Resolutions of the Nashville Convention.) Utterly opposed to the Clay's compromise, Davis and most other southern Democrats would join northern Whigs in attempting to kill it, although the latter group did so for very different reasons. Davis continued to denounce the Compromise of 1850 as a sellout of the South's equal rights. He later became Secretary of War under President Franklin Pierce (1853–57) and president of the Confederacy during the Civil War (1861–65).

Henry Foote

Senator Henry Foote, Democrat from Mississippi

A native Virginian, Foote moved to Mississippi and became an attorney, newspaper editor and politician. A Jacksonian Democrat, known for his flamboyant style, vituperative rhetoric and combativeness, Foote proved absolutely critical in forging what became the Compromise of 1850. Resolutely committed to defending the claim of Texas to all the land east of the Rio Grande River, Foote, quite unlike Davis and most southern Democrats, was prepared to admit California as a free state if territories were organized in the remainder of the Cession without the Proviso. From January 1850 on, against the wishes of Clay, Webster and Douglas, Foote insisted on the creation of a "select" Senate committee that would simultaneously consider all the slavery issues then before Congress, including a new fugitive slave bill. In April, this Select Committee of Thirteen was created, and in May it reported out an "omnibus bill" combining all proposals for the Mexican Cession in a single measure, as well as separate bills increasing federal enforcement in the North to capture fugitive slaves and abolishing public slave auctions in the District of Columbia. The omnibus strategy meant that California statehood could not pass without Northern concessions on territorial bills and the Texas boundary question, but it also meant that in order to obtain those concessions, southerners had to accept California as a free state. In 1851, Foote ran as Mississippi's Union pro-Compromise candidate for governor and defeated Jefferson Davis, the southern Rights candidate and his longtime rival. Foote was dissented against secession in 1860–61.

Senator Stephen A. Douglas, Democrat from Illinois

Small in stature but gifted as an orator, Douglas was known as the "Little Giant." He had been a lawyer and a judge. As a congressman, he was an expansionist, supporting the Mexican War. In 1850, he was chair of the Senate Committee on the Territories. An advocate of popular sovereignty, Douglas was ambitious to be president. He considered both Taylor's plan and Clay's initial proposal, with its emphasis that Mexico's antislavery law continue in force in the Mexican Cession, as too antislavery to satisfy the South, and he wanted to balance California's admission as a free state with the organization of territories in the rest of the Cession on the basis of popular sovereignty. However, like Clay, with whom he often cooperated despite being from different parties, Douglas steadfastly opposed bundling the various measures for the Cession into a single "omnibus" bill. When the exhausted Clay left Washington in early August, Douglas took over management of the Compromise in the Senate and secured passage, one by one, of the individual laws that together constituted it. Douglas remained in the Senate

Stephen Douglas

for the rest of his life, running successfully for reelection against Abraham Lincoln in 1858 (the "Lincoln-Douglas Debates"). In 1860, he won the Democratic presidential nomination, but the party split, and he lost the election to Republican Abraham Lincoln.

Thomas Hart Benton

Senator Thomas Hart Benton, Democrat from Missouri

Born and educated in North Carolina, Benton moved west to Tennessee and then St. Louis, Missouri, where he became a lawyer, editor and politician. A Jacksonian Democrat, who ardently supported the party's anti-central bank and anti-paper money policies and its elimination of property requirements for voters, Benton represented Missouri in the Senate from 1821 to 1852. Though living in a slave state, he identified with non-slaveholding whites, advocated free homesteads on western lands, and strongly opposed the extension of slavery. Benton argued against Texas annexation in 1844–45 and tried to reduce the size of Texas once its admission as a slave state was unstoppable. In 1850, he opposed both Clay and Calhoun's positions, and unlike almost all other southern Democrats, he openly championed Taylor's proposal for immediate statehood for California and New Mexico. But he devoted most of his time trying to redraw the Texas-New Mexico boundary in order to deny Texas's claims to the part of New Mexico east of the Rio Grande. In this effort, he frequently clashed with Mississippi's Henry Foote, who, at one point in the increasingly heated debates, drew a gun in the Senate chamber and threatened to shoot Benton. What were seen as anti-southern positions, cost him his Senate seat. (See Document 5: Floor remarks of Senator Hart Benton, 1850.)

Senator Salmon Chase, Free-Soiler from Ohio

Born in New Hampshire, Chase graduated from Dartmouth College and later moved to Cincinnati, Ohio, where he practiced law. Beginning with his defense of fugitive slaves, this former New Englander became a vehement opponent of slavery, a leader in the antislavery movement, and a founder of two Northern antislavery parties - the Liberty Party (1844) and the Free Soil Party (1848). Elected a Senator from Ohio in 1849, this Free Soiler opposed the Compromise of 1850. Like other Free Soilers, Chase welcomed California's admission as a free state, but he insisted on the organization of territorial governments with slavery explicitly prohibited by congressional statute in the remainder of the Cession and strenuously opposed any new fugitive slave act. Thus he opposed both the Taylor and Clay plans. One of the organizers of the Republican Party in 1854, Chase left the Senate in 1855 and was elected Republican governor of Ohio, serving until 1860 when he returned to the Senate. He competed unsuccessfully with Lincoln for the Republican presidential nomination in 1860. President Lincoln appointed Chase as his secretary of the treasury in 1861 and chief justice of the Supreme Court in 1864.

Salmon Chase

The Mediator: Senator William R. King, Democrat from Alabama and Senate president pro tempore

William R. King

Born to a well-to-do family of planters in North Carolina, King became a lawyer, congressman and briefly a diplomat to Russia (1816–17) and France (1844–46). In 1818, he moved to Alabama and within two years owned 80 slaves and a large plantation. Elected as one of the state's first two U.S. Senators in 1819, King served in the Senate for most of the next three decades. A Jacksonian Democrat, he supported opening public lands and opposed a central bank and a protective tariff. Yet he cooperated with Henry Clay in securing the compromise tariff of 1833. He and Senator James Buchanan (Pennsylvania Democrat), both lifelong bachelors, established a close personal relationship which influenced their attitudes towards the growing sectional dispute. Buchanan defended Southern interests from abolitionists' attacks and persuaded King that the majority of Northerners were not hostile to the South, thus encouraging the Alabamian's commitment to the national Democratic Party. King served as president pro tempore of the Senate from 1836-41 and 1850–52. Although King served on the Senate Select Committee of Thirteen, he did not vote for the Omnibus Bill. He did, however, defend the measures that made up the Compromise of 1850 against attacks by Southern Rights members of the Senate. In the 1852 election, King was the successful vice-presidential candidate on the Democratic ticket headed by Franklin Pierce of New Hampshire, but King died from tuberculosis six months later.

TEACHER INSTRUCTIONS

Preparation

1. Review the "Historical Background" with the class as either a lecture or a class reading. The maps will be an integral part of the negotiations, so if you present the material as a lecture, show the maps as overheads, post them around the room, and/or give the maps out as hand outs.
2. Once the class is comfortable with the background, distribute student handout: "Positions and Interests." Students should review all positions before they are assigned to take a particular side.
3. Distribute student handout: "The Participants." Again, have students review all the brief biographies before they are assigned a particular role.

Activity—Mock Congressional Mediation

Divide the class into groups of ten as follows:

Congressional Participants

Jefferson Davis (Democrat, Mississippi)

Henry Foote (Democrat, Mississippi)

Stephen Douglas (Democrat, Illinois)

Thomas Hart Benton (Democrat, Missouri)

POSITIONS AND INTERESTS

Party-*Section* Person	California	Utah	New Mexico	Texas border	Fugitive Slaves	District of Columbia
Whigs-*Southern* Henry Clay (Kentucky)	• Admit with compromise on other issues	• Organize territories with Mexican antislavery statute continuing in force	• Organize territory with Mexican antislavery statute continuing in force	• Set TX border to exclude NM area and pay TX for giving up claim to land	• Supports more rigorous fugitive slave trade law	• Supports abolition of slave trade
Whigs-*Northern* Daniel Webster (Massachusetts)	• Admit but willing to compromise on remainder of Cession	• Wilmot proviso unnecessary—Climate and terrain not conducive to slavery	• Wilmot proviso unnecessary—Climate and terrain not conducive to slavery	• Flexible on location of boundary and admitting more slave states from TX	• Supports rigorous fugitive slave law	• No stated position
William Seward (New York)	• Admit with no compromise elsewhere in Cession	• Insists on Proviso if any territorial government is organized	• Insists on Proviso if any territorial government is organized	• Set boundary at Nueces River and give land west of Nueces to NM	• Against new fugitive slave law	• Supports abolition of slave trade
Free Soil Party *Northern only* Salmon Chase (Ohio)	• Admit as free state	• Organize territorial government; bar slavery in new states	• Organize territorial government; bar slavery in new states	• Limit size of TX and give land to NM without payment to TX	• Strongly opposed to new fugitive slave law	• Supports abolition of slavery and slave trade in the capital
Democrats- *Northern* Stephen Douglas (Illinois)	• Admit as free state with compromise in rest of Cession	• Organize on basis of popular sovereignty	• Organize on basis of popular sovereignty	• Deny claim of TX to Rio Grande but pay TX for giving up claim to land	• Supports new fugitive slave bill	• Supports abolition of slave trade
Thomas Hart Benton (Missouri)	• Immediate statehood as free state	• Against attempt to organize territorial government	• Against attempt to organize territorial government; immediate statehood as free state	• Reduce size of TX but pay TX for giving up claim to land	• Supports new Fugitive Slave bill	• Supports abolition of slave trade
Democrats- *Southern* Jefferson Davis (Mississippi)	• Opposes admission as state; extend MO Compromise to Pacific; legalize slavery south of line	• Extend MO Compromise to Pacific and legalize slavery south of line—opposed to organization on popular sovereignty	• Extend MO Compromise to Pacific and legalize slavery south of line—opposed to organization on popular sovereignty	• Supports TX claim to land East of the Rio Grande and opposes any boundary that would reduce size of TX	• Supports stronger Fugitive Slave law	• Opposes abolition of slave trade as violation of slaveholders' rights
Henry Foote (Mississippi)	• Admit CA as free state ONLY as part of Omnibus bill with other concessions to the South	• Organize Territorial government based on popular sovereignty as part of Omnibus plan	• Organize Territorial government based on popular sovereignty as part of Omnibus plan	• Strongly opposed to any reduction in size of Texas—supports Texas claim to land East of the Rio Grande	• Supports new fugitive slave law	• Opposes abolition of slave trade

> Henry Clay (Whig, Kentucky)
>
> William Seward (Whig, New York)
>
> Daniel Webster (Whig, Massachusetts)
>
> Salmon Chase (Free Soil, Ohio)

The Mediator

> William R. King (Democrat, Alabama) and president pro tempore of the Senate

Observers/Reporters/Recorders

> Journalists for the Democratic *Washington Union*, the Whig *National Intelligencer* and the administration's newspaper, the *Washington Republic*.

2. Distribute student handout: "The Mock Congressional Mediation."

3. Review the setting and the directions with the students and have them proceed with their mock caucuses.

Debriefing

1. Bring the class back together for a discussion. Have the observers describe how the process of facilitated mediation worked in their group.

2. After discussing the process, summarize and compare the results each group obtained.

3. Either have the students read what actually happened in August 1850 ("The Facts Continued") or share it with the class as a lecture. Compare the group results and process with the historical reality.

4. Use the "Questions for Discussion" for essay topics or for further in-class discussion.

THE FACTS CONTINUED

The Senate logjam was broken in August 1850 when the Texas-New Mexico boundary issue was separated from the other issues. President Fillmore's August 6th message to Congress to immediately settle the Texas-New Mexico boundary issue created a sense of urgency before violence erupted on that border. Faced with the apparent emergency of Texas extremists bent on sending the state militia to seize Santa Fe, and provided with political cover by the president's appeal to avert bloodshed in the disputed territory, a coalition composed primarily of pro-compromise northern Democrats and southern Whigs (significantly joined by six New England Whigs) passed a compromise bill limiting the western boundary of Texas to its modern location.

The five individual laws enacted in September 1850 that subsequently became known collectively as the "Compromise of 1850" (See Document 9) included:

1. The Texas and New Mexico Act organized New Mexico as a territory; guaranteed that states formed out of the territory (modern day New Mexico and Arizona) could enter the Union as slave or free states as they desired; (popular sovereignty) established the Texas-New Mexico boundary at its modern location; and provided that in return for Texas's renunciation of all claims to New Mexican territory, the U.S. Government would pay the $10 million debt of the Republic of Texas, half of which was to be paid directly to the Texas

state government and half to compensate the holders of the unpaid bonds of the earlier Republic of Texas. (The entire U.S. budget in 1850 was $40 million). The act was adopted by votes of Southerners of each party plus most northern Democrats and a few northern Whigs, over the dissent of most northern Whigs and Free Soilers.

2. <u>Admission of California as a free state</u> under the constitution it had submitted to Congress in 1849. This act was adopted with solid Northern backing from both parties and support from a few Southerners from both parties. (Senate 34-18; House 150-56.) This is exactly what Taylor and Clay had requested originally, and it represented what Calhoun had protested.

3. The <u>Utah Act</u> established a territorial government for Utah (encompassing the modern states of Utah, Nevada, and western Colorado) with vague terms regarding the power of the territorial legislature over slavery (a gesture to popular sovereignty). However, the act included specific language that all states formed from the Utah Territory must subsequently be admitted by Congress as slave states *if* their constitutions prescribed it. None did. The Utah bill passed the Senate by a vote of 32-18 and 97-85 in the House (including 39 abstentions, mostly northern Whigs who could have killed the bill if they had voted). It was supported by the Democrats (North and South), and the southern Whigs. It was opposed by the Free Soilers, almost all northern Whigs and a smattering of southern Whigs and northern Democrats.

4. An <u>Act Prohibiting Public Slave Auctions in the District of Columbia</u> abolished public slave auctions but not private sales of slaves or slavery itself in the capital (Senate 33-19; House 124-47). Most Southerners— Whig and Democrat—voted against the bill. No Northerner, regardless of party, voted against the bill. However, there were 39 abstentions in the House.

5. A <u>Fugitive Slave Act</u> created a new and more effective process for the recovery of runaway slaves. The law established federal commissioners, appointed by the president, in northern states, who would hear cases involving alleged fugitive slaves. It denied blacks seized in the North the right to a jury trial or to

Compromise of 1850

215

testify in their defense. It awarded commissioners a $10 fee if they found fugitive slaves but only a $5 fee if they declared the alleged fugitive to be a free black. (For comparison: The average daily wage in 1850 for unskilled laborers in the North was under $1) It required Northerners, upon penalty of substantial fine and imprisonment, to help U.S. Marshals capture possible fugitive slaves. There was little debate on this bill. The vote in both houses (Senate 27-12; House 109-76) reflected the same sectional divisions as the votes on the Utah bill and the slave trade in the District of Columbia, including a large number of abstentions.

The extraordinary number of abstentions and absences on some of the votes, sometimes reaching 20 percent of the House and nearly 40 percent of the Senate membership, was the result of several factors. northern Whigs were pressured by the Fillmore administration to abstain rather than to follow the wishes of their constituents and vote against some of the compromise measures. Part of the nonvoting was due to sheer attrition. By the time the members were called upon to vote on the Fugitive Slave bill and the District of Columbia bill, which many members considered less important than the other measures, it was late summer and many Senators and Representatives had left the hot and muggy weather of Washington, D.C., for their homes.

The Aftermath

On September 9, 1850, California was admitted to the Union as a free state and the territories of New Mexico and Utah were created. Although some hailed the "Compromise of 1850" as the final settlement of the slavery extension issue, in reality it addressed only a few of the concerns expressed in the congressional debates. Despite southern Democrats' fears that the admission of California as a free state would shift the balance of power in the Senate to the North, throughout the 1850s, California sent only Democrats to the Senate and on sectional questions almost always voted with the South. Despite the possibility of slavery extension in the territorial bills, few slaves were ever taken into the New Mexico or Utah territories. There were no additional slave states.

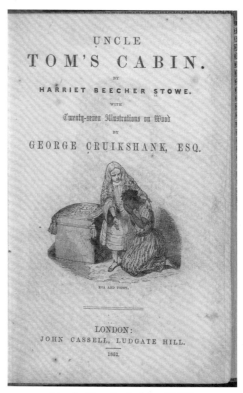

The little discussed Fugitive Slave Act of 1850 provoked far more controversy than Congress had imagined. northern Whigs denounced it as forcing northern states to aid the "Slaveocracy" in capturing slaves seeking their freedom. They also found it was deeply offensive to civil liberties by denying northern blacks due process and forcing northern whites to cooperate with the slave-catchers. Harriet Beecher Stowe's outrage inspired her to write her famous novel against slavery, *Uncle Tom's Cabin* (1852). Some northern states adopted more stringent "personal liberty" laws, and Northerners sometimes sued and occasionally mobbed southern slave-catchers seizing blacks. But the majority of the fugitive slaves in the 1850s were caught and returned to their masters.

The elections in 1850 and 1851 at the local, state and congressional levels indicated that the sectional and factional divisions within the Whig and Democratic parties were growing wider. In the South, most Whig candidates ran as defenders of the Compromise, but most Democrats continued to denounce it. In the North, most Democratic candidates lauded the Compromise for saving the Union and blasted northern Whigs and Free Soilers for endangering the nation. northern Whig candidates were caught

Uncle Tom's Cabin, 1852

in a dilemma. Only a minority supported the Compromise while the majority opposed it. The resulting split in the northern Whig Party led to sweeping victories in the North by pro-Compromise Democrats.

Political leaders in both major parties absorbed this lesson, and in the 1852 presidential election year, both the Whig and Democratic parties adopted national platforms that endorsed the Compromise of 1850 as a final settlement of the slavery question. The Democrats ran former Senator Franklin Pierce of New Hampshire for president and Alabama Senator William King for Vice President and adopted a pledge that their party would never again allow a discussion of any slavery-related matter in Congress. The Whigs nominated Mexican War General Winfield Scott, a Virginian, for president and William Graham, from North Carolina, for Vice President and adopted a platform accepting the Compromise of 1850, condemning further agitation of the slavery question and affirming states' rights. The Free Soil Party nominated Northerners for both positions, condemned slavery and the Compromise of 1850, and supported free homesteads in the West for settlers. The Democrats won a sweeping electoral victory in 1852. Pierce won 27 states and Scott only 4. Although the popular vote was much closer, the results led to the further disintegration of the Whig Party. The Free Soil Party received only half the votes that it had received in 1848.

The attempt to settle the issue of slavery in the territories through the Compromise of 1850 collapsed with the passage of the Kansas-Nebraska Act of 1854. (See Document 11: The Kansas-Nebraska Act.) Senator Stephen Douglas introduced a bill to organize the territories of Kansas and Nebraska through "popular sovereignty," thus permitting the admission of the territories with or without slavery. Douglas claimed that the popular sovereignty provisions applied to New Mexico and Utah territories in the Compromise of 1850 were meant to apply to all federal territories, including Kansas and Nebraska that had been part of the Louisiana Purchase. Since these two prospective territories were north of 36 degrees, 30 minutes latitude, the bill implicitly repealed the Missouri Compromise and thereby theoretically opened the rest of the West to slavery. Douglas's action infuriated the northern Whigs and many northern Democrats who claimed that he was betraying the Compromise of 1850 that some of them had reluctantly supported. Among the motives attributed to Douglas for introducing this controversial

"Bleeding Kansas": Northern view of
pro-slavery "border ruffians" arriving in
Kansas from neigboring Missouri

bill were his interest in building a transcontinental railroad along a central route west from Chicago, his need to court Southern support for his presidential ambitions, and his long-standing endorsement of local self-government and popular sovereignty.

Dred Scott

The Kansas-Nebraska Act was signed into law by President Pierce in May 1854. The result was permanently to polarize the Whig Party, because the southern Whigs supported the act and the northern Whigs unanimously opposed it. In the North, bipartisan, anti-Kansas-Nebraska coalitions soon emerged for political purposes. For the 1854 congressional elections, vigorous antislavery politicians united Free-Soilers, antislavery northern Whigs and antislavery northern Democrats to form a new, exclusively Northern-based, anti-Southern, political organization—the Republican Party.

Civil war broke out in Kansas over control of the territorial government between extremist pro-slavery and antislavery settlers, including abolitionist John Brown. The armed conflict and the future of Kansas as a free or slave state became the chief issue in the 1856 presidential election campaign. The Democrats nominated James Buchanan of Pennsylvania. The new Republican Party nominated John C. Fremont of California, who was supported by northern Whigs and Free Soilers. The American ("Know Nothing") nominated and the remnant of the Whig Party nominated former Whig President Millard Fillmore. Buchanan was elected president with 14 slave and 5 free states. The Whig Party disintegrated, most of its members dispersing into the Republican Party.

The U.S. Supreme Court attempted to end the controversy over the extension of slavery in 1857 by rendering a decision regarding the status of Dred Scott, a slave who had been brought to a free state and claimed that he was still free when he returned to a slave state. In a complex, splintered decision, the majority under Chief Justice Roger B. Taney of Maryland, held the Missouri Compromise unconstitutional in violation of the Fifth Amendment, which prohibits Congress from depriving persons of their property (slaves were legal property) without due process of law. Three of the justices , including Taney, explicitly denied that black slaves or free blacks who were descended from slaves were citizens of the United States or any of its states (only two of the justices affirmed that free blacks were citizens). The split decision and its vigorous denunciation indicated that the justices had not resolved the issue but rather had lowered the Court's prestige among Northerners and widened the sectional divide. (See Document 12: Excerpts from *Scott v. Sandford*)

In the 1858 Congressional and state elections, the emerging Republican swept the North. An exception to this was Illinois where Senator Stephen Douglas in his re-election campaign narrowly defeated Abraham Lincoln. However, the Lincoln-Douglass Debates propelled Lincoln to national prominence, especially through his argument regarding the extension of slavery. (See Document 13: Excerpts from Lincoln's "House Divided" Speech, June 1858.) The sectional divisions over the future of slavery finally led in the 1860 presidential election to the breakup of the Democratic Party into northern and southern wings, each with its own candidate. A candidate was also nominated by the remaining fragment of the old Whig Party and the American ("Know-Nothing") Party. With the end of the Whig Party and the sectional schism of the Democratic Party, the new Republican Party—a solely northern party composed of former northern Whigs, some northern members of the old Free Soil, Liberty and American parties, as well as independent, northern Democrats—catapulted their candidate, Abraham Lincoln of Illinois, to the presidency. He was elected solely with the electoral votes of northern states and on a platform opposed to any expansion of slavery. As a result, South Carolina, followed by other states from the Deep South, seceded from the Union and formed the Confederate States of America. The conflict over the extension of slavery had resulted in an attempt to form a separate southern nation and within a few months would lead to the beginning of a long and bloody civil war that would cost the lives of some 600,000 Americans. The war would settle permanently the issues of secession from the Union and the existence of slavery in the United States.

QUESTIONS FOR DISCUSSION

1. Given that the vast majority of Northerners had no intention of trying to abolish slavery in the states where it already existed and that plenty of fresh land for the expansion of plantation agriculture remained within the existing slave states, why did the issue of slavery expansion into the West repeatedly emerge and why did it provoke such intense conflict between Northerners and Southerners?

2. What role did national political parties (Whigs, Democrats) play in maintaining national cohesion? Why did they break apart?

3. How might other actions by Congress, the President, or the Supreme Court in 1850 and the 1850s have resolved the issues of the expansion of slavery, and, ultimately, slavery itself?

4. Suppose that Henry Clay had won the Whig nomination and the presidency in 1848 instead of Taylor. How might things have been different in 1850 with Clay in the White House rather than in the Senate?

    > Had Clay won the 1844 presidential election – and he came achingly close – there would have been no war with Mexico, no Wilmot Proviso, no territorial question to fight over. Had Whigs held a majority in the Senate in 1848, they would have amended the Treaty of Guadalupe Hidalgo to block any territorial acquisition, thus ending conflict over the Cession.

5. Alternatively, suppose that Zachary Taylor did not die in July 1850 but instead lived to serve out his full term. In that event, what might have happened to the crisis over slavery expansion into the Mexican Cession and to the political parties that confronted it?

    > It might also be argued that passage of Taylor's original plan without any new Fugitive Slave Act might have been more successful than the compromise that was eventually reached.

6. What alternatives to the Compromise of 1850 might have been more effective in avoiding a sectional split and the breakup of the Whig Party in the 1850s?

    > It could be argued that the Compromise of 1850 did avert a sectional split, at least temporarily.

    > If the southern Whigs had joined the northern Whigs in opposing the Fugitive Slave Act (instead of supporting it as a Southern issue), it would never have passed and would not have become a major issue in the 1850s. They could have attacked it as a partisan Democratic Party maneuver.

    > It is generally argued that it was the subsequent Kansas-Nebraska Act of 1854 that precipitated the breakup of the Whig Party, which as one of the two national political parties had helped to suppress sectional differences in the interest of larger national politics and policies. In its place in the North, there emerged a solely sectional party – the Republican Party. In 1854, had the southern Whigs joined northern Whigs in opposing the Kansas-Nebraska bill as a Democratic Party measure, for example, the measure would have been defeated and the immediate crisis would have been averted.

7. Great Britain ended slavery through an Act of Parliament, France through owner compensation, Spain by royal decree and several Latin American countries as part of an independence movement. Why do you think that only the United States had to engage in a civil war to resolve the issue of slavery?

8. Do you think that slavery could have ended in the United States without a war? Why or why not and how?

9. At what point did a civil war over slavery become unavoidable in the United States and why?

ADDITIONAL RESOURCES

Ayers, Edward L. *What Caused the Civil War: Reflections on the South and Southern History*. New York: Norton, 2005.

Blue, Frederick J. *The Free Soilers: Third Party Politics, 1848-1852*. Urbana: University of Illinois Press, 1973.

Brock, William R. *Parties and Political Conscience: American Dilemmas, 1840-1850*. Millwood, NY: KTO Press, 1979.

Ericson, David F. *The Debate over Slavery: Antislavery and Pro-slavery Liberalism in Antebellum America*. New York: New York University Press, 2000.

Fogel, Robert W. *Without Consent or Contract: The Rise and Fall of American Slavery*. New York: W.W. Norton, 1989.

Foner, Eric. *Free Soil, Free Labor, Free Men: The Ideology of the Republican Party before the Civil War*. New York: Oxford University Press, 1970.

Freehling, William W. *The Road to Disunion: Secessionists at Bay, 1776-1854*. New York: Oxford University Press, 1990.

Grant, Susan-Mary. *North over South: Northern Nationalism and American Identity in the Antebellum Era*. Lawrence: Kansas University Press, 2000.

Hamilton, Holman. *Prologue to Conflict: The Crisis and Compromise of 1850*. Lexington: University of Kentucky Press, 2005.

Holt, Michael F. *The Fate of their Country: Politicians, Slavery Extension and the Coming of the Civil War*. New York: Hill and Wang, 2004.

_____. *The Political Crisis of the 1850s*. New York: Norton & Co., 1978.

_____. *The Rise and Fall of the American Whig Party: Jacksonian Politics and the Onset of the Civil War*. New York: Oxford University Press, 1999.

Horton, James Oliver and Lois Horton. *In Hope of Liberty: Culture, Community, and Protest among Northern Free Blacks*. New York: Oxford University Press, 1997.

Levine, Bruce. *Half Slave and Half Free: The Roots of Civil War*. New York: Hill and Wang, 2005.

Lightner, David L. *Slavery and the Commerce Power: How the Struggle against the Interstate Slave Trade led to the Civil War*. New Haven: Yale University Press, 2006.

Oakes, James. The Ruling Race: *A History of American Slaveholders*. New York: Alfred A. Knopf, 1982.

Potter, David M. *The Impending Crisis, 1848-1861*. New York: Harper & Row, 1976.

Ratner, Lorman and Dwight L. Teeter, Jr. *Fanatics and Fire-eaters: Newspapers and the Coming of the Civil War*. Urbana: University of Illinois Press, 2003.

Smith, Elbert B. *The Presidencies of Zachary Taylor and Millard Fillmore*. Lawrence, KS: University Press of Kansas, 1988.

Stegmaier, Mark . Texas, New *Mexico, and the Compromise of 1850: Boundary Dispute and Sectional Crisis*. Kent, OH: Kent State University Press, 1996.

Voss-Hubbard, Mark . *Beyond Party: Culture of Antipartsanship in Northern Politics Before the Civil War*. Baltimore: Johns Hopkins University Press, 2002.

Walther, Eric H. *The Shattering of the Union: America in the 1850s*. Wilmington, DE: Scholarly Resources, 2004.

Waugh, John C. *On the Brink of Civil War: The Compromise of 1850 and How it Changed the Course of American History.* Wilmington, DE: Scholarly Resources, 2003.

DOCUMENTS ON CD

Document 1:	The Wilmot Proviso
Document 2:	President Taylor's Address to the House of Representatives, December 4, 1849
Document 3:	Senator Henry Clay's Proposals
Document 4:	Floor remarks by Senator Thomas Hart Benton
Document 5:	Speech by Senator Daniel Webster
Document 6:	Speech by Senator William Henry Seward
Document 7:	Speech by Jefferson Davis
Document 8:	Millard Fillmore's Address to the House of Representatives, August 6, 1850
Document 9:	The Compromise of 1850
Document 10:	Resolutions of the Nashville Convention critical of the 1850 Compromise
Document 11:	The Kansas-Nebraska Act, 1854
Document 12:	Excerpts *Scott v. Sandford*, 1857
Document 13:	Excerpt from Lincoln's "House Divided" Speech, June 1858

Teacher Overheads/Student Handouts on CD

1. Map of the Missouri Compromise, 1820

2. Timeline: Historical Background, 1787-1848

3. Map of the Mexican Cession, 1848

4. Timeline: Historical Background 1849-1850

5. The Immediate Facts

6. Brief biographies of the Participants

7. Positions on the Issues Chart

8. The Facts Continued

10. Questions for Discussion

Sources and Credits for Illustrations

p. 201: Map of Missouri Compromise, 1820, *National Atlas*

p. 202: Map of the Mexican Session, 1848, *National Atlas*

p. 203: William Lloyd Garrison, *LC-US262-10320*

p. 205: Four Proposals for Dividing Texas, *University of Texas Library*

p. 207: The Death of President Taylor, *Rare Images, Library of Congress*

p. 208: Sen. Henry Clay, *National Archives NWDNS-111-B-4201*

p. 208: Sen. Daniel Webster, National Archives *NWDNS-111-B-4205*

p. 209: Sen. William H Seward, *LC-USZ62-21907*

p. 209: Sen. Jefferson Davis, *LC-BH82- 2417*

p. 210: Sen. Henry Foote, *LC-USZ62-110163*

p. 210: Sen. Stephen A. Douglas, *LC-BH82- 2460*

p. 211: Sen. Thomas Hart Benton, *LC-USZ62-1112*

p. 211: Sen. Salmon Chase, *LC-USZ62-113378*

p. 212: Sen. William R. King, *LC-USZ62-3609*

p. 215: Map of the Compromise of 1850, *University of Nebraska Libraries*

p. 216: Cover of Uncle Tom's Cabin, *LC Rare Books Division*

p. 217: Lithograph of Bleeding Kansas, *Kansas.org*

p. 218: Dred Scott Wood Engraving, *LC-USZ62-5092*

Chapter Ten

The Struggle For Women's Rights in the Nineteenth Century

Objectives

- To analyze the origins of the movement for women's rights and how it emanated from women's involvement in abolition, temperance and other reform movements.

- To examine the goals of the 1848 Seneca Falls Declaration of Sentiments and how they were or were not implemented.

- To consider alternatives to the Fifteenth Amendment, giving black men the vote, that might have included women.

- To contrast the continuing and changing attitudes and roles regarding women in the nineteenth and twentieth centuries.

- To compare the legal and political rights and economic and social opportunities for women during the nineteenth and twentieth centuries.

Correlations with National History Standards

Era Four:
Standard 4C

The student understands changing gender roles and the ideas and activities of women reformers.

- Compare the North, South and West in terms of men's and women's occupations, legal rights and social status.

- Analyze the activities of women of different racial and social groups in the reform movements for education, abolition, temperance and women's suffrage.

- Analyze the goals of the 1848 Seneca Falls "Declaration of Sentiments" and evaluate its impact.

- Compare and contrast the antebellum women's movement for equality and twentieth century feminism.

Era Four:
Standard 3C

- Analyze how the Civil War and Reconstruction changed men's and women's roles and status in the North, South and West.

OVERVIEW

Women were a critical part of the development of the country in the colonial and Revolutionary periods. Yet, despite the ringing Revolutionary War rhetoric about "freedom" and "equality," women in the English colonies in North America were viewed as dependents, much like children. They had few legal rights and they were not able to vote or hold public office. If they were married, women were not even able to own property. The ideology that emerged, and to which most women subscribed, held that women were "naturally" dependent upon and subordinate to men in the political and economic realms while morally superior to males in their domestic roles as wives and mothers. In the nineteenth century, the struggle for women's rights began as a consequence of women's efforts for abolition, temperance, peace and social justice. Women began to focus on their immediate domestic needs, such as the right for married women to own property, to have custody of their children and to gain control of their own bodies. Only after obtaining some basic control over their domestic relations did women turn to their need for political rights. Even though male suffrage expanded dramatically during the early 1800s, the women's rights movement did not emphasize the right to vote until after the Civil War, and it took another fifty years to achieve national female suffrage. In the meantime, women's efforts resulted in the growth of a wide range of voluntary organizations. Women's struggles for social reform, whether for themselves, their families, their children or for the broader society, have been a major factor in the expansion and protection of individuals and individual rights, as well as for the welfare of society.

What was the source of the conflict over proposals in the 1860s to imbue women with the same legal and political rights as men? Why were women unable to obtain the vote as part of the expanded definition of American citizenship that extended suffrage to former male slaves in post-Civil War Reconstruction? Why did it take until 1920 for women to become recognized as full citizens themselves? What were the obstacles? Why has the enfranchisement of women not had the anticipated impact on elections and public policy? What issues raised by the nineteenth century women's movement remain significant today?

This case study includes two activities:

- A Mock Negotiation over priorities at the Seneca Falls Convention in 1848

- A Mock Mediation over whether women's rights advocates should support the Fifteenth Amendment in 1869.

HISTORICAL BACKGROUND

"I desire you would remember the ladies and be more generous and favorable to them than your ancestors," Abigail Adams wrote on March 31, 1777, to her husband John who was at the Continental Congress helping to determine national policies. Concerned that "all men would be tyrants if they could," she urged that the new government curb the "unlimited power" of husbands over wives. She also threatened: "if particular care and attention is not paid to the ladies, we are determined to foment a rebellion and will not hold ourselves bound by any laws in which we have no voice or representation." In his brief reply, John Adams made fun of his wife's concerns, dismissing her suggestion as a joke. Later, however, in writing to a male friend, he justified his dismissal of rights for women, as well as children, men without property, African Americans, and Indians, because he thought they lacked independent judgment as a result of their economic dependence on others (that is, white men). In the case of women, he added, "their delicacy renders them unfit for practice and experience in the great businesses of life." The majority of Americans, including most women, held views similar to those of John Adams in the late eighteenth century.

The legal status of eighteenth-century women derived from a combination of English common law, equity practices and provincial statutes, which varied from colony to colony. Married women had no right to own real or personal property, to sign contracts or to sue. The colonies continued to follow Blackstone's *Commentaries on English common law* (1865): "The very being or legal existence of the woman is suspended during the course of marriage, or at least incorporated and consolidated into that of the husband, under whose wing, protection and cover she performs every thing." This English common law practice of "coverture" gave the husband legal rights to all of a married couple's property, including any property brought into the marriage or inherited by the wife and to wages the wife earned during the marriage. The husband was given custody of children in the rare cases of divorce or separation since he controlled the means of support. And he had the right to sexual satisfaction and, thus, to his wife's body. Husbands also had the right to "correct" their wives and children, and physical punishment was assumed to be a necessary feature of such correction. In the more "progressive" states, the "rule of thumb" was applied, restricting men from beating their wives (or their children) with any rod or stick larger around than their thumb. Legally, a woman was largely at the mercy of her husband. If she married a wastrel, an alcoholic, a gambler, or a man who was simply mean and abusive, she had little legal recourse. In a period when over 90 percent of women married, the status of wives was essentially the status of women. And wives had few domestic or property rights.

Although widows automatically gained a dower right, that is, a life estate in one-third of her husband's real and personal property, and could sign contracts, sue and be sued; she could not sell or bequeath the property without special permission of a court or legislature. Widows often found themselves dependent on charity. Men held at least 90 percent of colonial wealth.

Beginning with the First Great Awakening, a revitalization of religious piety that swept through the American colonies between the 1730s and the 1770s, women had started to form female voluntary associations within their churches, giving them a separate but influential role. The American Revolution upgraded the value of domestic contributions of women. Spinning and weaving American cloth were transformed into patriotic acts. The Revolution also sanctioned group activities by women: secular, single-sex, voluntary organizations to support the war effort. Women made critical contributions to the patriotic cause—raising funds; providing clothing, bandages, and food for the army; storing ammunition and other war material; caring for the sick and wounded; serving as spies and couriers; managing farms, businesses, and families in the absence of husbands and fathers; and defending themselves and their homes when necessary.

The mobilization of women in such public roles challenged the traditional belief of female dependence on men and exclusion from the public realm. The contradiction between the growing activism by women and the predominant ideology that excluded women from the public forum was resolved by the concept of "republican motherhood," which gave women a patriotic duty to educate their sons to be virtuous citizens, rather than for them to be direct, active participants in the body politic. The ideology of republican motherhood emphasized women's domestic duty and inspired women to participate in the moral improvement of their communities, thus drawing women's areas of activity somewhat closer to that of men. However, most women emphasized their more conservative domestic roles rather than claiming a direct connection with political life as articulated in Britain by Mary Wollstonecraft in *The Vindication of the Rights of Women* (1792).

In the aftermath of the American Revolution, only New Jersey granted women the right to vote and then only to unmarried, property-owning (and therefore tax-paying) women—those who were not automatically represented by a husband and who had an independent economic stake in the government. Although these women formed a tiny percentage of New Jersey's electorate, ultimately they proved *too* independent for the all-male legislature. In 1806, a group of women voters formed a coalition with reform-minded men to turn out those in power. By a small margin, the coalition failed to achieve its ends, and in 1807, the New Jersey legislature retaliated by rescinding the vote for women and blacks. Since the Constitution did not specifically include women or blacks, a Constitutional amendment was not necessary to restrict the vote to "a free white male citizen."

Although the unmarried, propertied women of New Jersey were no doubt unhappy to lose their electoral privileges, this change in their political status placed them among the vast majority of Americans. Only a small minority of Americans—adult white men with property—could vote in the early 1800s. Therefore, only native-born, unmarried, white women who owned property could complain that they were *unfairly* denied the right to vote because of their gender. African-American, Native-American, and foreign-born women shared disfranchisement with most of the men of their groups, as did most poor white women, until the Jacksonian Era of the 1830s and 1840s, when property qualifications for voting were gradually eliminated.

Women voting in New Jersey in 1797, as depicted in Harper's Weekly *(1880)*

The Second Great Awakening, a religious revival that reached its peak in the 1820s, brought together religious beliefs and optimism for the possibilities of individual and communal improvement with the idea of female moral superiority. Emboldened by their sense of religious and civic mission, women built on their earlier organizing attempts and began to form secular, female voluntary organizations and associations for civic betterment. The Second Great Awakening marked the beginning of an alliance between women and ministers (almost all of whom were men): female moral superiority was endorsed by the clergy in exchange for women's support and activism. Women carved out a public space for themselves between the home and the formal institutions of government in voluntary organizations where they pursued reform efforts that were parallel to but separate from male efforts to effect social change through politics.

The doctrine of "women's sphere" was promoted by the changing work environment, the clergy and the popular ladies magazines that began to appear in the late 1820s. The "women's sphere" primarily reflected a change in the work force: the movement from an agrarian culture where the whole family worked on the farm to a wage labor economy where men went to work outside of the farm while middle class wives remained at home with domestic chores to do. The "separate sphere" doctrine increased women's authority at home and celebrated the new status of the middle class woman and a new consciousness of gender. Catharine Beecher contended in her *Treatises on Domestic Economy* in the 1840s that "the duties of the woman are as sacred and important as any ordained by men."

Women Advocating Change, 1830s and 1840s

Beginning in the 1830s, the public school system in the North began to expand and provide a decent, if all too brief, education to larger numbers of boys and girls. The need for low-paid teachers at the growing number of public schools as well as a public discussion about women's education stimulated the development of female seminaries and academies. Still, most women had little access to education that would prepare them for an occupation beyond housewife and mother. A small number of women earned their living as teachers, midwives, making textiles, shoes or hats, or taking in laundry or boarders. Beyond these, agricultural labor, domestic service, or prostitution offered poorly paid and sometimes dangerous ways for women to earn a living.

For black women, enslaved or free, the abolition of slavery was the major priority, as it was for the men of their race. The Northern states were slowly eliminating slavery: 1777 in Vermont; 1780 in Pennsylvania and Massachusetts; 1784 in Rhode Island, Connecticut and New Hampshire; 1787, by act of Congress, in the Northwest Territory (the future states of Ohio, Indiana, Illinois, Michigan, Wisconsin and part of Minnesota); 1799 in New York and 1804 in New Jersey. Concerned with protecting property rights, the state legislators adopted gradual emancipation of slaves. For example, in New York, children born to slave women after 1799 became free only after the males became 28 and the females became 24 years old. Slaves already in servitude remained slaves for life, although reclassified as "indentured servants." As late as 1830, there remained 3,568 black slaves in the Northern states. Similarly, American Indian women were more concerned about maintaining customary rights within their tribes and sustaining their communities on a shrinking land base than about gaining women's rights within the American political system. The women among the growing number of working-class European immigrants were focused, like their men, mainly on economic survival. Poor women with numerous children who were, for various reasons, the primary provider for their families hardly had a moment to think about the unfairness of their exclusion from voting and politics.

Given the constraints on women's lives, it is not surprising that when women—black, white, or Indian; native-born or foreign-born; poor, middling or rich; married or single; young, middle-aged, or old—thought about their rights, they focused on better education, higher wages, the right to their earnings and their property in marriage, the custody of their children and the control of their own bodies as both more critical

Women constrained by their clothes:
Antebellum women in corseted hoop skirts, 1830s

and more attainable. Woman's suffrage was only one of the issues that concerned women activists, and for many it was secondary to abolition, temperance, and reforming laws on property rights, child custody and divorce. It was not that most women would have rejected suffrage; indeed, it offered them respect as a citizen as well as a way for them to obtain and enforce their legal and civil rights.

In the early to mid-nineteenth century, women, like men, tried to address the harsh results of the rapid social and economic changes occurring in the United States through industrialization, urbanization and western expansion and engaged in a wide variety of organizations and reform movements to ameliorate poverty, disease, prostitution, drunkenness and other social problems. Rooted in ideals of republican motherhood, religious devotion, economic necessity, ideological principle, or some combination of these, many women widened their domestic sphere to participate in missionary and charitable societies; reform organizations dedicated to temperance, the abolition of slavery and prostitution, the improvement of working conditions; or more radical movements demanding rights for African Americans, Indians, workers, and women.

Different organizations and movements attracted different groups of women. Wealthier wives and daughters joined missionary and charitable societies. Women from middle class and upwardly-mobile families, many inspired by evangelical religious beliefs, engaged in moral reform efforts to eradicate drunkenness, prostitution, and slavery. And some white women from progressive religious traditions—especially the Society of Friends or Quakers—joined free black women in movements to abolish slavery, advance equal rights for African Americans and Indians, institute land reform, and improve working conditions. It was from this last group of women activists that the nation's first women's rights advocates emerged. They included women from across the economic spectrum: daughters of wealth and privilege who were especially cognizant of the restrictions imposed on them by their sex as well as women from farming communities and the urban working classes.

Women began to exercise the few rights they did have—most notably their First Amendment right to associate and petition the government—to promote change. Many women, who never imagined demanding rights for themselves, signed petitions opposing the removal of the Cherokee Indians from their traditional tribal lands or the expansion of slavery into Texas and other new western territories. For many of these women, the fight against slavery offered a model for analyzing their own oppression and for mobilizing to change the status quo. It also provided a small *coterie* of women with the skills—speaking, petitioning, fundraising and organizing conventions—that would be crucial to the struggle for women's rights.

The antislavery crusade began in 1831 when William Lloyd Garrison first published *The Liberator* and formed the New England Antislavery Society. Women joined immediately. Through the racially-integrated Philadelphia Female Anti-Slavery Society, a women's petition campaign was launched, and in the spring of 1837, the first Anti-Slavery Convention of American Women was organized and held in New York City. At this national convention, Angelina Grimké offered the following resolution:

> RESOLVED, That as certain rights and duties are common to all moral beings, the time has come for woman to move in that sphere which Providence has assigned her, and no longer remain satisfied in the circumscribed limits with which corrupt custom and a perverted application of Scripture have encircled her; therefore, it is the duty of woman, and the province of woman, to plead the cause of the oppressed in our land, and to do all that she can by her voice, and her pen, and her purse, and the influence of her example, to overthrow the horrible system of slavery.

The resolution was hotly contested. Some of the women thought that it was too radical and would hurt the cause to have it published with the convention proceedings. But with the support of Lucretia Mott, a Massachusetts Quaker and a founder of the Philadelphia Female Anti-Slavery Society, the resolution passed, though not unanimously. By 1838 the American Anti-Slavery Society had sent petitions with over 400,000 signatures to Congress. Almost 70 percent of those who signed the petitions were women.

Angelina Grimké

Sarah Grimké

Angelina and Sarah Grimké were daughters of a wealthy South Carolina slaveholder. They had come to abhor the institution of slavery, moved to Philadelphia, joined the Society of Friends and, in 1837, were hired by the recently formed American Anti-Slavery Society to lecture throughout New England on behalf of abolition. The Grimkés linked their religious devotion to their need to speak out against slavery. They also connected the oppression experienced by slaves to that experienced by women: "Women ought to feel a peculiar sympathy in the colored man's wrong, for like him, she has been accused of mental inferiority, and denied the privileges of a liberal education." And in the fight against slavery, they claimed, there was no reason for women to take a secondary place: "Men and women were CREATED EQUAL; they are both moral and accountable beings, and whatever is *right* for a man to do, is *right* for a woman to do."

Such radical claims and public activism by women infuriated many Northerners, including ministers and politicians as well as more moderate women activists. The clergymen of Massachusetts were horrified not only by the Grimkés' public proclamations on slavery, religion and women, but also by the huge "promiscuous" audiences. (In the early nineteenth century, the word "promiscuous" was used to indicate simply mixed groups of women and men.) In the midst of the Grimkés' New England tour, pastors throughout the region read a letter to their congregations asserting that "The power of woman is her dependence, flowing from the consciousness of that weakness which God has given her for her protection. . . . But when she assumes the place and tone of man as a public reformer . . . she yields the power which God has given her for her protection, and her character becomes unnatural." Many women embraced their ministers' words and limited their public efforts to those approved by the church, steering clear of anything tainted by political considerations. The most prominent opponent of women's public activism and equal rights was Catharine Beecher, the daughter of fiery abolitionist preacher Henry Ward Beecher and sister of Harriet Beecher Stowe, who would write *Uncle Tom's Cabin* in 1852. A moderate reformer who wrote petitions on behalf of the Cherokee Indians, advocated education for girls and household management for women, Catharine Beecher believed that it was "unwomanly" for women to engage openly in public debate.

The Emergence of Women's Rights

The debates at the Anti-Slavery Convention of American Women and the growing demands by women within the American Anti-Slavery Society to gain an equal place in the movement with men brought the issue of women's rights into the public arena. Antislavery preachers, like Samuel May of Syracuse, New York, would sermonize on women's rights in this same period, always linking women's moral duties to the fight against human bondage. Free black abolitionists, like Frederick Douglass, would advocate women's right to speak, vote and hold office in antislavery organizations. In this sense, the women's rights movement would, from its founding, tackle the intertwined issues of race and gender and do so in the heat of national struggles related to slavery, western expansion and industrialization. The disagreement over whether women should be included in leadership roles would split the ranks of the antislavery movement in two.

"Am I Not A Woman and a Sister?"
Cover of Lydia M. Child's
Authentic Anecdotes of
American Slavery, *1838*

At the World Anti-Slavery Convention held in London in 1840, the organizers refused to seat women delegates on the convention floor, much less let them speak. William Lloyd Garrison, a fiery orator and founder of the American Anti-Slavery Society, was so outraged by this discrimination against women that he moved to the balcony to sit with the women, abandoning his vote and his place on the floor. It was this public display of women's second-class citizenship that inspired Elizabeth Cady Stanton, the new bride of antislavery advocate Henry Stanton, who met Lucretia Mott at the Anti-Slavery Convention, to consider the need for a convention to address women's rights specifically, a convention that would occur eight years later when Mott and Stanton met again.

In the intervening years, antislavery women and men began boycotting slave-produced products such as sugar, rice, and cotton and arguing that only a refusal to participate in the system that supported slavery could end that system. Thus, in 1846, when the United States declared war with Mexico in a dispute over the border of slaveholding Texas, these same abolitionists spoke out against the war, and some refused to pay taxes to support what they called an unjust and immoral military effort. Joined now by other Northerners opposed to the war, a contingent of abolitionist men—many of them Quakers—and New England Transcendentalists such as Henry David Thoreau, refused to vote or to pay taxes.

While elite women most often formed benevolent associations and moral reform societies and middle-class women predominated in evangelical reform, women in the growing working classes, who were bearing the brunt of the changes in the working world from farms to factories, tried unsuccessfully to form labor organizations. Whereas the middle classes continued to idealize the mother-child relationship, poorer women often saw motherhood as a condition of extreme hardship. Sarah Trask, a factory worker in Massachusetts, kept a diary during the 1840s in which she recorded her concerns about work, wages, religion and marriage. Though she expected that she would be able to stay at home once she found a husband, she was nonetheless concerned about making a bad choice: "marriage to me seems a great responsibility," she wrote, "and almost all of the care comes upon the wife."

In the 1840s, women's rights advocates and their supporters worked in a number of states to obtain legal and economic rights for women—rights to property, custody of their children, and to their own earnings and inheritances. Several state legislatures considered moderate reforms for women, such as property rights for married women. For example, in 1848, New York passed a Married Women's Property Law, granting married women sole control over property that they brought into the marriage or received afterwards but not to property or wages they earned during the marriage. Since married women were not able to sue in court without their husband's permission, they still had little chance of securing their new rights, since no husband would approve a suit against himself. This led to efforts to expand the limited rights granted in the 1848 law as well as inspiring petition campaigns on behalf of other legal rights for women. More radical women, such as Margaret Fuller, a writer and intellectual from Massachusetts, wrote books and articles advocating compete autonomy for women, including equal rights and the vote.

In what would become an historic development, a group of women meeting in upstate New York, led by Elizabeth Cady Stanton, Lucretia Mott, her sister Martha Wright, as well as Mary Ann McClintock and Jane Hunt, who were both Quakers from Waterloo, New York, concluded that action was required and resolved to call a women's rights convention. The call for a Women's Rights Convention to be held in Seneca Falls, New York, July 19-20, 1848, was written just two weeks earlier. It was published both in the Seneca Falls *Courier* and Frederick Douglass' *North Star* in Rochester, New York, with only a few days notice to potential participants. Yet more than 200 women and about 40 men from the surrounding towns came to the meeting.

ACTIVITY ONE: MOCK NEGOTIATION PRIORITIZING GOALS AT THE SENECA FALLS CONVENTION, 1848

On July 19, 1848, more than 200 people, virtually all abolitionists, met at the Wesleyan Chapel in Seneca Falls, New York, to discuss women's conditions and rights. Although the original plan had been for only women to meet on the first day, so many men as well as women arrived on the first day that the organizers decided to invite them all in. The attendees included several husbands and well-known male abolitionists, including Frederick Douglass. The women bowed to the gender convention of having a man, Lucretia Mott's husband James, preside over the proceedings. James Mott proved to be an excellent facilitator for these boisterous debates. He was calm, judicious, widely respected and inscrutable as to his own stand on the issues.

At Elizabeth Cady Stanton's suggestion, the women used the Declaration of Independence as the model for their Declaration of Sentiments: "We hold these truths to be self-evident: that all men and women are created equal...." The Declaration of Sentiments presented a series of wrongs against American women and a series of resolutions intended to right those wrongs. (See Document 1: The Declaration of Sentiments.) Some of the most effective wording regarding women's roles in religious and reform activities was taken directly from the resolutions passed by the Anti-Slavery Convention of American Women in 1837. Other resolutions followed earlier antislavery petitions. Some were crafted on the spot, including the one demanding women's suffrage. The convention debated eleven resolutions over two days, including women's rights to equal treatment with men, occupations, education, spiritual equality, public speaking, the elective franchise and advocate change. Women's public rights were asserted on the basis of women's individual rights as citizens.

Your students will be playing the roles of various participants who were actually at the Seneca Falls Women's Rights Convention in 1848. Their task in this mock negotiation is to prioritize the resolutions in order to better understand their content and context. Although the actual participants were primarily in agreement about the nature of the rights that women should have, they did not make any effort to identify what they thought were the most important demands for rights. The exercise to prioritize the resolutions is purely hypothetical. One of the purposes is for your students to appreciate the context of the times, including the recognition that female suffrage was not the primary goal on the minds of most women or men who attended the Seneca Falls Convention in 1848. Another purpose is to appreciate that there were diverse views on what was most important, even among this group of feminists who mostly agreed, and to see if they could agree on a common list of priorities. This discussion will also help to set the stage for the second activity in this chapter: a mock mediation regarding the Fifteenth Amendment in 1869.

PARTICIPANTS

Lucretia Mott was born in 1793 into a Quaker family in the seafaring community of Nantucket, Massachusetts, where women managed the businesses and the families while most of the men were away at sea. She was educated at a school run by the Society of Friends, where she met and married James Mott in 1811. The two Motts taught at the school for a year. Lucretia received half the wages that her husband earned for the same job, as was the custom at the time. They then moved to Philadelphia where James became a successful merchant and Lucretia bore and raised six children, as well as speaking at meetings throughout the Northeast as a Quaker "minister." In 1833, she helped to found the interracial Philadelphia Female Anti-Slavery Society. She worked consistently for both the abolition of slavery in the South and the establishment of racial equality in the North. She was an active member of the Free Produce Society, which led boycotts against slave-produced goods, and she protested both slavery and the Mexican War. Mott also engaged in missions to the Seneca Indians in upstate New York and to fugitive African-American slaves in Canada, visited prisons regularly to work with prisoners to advance their education and assure their rights, and

Lucretia Mott

protested the use of capital punishment. Mott believed in equality in the family and in education and recognition of women's equal moral and religious capacity. She placed the abolition of slavery, rather than voting rights for women, as the primary concern of women's rights advocates in the mid-nineteenth century.

Amy Kirby Post

Amy Kirby Post was born in 1802 to a farming family in Long Island and attended Quaker schools. After her older sister Hannah, who had married Isaac Post and borne two children, died in 1828, Amy married Isaac and moved to Rochester, New York. Isaac worked as a butcher and then opened a pharmacy, while Amy raised her two stepchildren and bore four children of her own. Despite her domestic responsibilities and financial constraints, Amy became active in local and regional Quaker meetings, serving as a leader in the separate "women's" meetings which supervised women members, approved marriage bans and wrote testimonies on behalf of Indian rights, antislavery, temperance and other causes. During the 1840s, Post helped to found the interracial and mixed-sex Western New York Anti-Slavery Society, presided over numerous fundraising fairs, and worked with Isaac as a conductor on the Underground Railroad, helping slaves escape to Canada. From 1848 on, Post combined her antislavery activities with advocacy for women's rights. At the Rochester Woman's Rights Convention, held two weeks after Seneca Falls, Post insisted that a woman preside over the meeting. She helped form a Working Women's Protective Union among seamstresses. Amy Post was most concerned about how the limited access of black and white women to education and employment forced them into submission to men, immoral activities and impoverishment.

Frederick Douglass was born into slavery in Maryland in 1818. He worked as a field hand and dockworker for 20 years before escaping from his master while working in Baltimore. Using the papers of a free black sailor, he made his way to Boston and soon found employment as an antislavery lecturer for William Lloyd Garrison's

American Anti-Slavery Society. He toured throughout Europe and the northern United States before announcing plans in 1847 to start his own antislavery paper. Garrison and his followers in Boston disapproved, so Douglass moved west to Rochester, New York. There, as publisher of the *North Star*, he cemented his reputation as one of the leading spokespersons for abolition and racial equality for free blacks. A supporter of women's rights within antislavery circles as well as in the wider society, Douglass was, nonetheless, skeptical of wives holding equal rights within marriage. At about the time of the Seneca Falls Women's Rights Convention, Douglass turned away from Garrison's claims that the U.S. government was a pro-slavery institution and joined, instead, with a group of "political abolitionists," who argued that men must use their voting power to end slavery. His support for women's suffrage in Seneca Falls was linked to this agenda and to his demand for voting rights for Northern free blacks.

Frederick Douglass

Elizabeth Cady Stanton

Elizabeth Cady Stanton was born in 1815 in Johnstown, New York. Raised in wealth and ease, she received a substantial education for a girl of her day, including three years at a female seminary. She learned much about the law, including its inequities, by reading her father's law books and listening to him debate with the numerous law students who studied at his side. In 1840, she married Henry Stanton, a law student studying with her father who introduced her to the antislavery movement and to Boston social circles. Henry Stanton never fully approved of his wife's ventures into public life and was conspicuously absent from Seneca Falls during the women's rights convention of 1848. He believed abolition could only be achieved through political compromise and, as a congressman and lawyer, he feared being ridiculed for his wife's radical stands. He spent long periods in Washington, D.C., leaving Elizabeth to juggle childcare and activism. A Presbyterian, Cady Stanton had no experience with the Quakers' relatively egalitarian views on women, nor had she been deeply involved in antislavery politics before 1848. Although she believed that slaves should be freed, Stanton was also convinced that educated white women had a stronger claim to rights than the newly emancipated slaves or impoverished and illiterate Irish Catholic immigrants. She viewed suffrage as the most important weapon that women could wield to assure their rights.

TEACHER INSTRUCTIONS

Preparation

The class should read the background materials, the Declaration of Sentiments and Resolutions and the short biographies of the historical figures at the Convention, which include the participants' positions and interests.

Directions

1. Divide into groups of six or seven.

2. Assign each person a role:

   a. Elizabeth Cady Stanton

   b. Amy Kirby Post

c. Frederick Douglass

d. Lucretia Mott

e. An Observer/Recorder/Reporter—Thomas or Mary Ann McClintock

f. An Observer/Recorder/Reporter—Catharine Beecher who will be preparing an article about the Convention (She was not actually there, but we want to hear what she would say.)

g. Add James Mott as a mediator, if necessary.

The Roles

1. The four negotiators should try to come to an agreement as to which rights listed in the Declaration of Sentiments were the most important and should be given priority, using conflict resolution skills but also recognizing the constraints of their historical character.

2. The observer/recorder/reporters do not participate in the negotiation process. The role of the observer/recorder/reporter is to objectively observe, record and report on the negotiation process and results, using the negotiations evaluation form. Miss Beecher will listen to the deliberations and write an article explaining her views regarding the proceedings at the Women's Convention.

3. The role of the mediator is to help the negotiators to identify the issues and to come to a resolution.

Debriefing

1. Discuss the process and results from the mock negotiations or mediations.

2. Hand out and discuss "The Facts Continued: From Seneca Falls through the Civil War"

3. Compare the results of the mock negotiation with what actually occurred.

THE FACTS CONTINUED: FROM SENECA FALLS THROUGH THE CIVIL WAR

*O*n the second day of the Women's Rights Convention at Seneca Falls, New York, in mid-July 1848, the participants debated eleven resolutions. All but the ninth resolution passed unanimously. The ninth stated: "Resolved, That it is the duty of women of this country to secure themselves their sacred right to the elective franchise." In the end, the resolution did receive the support of a majority, albeit a narrow majority, of those in attendance but only as a result of the concerted efforts of Elizabeth Cady Stanton and Frederick Douglass. (See Document 2: Report of the Women's Rights Convention.)

In the decade following the Seneca Falls Convention, other women's rights meetings were held throughout the Northeast and Midwest. In 1850, Lucy Stone, a recent graduate of Oberlin College in Ohio (the first male institution of higher education to accept women and blacks) and lecturer for the Massachusetts Anti-Slavery Society, organized the first national women's rights convention and was instrumental in organizing several other women's rights conventions. By 1860, the women of New York finally secured the right to sue in court, and other Northern states began to consider women's legal rights. By 1865, twenty-nine states had enacted some form of married women's property reform. However, the battle for legal rights for women continued well into the twentieth century.

Even as women's rights advocates worked to advance women's legal rights, open the professions to women, and eradicate exploitative working conditions, alcoholism and wife abuse, the cause that gained the greatest attention from reform-minded women continued to be the abolition of slavery. As civil war loomed on the horizon, even the most ardent women's rights advocates, including Elizabeth Cady Stanton and the recently recruited Susan B. Anthony, set aside the battle for gender equality to focus on ending slavery.

The Civil War (1861-1865) required the efforts and sacrifices of women in the North and the South, as well as the men on the battlefields. Woman's rights advocates, led by Stanton and Anthony, formed the Women's National Loyal League to raise funds for the war and support for the Union. Amy Post, Lucretia Mott and other Quaker pacifists, along with black abolitionists, argued that the war was only worth supporting if its purpose was to end slavery. Abolitionists like Stone and Stanton hoped that an end to slavery and greater rights for African Americans would also bring expanded legal and political rights for women. Beginning with President Abraham Lincoln's Emancipation Proclamation of 1863 and concluding with the Thirteenth Amendment to the Constitution (ratified in 1865), which officially prohibited the practice of human bondage anywhere in the United States, the conflict became a war not just to preserve the Union but also to abolish slavery. However, it was not the abolition of slavery that posed grave problems for Americans in the war's aftermath but rather the status of freed blacks in the re-united nation. And it was the debates over this status—specifically over black citizenship and suffrage—that led to a major realignment within the women's rights movement in the late 1860s.

The Fifteenth Amendment, 1869

Woman's rights advocates like Elizabeth Cady Stanton and Susan B. Anthony hoped that the war would open the way for suffrage for women as well as black men. In 1866, with this agenda in mind, Stanton and Anthony joined former abolitionists, including Lucy Stone, Frederick Douglass, Sojourner Truth and Frances Harper, in establishing the American Equal Rights Association. Yet, almost immediately, African-American women divided, many like Harper made clear their belief that there was greater urgency for black men to gain suffrage than for women—black or white—to gain equal rights. Indeed, when the Fourteenth Amendment (ratified 1868) guaranteeing citizenship to African Americans inserted the word "male" in the Constitution for the first time, most African Americans—women and men—as well as many of their white abolitionist allies voiced their support. Anthony, Stanton and the legendary African-American lecturer Sojourner Truth, however, urged women's rights advocates to press for suffrage for women while the definition of U.S. citizenship was on the national political agenda. Although the threat of reduced representation in section two of the Fourteenth Amendment was never used to punish states which denied the vote "to any of the male inhabitants," the women's rights advocates saw this language as an affront to their claims to be equal citizens.

It was, however, the proposal for the Fifteenth Amendment to the Constitution that aroused the most serious debates among the women's rights advocates. Passed by Congress in February 1869, this amendment specifically enfranchised black men but not women. As the amendment headed to the states for ratification, the American Equal Rights Association met to discuss whether or not to support it.

Stanton and Anthony opposed the amendment, arguing that only a constitutional amendment that granted suffrage to women as well as black men should be supported because the vote was the right of ALL citizens. In contrast, Douglass, Harper and other abolitionists supported the amendment, believing that as Douglass said, "it was the Negro's hour," and that granting the vote to black men would eventually open the door to votes for women. Lucy Stone feared that simultaneous consideration of women's suffrage might jeopardize black male suffrage. Many women were torn by the issue—between principle and personal loyalty or between competing principles. Amy Post, for instance, had long supported racial and gender equality, and she believed deeply that universal rights were the only platform worthy of support. However, she chose to ally herself with the cause of black male suffrage. Sojourner Truth believed that newly freed African Americans required suffrage to ensure their rights, but she feared that granting black men (and not women) suffrage would give the men undue power over black women. Although Lucretia Mott believed that black men needed the protection of the suffrage more than women did, she was unwilling to speak out against her old friend and co-worker, Elizabeth Cady Stanton. Therefore, Mott refused to take any stand on the Fifteenth Amendment.

ACTIVITY TWO: MOCK MEDIATION WHETHER WOMEN'S RIGHTS ADVOCATES SHOULD SUPPORT THE FIFTEENTH AMENDMENT, 1869

*I*n May 1869, the Equal Rights Association, a coalition of blacks and whites, women and men dedicated to gaining rights for blacks and women, met in New York City. The Equal Rights Association included men and women who had worked together for years in support of both women's rights and abolition. Among the participants at the meeting in 1869 were Frederick Douglass, Susan B. Anthony, Frances Harper, Elizabeth Cady Stanton, Lucy Stone, Amy Post and Sojourner Truth. Chief among the issues for debate was whether or not to support the proposed Fifteenth Amendment, which read: "The right of citizens of the United States to vote shall not be denied or abridged by the United States or by any State on account of race, color, or previous condition of servitude."

The issue in this hypothetical mock mediation is, as it was at the Association's meeting in New York, whether during the Reconstruction debates in 1869 the Equal Rights Association should support an amendment to the U.S. Constitution that specifically guaranteed the right of *male* African Americans to vote but not the right of females to vote. Participants in this exercise will engage in a mock mediation on the issue of whether or not to support ratification of this proposed Constitutional amendment. Lucretia Mott will be the mediator. Catharine Beecher will be the observer/recorder/reporter.

PARTICIPANTS

Refer to the prior activity for short biographies of Elizabeth Cady Stanton, Amy Kirby Post, Frederick Douglass and Lucretia Mott.

Susan B. Anthony was born in 1820 in Adams, Massachusetts, to a Quaker father and a Baptist mother. She was brought up in a family with a long tradition of Quaker activism. She attended boarding school until the collapse of her father's textile business forced her into earning her own living. After teaching for fifteen years, she became active in the temperance movement to limit the consumption of alcohol, but because she was a woman, she was not allowed to speak at temperance rallies. Anthony did not attend the women's rights convention of 1848. She was frustrated by the inequalities between men and women and ready to embrace women's rights when she met Elizabeth Cady Stanton in Seneca Falls in 1852. Anthony was hired as a lecturer by the American Anti-Slavery Society and merged her antislavery work with efforts on behalf of women's rights to their own property and earnings and women's

Susan B. Anthony

labor organizations. Stanton, whose many children and other family responsibilities kept her at home, counted on the unmarried Anthony to deliver speeches and petitions that Stanton had written. The two formed a partnership that lasted fifty years. In 1869, Anthony joined Stanton in opposing the Fifteenth Amendment because it did not explicitly grant women the right to vote. Throughout the late 19th century, Anthony stayed focused on woman's suffrage. Ignoring opposition and abuse, she traveled, lectured and canvassed across the nation for the vote. She remained active until her death in 1906.

Sojourner Truth was born into slavery as Isabella Baumfree in Ulster County, New York, around 1797 and worked for a Dutch farming family. In 1827, when New York law emancipated all slaves, she claimed her freedom and moved to New York City, taking along her infant son. In 1843, she became a convert to evangelical religion,

Soujourner Truth

declared herself a preacher and took the name "Sojourner Truth." In 1846, she joined an antislavery, utopian community in Northampton, Massachusetts, where she was introduced to the abolitionist movement. She made her first speech on women's rights at a women's rights convention in Worcester, Massachusetts, in 1850. Her most famous speech was at a women's rights convention in Akron, Ohio, in 1851. Although this speech would later be reduced to the mantra of "Aren't I a woman," this phrase was never part of her original speech. (See Document 3: Sojourner Truth's Speech at the Akron Women's Rights Convention, Ohio, June 1851.) Truth became one of the most sought after lecturers on abolition and women's rights. Throughout her career, Sojourner Truth's main concern was promoting the rights of black women. For this reason, the Fifteenth Amendment posed a serious dilemma for her. She believed that newly freed African Americans needed political rights but she was also deeply concerned that black women not be subordinated to black men. She remained ambivalent about supporting the Fifteenth Amendment. Truth died in 1883.

Lucy Stone was born in Massachusetts in 1818. Even as a girl she chafed at the restrictions placed on members of the female sex. She graduated from Oberlin College in 1847 and became a lecturer for the Massachusetts Anti-Slavery Society, which granted her permission to devote part of each week to speaking on her own for women's rights. She helped to organize the first national women's rights convention in Worcester, Massachusetts, in 1850 and was also instrumental in organizing other women's rights conventions. In 1855, she married Henry Blackwell, an Ohio abolitionist and crusader for women's suffrage. By mutual agreement with her husband, she retained her maiden name. Stone and Blackwell chose to support the Fourteenth and Fifteenth Amendments even though they represented a setback for women's rights. After passage of the Fifteenth Amendment, Stone joined more conservative reformers to create the American Woman Suffrage Association and launched the weekly *Woman's Journal* in 1870. The schism in the women's movement was not healed until 1890 with the formation of the National American Woman Suffrage Association. Stone died in 1893.

Lucy Stone

Frances Watkins Harper

Frances Ellen Watkins Harper was born in 1825 in Baltimore, Maryland to free black parents, and orphaned when she was three years old. She attended Watkins Academy but could only find a job as a domestic servant. In 1852, she moved to Philadelphia where she gained fame as a poet. Starting in 1854, she began lecturing about abolition. She married, moved to Ohio, had four children and was widowed during the Civil War. Harper spoke on behalf of women's suffrage at a Women's Rights Convention following the war in May 1866 in New York City, where the American Equal Rights Association was founded. She continued to advocate for women's rights but believed that the most important issue at the moment was rights for blacks, and thus she supported the Fifteenth Amendment. (See Document 4: Frances Ellen Watkins Harper Speech, May 1866.) Harper continued to lecture in the South on black morality and on temperance and against white racial violence. She died in 1911.

Observer/Recorder/Reporter: Catharine Beecher was the daughter of fiery abolitionist preacher Henry Ward Beecher and sister of Harriet Beecher Stowe, author of *Uncle Tom's Cabin*. Catharine Beecher was a moderate reformer who wrote petitions on behalf of the Cherokee Indians, and advocated higher education and household management for women. She opened a female seminary in Hartford, Connecticut and the Western Female Institute in Cincinnati, Ohio, and was instrumental in founding women's colleges in Iowa, Illinois, and Wisconsin. Beecher believed that women should devote themselves to the moral development and education of their children and that it was "unwomanly" for women to engage openly in public debate. Although active in expanding higher education for women, Beecher opposed women's public activism, including providing women with the right to vote.

Catharine Beecher

TEACHER INSTRUCTIONS

Preparation

The participants, mediators and observer/recorder/reporters should read the background materials, the short biographies of the participants and any specific speeches, newspaper articles, or other written materials which provide background and understanding of their particular positions and/or interests.

Directions

1. Divide into groups of eight (for negotiation without a mediator) or nine (for mediation).

2. Assign each person a role:

a. Susan B. Anthony

b. Frederick Douglass

c. Frances Ellen Watkins Harper

d. Amy Kirby Post

e. Lucy Stone

f. Elizabeth Cady Stanton

g. Sojourner Truth

h. Lucretia Mott—mediator

i. Catharine Beecher—observer/recorder/reporter

The Roles

1. The participants should try to find a consensus that is consistent with the constraints of their historical characters.

2. The mediator should help the participants to come to a resolution that meets their underlying interests. The mediator should not try to impose his or her views on the participants.

3. The observer/recorder/reporters do not participate in the negotiation or mediation. They should

objectively observe, record and report on the mediation process and results. In this case, the observer/recorder/reporters might also write an article reporting on the proceedings from the perspective of Catharine Beecher.

Debriefing

1. Hand out and discuss "The Facts Continued" and "The Historical Effects."

2. Compare the results of the mock mediation with what actually occurred.

THE FACTS CONTINUED: 1869 TO 1920

*U*nable to find a compromise position on the issue of suffrage for women as well as black men (See Document 5: Proceedings of the Equal Rights Association, New York City, May 1869), the American Equal Rights Association split into two groups. Stanton and Anthony, who had demanded votes for both, formed the National Woman Suffrage Association (NWSA); Douglass and Harper, who accepted black male suffrage as a priority, joined Stone to form the American Woman Suffrage Association (AWSA). Over the next several decades, the AWSA recruited male as well as female members and focused exclusively on suffrage. Stanton and Anthony's NWSA allowed only women to be officials and promoted a broader agenda, including divorce reform and equal pay for women as well as suffrage. Stanton and Anthony's NWSA included working-class women, and it pushed for a national constitutional amendment for women's suffrage. Stone's AWSA was in many ways a more conservative organization, and its acceptance of men and its focus exclusively on the vote for women gained the support of the largest number of white abolitionists as well as most of the African-American activists of the age. Sojourner Truth, however, refused to break ties with her former supporters and friends, Stanton and Anthony. Amy Post maintained membership in both the NWSA and the AWSA, but she clearly stood on the side of black rights as the foremost priority in the postwar world. Mott sought to the end of her days to reconcile the two sides but to no avail.

Some see the women's debate over the Fifteenth Amendment as an early sign of white women's concern primarily for their own advancement. Stanton had made these critiques easier by her outrage at men she called "ignorant negroes and foreigners" gaining admittance to the polls before educated white women like herself. Yet the issues raised by this debate were more complex than they might seem at first glance. Sojourner Truth, for instance, agreed with Anthony that the Fifteenth Amendment would put black men "in the position of tyrants" over black women. And women did not divide along strictly racial lines, in spite of Harper's prediction. Rather, white women were themselves at odds over whether to support or oppose black male suffrage. At least as many white women sided with Stone's AWSA as with Stanton and Anthony's NWSA.

Following ratification of the Fifteenth Amendment in 1870, few men—black or white—continued to support the fight for women's suffrage. In fact, as Reconstruction waned, many men—primarily black men but also some poor white men—were effectively disenfranchised through exclusionary mechanisms such as poll taxes, grandfather clauses and literacy tests. As Stanton and Anthony had feared, once they had gained rights for themselves, few men bothered to battle on behalf of women's rights, for blacks or whites. Black women began to form their own suffrage organizations, feeling largely abandoned by black men and alienated from white women. The division into rival groups in 1869 proved an asset as well as a liability. It enabled the suffrage movement to involve a wider range of women nationwide and forced Stanton to tone down her intemperate rhetoric.

After 1869-1870, the battle for women's suffrage moved from the national level to the states and territories. Even in these smaller arenas, progress was very slow and often subject to the vagaries of partisan, ethnic and religious-group politics. In 1869, the territory of Wyoming was the first (after New Jersey's brief experiment) to grant women suffrage. The men in sparsely settled, frontier Wyoming were hoping to attract more women and families as permanent residents, rather than just transient men. In addition, Wyoming Democrats believed they could improve the position of their party by expanding the electorate to include women. When Wyoming became a state in 1890, its women not only had the right to vote but could also serve on juries and hold elective office. Colorado entered the Union in 1876, and in its first state constitution, women were granted the right to vote in local school elections. However, a referendum on full female suffrage was defeated in 1877. With an increasing number of men with more "liberal" views, the example of Wyoming and the rise of the People's Party (Populists), the Colorado legislature in 1893 authorized a referendum on women's suffrage which passed with the help of an intensive campaign by its proponents. Susan Anthony attributed these gains, in part, to less prejudice against suffrage in Western communities.

Utah applied for statehood with a constitution permitting women to vote, which was approved in 1895. The following year, a suffrage amendment in Idaho passed by a sweeping margin. In Idaho and Colorado, women were able to hold public offices as well as vote. In spite of an 1867 law in the territory of Washington that declared that "all white American citizens twenty-one years of age" were entitled to vote, the fact that several women had cast their ballot in 1869 without prosecution, and that the Washington legislature reaffirmed its support for women suffrage in 1883 and 1888, a federal court declared that the legislature had no right under the organic act of the territory to accord women the right to vote. Thus, by the close of the nineteenth century, women held voting rights in only four Western states—Wyoming, Colorado, Utah and Idaho.

The slow progress of the women's suffrage movement resulted from opposition at several levels. The Victorian ideology of the "cult of true womanhood," which confined women to the domestic sphere while men engaged in the worldly affairs of business and politics, retained a powerful hold, reinforced in the press and pulpit. In the North, many ethnic groups, particularly from agricultural regions of Europe, maintained a traditional view of the place of women. In the conservative post-Reconstruction South, many white Southerners, working to keep blacks from the polls, feared any attempts to extend the franchise. Some historians have suggested that the definition of separate spheres accompanied and made possible the replacement of patriarchal family relationships by companionate ones. The terms "separate spheres" expressed both a limiting ideology imposed on women and a set of boundaries expected to be observed by women, as well as a culture created by women.

Temperance Movement, cartoon from
Harper's Magazine, *1859*

Just as woman's reform efforts in the antebellum period were dedicated to abolition, so in the late nineteenth and early twentieth centuries far more women were engaged in battles for temperance or outright prohibition of alcohol or in campaigns to assist the poor and needy, for good government, and for international peace than in the fight for their own enfranchisement. During the late nineteenth century the most significant women's group in support of women's suffrage was the Woman's Christian Temperance Union (WCTU). Established in 1874, this reform group was committed to aiding women through numerous means including restricting domestic violence, abandonment and economic deprivation as a result of drunken husbands. In addition to temperance, women's efforts at social reform and improvement pushed and shaped the Populist and Progressive movements. Such efforts at reform also placed entrenched interests, such as the liquor industry and urban political machines, against woman suffrage, because they believed enfranchised women, emphasizing temperance, morality and good government, would vote against them.

Women, too, remained divided over their role in society and whether they should have the right to participate directly in political life, with many accepting the nineteenth century Victorian view of women as subordinate to men and not direct participants in political life. Some women, including prominent women such as Mrs. Grover Cleveland, First Lady in the mid-1890s, remained vigorously opposed to women's right to vote. These anti-suffragists argued that women's views were represented by the men of their social group, since it was presumed that their interests were the same.

During the late nineteenth century, opportunities for women in higher education expanded greatly. Separate women's colleges, including Vassar, Smith, Wellesley, as well as colleges for women affiliated with male universities, such as Barnard at Columbia University and Radcliffe at Harvard University, opened in the Northeast. A number of Western and Midwestern states created co-educational state colleges and universities. By 1880, 40,000 women (nearly a third of all college students) were enrolled in higher education. However, they faced a stark choice on graduation—marriage or a career. Many careers, such as teaching, were open only to unmarried or, at least, childless women. Nearly half of all college-educated women in the late nineteenth century never married; and those who married did so later and had fewer, if any, children.

In 1873, Susan Anthony attempted to cast a ballot in New York and was tried, convicted and fined for this offense. The following year, the U.S. Supreme Court affirmed in *Minor v. Happersett,* 88 US 162 (1874), that it was constitutional for a state to deny women the right to vote. Virginia Minor, an official in a local suffragist organization, had tried to vote in Missouri in 1872. She filed a suit with her lawyer husband (since as a married woman she could not bring her own suit) against the registrar who had excluded her from the polls. The Minors argued that suffrage was a privilege of citizenship and that the Fourteenth Amendment prohibited the states from interfering with this privilege. However, the U.S. Supreme Court, affirming the lower court's decision, held that suffrage was not a privilege of citizenship. This forced the suffragists back to Congress for a constitutional amendment.

Recognizing that a divided movement was hurting their success, the two women's suffrage organizations finally overcame their antagonism and merged into the National American Woman Suffrage Association (NAWSA) in 1890 with Stanton as the first president and Anthony as her successor. However, the organization remained internally divided over strategy. The resulting compromise was to work at both the state and national levels. Between 1870 and 1910, some 480 local suffrage campaigns produced 17 referenda, but only two of those resulted in a victory for woman suffrage. At the same time, suffragists added new arguments to their Enlightenment tradition of individual rights. No longer focused primarily on women's just claim to equal rights as citizens, they now argued that the state needed women precisely because of their difference from men. They claimed that the state needed women to vote because female morality would help improve society and clean up corruption, protect children, and enhance women's ability to carry out their traditional roles as wives and mothers. These arguments, developed as Victorian ideas about the separate roles for men and women, were beginning to crumble between 1900 and 1915 with the growth of working women, labor unions, women's clubs, settlement houses and progressive ideas.

After 1910, the suffragists broadened and intensified their methods. They moved from polite letter-writing campaigns to large-scale parades and other public demonstrations and intense political efforts at the national level. Elizabeth Cady Stanton's daughter, Harriet Stanton Blatch, whose marriage to an Englishman made her familiar with the more militant approach taken by British suffragists, and Alice Paul, a New Jersey Quaker who had studied in London, brought these militant tactics to the suffrage movement in the United States. At one point, Blatch and other suffragists chained themselves to the White House fence, demanding that President Woodrow Wilson support women's suffrage. After defeats in state referenda in four key eastern states—Massachusetts, New Jersey, New York and Pennsylvania—a new generation of younger women assumed control of the women's rights movement after 1915. These leaders, including Carrie Chapman Catt as well as Paul and Blatch, were committed to national action.

Suffragists Demonstrating at the Capitol,
1913

By 1916, suffrage for women had become a national political issue. Suffragists besieged both Republican and Democratic National Conventions that year. Initially ambivalent about the issue, Democratic President Woodrow Wilson announced his support for suffrage at a NAWSA convention in 1916 but reiterated that it should be accomplished on a state by state basis. Republican presidential candidate Charles Evans Hughes supported a national suffrage amendment, but the Republican convention favored state action. The attempt to gain voting rights for women became merged with the issue of U.S. entry into World War I. (See "U.S. Entry into World War I," Volume Two, Chapter Six.) Many prominent women reformers and peace advocates, such as Jane Addams, as well as women's organizations like the Women's Peace Party (predecessor of the Women's International League for Peace and Freedom), pressed for international mediation rather than U.S. entry into the war. Women peace advocates, like the progressive reformers—male and female, including Alice Paul—had supported Wilson's re-election. After his re-election, militant suffragists from the National Woman's Party picketed Wilson at the White House in early 1917, with banners asking "How Long Must Women Wait for Liberty?" Several were arrested and sent to prison where they continued their protests with hunger strikes, generating both support and antipathy. Once the U.S. declared war in April 1917, some women continued to oppose war mobilization, but the majority of women worked long hours supporting the war effort at home. Many women expected that their efforts would be rewarded with expanded political rights. Indeed, President Wilson lent his support to women's suffrage as he called upon American women to support his crusade to make the world "safe for democracy."

With the nation at war, the government calling for all Americans to do their duty, and the power of the brewers and liquor interests as well as the urban machines temporarily curtailed, the political movement for enfranchising women gained momentum. During 1917, women gained the right to vote in Arkansas, Indiana, Michigan, Nebraska, North Dakota (presidential election only), Ohio (repealed later that year), New York and Rhode Island. In 1918, Oklahoma, South Dakota and Texas (primaries only) followed suit. By that time, women had been granted the right to vote in a growing number of countries: New Zealand (1893); Australia (1902—white women only); Finland (1906); Norway (1907—economic requirements until 1913); Denmark (1915); Iceland (1915—women age 40 or above); Russia (1917), Austria, Czechoslovakia, Germany, and Hungary (limited); Luxembourg, Poland and the United Kingdom (married women, women householders and women university graduates age 30 and over); Rhodesia (Zimbabwe); and Sweden (1918).

In 1919, a year after the war's end and a year before the next presidential election, Congress passed and President Wilson signed the Nineteenth Amendment granting women suffrage nationally. It took another year for the required three-quarters of the states to ratify the amendment, the most substantial opposition coming in the South. The final state to approve ratification was Tennessee. The constitutional amendment was passed in that state in 1920 by a one-vote margin—the vote of a young congressman whose mother was a long-time suffragist.

Legacies for Today

The Nineteenth Amendment granted 26 million women the right to vote, beginning with the presidential election of 1920. However, most black women, like most black men, were prevented from exercising their right to vote through discriminatory laws and practices, primarily in the Southern states, until the Civil Rights Movement and laws of the 1960s. During the 1920s, after the passage of women's suffrage, the National American Women's Suffrage Association evolved into The League of Women Voters, a nonpartisan political organization that influenced public policy through education and advocacy. Alice Paul's National Woman's Party shifted its goal to an Equal Rights Amendment, which the League of Women Voters opposed as a threat to the protective legislation that women had achieved.

By the mid-1920s, it was clear that supporters and opponents of women's suffrage had overestimated the impact that woman's suffrage would have on the political life of the country. Women have tended to vote in smaller proportions than men. They have not voted as a block. With few exceptions, women have followed the voting patterns of

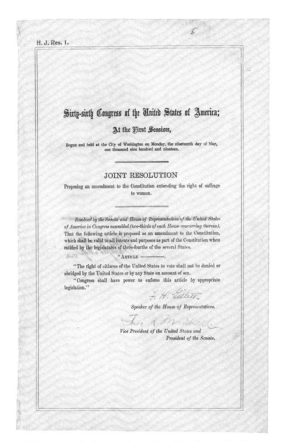

Nineteenth Amendment to the Constitution (1919)

the educational, social or economic class or group to which they belong, much like the men. And although the number of women in elective office has grown steadily, progress has been slow. In 1916, Jeanette Rankin (MT) was the first woman elected to serve in Congress. In 1940, Margaret Chase Smith (ME) became the first woman elected to the Senate without having first been elected or appointed to fill a vacant Senate seat. According to the Center for American Women and Politics at Rutgers, The State University of New Jersey, 16 percent of the 100 seats in the U.S. Senate and 16 percent of the 435 seats in the House of Representatives were held by women at the start of the 110th Congress (2007-2009). In 2007, women served as governors in nine of the fifty states;

represented 23.5 percent of the 7,382 seats in state legislatures and served as mayors for 12 of the 100 largest American cities. This is an increase in comparison to 1979, when women held 3 percent of the seats in Congress, 11 percent of statewide legislative offices and 10 percent of state legislative offices. With Nancy Pelosi (CA) becoming the first female Speaker of the House in 2007, women are finally claiming leadership positions in Congress. The campaign of Senator Hillary Clinton (D-NY) as the first female to pose a major challenge to the hegemony of men as a presidential candidate for one of the two major political parties demonstrates both the progress made by women and the lingering sexism. Full political equality for women still remains elusive at the start of the twenty-first century.

Women in the early twenty-first century continue to argue over the definition of women's issues and the importance of and priorities for particular issues in advancing women's rights and equality. Is an Equal Rights Amendment to the Constitution the best way to ensure gender justice or must attitudes and images of women be transformed before legal changes can make a significant difference? Since women have the right to vote, should the franchise be exercised to advance equality of the sexes or are there other issues that have a greater impact on how women vote in any given election? Should women choose candidates who are pro-choice or anti-choice on the issue of abortion, for instance, assuming that single-issue politics is most effective? Or do women need to think about broader platforms and visions that get lost by concentrating too closely on any one issue?

Why, for instance, is there a greater public outcry over sexual harassment cases than over cuts in social welfare when reduction in social welfare funding negatively affects a far greater number of women? How does women's economic insecurity make them more vulnerable to sexual abuse, whatever its form? How can women forge alliances to advance social change when they have such diverse experiences and needs? Moreover, given the very different educational and occupational opportunities available to women of different racial, ethnic and class backgrounds, how can coalitions be built to address the needs of diverse women? When is it important to include men in those coalitions, and when is it necessary for women to organize on their own?

Far too many of the issues raised in the nineteenth century are still relevant to women's lives today. Remnants of the ideology of "separate spheres" for men and women persist as symptoms of a gendered system of power relations that has long historical roots. The slow pace of improvement in the legal and political rights of women in the United States in the nineteenth century and the gender inequities that continue into the twenty-first century reflect how glacially social attitudes change. (For a continuation of the struggle for women's rights, see Volume Two, Chapter 8: "Women in the Workforce after World War II".)

QUESTIONS FOR DISCUSSION

1. How did the antislavery movement challenge established notions regarding women's roles in society?

2. Why was suffrage for women considered a radical idea in 1848?

3. Which particular groups supported and which opposed women's suffrage in the nineteenth and early twentieth centuries and why? How could the conflict over women's enfranchisement have been resolved?

4. Why were women not given the right to vote along with black men in the Fifteenth Amendment in 1869? What do you think were the most compelling arguments for and against woman's suffrage in 1869?

5. What might have been the impact on U.S. domestic and foreign policies had women been given the right to vote in 1869?

6. How do women decide when their own needs are more important than helping others in need?

7. How can people of different genders, races, classes and ethnic groups work together to develop an agenda that will benefit them all?

ADDITIONAL READINGS

Bacon, Margaret Hope. *Mothers of Feminism: The Story of Quaker Women in America.* San Francisco: Harper and Row, 1986.

Boydston, Jeanne. *Home and Work.* New York: Oxford University Press, 1990.

Crocco, Margaret Smith, "The Road to the Vote." *Social Education* (Sept. 1995): 257-264.

Evans, Sara M. *Born for Liberty: A History of Women in America.* New York: The Free Press, 1989.

DeGezelle, Terri. Susan B. *Anthony and the Women's Movement.* Chicago: Heinemann, 2007.

DuBois, Carol and Richard Candida Smith, eds. *Elizabeth Cady Stanton, Feminist Thinker: A Reader in Documents and Essays.* New York: New York University Press, 2007.

Foner, Philip S., ed. *Frederick Douglass on Women's Rights.* Westport, CN: Greenwood Press, 1976.

Ginzberg, Lori D. *Women in Antebellum Reform.* Wheeling, IL: Harlan Davidson, Inc., 2000.

Gordon, Ann D., ed. *The Selected Papers of Elizabeth Cady Stanton and Susan B. Anthony,* 4 vols. New Brunswick, NJ: Rutgers University Press, 1997-2007.

Hewitt, Nancy. "Feminist Friends: Agrarian Quakers and the Emergence of Women's Rights in America." *Feminist Studies* (Spring 1986): 27-49.

Jeffrey, Julie Roy. *The Great Silent Army of Abolitionism: Ordinary Women in the Antislavery Movement.* Chapel Hill: University of North Carolina Press, 1998.

Kerber, Linda K., *No Constitutional Right to be Ladies: Women and the Obligations of Citizenship.* New York: Hill and Wang, 1998.

_____. *Women of the Republic: Intellect and Ideology in Revolutionary America.* New York: W.W. Norton, 1986.

_____. *Women's America: Refocusing the Past.* 6th ed. New York: Oxford University Press, 2004.

_____. "Separate Spheres, Female World, Woman's Place: The Rhetoric of Women's History." *The Journal of American History* 75.1 (June 1988).

Klinghoffer, Judith and Lois Elkis. "The Petticoat Elections: Women's Suffrage in New Jersey, 1776-1807." *Journal of Early Republic* 12 (1992).

Lerner, Gerda. *The Grimké Sisters from South Carolina: Pioneers for Women's Rights and Abolition.* New York: Schocken Books, 1971.

_____. *The Majority Finds Its Past: Placing Women in History.* New York: Oxford University Press, 1979.

Marshall, Susan. *Splintered Sisterhood: Gender and Class in the Campaign against Woman Suffrage.* Madison: University of Wisconsin Press, 1997.

McCarthy, Kathleen D. *Lady Bountiful Revisited: Women, Philanthropy and Power.* New Brunswick: Rutgers University Press, 1990.

McGoldrick, Neale and Margaret Crocco. *Reclaiming Lost Ground: The Struggle for Woman Suffrage in New Jersey.* Trenton: NJ Historical Commission and NJ Council for the Humanities, 1994.

Painter, Nell Irvin. *Sojourner Truth: A Life, a Symbol.* New York: W.W. Norton, 1996.

Sklar, Kathryn Kish. *Women's Rights Emerges within the Antislavery Movement, 1830-1870.* New York: Bedford/St. Martin, 2000.

Sprague, William Forrest. *Women and the West.* New York: Arno Press, 1972.

Terborg-Penn, Rosalyn. *African American Women in the Struggle for the Vote, 1850-1920.* Bloomington: Indiana University Press, 1998.

Wellman, Judith. *The Road to Seneca Falls: Elizabeth Cady Stanton and the First Woman's Rights Convention.* Chicago: University of Illinois Press, 2004.

Woloch, Nancy. *Women and the American Experience.* New York: McGraw Hill, 1984.

Yellin, Jean Fagan and John C. Van Horne, eds. *The Abolitionist Sisterhood: Women's Political Culture in Antebellum America.* Ithaca, NY: Cornell University Press, 1994.

Women's Rights National Historical Park created by an Act of Congress in 1980 in Seneca Falls, NY. See www.nps.gov/wori/ .

DOCUMENTS ON CD

Document 1:   *Declaration of Sentiments at the Women's Rights Convention,* Seneca Falls, NY, July 1848

Document 2:   *Report of the Women's Rights Convention,* Seneca Falls, NY, July 1848

Document 3:   Sojourner Truth Speech at Akron Women's Rights Convention, Ohio, June 1851, from *Anti-Slavery Bugle*, Salem, Ohio, June 21, 1851.

Document 4:   Frances Ellen Watkins Harper Speech, *Proceedings of the Eleventh Woman's Rights Convention,* New York, May 1866

Document 5:   *Proceedings of the Equal Rights Association,* New York City, May 1869

Teacher Overheads/Student Handouts on CD

1: Timeline: The Struggle for Women's Rights, 1780-1860

2: Directions for Mock Negotiations: Prioritize the resolutions at the Women's Rights Convention in Seneca Falls, 1848

3: Resolutions from the Declaration of Sentiments at the Women's Rights Convention in Seneca Falls, July 1848

4: Directions for Mock Mediation: Should Women's Rights Organizations Support the Fifteenth Amendment in 1869?

5: Timeline: The Struggle for Women's Rights Continues, 1848-today

Sources and Credits for Illustrations

p. 226: Women Voting in New Jersey in 1797, *Rutgers University Libraries*

p. 227: Antebellum women in corseted hoop skirts,1830s, *University of Waterloo*

p. 228: Angelina Grimké, *LC-USZ61-1609*

p. 228: Sarah Grimké, *LC-USZ61-1608*

p. 230: Cover of Lydia M. Child's *Authentic Anecdotes of American Slavery*, 1838, *LC Rare Book Division*

p. 232: Lucretia Mott, *LC-USZ62-42559*

p. 232: Amy Kirby Post, *Rochester Public Library*

p. 233: Frederick Douglass, *LC-USZ62-15887*

p. 233: Elizabeth Cady Stanton, *LC-USZ62-28195*

p. 236: Susan B. Anthony, *University of Pennsylvania Libraries*

p. 237: Sojourner Truth, *LC-USZ62-119343*

p. 237: Lucy Stone, *LC-USZ62-29701*

p. 237: Frances Watkins Harper, *University of Alabama*

p. 238: Catharine Beecher, *The Library of Congress*

p. 240: Temperance Movement Cartoon from *Harper's Magazine*, 1859, *University of Wisconsin*

p. 242: Suffragists Demonstrating at the Capitol, 1913, *LC-USZ62-22262*

p. 243: Nineteenth Amendment to the Constitution, 1919, *National Archives 100 Most Important Documents*

Chapter Eleven

Post-Civil War Reconstruction

Objectives

- To understand the conflicts and possibilities and involved in Reconstruction.

- To compare the policies of Presidents Lincoln and Johnson and key members of the Congress regarding Reconstruction in the southern states.

- To explain the range of possible approaches to Reconstruction and how they were limited by the prevailing social values shared by the North and the South in the mid-nineteenth century.

- To understand the efforts made by recently emancipated African Americans to improve their economic, legal and political positions in the mid-nineteenth century.

- To assess the degree of progress made by the federal and state governments towards multiracial political democratization and economic and social justice during the Reconstruction period.

- To examine the legacy of Reconstruction.

Correlations with National History Standards

Era Five
Standard 3A

- Contrast the Reconstruction policies advocated by Lincoln, Andrew Johnson and sharply divided Congressional leaders, while assessing these policies as responses to changing events.

- Analyze how shared values of the North and South limited support for social and racial democratization, as reflected in the Compromise of 1877.

- Analyze the role of violence and the tactics of the "redeemers" in regaining control over the southern state governments.

Standard 3B

- Explain the economic and social problems facing the South and appraise their impact on different social groups.

- Describe the ways in which African Americans laid foundations for modern black communities during Reconstruction.

- Analyze how African Americans attempted to improve their economic position during Reconstruction and explain the factors involved in their quest for land ownership.

Standard 3C

- Assess the progress of "Black Reconstruction" and legislative reform programs promoted by reconstructed state governments.

- Analyze how the Civil War and Reconstruction changed men's and women's roles and status in the North and South.

OVERVIEW

The Reconstruction Era, 1865–1877, involved years of intense conflict over the kind of society that Americans wanted after fighting a brutal Civil War and ending slavery. On the surface, the Reconstruction Era was marked by attempts by elected representatives from the Northern states to force the South to adhere to one of the most important objectives of the Civil War—the end of black enslavement—as well as to ensure full acceptance by the South of the restoration of the Union and government by those who had been loyal to it. Yet, that issue raised many other equally difficult questions, such as the political, economic, and social status of the former slaves, and the proper role of the federal government vis-à-vis the states. Since the issue of civil rights for blacks had never before been considered on such a large scale, it was fraught with conflict between those who advocated strong federal initiatives designed to protect the historically disparaged and exploited people of African ancestry and those who sought to give southern states control over the destiny of the former slaves. The desperate need to address the dramatic consequences of emancipation conflicted with a long tradition of local autonomy and also of racial oppression. At the same time, black men and women, those recently emancipated as well as former free blacks, sought actively to gain as much autonomy as possible, to strengthen their family and community ties, and to stake a claim to equal citizenship. The dynamics of Reconstruction were also affected by changing relationships among the planters, merchants, and yeomen farmers within the southern white community. Reconstruction included conflicts involving the federal versus the state governments, the Republican Party versus the Democratic Party, the executive versus the legislative branch, and southern planters and their supporters versus the black freedmen and women and their white allies seeking new economic and political directions for the South.

HISTORICAL BACKGROUND

Even before Confederate General Robert E. Lee surrendered to Union General Ulysses S. Grant on April 9, 1865 at Appomattox, Virginia, the battle had begun over how to politically reintegrate or "reconstruct" the eleven southern states that had seceded from the Union. As an interim war measure, President Abraham Lincoln had issued a preliminary Emancipation Proclamation in 1862. It declared that all enslaved Africans in states or parts of states still in rebellion on January 1, 1863 "shall be then, henceforward, and forever free." (See Document 1: The Emancipation Proclamation, and Document 2: Lincoln's defense of the Emancipation Proclamation in a letter to his friend, James Conkling, August 1863.) The Emancipation Proclamation not only freed slaves in areas still under Confederate control but also authorized the enlistment of former slaves into the Union army and navy. Hundreds of thousands of slaves fled from their masters to the freedom brought by the Union forces, and thousands enlisted in the Union Army or Navy. As the blue-clad forces occupied secessionist states, Lincoln appointed provisional military governors to maintain security and U.S. interests and protect freed slaves.

In December 1863, several months after the crucial Union victories at Gettysburg and Vicksburg, President Lincoln announced a method for bringing the states that had seceded back into the Union. Except for Confederate leaders, there would be complete amnesty for Southerners who took an oath of loyalty to the United States. When 10 percent of a state's voters took the oath and when a state agreed to emancipation, the president would recognize civil authority in that state. However, some members of Congress, jealous of the Executive's expanded power during the war and fearful of a reunified Democratic Party, introduced the Wade-Davis Bill that required a majority to take the oath. (See Document 3: The Wade-Davis Bill.) These "Radical" Republicans in Congress wanted the legislative branch to have a strong voice in Reconstruction. Lincoln, however, pocket-vetoed the 1864 Wade-Davis Bill. In February 1865, Congress proposed the Thirteenth Amendment, officially prohibiting slavery and "involuntary servitude, except as punishment for a crime." (See Document 4: The Thirteenth Amendment.) It was ratified by December 1865.

After his reelection, with the end of the war rapidly approaching, Lincoln, in his Second Inaugural Address (March 1865), appealed for unity and peace rather than vengeance. "With malice toward none; with charity for all . . . let us strive on to finish the work we are in; to bind the nation's wounds. . . to do all which may achieve and cherish a just and lasting peace." (See Document 5: Lincoln's Second Inaugural Address.) Lincoln showed evidence of flexibility towards restoring the seceded states to Union as long as the institution of slavery was brought to an end. For the first time, he publicly called for limited black suffrage in the South. He also considered compensating slaveholders, but his cabinet rejected that suggestion.

Wreckage of Richmond, Virginia, 1865

After four bloody years of warfare, the guns fell silent in April 1865 as the Confederate commanders surrendered their forces. The Union dead numbered 360,000; the Confederate dead 260,000. The former Confederacy lay prostrate, militarily defeated, economically destitute, psychologically disillusioned and embittered. Small farmers were devastated by the loss of farm animals and tools. The planter elites who had led the South out of the Union had lost much of their wealth (since most of it was invested in slaves and land). The small slaveholders, who had owned only a few slaves but who cumulatively made up the majority of the one-third of southern white families that owned slaves, also lost their slave laborers. The southern whites who had not owned slaves (two thirds of the South's white families) were less affected economically by the end of slavery, but many of them had believed in black slavery as a form of white superiority and racial control. Those in the white South who had supported the Confederate cause sought to come to terms with the meaning of defeat as former secessionists began to develop the romantic myth of the worthy "Lost Cause." The victorious North sought to define the meaning of the victory—the Union and a new birth of freedom—and to determine the direction of the country. Black Americans, the overwhelming majority of whom were now freed slaves living in the South, sought to use their newly-won freedom. The former slaves now were legally free but penniless in the land of their former masters. They wanted to make their own way, but their former owners wanted to keep them tied to the land as the basic agricultural labor force.

President Lincoln repeated his plea for reconciliation at the cabinet meeting held the morning of April 14, 1865. That evening, while watching a play at Ford's Theatre in Washington, D.C., the president was assassinated by a Southern sympathizer, actor John Wilkes Booth. The vice president, Andrew Johnson, took the oath of office as president at 10:30 a.m. the next morning.

President Johnson and the Congress

Andrew Johnson had been vice president for just over a month when Lincoln's assassination elevated him to the presidency. Like Lincoln, he had risen from humble origins, but he lacked the depth, understanding, and flexibility of his predecessor. Lincoln had chosen this Tennessee Democrat as his running mate in 1864 because of Johnson's loyalty when his state seceded and because, as a Democrat and a Southerner, Johnson broadened the National Union (Republican) ticket. As president, Johnson announced and began to implement Lincoln's reconstruction plan (with minor changes) in the summer and

Lincoln-Johnson Campaign Poster, 1864

fall of 1865 while Congress was in recess. Johnson excluded the southern planters from pardons at first but then pardoned some members of the Confederate elite who personally petitioned him. Unlike Lincoln, however, Johnson had no empathy for blacks and no desire to assist or enfranchise former slaves. He wanted to limit the vote to white men. He ordered land restored and blacks dispersed if they would not sign contracts to labor on land returned to its former owners. Although Johnson accepted the end of slavery, he remained a white Southerner and a Democrat, and never abandoned his racial prejudices that African Americans were inferior. He also denied that the federal government had any right to dictate suffrage requirements to the states.

By the time the new Congress convened in December 1865, Johnson claimed that Reconstruction had been successfully completed. All but one of the former Confederate states had fulfilled Johnson's minimal requirements, including the formal abolition of slavery through the ratification of the Thirteenth Amendment. However, white southern voters had reelected many former Confederate leaders to power. With the all-white Democratic Party in control, the southern legislatures began systematically to restrict African Americans, limiting or prohibiting them from voting, serving on juries, possessing firearms, buying property or from refusing to sign yearlong labor contracts. Any adult male without a job could be declared a "vagrant," arrested and assigned by local sheriffs to work for local planters or other employers to pay off their fines. These so-called "black codes" were enforced by white violence against freed blacks to maintain the system of white supremacy. (See Document 5: Black Codes of Mississippi and Louisiana, 1865.)

To many Northerners, such actions were an insult to those who had shed so much blood to preserve the Union and free the slaves. Radical Republicans sought to ensure full citizenship and the vote for black freedmen and to deprive rebels from voting for a period of years. Moderate Republicans supported blacks' basic civil rights but were initially ambivalent about black suffrage and sought mainly to exclude former Confederate leaders from public office. northern Democrats opposed black suffrage and equal rights and wanted to restore southern Democrats to power. Meanwhile, white southern elites, particularly the planters and their allies, who led the Democratic Party in the South, sought to retain as much of the prewar racial and economic conditions as possible. Freed blacks sought security and opportunity: They wanted land, equal rights, including the right to vote, and the autonomy to establish their own community institutions, such as black churches and benevolent associations. Their desires alarmed President Johnson and many southern whites and helped put these issues on the national agenda. In Washington, conflict between the new, Southern, Democratic President and the northern, Republican-dominated Congress went beyond partisan

Northern Cartoon of President Johnson Pardoning
Southern Rebels at the White House, 1865

politics to the proper roles of Congress and the Executive, the direction of Reconstruction, the rights of the freedmen, and ultimately the nature and future of democracy in America.

On the first meeting of the new Congress, December 5, 1865, the Republican radicals, moderates and conservatives united to prevent the seating of the senators and representatives from the eleven former Confederate states who sought to take their places under Johnson's Reconstruction program. Ideologically, they opposed this affront to the meaning of the Union victory. Politically, they feared that if the currently elected southern Democrats were united with northern Democrats, the Democratic Party might reestablish a majority in Congress as well as the national electorate.

The Republicans challenged the president's leadership as well as the southern whites' actions and began to enact legislation to protect the former slaves. The U.S. Army's Freedman's Bureau, which was created in 1865 to provide assistance, protect the civil rights and prevent the exploitation of former slaves, was set to expire in 1866. Congress passed a bill to extend the life of the Freedman's Bureau. President Johnson vetoed the bill, arguing that federal aid to poor blacks encouraged laziness and constituted discrimination against whites. Johnson also vetoed a Civil Rights bill that declared that blacks born in the United States were citizens, arguing that blacks did not deserve to be American citizens. However, the Republican Congress overrode the president's veto with a two-thirds majority, and, in March, 1866, passed the Civil Rights Act that declared African Americans to be U.S. citizens and entitled to equal protection under the law as well as civil rights, including the right to buy, lease, and sell property, make legally enforceable contracts, and sue and testify in court. (See Document 7: The Civil Rights Act of 1866 and Johnson's veto.) Later in the year the Republican Congress similarly adopted an extension of the Freedman's Bureau.

As a result of the intensifying conflict in Washington, the Congress established a powerful ad hoc committee, the Joint Committee on Reconstruction (also known as the Joint Committee of Fifteen), composed of six senators and nine representatives (a mix of radical, moderate and conservative Republicans plus a few Democrats). The committee met from January 1866 to February 1867. The mandate of the Joint Committee was to investigate and recommend to Congress policies concerning the issues of suffrage, conditions for blacks in the South, and Southern representation in Congress. The committee members were also mindful that 1866 was an election year for one-third of the Senate and all of the members of the House of Representatives.

THE MOCK CONGRESSIONAL HEARINGS AND FACILITATED NEGOTIATION

*T*he Joint Committee on Reconstruction was holding its hearings in January through May 1866 on conditions in the South and the proposed scope and role for the federal government in Reconstruction. Senator William Pitt Fessenden served as the chair of the committee.

It is April of 1866. We will be conducting a mock congressional hearing with testimony by witnesses before the Joint Committee on Reconstruction. This will be followed by a committee debate and decision regarding a report from the Committee to the Congress. Our Joint Committee will include only a representative sample (five) of the actual total committee members (15). In our mock hearings, as the committee members did in the actual hearings, we will be considering the following issues:

1.   What should be the scope of freedom to be granted to the freed slaves, that is, what specific rights and resources should the freedmen and freedwomen have? Should adult freed blacks receive the suffrage? Which ones? Should any resources, such as land or other materials assistance, be awarded to them?

2.   What should be the scope of authority of the states and of the national government in regard to the citizens in a state?

3.   What conditions, if any, should be imposed on the defeated southern states before they could be readmitted to representation in Congress? Should there be any penalties for those former Confederates who voluntarily encouraged, supported, or led secession from the Union and the war against the United States?

THE PARTICIPANTS

Selected members of the Joint Congressional Committee on Reconstruction

The actual joint committee consisted of six members from the Senate and nine from the House, of whom twelve were Republicans and three Democrats. Some of the leading radical Republicans served on the committee, but the moderate Republicans actually controlled it, as they did the Congress as a whole. We have selected five members of the committee to reflect the various views held.

Senator William Pitt Fessenden, moderate/conservative Republican from Maine

Senator Fessenden was chairman of the Joint Committee on Reconstruction. "Pitt" Fessenden was a man of great intellectual force and commanding ability. A prominent lawyer and Whig Party activist, Fessenden helped found the Republican Party. During the Civil War, he came slowly to support emancipation and opposed radical measures for the confiscation of secessionists' property. He believed that Congress and not the Executive had responsibility for Reconstruction, and he disagreed with both Lincoln's and Johnson's lenient 10 percent plan. Instead, Fessenden demanded that a majority

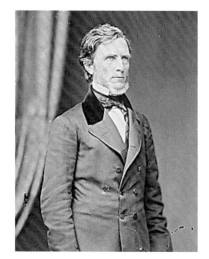

William Pitt Fessenden

in each former Confederate state swear allegiance to the Union. Fessenden also opposed the Republican radicals. He did not share their idealism and passion. Instead, he recommended ratification of the Fourteenth Amendment as a reasonable requirement for southern Reconstruction and as a way of keeping the party united. As Republican Reconstruction became more militant in 1867, Fessenden's conservatism led him to try to limit the intervention of the federal government, particularly in regard to property rights and what he came to consider excessive congressional action. He led the opposition to the attempt in 1868 to impeach and remove Johnson from office, casting a deciding vote for acquittal. He died in 1869.

Senator James Wilson Grimes, moderate/conservative Republican from Iowa

Despite being initially allied with the radical Republicans during the war because of his lifelong antislavery views, Grimes was a maverick who became, like his friend, William Pitt Fessenden, a moderate to conservative Republican. In the postwar period, this idiosyncratic reformer and strict constitutionalist turned against increasingly radical proposals. He opposed Thaddeus Steven's proposal for redistributing land confiscated from affluent Confederates to former slaves. Grimes had opposed Lincoln's expansion of executive power and continued to reject Johnson's attempt to dominate Reconstruction policy. He believed that unlike Lincoln, who he saw as a skilled and effective statesman, Johnson was "a man of low instincts, vindictive, violent and of bad habits." Grimes helped draft the Fourteenth Amendment and the Joint Committee's plan for Reconstruction, and he repeatedly helped override Johnson's vetoes. Later, at President Johnson's impeachment trial, Grimes voted "not guilty" against the wishes of many of his Republican constituents. His health broken, Grimes resigned from Congress in 1870.

James Wilson Grimes

Representative Thaddeus Stevens, radical Republican from Pennsylvania

Stevens was the Republican majority leader, chairman of the House Ways and Means Committee, and the most influential radical in the House of Representatives. Born to poverty and raised with his siblings by his mother after their alcoholic father deserted the family, the highly intelligent and ambitious Stevens graduated from Dartmouth College and became a successful lawyer and politician in Lancaster, Pennsylvania. His initial poverty, lameness due to a clubfoot and his strong Baptist faith imbued him with a lifelong sympathy for the disadvantaged. Since the 1830s, Stevens had demanded full civil and political rights as well as social-economic opportunity for blacks. He personally assisted runaway slaves in violation of the law. During the Civil War, he prodded Lincoln for emancipation, enlistment of black troops, and full civil rights for blacks. In 1865, the crusty, 73-year-old Pennsylvanian was outraged at white, southern, Democratic Reconstruction.

Thaddeus Stevens

He sought to break the power of the southern planters and create an independent black yeomanry in the South by confiscating the land of the rebel elites and redistributing it as small homesteads to former slaves, but his proposal was defeated in February 1866. Opponents at the time and later branded Stevens a fanatical extremist. Although Stevens did hold advanced racial views, as majority leader he worked for the passage of moderate compromises that he had previously opposed. His dislike of Johnson was intense, and he was bitterly disappointed in the president's acquittal. Stevens died shortly afterwards.

Representative Roscoe Conkling, radical Republican from upstate New York

Roscoe Conkling

Conkling was a successful corporate lawyer and former mayor of Utica, New York, long identified with bankers and railroad financiers. He was concerned that the U.S. government not repudiate its war debts. Conkling was initially a Whig and later a Republican. A wealthy, young man in his thirties during the Reconstruction debates, Conkling was proud of his commanding demeanor and physique. Supremely self-assured, aloof and remote, Conkling was an eminent careerist, who devoted himself to party politics rather than legislation. Pragmatic rather than idealistic, he would do whatever was necessary to strengthen the party, including support for black suffrage in the South. In the postwar period, he was a rising star in intricate New York politics, who tied his fate with the radical positions of Thaddeus Stevens and often stood beside the sharp-tongued but ailing Stevens as a body-guard. In 1867, Conkling won election to the Senate. In 1870, he refused the attempt by the radicals to impose conditions on southern state constitutions that went beyond the Reconstruction Acts of 1867. Still, he was instrumental in passage of the Civil Rights Act of 1875.

Representative Andrew Jackson Rogers, Democrat from New Jersey

Andrew Jackson Rogers

Rogers was a "Peace Democrat" from northwestern New Jersey, an area of small farms and dairies and a stronghold of old Jacksonian Democrats. Born in 1828, Rogers attended common schools, was a hotel and grocery clerk and a teacher, before becoming a lawyer. When the northern Democratic Party split between War Democrats or Unionists who supported the war and the Peace Democrats who opposed it, Rogers was part of the latter, who were derided as "Copperheads" or snake-like traitors. The "Copperheads" advocated a Union restored by negotiation rather than war. They denounced military arrests, conscription, emancipation, and other war measures. Many like Rogers were ardent white supremacists not opposed to slavery. The successful termination of the war discredited the Copperheads. Rogers was a colorful demagogue whose oratory often pitted the poor against the rich. In February and again in June 1866, Rogers assailed the Fourteenth Amendment and denounced the majority on what he called the "Committee on Destruction" as despots bent on destroying the Constitution, radicals who would dangerously give "negroes... the right of suffrage, and hold office and marry whites." Rogers praised Andrew Johnson as an enemy of the aristocracy "who believes that this Government was made for the benefit of white men and white women." "Andrew Johnson," he declared, "is an instrument in the hands of God to save this country." After being defeated for reelection in the Republican landslide of 1866, Rogers moved to New York City and became counsel for the city. He later moved to Denver in 1892 where he became city police commissioner.

Witnesses/Lobbyists

Most of the actual witnesses before the Joint Committee on Reconstruction in 1866 were military governors or generals in the various states subject to Reconstruction who testified about the conditions that they observed and the opposition and resistance to Reconstruction efforts. Instead, we have identified a more diverse group of individuals who lived during the Civil War and Reconstruction, whose views might have helped the Committee on Reconstruction to better understand the problems and conditions that existed at the time. While in reality, the committee did not ask for testimony by Frederick Douglass, Charlotte Forten Grimké or any other prominent black citizens in 1866, we believe that including such views may lead students to a better understanding of the opportunities and problem that existed in 1866. Of the following witnesses in the mock congressional hearing, only Alexander Stephens, a white southern Democrat, and Clara Barton, a Northern, white humanitarian who provided medical assistance during the Civil War and visited prisoner of wars camps afterwards, actually provided testimony to the Committee on Reconstruction in 1866.

Clara Barton, Northern white humanitarian, Unionist, and founder of the American Red Cross

Born in Massachusetts in 1821 to an old and prosperous New England family, Clara Barton became a schoolteacher, educational reformer, and feminist, demanding wages equal to male colleagues. In Bordentown, New Jersey, she introduced the Massachusetts model of free public schools. One of the few female government clerks in Washington when the Civil War began, Barton helped with medical assistance to wounded soldiers on and near the battlefields, becoming known as the "angel of the battlefield." At the end of the war, she returned to the South to search for missing soldiers and to mark graves at the infamous prisoner of war camp in Andersonville, Georgia. In February 1866, Barton testified before a subcommittee of the Joint Committee on Reconstruction about the conditions she had seen among blacks during her visit to Georgia in 1865. She reported that blacks had flocked to her tent, asking whether they were still free now that Lincoln was dead and telling her that their masters were still working them without pay. She told the committee that the blacks sometimes reported instances of cruelty and, in one case extreme cruelty, an overseer had repeatedly

Clara Barton

whipped a pregnant woman for refusing to work in the field. Barton reported the former slaves to be "friendly, full of confidence in the United States government, loving the Northern people." Barton later founded and for two decades headed the American Red Cross. She also continued her support for social reform, equal rights for women, and aid to blacks. Barton died in 1912.

257

Frederick Douglass, leading black abolitionist and civil rights activist

Frederick Douglass was born in Maryland of a white father and a black slave mother. He taught himself to read and write. Escaping from slavery in 1838, he went to New York and Massachusetts, and became active in the Anti-Slavery Society. From Rochester, New York, he published an abolitionist paper, the *North Star*, lectured on slavery and supported women's suffrage. Douglass was a commanding presence, over six feet tall, with a leonine head and a booming voice. During the Civil War, he thundered against slavery and urged black men to fight in the Union Army for their freedom and full citizenship. Douglass insisted that emancipation was only the first step in the elevation of blacks. He complained that the freedmen "were sent away empty handed, without money, without friends, and without a foot of land to stand upon. Old and young, sick and well, they were turned loose to the open sky, naked to their enemies." He urged that the freedmen not only be given civil and political rights but also some initial economic assistance. He worked to get rid of the repressive southern "black codes" that were threatening to reinstitute another form of bondage. He remained a Republican even while denouncing the party's abandonment of southern blacks in the 1870s. Douglass died in 1895.

Frederick Douglass

Charlotte Forten Grimké, Northern black woman educator and humanitarian

Born in Philadelphia, Pennsylvania, in 1837 to Robert and Mary Wood Forten, prominent free blacks and active reformers and abolitionists, Charlotte Forten was educated in Massachusetts, became a teacher and joined the antislavery movement. William Lloyd Garrison published some of her poetry in the *Liberator*. Her diaries, beginning in 1854, reveal the struggles of a young African-American woman. During the Civil War, Forten became one of the "Yankee School Marms" following the Union Army to educate newly freed slaves. From 1862-64, she was the first African-American teacher at Port Royal on St. Helena, one of the Sea Islands off South Carolina occupied by the Union Army. The journal of her experiences during the war was published in the 1864 spring issues of the *Atlantic Monthly*.

Charlotte Forten Grimke

She found that the black children and adults were eager to learn to read and write, and that they could learn rapidly. She was horrified by the cruelty of slavery they described to her-- the meager rations, the use of the lash, and especially the selling away of the children. An old woman told her what a happy year it was when the Union forces arrived in 1862: "Nobody to whip me, nor drive me, and plenty to eat." Forten served as secretary of a Boston organization providing Northern assistance to teachers working with the former slaves throughout the South from 1865-1870, then taught in Charleston and Washington, D.C. In 1878, she married Francis Grimké, a Presbyterian minister in Washington, D.C., the son of a white South Carolina planter and one of his slave women, and the nephew of two of the most famous white female abolitionists, Angelina and Sarah Grimké (the planter's sisters). Charlotte Forten Grimké died in 1914.

General Oliver O. Howard, professional soldier, general in the Union Army and head of the Freedmen's Bureau

As a boy working on his father's farm in Maine, Oliver Howard had labored alongside a young black farmhand, and he later credited this experience with the origins of his liberal racial views. Howard graduated from West Point and served as a Union general throughout in the Civil War, even after a shell cost him his right arm in 1862. After the war, when Congress created the Freedmen's Bureau under the War Department, President Johnson appointed Howard to lead it. He proved a competent and conscientious manager, with good intentions, humanitarian passion and religious enthusiasm for the job. However, he was inclined to believe the best of everyone and refused to give credence to any charges of misconduct against Bureau officials. Although the Freedmen's Bureau was hated by many white Southerners, the bureau issued more than 15 million food rations, gave medical care to one million people, administered the small sums that Congress appropriated for schools for the freed slaves, and tried to protect the freedmen's rights. Reports to the Freedmen's Bureau about conditions in each state subject to reconstruction were submitted to the Joint

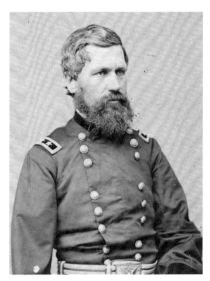

Oliver O. Howard

Congressional Committee on Reconstruction. By the end of 1868, Congress had virtually eliminated the Bureau. Instead, Howard, along with others, founded a black university (Howard University) in Washington, D.C. in 1867. He served as its president between 1869 and 1874 before being assigned by the Army to the wars against the Plains Indians in the American West.

James Longstreet

James Longstreet, former Confederate General; became a Republican after the Civil War

Born into a family of South Carolina planters, James Longstreet grew up in Georgia under the tutelage of an uncle, who was a noted jurist, educator and clergyman. He graduated from West Point in 1842, fought in the Mexican War, and became Robert E. Lee's second-in-command, confidant and adviser during the Civil War. After the war, Longstreet, moved to New Orleans and became a cotton broker. Although he remained a conservative and a believer in white supremacy, his political ideas began to change, and in 1867, he became what southern Democrats denounced as a "scalawag," a native white Southerner who supported the Republican Party. He believed that cooperation with the Republicans would minimize the length and impact of Reconstruction. Although denounced by southern Democrats, Longstreet supported Republican candidates and was rewarded with a series of governmental appointments at both the state and national level.

Senator John Sherman, moderate/conservative Republican from Ohio

John Sherman

Sherman was a younger brother of Union General William T. Sherman. He became a lawyer, launched a lumber concern and bought real estate wisely. He exercised the same self-restraint in politics that enabled him to stay in office for nearly half a century. He understood how to compromise his personal preferences with the needs and attitudes of his constituents. He was elected in 1854 as a compromise candidate and his views remained moderate and restrained. A tall, spare man, he found the field of finance to his liking and helped in the planning of the national banking system. His moderate views carried through to the issue of Reconstruction where he often advanced less drastic alternatives to those of the radicals. Sherman wanted to settle the Reconstruction issue as quickly as possible. He supported the Civil Rights Bill of 1866. Sherman opposed Johnson largely for abandoning the Republican Party and its policies on Reconstruction, and he voted to remove him from office. Sherman's career as a financial expert in Congress and then in the cabinet continued through 1898. He authored the Sherman Anti-Trust Act of 1890.

Robert Smalls, Southern black Republican and Union war hero

Born in 1839 a slave in Beaufort, South Carolina, Robert Smalls became a skilled seaman and expert coastal pilot. In 1862, he led a group of slaves in seizing a Confederate dispatch boat from its dock and sailing it out to the Union Navy blockading the Carolina coast. Smalls' heroic action was widely praised in the North, and it helped persuade Secretary of War Edwin Stanton to authorize an experiment in recruiting escaped slaves in northern occupied areas of the South as soldiers of the Union Army. Smalls served as captain of his captured dispatch boat with the Union Navy during the war. Union forces occupied many of the Sea Islands of the Carolinas, and the land was given to former slaves. After the war, Smalls protested Johnson's policy of returning the Sea Islands properties held by blacks back to the former white owners. Under Congressional Reconstruction, he became one of the newly enfranchised freedmen and a delegate to the state's constitutional convention where he helped draft a resolution giving South Carolina its first system of free, public education. In 1868, he was elected to the state legislature where he served until 1875. He also served in the state militia, rising to the rank of brigadier general, and was elected several times to Congress. He later served as U.S. customs collector at Beaufort. Smalls died in 1915.

Robert Smalls

Alexander Stephens, white Southern Whig/Democrat

Born in rural Georgia, Alexander Stephens attended what became the state university, taught for a while, then read law. He was elected to the Georgia legislature, and then to Congress. Politically, he was a Whig, but when that party disintegrated in the 1850s, he became a Democrat. He defended slavery on biblical grounds, although he saw it mainly as a way of controlling a subordinate race. Personally, he was a kindly master to his slaves. Like many other southern Whigs, he opposed secession. However, after Georgia seceded, he helped draft the Confederate Constitution, and he was elected vice president of the Confederacy in1861. He argued that a state's right to secede was essential for keeping the national government within the bounds of constitutionality, moderation and equity. During the war, he bitterly criticized Confederate President Jefferson Davis. In 1865, under Andrew Johnson's Reconstruction program, Stephens was elected to the U.S. Senate, but was excluded by the Republican Congress along with all others from the former Confederate states. He supported Johnson's Reconstruction policies, and in April 1866, he testified before the Joint Congressional Committee that while not repudiating the theoretical right of secession, the people of Georgia would not use it again and also acquiesced in the abolition of slavery. He stressed that white Georgians were, however, opposed to granting the freedmen the right to vote. He also denied the constitutional power of the federal government to impose conditions for the restoration of the former Confederate states to the Union.

Alexander Stephens

Senator Charles Sumner, radical Republican from Massachusetts

Sumner was a graduate of Harvard College and Law School, and a man of independent thought. He was outspoken in his condemnation of slavery and an earnest advocate of equal rights for blacks. He helped found the Republican Party in the 1850's. As early as 1862 he announced that the seceded states had abdicated all rights under the Constitution. He insisted that Reconstruction should be controlled by Congress rather than the President. It was Sumner's insistence that led the Senate to add to the requirements for "readmission" of the seceded states the insertion in their constitutions of a provision for equal suffrage rights for whites and blacks. He also would have liked to require that the states provide free schools and free farmsteads to the freedmen. Sumner was no favorite of the business community in his state. However, he was a protector of textile industries and interests in government securities. Sumner was not a shrewd scheming politician but rather a humanitarian idealist and an ardent supporter of numerous reform movements both before and after the Civil War. He would hear of no compromise on the subject of human rights. Sumner was six feet four inches tall, with a powerful voice which he used with great skill. In 1868, he was a leading advocate for impeaching and removing President Johnson.

Charles Sumner

William H. Trescot, white Southern planter and Democrat

Born in Charleston, South Carolina, William Trescot attended private schools, read law, studied diplomacy and married into a southern planter family. He was small in stature and noted for the instability of his opinions, but he was impressive in manners and brilliant in conversation. In 1850, he wrote *The Position of the South,* a summary of the southern social and economic view. He also wrote several treatises about diplomacy. He held a series of positions with the state of South Carolina both before and after secession. During the Civil War, he was an intermediary between the Confederate government and the British and French consuls. After the war, he served as the Washington lobbyist for the governor of South Carolina and the state's planter elite in their attempts to recover properties taken by the Union Army and given to freed slaves. Trescot argued that this would preclude the cotton and rice planters of South Carolina from obtaining the disciplined labor force they required. As Trescot wrote to President Johnson in 1866, even if relatively few freedmen established themselves as independent farmers, plantation discipline would dissolve since "it will be utterly impossible for the owner to find laborers that will work contentedly for wages alongside of these free colonies."

William H. Trescot

POSITIONS AND INTERESTS

During the Civil War, and immediately afterwards, the positions of the political parties and individual politicians were in a state of flux. There were several important political divisions over the status of former black slaves, the status of the states that had seceded and those who led them, and the balance of power between the state and national governments, as well as between the legislative and executive branches of the federal government.

Democrats *(Alexander Stephens, William Trescot and Rep. Rogers)*

Positions

Freed slaves

Accepted the end of slavery as a result of the North's victory but argued that blacks were inferior to whites and should not be given legal and political rights equal to those possessed by adult white men.

Secessionists and Seceded States

Southern states had not successfully seceded and therefore had never legally left the Union. Once 10 percent of the electorate took an oath of loyalty to the United States and state constitutions rejected secession and slavery, the voters, including pardoned Confederates, should resume their rights and elect their representatives and senators to Congress immediately.

Locus of Constitutional Authority

Committed to states' rights, distrusting national power over social and cultural as well as political issues on racial, ethnic, or religious grounds. The president, rather than the Congress, should exercise primary constitutional authority for Reconstruction.

Interests

<u>Political</u>

Northern and southern Democrats had a political interest in reuniting the party in hope of a winning a Democratic majority in Congress and the presidency in 1868.

<u>Economic</u>

Southern planters, mainly white Democrats, located primarily in the low country and in the rich soil areas ("the black belt") of the deep south, wanted the freed men and women to provide the labor for their staple crops (primarily cotton, but also rice and sugar) without having to pay high wages. They wanted to restrict the ability of blacks to obtain their own land and to restore gang labor from sunup to sundown under white supervision.

Southern white yeomen and non-slaveowning white farmers, particularly in the mountain and up-country areas where there were fewer planters and blacks, were interested in escaping from debt. The physical destruction of their farms during the war made it very difficult for them to begin farming again without getting into even more debt and losing their farms to creditors.

Those northern industrial workers who were foreign-born, Irish and German Roman Catholics, generally holding unskilled or less skilled jobs, were Democrats who were concerned with the possibility of blacks competing against them for unskilled jobs.

Poorer white Northern farmers and tenant farmers, heirs of the Jacksonian tradition and located in the rural North or border states or the southern tier of the Midwest populated especially by former Southerners, tended to support the Democratic Party's position on Reconstruction

<u>Social</u>

While non-slaveowning white farmers and freed black slaves could have cooperated along class lines (since the blacks wanted the land of their former masters, not that of the up-country whites) in opposition to the rule by the planters for the planters' economic benefit. The planter elites kept the non-slaveowning whites aligned with them by emphasizing the psychological and security interest of poorer southern whites in keeping blacks in subordinate and inferior positions as a form of white superiority and of race control.

Moderate/Conservative Republicans *(Senators Fessenden, Grimes and Sherman)*

Positions

<u>Freed slaves</u>

Argued that the great human and material sacrifices of the war would have been given in vain if the South were allowed to keep blacks degraded. Some of this patriotic rhetoric may have reflected vindictiveness towards the slaveowning elites who had caused so much bloodshed. Moderates supported free labor and at least some legal rights for blacks, but most were not enthusiastic about the prospect of black suffrage (most northern states also excluded blacks from voting). Initially, the moderates supported Johnson.

Secessionists and Seceded States

On the whole, moderate and conservative Republicans believed that the secessionist states had abandoned the Union and, therefore, could be made to fulfill certain requirements before their representatives were readmitted to the national government. They came to this view after the unrepentant attitude of many of the former secessionists, including top Confederate officials elected to Congress in 1865 by the white Democrats.

Locus of Constitutional Authority

The moderate and conservative Republicans had initially hoped that the president would take the lead during the summer of 1865, while Congress was in recess, to accomplish Reconstruction quickly and smoothly. They wanted to focus on other national issues, especially the enormous war debt, the need to encourage economic development, and the desire to consolidate the Republican Party and expand it into the South. They also believed that with the end of the wartime emergency, some of the power assumed by the federal government and the executive should properly flow back to the Congress and to the states. In 1865-66, however, they came to believe that the former Confederate states were incapable of reforming their laws regarding the freedmen without more active involvement by the federal government than that proposed in President Johnson's Reconstruction plan.

Interests

Political

The Republican Party was only in the North, was only a decade old and had won the presidency in 1860 with only 40 percent of a popular vote. It needed to expand its political base into the South.

Economic

Some northern industrialists and financiers, former Whigs, now primarily Republicans, support the pro-business attitude and achievements of the Republican Party, and seek profits from investments in cotton and textile mills.

Some northern industrial Protestant workers, generally holding more skilled jobs, believed in "free labor, free men" slogans of the Republican Party.

Feared that the rapid reentry of the southern states under the Democratic Party would imperil many of the Republican Party's achievements during the war, including protective tariffs, homestead acts, grants to build railroads, state universities, and a national banking and currency system. These initiatives, which Republicans viewed as essential for the United States to become a strong and unified nation, were seen as inimical to the interests of the planter-led southern Democrats.

Radical Republicans *(Senator Sumner, Reps. Stevens and Conkling)*

Positions

Freed Slaves

Determined to wipe out the blot of slavery and the ideology of racial inferiority perpetrated by the planter-driven "Slave Power" and to impose upon a recalcitrant white South freedom and equality for African Americans.

Saw the Civil War and Reconstruction as providing a rare opportunity to make far-reaching changes and achieve a "multiracial democracy." While radicals may have disagreed over the economic issues of the day—tariff, currency, and railroad assistance—they agreed on the moral imperative of redefining and expanding American citizenship to include blacks.

Secessionists and Seceded States

The more extreme radicals saw secession and the waging of war against the Union as "treason" and, therefore, held the former Confederate states to be either "conquered enemy lands" or states that had reverted back to the condition of mere territories. Stevens' plan was for the government to confiscate the land of disloyal planters, give 40 acres (and perhaps a mule from army surplus) to black families and Union Army veterans, and sell the rest to raise money to pay off the enormous federal war debt.

Locus of Constitutional Authority

Asserted that Congress rather than the president had traditionally under the Constitution determined when and under what conditions territories would be admitted to the Union as states with duly elected representatives to Congress. Also committed to expanding the scope of the federal government, based on the constitutional need to guarantee each state a republican form of government.

Interests

Political

Like the other Republicans, the radicals also had a political interest in achieving a national, not just a northern, base for their fledgling political party. Enfranchisement of several million freedmen, whom they believed could (along with many former Whigs) become loyal supporters of the Republican Party in the South, would expand the strength of the party at the expensive of the Democrats.

Southern blacks saw their most important interest in having the rights of citizens and suffrage.

Economic

Southern blacks wanted autonomy over their lives. They wanted their own land, or at least the right to supervise their own labor and to decide which members of their families (men, women and children) would work in the fields, compensation for their labor, and respect and recognition as citizens and the political means to protect their interests. They also saw white Republicans, North and South, as their allies against postwar repression initiated by white Democrats.

Northerners, white and black, who relocated to the South, such as Union army officers turned politicians or entrepreneurs as well as civilian business and professionals, as well as those southern urban business interests, had a more Northern vision of progress through a market driven system of industrial as well as agricultural goods and labor.

Economic/political

More affluent farmers and those who lived in the areas of the upper Midwest settled by New Englanders or by antislavery, Protestant Germans and Scandinavians usually supported the Republican Party.

TEACHER INSTRUCTIONS

Preparation

1.   Review the "Historical Background" with the class. Assign it as a reading or present the material as a lecture.

2.   Once the class is comfortable with the background, distribute student handout: "Positions and Interests." Students should review all positions before they are assigned to take a particular side.

3.   Pass out student handout: "The Participants." Again, have students review all the brief biographies before they are assigned a particular role.

Directions

1.   Divide the class into groups of 18–20 as follows:

     Members of the Joint Committee
     •   Senator William Pitt Fessenden, chair
     •   Senator James Wilson Grimes
     •   Rep. Thaddeus Stevens
     •   Rep. Roscoe Conkling
     •   Rep. Andrew Jackson Rogers

     Witnesses
     •   Clara Barton
     •   Frederick Douglass
     •   Charlotte Forten-Grimké
     •   General Oliver Howard
     •   James Longstreet
     •   Senator John Sherman
     •   Robert Smalls
     •   Alexander Stephens
     •   Senator Charles Sumner
     •   William Trescot

     Observers/Reporters/Recorders
     •   Assign the remaining 3–5 students to be newspaper reporters who will act as observers/reporters/recorders

2.   Have the members of the Joint Committee, the witnesses, and the observers in each group form a team. As a team, they should then review the positions and interests of the participants.

3.   The participants and observers should, as a team, identify possible options that might by acceptable.

4.   Distribute student handout: "The Mock Congressional Hearing and Debate."

5.   Review the setting and the directions with the students and have the teams come together in their groups and proceed with their mock hearings and debates.

Debriefing

1.   Once the groups have finished, bring the class back together for a discussion. Have the observers describe how the process of conducting a hearing and debate worked in their group.

2.   After discussing the process, summarize and compare the results each group obtained.

3.   Either have the students read what actually happened during Reconstruction ("The Facts Continued") or share this information with the class as a lecture. Compare the group results and process with the historical reality.

4.   Keep in mind that while, in reality, most of the testimony before the Joint Committee was from generals and other military personnel in the South rather than from prominent African Americans, such as Frederick Douglass, we have intentionally included testimony from a broader range of perspectives.

5.   Discuss the legacy of Reconstruction ("The Legacy of Reconstruction").

6.   Use the "Questions for Discussion" for essay topics or for further in-class discussion.

THE FACTS CONTINUED

Following its hearings, the Joint Committee on Reconstruction formulated an Amendment to the Constitution (what would become the Fourteenth Amendment) to ensure that the protections of the Civil Rights Act of 1866 would not be repealed. The Committee made its recommendation on April 28, 1866, without the support of the three Democrats. The proposed Fourteenth Amendment was a compromise: while confirming blacks' citizenship, it did not guarantee them the right to vote. Rather, it left to each state to decide who would have the suffrage. The most important section defined for the first time national (as opposed to state) citizenship: "All persons born or naturalized in the United States and subject to its jurisdiction" were declared American citizens, a definition that included the former slaves. The Amendment then authorized federal protection against state action abridging the "privileges or immunities of citizens of the United States" or denying any person "due process" and "equal protection" of the laws. The second section provided that if a state excluded any adult male citizens from voting, its representation in Congress would be proportionately reduced. The initial version excluded those who had voluntarily aided the Confederacy from voting in national elections until 1870; however, moderates and conservatives disliked this broad disfranchisement as too vindictive, and Congress changed it to simply exclude from public office southern officials or military officers who had previously sworn allegiance to the U.S. Constitution and then voluntarily aided the Confederacy. The fourth section repudiated the Confederate debt, and the fifth section empowered Congress to enforce the amendment through appropriate legislation.

The full report of the Joint Committee on Reconstruction issued in June 1866 defended what the committee had proposed to Congress on April 28th. The status of the former Confederate states was dismissed as a "profitless abstraction." The report declared the freedmen to be "free men and citizens" not to be abandoned, but did not demand that they be granted immediate suffrage. The committee supported the "representation clause" as a reasonable compromise that continued the tradition of leaving voting qualifications to the states; but it predicted that these policies would lead to black suffrage "at no distant day." On the issue of seating the Southerners newly elected to Congress, the committee declared the former secessionist states to be so recalcitrant that they were not yet entitled to representation in the national government. The committee also declared that the Constitution gave Congress rather than the president authority over Reconstruction policy. (See Document 8: Report of the Joint Committee on Reconstruction, June 1866.)

Following a brief debate, Congress passed the proposed Fourteenth Amendment on June 13, 1866, despite opposition of the Democratic minority, and submitted it for ratification. Congress required the former secessionist states to ratify the Amendment to qualify for readmission. However, with President Johnson's encouragement, almost all the white Democratic governments in the South rejected the Fourteenth Amendment. Only Republican-governed Tennessee ratified it in 1866, and that state was quickly restored to the Union.

The congressional election in fall 1866, the first national election since the end of the war, was an important watershed. Democrats had hoped that voters would repudiate Republicans and their Reconstruction policies. During the summer, white mobs killed or maimed peacefully demonstrating blacks in New Orleans and Memphis, reinforcing the Republican contention that the South was still controlled by recalcitrant slaveowners who sought to undo the Union victory. Running on their wartime military and economic achievements as well as their Reconstruction policies, Republicans won handily throughout the North. They even gained several additional seats in Congress, thus solidifying their two-thirds, veto-proof majorities in both houses.

With the Republicans firmly in control, Congressional Reconstruction (sometimes called "Republican" Reconstruction or inaccurately "Radical" Reconstruction) began. Over President Johnson's veto, Congress enacted the Reconstruction Act of 1867. "No legal State governments or adequate protection for life or property now exist in the rebel States," the act declared, "and it is necessary that peace and good order should be enforced in said States until loyal and republican State governments can be legally established." The act divided the former rebel states (except for readmitted Tennessee), into five military districts, each with a federal military commander whose powers were superior to those of the state governments. These states were required to conduct elections involving all male citizens "of whatever race, color, or previous conditions" for the drafting of new state constitutions that would guarantee black suffrage and ratify the Fourteenth Amendment. Each state would then be eligible, contingent upon congressional approval, for representation in the national government. When southern Democrats refused to accept these conditions, Congress required the military commanders to enroll all voters, which they did (in the process, 703,000 blacks and 627,000 whites were added to the voter rolls) and to arrange new elections. The result was that new state constitutions were adopted, which provided for the universal suffrage of adult males, civil rights for blacks as well as whites, and the disqualification of ex-rebels.

Looking toward the November 1868 presidential election, Johnson sought to build an electoral base among southern and northern Democrats, former southern Whigs, and perhaps some moderate and conservative Republicans. He portrayed the Republicans in Congress as fanatical extremists. The conflict between President Johnson and the Republican Congress revolved around the role of the national government in the affairs of the defeated southern states and the future of blacks as members of the body politic. But the pugnacious president's ineptness, coarseness, racism and political ambitions, combined with the blatant actions of

SIGNIFICANT ELECTION SCENE AT WASHINGTON, June 3, 1867.—[Sketched by A. W. M'Callum.]

Northern view of African-American Men Voting in Washington, D.C., 1867

the reconstituted Democratic southern governments, alienated moderates and even many conservatives in the Republican Party. The emotions stirred by the conflict between the two branches of government set the stage for an unsuccessful attempt by the congressional Republicans to remove the president from office.

On February 24, 1868, the House of Representatives voted to impeach President Johnson. Under the Constitution, impeachment required "high crimes or misdemeanors." Therefore, most of the charges related to his violating the Tenure of Office Act by firing his Secretary of War, Edwin Stanton (who had been working with the Radicals to undermine Johnson's reconstruction plans). The constitutionality of this law was questionable and had never been tested in the courts. Johnson's trial began in the Senate on March 30. Seven House members, including Thaddeus Stevens, served as the prosecutors. Five lawyers defended Johnson. The president himself never appeared in the Senate during his trial, which lasted over a month. The Senate failed by one vote to convict Johnson and remove him from the presidency. (See Document 9: The Impeachment of President Johnson.)

Impeachent Trial of President Johnson, 1868

In July 1868, the Fourteenth Amendment was ratified (See Document 10: The Fourteenth Amendment), and the Democratic state governments set up under Johnson's policy were replaced by Republican state governments. In a notable expansion of American democracy, the biracial Republican coalition in the South elected black as well as white office holders. During Republican Reconstruction, whites continued to hold the governorships and the majorities in every house of every southern state government (except South Carolina, one of the most populous black states with one of the wealthiest and best-educated free black communities, which for a brief period had an African-American majority in both the Assembly and the Senate). Nearly half the elected African-American officials at the state and national level had been educated, urban, free blacks (ministers, teachers, storekeepers, farmers, artisans) before the war, and the majority of former slaves who held state or national office had been skilled workers: carpenters, barbers, blacksmiths, masons, and boatmen or such.

The Democratic Party bypassed Johnson for its presidential nomination, instead selecting Horatio Seymour, a former governor of New York, as the Democratic presidential candidate. Seymour was defeated by Republican war hero, General Ulysses S. Grant. Johnson returned home embittered but in 1875 was reelected to the Senate from Tennessee. He died, however, before resuming his old seat.

The Republican experiment in multiracial democracy in the South in the late 1860s and early 1870s bore tangible fruits for thousands of recently freed black Southerners, as well as for thousands of up-country and mountain region whites who had long been antagonistic to the planter elites and many of whom had opposed the Confederacy. The establishment of schools, the granting of equal citizenship to blacks, and the effort to revitalize the devastated South were commendable achievements which refuted the traditional description of the period primarily as a tragic era of rampant misgovernment. southern black men were enfranchised, which enabled them, for the first time, to express their interests and preferences in a democratic setting. Blacks were elected to local, state and federal offices. For the first time, they served as sheriffs, tax assessors, and jurors, challenging long-held beliefs that blacks were incapable of participating in democratic affairs. As elected officials, blacks helped to pass legislation in southern states that enfranchised poor whites, established the South's first free public school system and public health facilities, rebuilt and modernized the transportation system, and abolished many cruel forms of punishment.

Yet these biracial Republican governments also faced enormous obstacles and bitter adversaries, who eventually triumphed against them. Economically, they had to raise taxes to pay for the rebuilding and the new governmental services, a painful task in a region impoverished by the war and then a national depression that began in 1873. Ideologically, they faced centuries-old racism that had been intensified in the prewar defense of slavery. Politically, the Republican Party was identified with the military defeat of the South in the Civil War. And the southern Republican governments were also competing with a Democratic Party that used fraud, racial hatred, violence, and even terrorism to win elections and to remain in power (Republicans also used fraud to remain in power). In Virginia and Tennessee, which had vast white majorities, the Democrats reestablished control by 1869. In other states throughout the South, paramilitary groups, such as the Ku Klux Klan, emerged. Armed night riders, their identity concealed by masks and hood, terrorized blacks and their white supporters in the Republican Party to prevent them from voting or to drive them out of office and maintain white Democratic supremacy. Hundreds were killed and hundreds more whipped or maimed. Although overall President Grant was rather passive, the federal government took some action to protect voters and officeholders against the Klan and other attempts to disenfranchise black Americans. (See Document 11: Organization and Principles of the Ku Klux Klan, 1868.)

Northern view of Anti-Black Riots in New Orleans, 1874

The Fifteenth Amendment, which declared that the right to vote "shall not be denied or abridged…by any State on account of race, color, or previous condition of servitude," was passed in 1869 and ratified in 1870. (See Document 12: The Fifteenth Amendment, 1869.) The Ku Klux Klan Acts and the creation of the Department of Justice expanded federal power to deal with violations of citizens' rights. But the continued violence and fraud at election time, the nationwide, decade-long depression of 1873, and the costs of enforcing the new laws, all eroded the political will to sustain Republican Reconstruction. The Democrats regained control of the House of Representatives as well as a number of southern states in 1874. The 1876 election and the resulting Compromise of 1877, in which Republican president-elect, Rutherford Hayes, agreed to stop using military force to help maintain Republican governments in the South, brought an end to Reconstruction. In the 1883 *Civil Rights Cases*, brought by African Americans who had been denied an accommodation or privilege on account of color in violation of the Civil Rights Act of 1875, the U.S. Supreme Court held that the rights which the Civil Rights Act attempted to protect were social rather than civil rights, and that the Federal Government had no jurisdiction over these matters, thus ending the federal governments legal efforts to enforce the due process and equal rights guarantees of the Fourteenth Amendment. (See Document 13: *Civil Rights Cases*, 1883.)

The Legacy of Reconstruction

Although Reconstruction may have succeeded in formalizing an end to slavery and offering a brief experiment in multiracial democracy, it failed to realize the dreams of equal opportunity for African Americans as citizens and free laborers. Nor was Reconstruction able to curtail the power of the planter elites or create a permanent Republican Party in the South. The Civil War brought an end to black slavery that had existed in the South for two centuries, but it left deep scars and conflicting attitudes and interests.

The persistence of racism, the widespread use of violence and other forms of coercion, the failure to provide an economic basis for the new freedom, such as the provision of land in the predominantly agricultural society, prevented the freed slaves from achieving true autonomy. The gang labor system under direct white supervision and punishmnt was ended, but it was replaced by a sharecropping system in which blacks lived in peonage on small family plots and grew cotton on the planter's land for a share of the crop's value, restricted by debt under a rapacious crop-lien system. Black codes made their new civil and political rights all but meaningless. Complete disenfranchisement of blacks came in the 1890s and the first two decades of the twentieth century. In the long run, the experiment in multiracial democracy was ended by the reassertion of white Democratic planter control in the South with the acquiescence of distracted or disillusioned elements in the North. Politically, the one-party (Democratic Party) rule and disfranchisement of a sizable proportion of the South's population helped keep that region under the control of a conservative, planter-oriented elite. Not only did this white elite dominance limit the South to a largely impoverished, backwater region, but through the South's conservative Democratic representatives in Washington, D.C., it also impeded national legislation on racial and other progressive issues for decades to come.

For the progeny of the freedmen and freedwomen, the Reconstruction Era was a sad episode of broken promises and shameless reaction to racial reforms. Writing in 1903, black sociologist W.E.B. Du Bois observed: "For this much all men know: despite compromise, war and struggle, the Negro is not free. In the backwoods of the Gulf States, for miles and miles, he may not leave the plantation of his birth; in well-nigh the whole rural South the black farmers are peons, bound by law and custom to an economic slavery, from which the only escape is death or the penitentiary." Martin Luther King, Jr. would strike a similar cord in 1963, observing that a century after President Lincoln issued that Emancipation Proclamation, "We must face the tragic fact that the Negro is still not free. One hundred years later, the life of the Negro is still sadly crippled by the manacles of segregation and the chains of discrimination."

Costs and Benefits of the Civil War and Reconstruction

The South

- 260,000 Confederate soldiers died in the Civil War
- 60 percent of southern wealth was lost
- Sharecropping and crop liens pervented crop diversification a development

The North

- 360,000 Union soldiers died in the Civil War
+ War gave the North an industrial boost

African Americans

+ Slavery abolished--3.5 million former slaves freed
+ Fourteenth and Fifteenth Amendments enacted protecting African Americans and the right of black males to vote
+ Growth of black churches and schools
+ African Americans participated in democratic government
- Rise of vigilantism and violence against African Americans
- Federal courts increasingly did not support laws to protect freedmen's rights
- After 1877, states reinstated laws discriminating against African Americans

---

Reconstruction was a period in which the turmoil of the Civil War was turned toward an attempt to reform public life. Despite intense opposition, it produced three enormously important constitutional amendments that abolished slavery, established a new, more expansive definition of U.S. citizenship and the citizens' rights within the states, and tried to guarantee black men the right to vote. Had Reconstruction gone the route envisioned by Thaddeus Stevens, the future of blacks in American society might have been significantly better. On the other hand, had Reconstruction followed the desires of President Johnson, the future of blacks in American society would have probably been even worse. It was the crisis of Reconstruction itself that was the creative element in the situation, pushing individuals toward new ideas and uncharted paths. Black Americans looked upon the period as the first opportunity for them to protect their interests as citizens. Knowing that such an opportunity existed, flawed as it was, helped African Americans later to challenge with greater determination the obstacles to their freedom and a better life. Looking back on it more than a century later, Reconstruction was a missed opportunity for the United States to set an example to the world for the attainment of a successful multiracial democracy.

QUESTIONS FOR DISCUSSION

1. Why did Reconstruction develop the way it did?

2. If the various parties to the Reconstruction debate had used conflict resolution skills, such as active listening and interest-based negotiation, could they have negotiated a Reconstruction Plan that might have avoided the excesses and turmoil created by the dramatic changes from Presidential Reconstruction to Congressional Reconstruction to more conservative Reconstruction?

3. Were the participants in the Reconstruction drama fully aware of the implications for expanding the federal government and changing the relations between the states and the federal government inherent in the passage of the Civil Rights Act and the Thirteenth, Fourteenth, and Fifteenth Amendments?

4. How did the Reconstruction debates about the definition of citizenship impact the growing movement for the women's rights movement in the 19th century?

5. Do you think that the federal civil war amendments were able to change the class structure and the attitudes about race relations in the south? Why or why not? do you think that it is possible to change social attitudes through the enactment and enforcement of federal laws?

POSSIBLE ALTERNATIVES IN 1866

*   The Republican Party might have tried to find a way to appeal to white as well as black voters in the South on economic issues. The Populist movement of the 1890s indicates that in some states poor whites and blacks might have learned to act together for their common economic grievances and goals.

*   Whites and blacks in the South could have conceivably cooperated along class lines as yeomen farmers against the large landowning planters (and with the support of northern Republican allies). Their benefits might have been land redistribution of leading Confederates' land into parcels for small farmers, white and black; government aid to provide a system of public education and public health facilities for the South (which had not existed before the war). Belief in private property interfered with the first. The latter would have been difficult due to racial prejudice as well as hostility towards the Yankees, former abolitionists, and Republican Party.

*   Southern planters might have appealed to conservative interests in the North in support of their need for a disciplined, gang labor force to produce cotton and other staples that profited them but also provided profits for many investors, business, and financial interests in the North.

*   President Andrew Johnson might have played a stronger role in directing social and political reconstruction of the South if he had taken into account predominant public opinion in the North. For example, instead of being so lenient to the secessionist, white South and essentially turning over the process of Reconstruction to the dominant prewar planter elites, Johnson might have worked to build up a yeoman class of blacks and whites and thus sought to achieve recognition of the social revolution in the South as inevitable but also economically beneficial by making landownership more widespread and agricultural more diversified.

*   The federal government might have been stronger in enforcing the Civil War Amendments in the South, as President U.S. Grant did in 1871 when he suppressed the Ku Klux Klan temporarily, and as the federal government under Presidents John Kennedy and Lyndon Johnson did in the 1960s in responding to resistance to new civil rights laws and court orders. However, this often produces a backlash against the use of governmental power.

ADDITIONAL RESOURCES

Abbott, Richard H. *The Republican Party and the South, 1855-1877: The First Southern Strategy.* Chapel Hill: University of North Carolina Press, 1986.

Ash, Stephen V. *A Year in the South: Four Lives in 1865.* New York: Macmillan, 2002.

Bagget, James Alex. *The Scalawags: Southern Dissenters in the Civil War and Reconstruction.* Baton Rouge: Louisiana University Press, 2003.

Cimbala, Paul A. *Under the Guardianship of the Nation: The Freedmen's Bureau and the Reconstruction of Georgia, 1865-1870.* Athens: University of Georgia Press, 1997.

Donald, David. *The Politics of Reconstruction, 1863-1867.* Baton Rouge: University of Louisiana Press, 1965.

Du Bois, W.E.B. *Black Reconstruction in America: An Essay Toward a History of the Part Which Black Folk Played in the Attempt to Reconstruct Democracy in America, 1860-1880.* New York: Macmillan, 1992. Originally published in 1935.

Duncan, Russell. *Freedom's Shore: Tunis Campbell and the Georgia Freedmen.* Athens: University of Georgia Press, 1986.

Foner, Eric, and Olivia Mahoney. *America's Reconstruction: People and Politics after the Civil War.* New York: Harper, 1995.

Foner, Eric. *Freedom's Lawmakers: A Directory of Black Office Holders during Reconstruction.* New York: Oxford University Press, 1993.

_____. *Give Me Liberty! An American History.* New York: Norton, 2004.

_____. *Reconstruction: America's Unfinished Revolution, 1863-1877.* New York: Harper, 1988.

Gillette, William. *Retreat from Reconstruction, 1869-1879.* Baton Rouge: Louisiana University Press, 1979.

_____. *The Right to Vote: Politics and the Passage of the Fifteenth Amendment.* Baltimore, Md.: The Johns Hopkins University Press, 1969.

Holt, Thomas C. *Black over White: Negro Political Leadership in South Carolina During Reconstruction.* Urbana: University of Illinois Press, 1977.

Perman, Michael. *The Road to Redemption: Southern Politics, 1869-1879.* Chapel Hill: University of North Carolina Press, 1984.

_____. *Reunion Without Compromise: The South and Reconstruction, 1865-1868.* Cambridge: Cambridge University Press, 1973.

Stampp, Kenneth M. *The Era of Reconstruction, 1865-1877.* New York: Knopf, 1965.

Documents On CD

Document 1:	The Emancipation Proclamation
Document 2:	Lincoln defense of the Emancipation Proclamation in a letter to James Conkling, August 26, 1863
Document 3:	Wade-Davis Bill, July 1864
Document 4:	Thirteenth Amendment, 1865
Document 5:	Lincoln's Second Inaugural Address, March 4, 1865
Document 6:	Black Codes of Mississippi and Louisiana, 1865
Document 7:	Civil Rights Act of 1866 and Johnson's Veto
Document 8:	Report of the Joint Committee on Reconstruction, June 20, 1866
Document 9:	Impeachment of President Johnson
Document 10:	Fourteenth Amendment, 1868
Document 11:	Organization and Principles of the Ku Klux Klan, 1868
Document 12:	Fifteenth Amendment, 1869
Document 13:	Civil Rights Cases, 109 US 3, 1883

Teacher Overheads/ Student Handouts On CD

1. Objectives

2. Background to the Reconstruction Debate, 1787-1864

3. Election of 1864

4. Wreckage of Richmond, Virginia, 1865

5. Background to the Reconstruction Debate

6. President Johnson pardoning southern planters

7. Mock Legislative Hearing, Debate, Lobbying and Decision

8-13.Selected Members of the Joint Committee on Reconstruction

14. Positions and Interests

15-25.Witnesses/Lobbyists

26. Directions for Mock Congressional Hearing and Negotiations

27 Debriefing

28. What Really Happened?

29. Impeachment Trial of President Johnson

30. Reconstruction

31. Rule of Terror in New Orleans

32. Results of the Civil War and Reconstruction

33. Questions for Discussion

SOURCES AND CREDITS FOR ILLUSTRATIONS

p. 251   Wreckage of Richmond, Virginia, 1865, *Library of Congress (LC)-B811-3181*

p. 252   Lincoln-Johnson Campaign Poster, 1864, *LC-USZ62-14616*

p. 253   Northern cartoon of President Johnson pardoning southern rebels at the White House, *Harper's Weekly,* 1865

p. 254   Sen. William Pitt Fessenden, *National Archives NWDNS-111-B-5895*

p. 255   Sen. James Grimes, *LC-BH83- 158*

p. 255   Rep. Thaddeus Stevens, *United States Congress*

p. 256 Rep. Roscoe Conkling, *Matthew Brady, ca. 1860 - ca. 1865*

p. 256   Rep. Andrew Rogers, *LC-BH82- 4906 C*

p. 257   Clara Barton, *LC-USZ62-19319*

p. 258   Frederick Douglass, *LC-USZ62-15887*

p. 258   Charlotte Forten-Grimké, *Salem State College*

p. 259   Gen. Oliver Howard, *LC-B813- 3719 A*

p. 259   James Longstreet, *LC-B813- 2014 B*

p. 260   Sen. John Sherman, *LC-BH832- 1961*

p. 260   Robert Smalls, *LC-BH826- 825*

p. 261   Alexander Stephens, *LC-B813- 1430 B*

p. 261   Sen. Charles Sumner, *LC-BH82- 5237*

p. 262   William Trescott, *LC-USZ62-94551*

p. 268   Northern view of African-American Men Voting in Washington, 1867, *Harper's Weekly*

p. 269   Impeachment Trial of Andrew Jackson, *LC-USZ62-75616*

p. 270   Northern view of Anti-Black Riots in New Orleans, 1874, *LC-USZ62-55606*

INDEX

A

Abolition 227, 228
Active listening 27, 33, 39
Adams, Abigail 224
Adams, John 123, 130, 224
Adams, Samuel 64, 116
Adams-Onís Treaty 181
Addams, Jane 5, 63, 242
African moots 10
African slave trade 136–139
    constitutional provisions 151
Alamo 181
Allen, Richard 138
Alternative dispute resolution;
    See Conflict resolution
Alternatives in History 15
American Revolution 18, 60, 61, 63–65, 106,
       136–138, 160, 224
    role of women 225
Annapolis Convention 139
Annawon 79, 80, 84
Annexation of Texas
    boundary disputes 182
    positions and interests 185
Anthony, Susan B. 64, 235–236, 239–241
Anti-Federalists 153
Antislavery movement 229–231
Apartheid, South Africa and 7
Arbitration 30
Articles of Confederation 135, 139

B

Bargaining 34
Barton, Clara 257
Barton, Keith C. 14
Battle of Buena Vista 189
Beecher, Catharine 64, 226, 229, 238
Beecher, Henry Ward 229
Begin, Menachem 35, 47
Benton, Thomas Hart 187, 204, 211
Best Alternative To a Negotiated Agreement (BATNA)
    37, 54
Black codes 252–253
Blackstone's Commentaries 225
Blatch, Harriet Stanton 242
Bloom's Taxonomy 14
Boston Massacre 111

Boston Tea Party 112
Boudinot, Elias 164, 167, 169, 173
Bowie, Jim 181
Brainstorming solutions 36, 40
British Peace Commission 70, 130
Brown, John 218
Brown v. Board of Education 32
Buchanan, James 218
Burke, Edmund 68, 112, 114
Butler, Pierce 141–142, 144

C

Calderon, Felipe 193
Calhoun, John C. 203, 206
California gold rush 202
Camp David Accords 35, 48
Canonchet 78, 80, 84
Carr, E.H. 16
Carter, Jimmy 47
Cass, Lewis 164, 166, 168, 201
Catt, Carrie Chapman 242
Caucus 48, 116
Center for American Women and Politics 243
Chase, Salmon 211
Cherokee Nation
    civilizing program 161–162
    culture 173–174
    land treaties 161, 162
Cherokee Removal 18, 67, 159, 164, 173, 228
    positions and interests 168
Cherokee syllabary 162
Chickasaws
    civilizing program 161
    land treaties 162, 164
Choctaws
    civilizing program 161
    land treaties 162, 164
Citizens, Development of 20
Civil Rights Act of 1866 253
Civil Rights Act of 1875 271
Civil Rights Cases 271
Civil Rights Movement 7
Civil War 18, 71, 136, 224, 235, 250–251, 272
Clay, Henry 16, 70, 204, 206, 208
Cleveland, Grover 241
Clinton, Hillary 244
Coercion 4
Coercive Acts 62, 112–115

Cold War 8
Collective memory;
    See Public memory
Common Sense 130
Compromise 27, 30
Compromise of 1850 18, 61, 153
    consequences 216–218
    provisions 214–216
Conciliatory Proposal 129
Conflict
    definition of 24
    responses to 29
    sources of 21, 25
    triggers of 33, 38
Conflict resolution activities
    Conflict Resolution Bingo Game 22
    Do I Understand You 39–40
    Downtown 50, 51
    Going to the Cleaners 43–45
    John and Matt 41–42
    Student Attitudes about Conflict 22
    The Bloody Conflict 25
    The Noisy Neighbor 54
    Triggers 38
    What is Mediation? 47
Conflict resolution skills 9
Conkling, Roscoe 256, 264
Conservatives
    at First Continental Congress 64, 121
Constituent groups 68
Constitution
    ratification of 152
Cotton gin 200
Cox, Laurence 93, 95, 97
Crazy Horse 159
Creeks
    civilizing program 161
    land treaties 162, 164
Crockett, Davy 181
Cuban independence 70
Cuban Missile Crisis 10, 18, 60, 67, 68
Curriculum, Goals of 1

D

Dalai Lama 8
Davis, Jefferson 209
Deane, Silas 118
Debriefing 65–66
Declaration of Rights and Resolves 123
Declaration of Sentiments 231
Declaratory Act 109
Delaware Nation 90

Democracy, Basis of 2
Deutsch, Morton 28
Dewey, John 19
Diamond, Jared 16
Dickinson, John 110, 144
Dilbeck, Mierka 94, 97
Discipline 4
Douglas, Stephen A. 207, 210, 217–219
Douglass, Frederick 229, 232, 236, 239, 258
Dred Scott 218
Du Bois, W.E.B. 272
Duane, James 64, 118
Dutch settlers 96

E

Easton, John 62, 79, 81, 84
Echevarria, Antulio J. 13
Economic sanctions 37
Emancipation Proclamation 154, 235, 250, 271
English Civil War 91
Enlightenment 106
Equal Rights Amendment 243
Evaluation of Curriculum 20

F

Federal Convention of 1787 18, 66
    background 139–140
    slavery and 66
Federal Trade and Intercourse Acts 160
Federalist Papers 152
Ferguson, Niall 16
Fessenden, William Pitt 254, 263
Fifteenth Amendment 239, 271
    women's advocacy 235
Fillmore, Millard 207
First Continental Congress 60–61, 63–65, 70, 106, 123
    positions and interests 120–121
First Great Awakening 225
Fisher, Roger 32
Flight 30, 31
Foote, Henry 204, 210
Force 3
Fourteenth Amendment 268, 269
Fox, Vincente 193
Franco-American Alliance 130
Franklin, Benjamin 60–62, 64–65, 67–68, 106, 124, 144
Free African Society 138
Free-Soil Party 201–203
    slavery in the territories 206

Freedman's Bureau 253
Frelinghuysen, Theodore 164–165, 169
Fremont, John C. 218
French and Indian War; *See* Seven Years War
Freud, Sigmund 5
Fugitive Slave Act of 1793 153, 204
Fugitive Slave Act of 1850 153, 215;
  See also Compromise of 1850: provisions
Fugitive slaves 142, 143
  constitutional provisions 152
Fukuyama, Francis 8
Fundamental rights 31

G

Gadsden, Christopher 64, 116, 123
Gage, General Thomas 115, 128
Galloway, Joseph 61, 64, 115, 119, 123
Garrison, William Lloyd 203, 228, 230
Gerry, Eldridge 152
Getting to Yes 32
Glorious Revolution 109
Gradual emancipation 138, 227
Grant, Ulysses S. 189, 250, 270
Great Awakening 106
Grenville, George 108–109
Grimes, James Wilson 255, 263
Grimké, Angelina 228–229
Grimké, Sarah 229
Grimké. Charlotte Forten 258
Guerrilla war tactics 86

H

Hamilton, Alexander 141
Hand, Judith 5
Harper, Frances 235, 237, 239
Harvard Negotiation Project 21
Henry, Patrick 108
Herrera, José Joaquín de 182, 187
Historical inevitability 15
Hobbes, Thomas 5
Holy experiment 92
Hoover, Herbert 194
House of Burgesses 108
Houston, Sam 181
Howard, Oliver O. 259
Hughes, Charles Evans 242
Human Security Report 8
Hunt, Jane 231
Huntington, Samuel P. 9, 28

I

Intolerable Acts;
  See Coercive Acts
Iraq
  American invasion of 71

J

Jackson, Andrew 161, 181
  indian removal policies 163–164
Jefferson, Thomas 129–130, 139, 160, 180, 194
Johnson, Andrew 173, 251, 253, 268–269
  impeachment 269
Joint Committee on Reconstruction 253–254, 267
Jones, Evan 164, 166, 169
Just war theory 6

K

Kagan, Robert 4, 8
Kansas-Nebraska Act 217–218
Kant, Immanuel 8
Kennedy, John F. 68
Khrushchev, Nikita 68
King George III 108, 112
King, Jr., Martin Luther 7, 272
King Philip;
  See Metacom
King Philip's War
  costs 87
  positions and interests 82
King, Rufus 141, 145
King, William R. 212, 217
Knowledge of history, Americans and 14
Knox, Henry 160
Ku Klux Klan 270

L

Labor management relations 10
League of Women Voters 243
Learning Pyramid 19
Lee, Richard Henry 64, 117, 123
Lee, Robert E. 189, 250
Lenni Lenape 60, 90–91, 92, 93
  positions and interests 97
Levstik, Linda S. 14
Lincoln, Abraham 153, 218, 235, 250–251

Litigation 30
    role of 29
Little Big Horn 159
Livingston, William 64, 117
Longstreet, James 259
Lord Aberdeen 190
Lord Chatham;
    See Pitt, William
Lord North;
    See North, Lord Frederick
Lorenz, Konrad 5
Los Angeles Riots 61
Louisiana Purchase 181, 200, 217
Lumpkin, Wilson 167, 168

M

Madison, James 140–141, 145, 160
Mandela, Nelson 7
Manifest Destiny 194
Markham, William 92, 93, 94, 97
Married Women's Property Law 230
Marshall, John 164
Mason, George 141, 145, 152
Mason, James 204
Mason-Dixon Line 142
Massachusetts Bay Colony 76
Massasoit 75–76, 83
Mather, Increase 80, 84, 87
May, Samuel 229
McClintock, Mary Ann 231
McCullough, David 12
Mediation 31, 47
Mediation, Community 10
Mediation, Peer 11
Mediation, Third-party 9
Mediator/facilitator 62
Mennonites 96, 100
Merton, Thomas 14
Metacom 62, 78–79, 81, 84, 85–86, 159
Mexican Cession 191, 202–203
Mexican Revolution 193
Mexican War 18, 60, 62, 67, 70, 180, 194, 200–201
Middle East 10
Minor v. Happersett 241
Minor, Virginia 241
Missouri Compromise 153, 199, 200, 217
Moderates
    at First Continental Congress 64, 121
Mohegans 86
Monroe, James 160
Montgomery Bus Boycott 31, 61

Morris, Gouverneur 141, 146
Mott, James 231
Mott, Lucretia 230–232, 235
Multicultural 2, 13

N

Napoleonic wars 181
Narragansetts 85
National American Woman Suffrage Association 241
National Assessment of Educational Progress 14
National History Standards 59
National pride 21, 28
Native Americans
    civilizing program 160–162
Native Americans and Quakers
    positions and interests 95–96
Negotiation 31, 42
New Jersey Plan 140
New York Metropolitan Transit Authority 34
Nineteenth Amendment 243
Non-importation 110–112
North American Free Trade Agreement 194
North, Lord Frederick 60–62, 64–65, 67–68, 70, 106, 112, 114, 124, 129
Northwest Ordinance 142, 200
Northwest Territory 71
Nuclear war 18

O

Objective criteria 36
Observer/recorder/reporter 63
Olive Branch Petition 129–130
Omnibus Bill of 1850 206–207
Oregon Treaty 190

P

Pacifists 7
Paine, Thomas 130
Paredes y Arrillaga, Mariano 187, 188
Parliament 68, 109, 112, 114, 123–124
Paterson Silk Strike 60
Paterson, William 140, 146
Paul, Alice 242–243
Peace subculture, Characteristics of 6
Peel, Robert 190
Pelosi, Nancy 244

Peña y Peña, Manuel de la 60, 62, 184, 186, 190
Penn, William 91–92, 98–99
Pequot War 77
Pierce, Franklin 217–218
Pilgrims 75, 84
Pinckney, Charles 141, 143, 146
Pitt, William 70, 112, 114
Plan of Union 61
Plausibility 17
Polk, James K. 16, 183, 187, 200
Pontiac 159
Positional negotiation; *See* Bargaining
Positions and Interests 64
Post, Amy Kirby 232, 235
Printz, John 94, 97
Problem solving 24
Proclamation Line of 1763 107–108
Public memory 12
Public slave auctions;
      See Compromise of 1850: provisions
Pullman Strike 32, 60, 63, 68, 71
Puritans 60, 75–77, 83, 93, 136

Q

Quakers 60, 91, 100–101, 136, 228, 230–231
      positions and interests 95–96
Quartering Act of 1765 110
Quebec Act;
      See Coercive Acts

R

Radical Republicans 67
Radicals
      at First Continental Congress 64, 120
Ramirez, José Fernando 187
Randolph, Edmond 140, 152
Randolph, Peyton 61, 63, 115, 119
Rankin, Jeanette 243
Read, George 64, 118
Reconstruction 16, 60, 67, 250
      positions and interests 262–265
Reconstruction Act of 1867 268
Rejón, Manuel Crescencio 187, 191
Republican Party
      origins 218
Revere, Paul 110, 115, 123
Revolutionary War;
      See American Revolution
Ridge, John 164, 173

Ridge, Major 164, 173
Rogers, Andrew Jackson 256, 262
Roleplaying 18
Roleplaying
      directions 61–62
Roleplaying activities
      parallel studies 60
Roosevelt, Franklin D. 194
Roosevelt, Theodore 194
Ross, John 162, 164–165, 170, 172
Rousseau, Jean-Jacques 5
Rule of law 2

S

Sachems 74
Sadat, Anwar 35, 47
Sanchez, George 28
Santa Anna, Antonio Lopez de 181–182, 187
Santayana, George 12
Schlesinger, Jr., Arthur M. 13
Scott v. Sandford;
      See Dred Scott
Scott, Winfield 190, 217
Second Continental Congress 125, 128, 139
Second Great Awakening 226
Self interest 6
Seneca Falls Women's Rights Convention 64, 231, 234
Separatists 74
Sequoyah 162
Seven Years War 107–108
Seward, William H. 209
Sherman, John 260, 263
Sherman, Roger 130, 143, 147
Sitting Bull 159
Slave trade 151–152
Slavery
      18th century attitudes toward 138–139
      and the American Revolution 137
      and the Constitution 61, 199
      Federal Convention of 1787 and 66
      in the Colonies 136–139
      positions and interests 71, 147–148, 203
      women and 229;
            See also Antislavery movement
Slidell, John 60, 62, 183–184, 186, 188
Smalls, Robert 260
Smith, Margaret Chase 243
Sons of Liberty 109
Southern secession 218
Squanto 75
Stamato, Linda 5

..p Act 108–109
Stanton, Edwin 269
Stanton, Elizabeth Cady 230–231, 233–234
Stanton, Henry 230
Stephens, Alexander 261, 262, 264
Stevens, Thaddeus 67, 255, 269
Stone, Lucy 64, 234, 235–237, 239
Stowe, Harriet Beecher 216, 229
Student assessment 45, 54
Suffolk Resolves 61, 115, 123–124
Suffrage
    and African Americans 239;
        See also Fifteenth Amendment
    and women 225–227, 239–243;
        See also Nineteenth Amendment
Sugar Act 108
Sumner, Charles 261, 264
Swedish settlers 96

T

Taft, William Howard 194
Tamany 94, 97
Taylor, Zachary 188–189, 201, 203, 207
Tea Act 112
Teachable moments 56
Tecumseh 159
Temperance 241
Texas and New Mexico Act 214;
    See also Compromise of 1850: provisions
Thirteenth Amendment 154, 235, 250
Thomson, Charles 64, 120
Thoreau, Henry David 189, 230
Three-fifths Clause 140–142, 151, 199, 200
Thucydides 13, 27
Tocqueville, Alexis de 170
Tomackhickon 94, 97
Townshend, Charles 109
Townshend duties 109–111
Trade
    and slavery 143, 151–152
    between Britain and Mexico 183
    between England and North American colonies 109–112
    between English settlers and Indians 77, 90
    debates in First Continental Congress 123
    England and the South 200
Trail of Tears 171, 172
Transcendentalists
    abolition and 230
Trask, Sarah 230
Treaty of Guadalupe Hidalgo 201
Treaty of Holston 160

Treaty of Hopewell 160
Treaty of New Echota 164, 172–173
Treaty of Paris 107
Treaty of Shackamaxon 99
Treaty of Versailles 37
Trescot, William H. 262
Trevor-Roper, Hugh R. 17
Triggers;
    See Conflict, Triggers of
Trist, Nicholas 190, 191, 194
Trolloppe, Frances 170
Troup, George M. 167, 168
Truth and Reconciliation Commission 7
Truth, Sojourner 235, 236
Tuchman, Barbara 6, 27
Tyler, John 182, 200

U

Uncle Tom's Cabin 216
Underground railroad 204
Underlying interests 21, 34, 40
United Colonies of New England 77, 85
Urban riots 10
Ury, William L. 32
Utah Act 215;
    See also Compromise of 1850: provisions

V

Van Buren, Martin 201
Van Evera, Stephen 27
Victory 3
Vietnam War 60, 71
Violence, America and 2
Virginia Plan 140
Voltaire 15, 98
Voting rights;
    See Suffrage

W

Wade-Davis Bill 250
Walker, David 202
Walking Purchase 99
Wampanoags 60, 62, 74–79, 85, 93
Wampum 77, 98
Ward, Nancy 164–165
Washington, George 129, 140, 144–145, 160

Webster, Daniel 71, 206, 208
Weetamoo 81, 85
Whig factions in England 112–114
Whig Party 16
Whigs
    opposition to Mexican War 200
    slavery in the territories 206, 217–218
Whitney, Eli 200
Williams, Roger 76, 82, 84
Wilmot Proviso 201–202
Wilson, James 141, 147
Wilson, Woodrow 194, 242–243
Win-win solution 9
Winslow, Josiah 77, 79, 84
Winthrop, John 75–76
Winthrop, Jr., John 78, 80, 84
Wollstonecraft, Mary 225
Woman's Christian Temperance Union 241
Women in the Workforce After World War II 62
Women's rights
    economic rights 230
    education 227
    marriage 225
Women's Rights Movement 7
Women's sphere 226
Worcester, Samuel 164
Worcester v. Georgia 164
World War I 18
Worst Alternative to a Negotiated Agreement (WATNA)
        37, 54, 71
Wounded Knee 159
Wright, Martha 231

Z

Zedillo, Ernesto 193
Zero-tolerance 4